THE M. & E. H

COMMERCIAL and INDUSTRIAL LAW

G. ROBERTS, LL.B.
and
W. T. MAJOR, M.A., LL.B.
Barrister-at-Law

SECOND EDITION

MACDONALD & EVANS LTD
8 John Street, London WC1N 2HY

First published November 1967
Reprinted March 1969
Reprinted August 1970
Second edition November 1972
Reprinted September 1974
Reprinted September 1975

©
MACDONALD AND EVANS LIMITED
1972

ISBN: 0 7121 0337 6

*Printed in Great Britain by Butler & Tanner Ltd
Frome and London*

This book is due for return on or before the last date shown below.

Gresswell Ltd., London, N.21 Cat. No. 1207

PREFACE TO THE SECOND EDITION

FOR THE new edition of this HANDBOOK, which attempts to present the outlines of commercial and industrial law in one volume, the chapters on industrial law have been rewritten so as to incorporate the provisions of the *Industrial Relations Act, 1971*. In other respects, the text has been updated and, we hope, improved.

We are happy to express again our gratitude to Mrs Mary Oliver, M.A., who has generously given her time and attention to the revision of the chapters on company law.

We hope that students preparing for examinations in commercial and industrial law will continue to find in these pages a useful supplement to the standard textbooks, both for initial learning and for examination revision.

June 1972

G. ROBERTS
W. T. MAJOR

NOTICE TO LECTURERS

More and more lecturers are now using HANDBOOKS as working texts to save time otherwise wasted by students in protracted note-taking. The purpose of the series is to meet practical teaching requirements as far as possible, and lecturers are cordially invited to forward comments or criticisms to the Publishers for consideration.

P. W. D. REDMOND
General Editor

CONTENTS

		PAGE
Preface to the second edition .	. .	v
Table of cases	.	xiii

PART ONE: LAW OF CONTRACT

CHAP.

I The formation of a contract
The classes of contract	.	1
Agreement	.	2
The legal effect of a binding contract	.	3
The offer must be definite . .	.	3
Communication of the offer . .	.	5
Acceptance must be unqualified .	.	6
Acceptance of a tender . .	.	7
Communication of acceptance. .	.	8
Revocation	.	10
Lapse	.	11
Rejection	.	12
Intention to create legal relations .	.	12

II Consideration and terms of contract
Consideration	.	15
Waiver must be supported by consideration	.	18
Equitable estoppel . . .	.	19
The terms of a contract . .	.	19
Implied terms . . .	.	23
Conditions and warranties . .	.	24
Matters affecting the validity of a contract	.	25

III Contractual capacity
Capacity, persons and rights . .	.	28
Infants as contracting parties . .	.	28
Insane or drunken persons . .	.	31
Corporations	.	32

IV Mistake, misrepresentation and coercion
Mistake—its effect upon agreement .	.	34
Mistake at common law . . .	.	35
Mistake in equity . . .	.	42

vii

CHAP.   PAGE
        Misrepresentation: representations distinguished
            from express terms   43
        Misrepresentation may be innocent or fraudulent   45
        Duress and undue influence   48

  V   Illegal, void and unenforceable contracts
        Illegality generally   52
        Scope of illegality in contracts   .   .   .   53
        The consequences of illegality   55
        Void contracts generally   56
        Contracts made void by statute   .   .   .   57
        Contracts void at common law as being against
            public policy   57
        Consequences where a contract is void as being
            against public policy   61
        Restrictive trade practices   62
        Unenforceable contracts.   63
        The *Hire-Purchase Act*, 1965   66

 VI   Privity and assignment
        Privity of contract   69
        Assignment of contractual rights   .   .   .   70
        Assignment of contractual obligations   .   .   73
        Negotiable instruments   73

VII   Discharge and breach
        The end of a contract   76
        Discharge by performance   76
        Discharge by agreement.   78
        Discharge by frustration   79
        Discharge by acceptance of breach .   .   .   82
        Remedies for breach of contract   .   .   .   83
        Unliquidated damages   85
        Liquidated damages   87
        Claim for a specific sum as damages   .   .   89
        Quantum meruit as a remedy for breach   .   .   90
        Recovery of a reasonable price for goods .   .   91
        Limitation Act, 1939   92
        Specific performance   92
        Injunction   93

VIII Quasi-contract
        The meaning of quasi-contract   .   .   .   96
        Actions in quasi-contract   97

Part Two: COMMERCIAL LAW

CHAP.   PAGE

IX Agency
    The principal–agent relationship . . . 100
    Position of principal and agent with regard to
        third parties 102
    Position as between principal and agent . . 104
    Breach of warranty of authority . . . 105
    Termination of the agency relationship . . 106
    Particular classes of agents 107

X   The law of partnership
    Nature of a partnership 110
    Relationship between partners . . . 112
    Relationship of partners and third parties . 114
    Dissolution of partnership 118
    Limited partnerships 121

XI Negotiable instruments
    Bills of exchange 123
    Acceptance of a bill 125
    Negotiation of a bill 128
    Payment of a bill 129
    Consideration for a bill: holders . . . 132
    Liability of parties: discharge . . . 134
    Cheques 136
    Promissory notes 139

XII Sale of goods
    The contract of sale 142
    Duties of seller and buyer . . . 144
    Transfer of ownership 149
    Rights of unpaid seller against the goods . 153
    Seller's personal remedies . . . 154
    Buyer's personal remedies . . . 156
    Auction sales 159
    International trading contracts . . . 160

XIII Hire-purchase and conditional sale agreements
    Hire-purchase at common law . . . 163
    The *Hire-Purchase Act*, 1965 . . . 164

XIV Commercial arbitration
    Reference to arbitration 169
    Arbitration agreements 171

XV Restrictive trade practices
    Restrictive agreements generally . . . 175
    Resale price maintenance . . . 179

Part Three: COMPANY LAW

CHAP.		PAGE
XVI	Formation of companies	
	Nature and formation of companies	182
	Shares	190
XVII	The operation of companies	
	Directors	197
	Meetings	198
	Company accounts	201
	Contractual capacity of companies	206
	Contracts to borrow money	207
XVIII	Winding up of companies	
	Winding up	212
	Compulsory winding up	212
	Voluntary winding up	215
	Contributories and creditors	218
	Reconstruction and amalgamation	220

Part Four: INDUSTRIAL LAW

CHAP.		PAGE
XIX	The law of master and servant	
	The contract of service	222
	Duties of the employer	228
	Duties of the employee	234
	Discharge of contract of service	237
	Unfair dismissal	240
	Redundancy	243
	Employer's vicarious liability	252
XX	Industrial relations	
	Industrial Relations Act, 1971	256
	The institutions	258
	Registration	260
	Collective agreements	267
	Rights of workers	269
	Industrial action	273
XXI	Industrial injury and disablement	
	Scope of the scheme	278
	Industrial injury	281
	Industrial diseases	286
	Benefit	286
	Administration of the scheme	289
	Law Reform (Personal Injuries) Act, 1948	293

CHAP.   PAGE

XXII   National insurance
       Scope of the scheme   296
       Conditions of unemployment and sickness benefit   298
       Unemployment   300
       Sickness   304
       Benefits   304
       Administration of the scheme.   .   .   .   305

XXIII Statutory control of working conditions: Factories
       The Factories Act, 1961   307
       Health (general provisions)   .   .   .   311
       Safety (general provisions)   .   .   .   314
       Welfare (general provisions)   326
       Special health, safety and welfare provisions   .   328
       Accidents and industrial diseases   .   .   .   330
       Employment of women and young persons   .   331
       Health and safety provisions for women and
           young persons   334
       Miscellaneous provisions   335
       Observance of the Act   336
       Administration of the Act   337

XXIV   Statutory control of working conditions: Offices, etc.
       The Offices, Shops and Railway Premises Act, 1963   340
       Health, safety and welfare provisions   .   .   341
       Miscellaneous provisions   346
       Observance of the Act   347
       Administration of the Act   349

Appendix: Examination technique   353
Index   357

TABLE OF CASES

A

Allcard *v.* Skinner (1887), 36 ChD. 145 49
Andrews *v.* Hopkinson, [1957] 1 Q.B. 229; [1956] All E.R. 422 . 163
Appleson *v.* Littlewood Ltd., [1939] 1 All E.R. Rep. 55 . . *13*
Armstrong Whitworth Rolls *v.* Mustard, [1971] 1 All E.R. 598 . *250*
Ashbury Railway Carriage Co. *v.* Riche (1875), L.R. 7 H.L. 653 188
Ashington Piggeries *v.* Hill, [1971] 1 All E.R. 847 . . . *146*
Attwood *v.* Lamont, [1920] 3 K.B. 571; [1920] All E.R. Rep. 55 *61*
Automatic Woodturning Co. *v.* Stringer, [1957] A.C. 457; [1957]
1 All E.R. 90 . . . . *317*
Avery *v.* Bowden (1855), 6 E. & B. 953, 962 83

B

Baily *v.* De Crespigny (1869), L.R. 4 Q.B. 180 . . . 80
Baker *v.* Jones, [1954] 2 All E.R. 553 58
Balfour *v.* Balfour, [1919] 2 K.B. 571; [1918–19] All E.R. Rep.
860 . . . . *13*
Ball *v.* Thomas and Baldwins, [1968] 1 W.L.R. 192 . . *321*
Ballett *v.* Mingay, [1943] 1 K.B. 281; [1943] 1 All E.R. 143 . 29
Bank voor Handel en Scheepvaart N.V. *v.* Slatford, [1953] 1 Q.B.
248 226
Bell *v.* Lever Bros., Ltd., [1932] A.C. 161; [1931] All E.R. Rep. 1 36
Beresford *v.* Royal Insurance Co., Ltd., [1938] A.C. 586; [1938]
2 All E.R. 602 53
Beswick *v.* Beswick, [1966] 3 All E.R. 1; [1967] 2 All E.R. 1197 . 69
Bigos *v.* Bousted, [1951] 1 All E.R. 92 56
Bissett *v.* Wilkinson, [1927] A.C. 177; [1926] All E.R. Rep. 343 . 44
Black *v.* Fife Coal Co., Ltd. 232
Boulton *v.* Jones (1857), 2 H. & N. 564 . . . . 6, 37
Bowmakers Ltd. *v.* Barnet Instruments Ltd., [1945] K.B. 65;
[1944] 2 All E.R. 579 56
Bradbury *v.* Morgan (1862), 1 H. & C. 249 12
Branca *v.* Cobarro, [1947] K.B. 854; [1947] 2 All E.R. 101 . 7
Bridge *v.* Campbell Discount Co., Ltd., [1962] A.C. 600; 1 All E.R.
385 88
British Celanese *v.* Moncrieff, [1948] Ch. 564; [1948] 2 All E.R. 44 236
British Railways Board *v.* Liptrot, [1969] 1 A.C. 136; [1967] 2 All
E.R. 1072 319
British Reinforced Concrete Co., Ltd. *v.* Shelff, [1921] 2 Ch. 563;
[1921] All E.R. Rep. 202 61
British Syphon Co. *v.* Homewood, [1956] R.P.C. 27 . . . 236
British Wagon Co. *v.* Lea & Co. (1880), 5 Q.B.D. 149 . . 73

PAGE

Brooks Wharf and Bull Wharf Ltd. *v.* Goodman Bros., [1937]
1 K.B. 534; [1936] 3 All E.R. 696 97
Brown & Son *v.* Craiks, [1970] 1 W.L.R. 752; [1970] 1 All E.R.
823 147
Butchart *v.* Dresser (1853), 4 De G.M. & G. 542, 545 . . . 115
Byrne *v.* Van Tienhoven (1880), 5 C.P.D. 344 11

C

Cammell, Laird & Co., Ltd. *v.* Manganese Bronze Co., Ltd., [1934]
A.C. 402 144
Campbell Mostyn (Provisions) *v.* Barnett, [1954] C.L.Y. 2985, *156*
C.A. .
Carlill *v.* Carbolic Smoke Ball Co., [1892] 2 Q.B. 484; [1891–94]
All E.R. Rep. 127 . . . . 6, 9
Cassidy *v.* Minister of Health, [1951] 2 K.B. 343; [1951] 1 All E.R.
574 224
Central London Property Trust, Ltd. *v.* High Trees House, Ltd.,
[1947] K.B. 130; [1956] 1 All E.R. 256 19
Century Insurance Co., Ltd. *v.* Northern Ireland Road Transport
Board, [1942] A.C. 509; [1942] 1 All E.R. 491 . . . *252*
Chapelton *v.* Barry U.D.C., [1940] 1 K.B. 532; [1940] 1 All E.R.
356 . . . . *21*
Charter *v.* Sullivan [1957] 2 W.L.R. 528; [1957] 1 All E.R. 809 . *156*
City Equitable Fire Insurance Co., Ltd., *Re*, [1925] Ch. 407 . 198
Clayton & Waller Ltd. *v.* Oliver, [1930] A.C. 209 . . . 231
Clifford *v.* Challen (Charles H.) & Son, Ltd., [1951] 1 K.B. 295;
[1951] All E.R. 72 . . . . *233*
Close *v.* Steel Company of Wales, Ltd., [1961] 2 All E.R.
953 . . . . 316, 318, *319*
Compagnie de Commerce et Commission S.A.R.L. *v.* Parkinson
Stove Co., Ltd., [1953] 2 Lloyds Rep. 487 C.A. . . . 9
Couchman *v.* Hill, [1947] K.B. 554; [1947] 1 All E.R. 103 . 20, 45
Cowan *v.* Milbourn (1867), L.R. 2 Ex. 230 56
Cranleigh Precision Engineering *v.* Bryant, [1965] 1 W.L.R. 1293;
[1964] 3 All E.R. 289 . . . . *235*
Craven-Ellis *v.* Canons Ltd., [1936] 2 K.B. 403; [1936] 2 All E.R.
1066 99
Cross *v.* Midland and Low Moor Iron and Steel Co., [1965] A.C.
343; [1964] 3 All E.R. 752 316
Cundy *v.* Lindsay (1878), 3 App. Cas. 459 . . . . *39*
Currie *v.* Misa (1875), 1 App. Cas. 554 15
Curtis *v.* Chemical Cleaning and Dyeing Co., [1951] K.B. 805;
[1951] 1 All E.R. 631 21
Cutter *v.* Powell (1795), 6 Term Rep. 320 76

D

D. & C. Builders *v.* Rees, [1966] 2 Q.B. 617; [1965] 3 All E.R. 837 79
Davies *v.* London and Provincial Marine Insurance Co. (1878),
8 Ch.D. 469 47

  PAGE

Davis Contractors, Ltd. *v.* Fareham U.D.C., [1956] A.C. 696;
  [1956] 2 All E.R. 145   80
De Bernady *v.* Harding (1853), 8 Ex. 822 . . . . *91*
Denyer *v.* Skipper and East, [1970] 1 W.L.R. 1087; [1970] 2 All E.R.
  382 . . . . *334*
Derry *v.* Peek (1889), 14 A.C. 337; [1886–90] All E.R. Rep. 1 .   45
Dickinson *v.* Barrow, [1904] 2 Ch. 339   66
Doyle *v.* White City Stadium Ltd., [1953] 1 K.B. 110; [1934] All
  E.R. Rep. 252   31
Dunlop Pneumatic Tyre Co., Ltd., *v.* New Garage & Motor Co.,
  Ltd. [1915] A.C. 79; [1914–15] All E.R. Rep. 333 . . 81, 87
Dunlop Pneumatic Tyre Co., Ltd. *v.* Selfridge & Co., Ltd., [1915]
  A.C. 847; [1914–15] All E.R. Rep. 333 . . . . 69, *179*

                                 E

Eaves *v.* Morris Motors Ltd., [1961] 2 Q.B. 385; [1961] 3 All E.R.
  233 317
Eccles *v.* Bryant and Pollock, [1948] Ch. 93; [1947] 2 All E.R. 865   *7*
Ehrman *v.* Bartholomew, [1898] 1 Ch. 671 . . . . *94*
Eley *v.* Positive Life Assurance Co. (1876), 1 Ex.D. . . . 190
Ellen *v.* Topp (1851), 6 Ex. 424 . . . . . . *83*

                                 F

Felthouse *v.* Bindley (1862), 11 C.B. (N.S.) 869 (1863) 1 New Rep.
  401 . . . .   *8*
Fenton *v.* Thorley & Co., [1903] A.C. 443 281
Fibrosa Spolka Akcyjna *v.* Fairbairn Lawson Combe Barbour,
  Ltd., [1943] A.C. 32; [1942] 2 All E.R. 122 . . .   97
Fisher *v.* Bell, [1961] 1 Q.B. 394; [1960] 3 All E.R. 731 . .   *4*
Fisher *v.* Bridges (1854), 3 E. & B. 642   55
Fitch *v.* Dewes, [1921] 2 A.C. 158; [1921] All E.R. Rep. 13 .   *60*
Fitzgerald *v.* Hall Russell, [1969] 3 All E.R. 1140 . . *251*
Foster *v.* Driscoll, [1929] 1 K.B. 470; [1928] All E.R. Rep. 130 .   54
Frost *v.* Aylesbury Diary, [1905] 1 K.B. 608 . . . *146*

                                 G

Gallagher *v.* Shilcock, [1949] 1 All E.R. 921 . . . 154
Galloway *v.* Galloway (1914), 30 T.L.R. 531 . . .   *37*
Garner *v.* Murray, [1904] 1 Ch. 57 120
Gaussen *v.* Morton (1830), 8 L.J. (O.S.) K.B. 313 . . 107
General Billposting Co. *v.* Atkinson, [1909] A.C. 118 . . 238
General Cleaning Contractors, Ltd. *v.* Christmas, [1953] A.C. 180;
  [1952] 2 All E.R. 1110 . . . . *233*
German Date Coffee Co., *Re*, (1882), 20 Ch.D. 169 . . 188
Gluckstein *v.* Barnes, [1900] A.C. 240 187
Gordon *v.* Gordon (1821), 3 Swan. 400   48
Gorse *v.* Durham C.C., [1971] 1 W.L.R. 775; [1971] 2 All E.R.
  666 222
Graham *v.* Co-operative Wholesale Society Ltd., [1957] 1 All E.R.
  654 328

PAGE

Grant v. Australian Knitting Mills, Ltd., [1936] A.C. 85 . . 147
Greenwood v. Greenwood (1863), 2 De G. J. & Sm. 28 . . 48
Grist v. Bailey, [1966] 2 All E.R. 42

H

Hands v. Simpson, Fawcett & Co., Ltd. (1928), 44 T.L.R. 295 . *46*
Harris v. Nickerson (1873), L.R. 8 Q.B. 286 . . . *4*
Harrison & Jones, Ltd. v. Bunton and Lancaster, Ltd. (1953),
   1 Q.B. 646; [1953] 1 All E.R. 903 . . . . *35*
Hartley v. Ponsonby (1857), 7 E. & B. 872 . . . *16*
Hartog v. Colin & Shields, [1939] 3 All E.R. 566 . . . *39*
Harvey v. Facey, [1893] A.C. 552 . . . . . *5*
Henthorn v. Fraser, [1892] 2 Ch. 27; [1891–94] All E.R. Rep. 908   9
Herman v. Jeuchner (1885), 15 Q.B.D. 561 . . . 55
Hermann v. Charlesworth, [1905] 2 K.B. 123 . . . 61
Herne Bay Steamboat Co. v. Hutton, [1903] 2 K.B. 683; All E.R.
   Rep. 627 81
Heron II, The. *See* Koufos v. Czarnikow.
High Trees House Case. *See* Central London Property Trust Ltd.
   v. High Trees House, Ltd.
Hindle v. Percival Boats, [1969] 1 W.L.R. 174; [1969] 1 All E.R.
   836 . . . . *246*
Hivac v. Park Royal Scientific Instruments, [1946] 1 Ch. 169 . *235*
Hoenig v. Isaacs, [1952] 2 All E.R. 176 77
Holman v. Johnson (1775), 1 Cowp. 341 52
Holt v. Markham, [1923] 1 K.B. 504; [1922] All E.R. Rep. 134   98
Home Counties Dairies v. Skilton, [1970] 1 All E.R. 1227 . . *60*
Hood v. West End Motor Car Packing Co., [1917] 2 K.B. 38 . 47
Household Fire Insurance Co. v. Grant (1879), 4 Ex.D. 216 . 10
Hudson v. Ridge Manufacturing Co., Ltd., [1957] 2 Q.B. 348;
   [1957] 2 All E.R. 229 232
Hughes v. Liverpool, etc., Friendly Society, [1916] 2 K.B. 482;
   [1916–17] All E.R. Rep. 918 56
Humberstone v. Northern Timber Mills, [1949] A.L.R. 985 . . 225
Humble v. Hunter (1848), 12 Q.B. 310 104
Hyde v. Wrench (1840), 3 Beau. 334 . . . . . *6, 12*

I

Inche Noriah v. Shaik Allie Bin Omar, [1929] A.C. 127; [1928]
   All E.R. Rep. 189 . . . . *50*
Ingram v. Little, [1961] 1 Q.B. 31; [1960] 3 All E.R. 332 . . *37*
Ionides v. Pender (1874), L.R. 9 Q.B. 531 47
Irwin v. White, Tompkins & Courage, [1964] 1 W.L.R. 387; [1964]
   1 All E.R. 545 319

J

Jenkins v. Allied Ironfounders, [1970] 1 W.L.R. 304; [1969] 2 All
   E.R. 1609 . . . . *323*
Joel v. Morrison (1834), 4 C. & P. 253
Johnson v. Callow, [1970] 1 All E.R. 129 . . . . *316*

PAGE

Jones v. Padavatton, [1969] 2 All E.R. 616 13
Jordan v. Norton 12
Joyce v. Boots Cash Chemists (Southern) Ltd., [1950] 2 All E.R.
719 308

K

Kaufmann v. Gerson, [1907] 1 K.B. 591; [1904–7] All E.R. 719 . *49*
Keighley, Maxsted & Co. and Durant & Co., Re, [1893] 1 Q.B. 405 104
Kelly v. Dale, [1965] 1 Q.B. 185; [1964] 2 All E.R. 497 . . 315
Kelner v. Baxter (1866), L.R. 2 C.P. 174 186
Kendall v. Lillico, [1968] 2 All E.R. 444 . . . . *146*
Keppel v. Wheeler, [1927] 1 K.B. 577; [1926] All E.R. Rep. 207. 104
King v. Magnatex, Ltd. (1951), 44 R. & I.T. 742; [1951] C.L.Y.
1382 310
Koufos v. Czarnikow, [1969] 1 A.C. 350; [1967] 3 All E.R. 686 . 86
Krell v. Henry, [1903] 2 K.B. 740; [1900–3] All E.R. Rep. 20 . 81

L

Larner v. L.C.C., [1949] 2 K.B. 683; [1949] 1 All E.R. 964 . *98*
Latimer v. A.E.C. Ltd., [1953] A.C. 643; [1953] 2 All E.R. 449 . 232
Laws v. London Chronicle, [1959] 1 W.L.R. 698; [1959] 2 All E.R.
285 234
Leslie v. Sheill, [1914] 3 K.B. 607; [1914–15] All E.R. Rep. 511 29
L'Estrange v. Graucob, Ltd., [1934] 2 K.B. 394; [1934] All E.R.
Rep. 16 21
Lewis v. Averay, [1972] 1 Q.B. 198; [1971] 3 All E.R. 907 . . *38*
Lloyd v. Grace, Smith & Co., [1912] A.C. 716 . . . *254*
Locker and Woolf, Ltd. v. Western Australian Insurance Co., Ltd.,
[1936] 1 K.B. 408 47
Lumley v. Wagner (1852), 21 L.J.Ch. 898 93
Luttman v. Imperial Chemical Industries Ltd., [1955] 3 All E.R.
481 310

M

McCarthy v. Daily Mirror Newspapers, Ltd., [1949] 1 All E.R.
801 337
McManus v. Fortescue, [1907] 2 K.B. 1; [1904–7] All E.R. Rep. 707 159
McRae v. Commonwealth Disposals Commission (1951), 84 C.L.R.
377 36
Maredelanto Compania Naviera S.A. v. Bergbau-Handel G.m.b.H.;
The Mihalis Angelos, [1970] 3 All E.R. 125 . . . 84
Marriott v. Oxford and District Co-operative Society, (1967) 3
K.I.R. 620 . . . . 238, *245*
Martin v. Gale (1876), 4 Ch.D. 428 30
Mason v. Provident Clothing and Supply Co. Ltd., [1913] A.C.
724; [1911–13] All E.R. Rep. 400. . . . . . *60*
Mercantile Union Corporation Ltd. v. Ball, [1937] 2 K.B. 498;
[1937] 3 All E.R. 1 31

PAGE

Midland & Low Moor Iron & Steel Co., Ltd. v. Cross, [1965]
A.C. 357; [1964] 3 All E.R. 752 316
Millard v. Serck Tubes, [1969] 1 W.L.R. 211; [1969] 1 All E.R. 598 *318*
Minister of Social Security v. Amalgamated Engineering Union,
[1967] 1 A.C. 725; [1967] 1 All E.R. 210 . . . . *292*
Mitchell v. Westin, [1965] 1 W.L.R. 297; [1965] 1 All E.R. 657 . 316
Moorcock, The (1889), 14 P.D. 64 . . . . . . *24*
Morren v. Swinton and Pendlebury B.C., [1965] 1 W.L.R. 576;
[1965] 2 All E.R. 349 . . . . *223*

N

National Coal Board v. Galley, [1958] 1 W.L.R. 16; [1958] 1 All
E.R. 91 240
Napier v. National Agency Ltd., [1951] 2 All E.R. 264 . . *53*
Nelson v. Larholt, [1948] 1 K.B. *97*
Nimmo v. Cowan & Sons, [1968] A.C. 107; [1967] 3 All E.R. 187 *323*
Nokes v. Doncaster Amalgamated Collieries, [1940] A.C. 1014 . 222
North Riding Garages v. Butterwick, [1967] 2 Q.B. 56; [1967] 1
All E.R. 644 . . . . *246*

O

O'Brien v. Associated Fire Alarms, [1968] 1 W.L.R. 1916; [1969]
1 All E.R. 93 . . . . *245*
Oliver v. Davis, [1949] 2 K.B. 727; [1949] 2 All E.R. 353 . 132
Olley v. Marlborough Court Hotel, Ltd., [1949] 1 K.B. 532; [1949]
1 All E.R. 127 21
Overstone, v. Shipway, Ltd., [1962] 1 All E.R. 52 . . . *89*

P

Page One Records v. Britton, [1967] 3 All E.R. 822 . . *240*
Parkinson v. College of Ambulance, Ltd., [1925] 2 K.B. 1; [1924]
All E.R. Rep. 325 . . . . *54*
Parvin v. Morton Machine Co., Ltd., [1952] A.C. 515; [1952] 1 All
E.R. 670 . . . . *319*
Payne v. Cave (1789), 3 T.R. 148 . . . . . . *10*
Pearce v. Brooks (1866), L.R. 1 Ex. 213 . . . . *54*
Pepper v. Webb, [1969] 1 W.L.R. 514; [1969] 2 All E.R. 216 . *239*
Pharmaceutical Society of Great Britain v. Boots Cash Chemists,
Ltd., [1953] 1 Q.B. 401; [1953] All E.R. 482 . . . 4
Phillips v. Brooks, [1919] 2 K.B. 243; [1918–19] All E.R. Rep. 246 *38*
Phonographic Equipment, Ltd. v. Muslu, [1916] 3 All E.R. 626 88
Pinnel's Case (1602), 5 Co. Rep. 117a *18*
Planché v. Colbourn (1831), 8 Bing. 14 . . . . . *91*
Poland v. John Parr & Sons, [1927] 1 K.B. 236; [1926] All E.R.
Rep. 177 C.A. *253*
Prager v. Blatspiel, Stamp and Heacock, Ltd., [1924] 1 K.B. 566;
[1924] All E.R. Rep. 524 102
Price v. Mouat (1862), 11 C.B. (N.S.) 508 234
Pullen v. Prison Commissioners, [1957] 3 All E.R. 470 . . 309

PAGE

R

R. *v.* Industrial Injuries Commissioner, *ex p.* Amalgamated
Engineering Union, [1966] 2 All E.R. 97 . . . . *285*
R. *v.* National Insurance Commissioner, *ex p.* Jones, [1970] 1 All
E.R. 97 292
R. *v.* National Insurance (Industrial Injuries) Commissioner,
ex p. Richardson, [1958] 2 All E.R. 689 . . . 283
Raffles *v.* Wichelhaus (1864), 2 H. & C. 906 . . . *37*
Ramsgate Victoria Hotel Co. *v.* Montefiore (1866), L.R. 1 Ex.
109 . . . . *11*
Rawlinson *v.* Ames, [1925] 1 Ch. 96 66
Ready Mixed Concrete (South East) *v.* Minister of Pensions and
National Insurance, [1968] 2 Q.B. 497; [1968] 1 All E.R. 433 . *223*
Richards *v.* Highway Ironfounders (West Bromwich), Ltd., [1955]
3 All E.R. 205 . . . . *328*
Roberts *v.* Gray, [1913] 1 K.B. 520; [1911–13] All E.R. Rep. 870 31
Robinson *v.* Davison (1871), L.R. 6 Ex. 269 . . . 81
Robinson *v.* Graves, [1935] 1 K.B. 579 143
Robson and Sharpe *v.* Drummond (1831), 2 B. & Ad. 303 . 73
Roscorla *v.* Thomas (1842), 3 Q.B. 234 . . . . *17*
Rose and Frank Co. *v.* Crompton Bros., Ltd., [1925] A.C. 445;
[1924] All E.R. Rep. 245 . . . . . . *13*
Rotherham Alum Chemical Co., *Re*, (1883), 25 Ch.D. 103 . 190
Rowland *v.* Divall, [1923] 2 K.B. 500 . . . . *145*
Royal British Bank *v.* Turquand (1855), 5 E. & B.; (1856) 6
E. & B. 327 190

S

St. John Shipping Corporation *v.* Joseph Rank, Ltd., [1957] 1 Q.B.
267; [1956] 3 All E.R. 683 53
Sajan Singh *v.* Sardara Ali, [1960] A.C. 167; [1960] 1 All E.R. 269 56
Salomon *v.* Salomon & Co., Ltd., [1897] A.C. 22 . . *182*
Saunders *v.* Anglia Building Society, [1971] A.C. 1004; [1970] 3 All
E.R. 961 . . . . *41*
Scammell and Nephew *v.* Ouston, [1941] A.C. 251; [1941] 1 All
E.R. 14 . . . . *4*
Scriven *v.* Hindley, [1913] 3 K.B. 564 . . . . *37*
Scruttons, Ltd., *v.* Midland Silicones, Ltd., [1962] A.C. 446; [1962]
1 All E.R. 1 69
Simpkins *v.* Pays, [1955] 3 All E.R. 10 . . . . *13*
Sinclair *v.* Neighbour, [1967] 2 Q.B. 279; [1966] 3 All E.R. 988 . 236
Solle *v.* Butcher, [1950] 1 K.B. 671; [1949] 2 All E.R. 1107 35, 42
Southern Foundries, Ltd. *v.* Shirlaw, [1940] A.C. 701. . 189
Springer *v.* Great Western Railway Co., [1921] 1 K.B. 257; [1920]
All E.R. Rep. 361 102
Spurling *v.* Bradshaw Ltd., [1956] 2 All E.R. 121 . . 21
Stanbrook *v.* Waterlow & Sons, [1964] 1 W.L.R. 825; [1964] 2 All
E.R. 506 315
Stanger *v.* Hendon Borough Council, [1948] 1 K.B. 571 . *310*

PAGE

Steinberg *v.* Scala (Leeds), Ltd., [1923] 2 Ch. 452; [1923] All
    E.R. Rep. 239 . . . .   *30*
Steven & Co. *v.* Bromley & Son, [1919] 2 K.B. 722 . . .   *90*
Stevenson *v.* McLean (1880), 5 Q.B.D. 346 . . . . 7, 12
Stevenson Jordan & Harrison *v.* Macdonald & Evans, [1952] 1
    T.L.R. 101 . . . . 224, 226
Stilk *v.* Myrick (1809), 2 Camp. 317. . . . . .   *16*
Stone (J. & F.) Lighting & Radio *v.* Haygarth, [1966] 3 All E.R.
    539 . . . .   *309*
Suisse Atlantique Societé D'Armemant Maritime S.A. *v.* N.V.
    Rotterdamsche Kolen Centrale, [1966] 2 All E.R. 61 .   *22*
Summers (John) & Sons, Ltd. *v.* Frost, [1955] A.C. 740; [1955]
    1 All E.R. 870 . . . .   *317*

T

Tate *v.* Williamson (1866), 2 Ch.App. 55 . . . .   *48*
Taylor *v.* Caldwell (1863), 3 B. & S. 826   80
Taylor *v.* Kent C.C., [1969] 3 W.L.R. 156; [1969] 2 All E.R. 1080.   *248*
Taylor *v.* Laird (1856), 25 L.J. Ex. 329   5
Thomas *v.* British Thomson-Houston Co., Ltd., [1953] 1 All E.R.
    29   311
Thomas *v.* Brown (1876), 1 Q.B. 714   65
Thompson (W. L.), Ltd. *v.* Robinson (R.) (Gunmakers), Ltd.,
    [1955] Ch. 177; [1955] 1 All E.R. 154   156
Thornton *v.* Fisher & Ludlow, [1968] 1 W.L.R. 655; [1968] 2 All
    E.R. 241 . . . .   *313*
Thornton *v.* Shoe Lane Parking, [1971] 2 Q.B. 163; [1971] 1 All E.R.
    686 . . . .   *23*
Torkington *v.* Magee, [1903] 1 K.B. 644; [1900–3] All E.R. Rep.
    991   70
Trevor *v.* Whitworth (1887), 12 App. Cas. 409 . . .   194
Triplex Safety Glass Co. *v.* Scorah, [1938] Ch. 211; [1937] 4 All
    E.R. 693   237
Trueman *v.* Loder (1840), 9 L.J.Q.B. 165 . . . .   *101*
Tsakiroglou & Co. *v.* Noblee Thorl, G.m.b.H., [1962] A.C. 93;
    [1961] 2 All E.R. 179   80
Turner *v.* Goldsmith [1891] 1 Q.B. 544   231
Turner *v.* Sawdon & Co., [1901] 2 K.B. 653 . . .   231
Twycross *v.* Grant, [1952] 2 Q.B. 100; [1952] 1 All E.R. 613 .   186

U

Upton R.D.C. *v.* Powell, [1942] 1 All E.R. 220 . . . .   *90*

V

Valentini *v.* Canali (1889), 24 Q.B.D. 166; [1886–90] All E.R. Rep.
    883   29
Varley *v.* Whipp, [1900] 1 Q.B. 513. . . . .   *145*
Victoria Laundry Ltd. *v.* Newman Industries, Ltd., [1949] 2 K.B.
    528; [1949] 1 All E.R. 997 . . . . . . 85, 155

W

Warner Brothers Pictures Inc. *v.* Nelson, [1937] 1 K.B. 209;
    [1936] 3 All E.R. 160 . . . . *94*
Warren *v.* Henlys, Ltd., [1948] 2 All E.R. 935 . . . *253*
Whelan, *Re*, [1897] 1 I.R. 575 . . . . . . *12*
Williams *v.* Carwardine (1833), 4 B. & Ad. 621 . . . 6
Wilson *v.* Rickett, Cockerell & Co., Ltd., [1954] 1 All E.R. 868 . *147*
With *v.* O'Flanagan, [1936] 1 Ch. 575; [1936] 1 All E.R. 727 . 47

Y

Yewens *v.* Noakes (1880), 6 Q.B.D. 530 223

PART ONE

LAW OF CONTRACT

CHAPTER I

THE FORMATION OF A CONTRACT

THE CLASSES OF CONTRACT

1. Two classes of contract. A contract is made where the parties have reached agreement, or where they are deemed to have reached agreement, and the law recognises rights and obligations arising from the agreement. Contracts are traditionally divided into two broad classes:

(a) *Specialty contracts.*
(b) *Simple contracts* (sometimes known as parol contracts).

2. Specialty contracts. A specialty contract is a contract made under seal, *i.e.* it is written on paper or parchment and is signed, sealed and delivered.

A contract under seal is the most solemn and formal way in which an agreement can be made under English law. Certain transactions are *void* if not carried out under seal; the most important of these are:

(a) *A promise to make a gift.*
(b) *Conveyances of land*, or of any interest in land. (There is an exception in the case of leases for a term not exceeding three years.)
(c) *Any transfer of ownership of a British ship*, or any share therein.
(d) *Gratuitous promises.*

3. Simple contracts. All contracts which are not made under seal are *simple contracts*. This **HANDBOOK** is mainly concerned with simple contracts, but special reference will be made, where appropriate, to specialties.

1

There are three fundamental elements in any *simple contract*. They are:

(a) *Agreement:* the parties must have reached, *or be deemed to have reached*, agreement.

(b) *Intention:* the parties must have intended, *or be deemed to have intended*, to create legal relations: *see* **6** below.

(c) *Consideration:* usually, according to the terms of an agreement, some advantage moves from one party to another. The giving of mutual advantages by the parties is the essence of a bargain. An advantage or benefit moving from one party to another is known as consideration: *see* II, 1–3.

NOTE: There is no contract where any of these three elements is missing.

AGREEMENT

4. Manner of agreement. An agreement may be made in any manner whatsoever, provided the parties are in communication. An agreement may be made:

(a) *in writing, or*

(b) *by word of mouth,* or

(c) *by inference from the conduct* of the parties and circumstances of the case, or

(d) *by any combination* of the above modes.

5. The test of agreement. Adequate tests are necessary to enable the court to decide cases involving dispute:

(a) as to whether agreement was reached at all, or

(b) as to the extent of the agreement, *i.e.* the terms of the agreement.

In both issues the *intention* of the parties is paramount.

6. Intention and agreement. The intention of the parties is gathered from what they said or wrote to each other during their negotiations. Also, where necessary, the conduct of the parties is taken into account, for much can be inferred from conduct. The court is not concerned with the inward mental intent of the parties, but rather, with what a *reasonable man* *would say was the intention* of the parties, having regard to all the circumstances. Wherever necessary, the court will infer terms to give effect to the presumed intentions of the parties. Notice that the presumed intention may or may not be the same as the actual intention.

In order to discover whether agreement was reached between parties, the courts analyse the negotiations into "offer and acceptance."

"It must, to constitute a contract, appear that the two minds were at one, at the same moment of time, that is, that there was an offer continuing up to the time of acceptance": *Dickinson* v. *Dodds*, per JAMES, L.J.

THE LEGAL EFFECT OF A BINDING CONTRACT

7. Rights and obligations. Where parties have made a binding contract, they have created rights and obligations between themselves. The contractual rights and obligations are correlative, *e.g.* X agrees with Y to sell his car for £500 to Y. In this example, the following rights and obligations have been created:

(a) X is under an obligation to deliver his car to Y: Y has a correlative right to receive the car.
(b) Y is under an obligation to pay £500 to X: X has a correlative right to receive the £500.

8. Breach of contract. Where a party neglects or refuses to honour a contractual obligation, there is a breach of contract. A breach by one party causes a right of action to accrue to the other party.

The usual remedy for breach of contract is damages, *i.e.* the award of a sum of money to put the aggrieved party in the position he would have enjoyed had the contract not been broken. The sum is paid, of course, by the contract-breaker following the award of the court. In certain special circumstances, the court may order the contract-breaker to carry out his contractual promise specifically. This is known as the equitable remedy of *specific performance*. Specific performance is never awarded where damages will suffice.

THE OFFER MUST BE DEFINITE

9. The terms must be certain. The offer is an undertaking by the offeror to be contractually bound in the event of a proper acceptance being made. The offer must, therefore, be clear, complete and final.

> *Scammel* v. *Ouston* (1941), H.L.: O ordered a motor van from S "on the understanding that the balance of the purchase price can be held on hire purchase terms over a period of two years." HELD: the order (*i.e.* the offer) was so vague that it had no definite meaning. Further negotiations would be required before agreement could be reached.

10. An offer may be partly or wholly implied. It is always presumed that the offeror has expressed all the terms of his offer but, where necessary to give effect to his obvious intentions, the law will draw inferences from the circumstances. For example, when a customer takes goods from the shelves of a self-service store and presents them at the cashier's desk, there is an offer implied from conduct: *Pharmaceutical Soc.* v. *Boots* (1953). But an offer will be implied by law only where it is necessary to give effect to the clear intention of the offeror, *i.e.* it must be certain.

11. An invitation to treat is not an offer. An offer must be distinguished from a mere invitation to treat. An invitation to treat is a first step in negotiations which may, or may not, be a prelude to a firm offer by one of the parties.

> *Harris* v. *Nickerson* (1873): N, an auctioneer, advertised that he would sell certain goods, including office furniture, on a specified date. H attended the sale with the intention of buying some office furniture. N withdrew the office furniture from the sale. H claimed damages for breach of contract, contending that the advertisement was an offer which he had accepted by attending the sale. HELD: the advertisement was a mere statement of intention amounting to an invitation to treat.

> *Fisher* v. *Bell* (1960): B displayed in his shop window a flick-knife behind which was a ticket bearing the words "Ejector knife—4s." He was charged with *offering for sale* a flick-knife, contrary to the provisions of the *Restriction of Offensive Weapons Act*, 1959. HELD: the displaying of the flick-knife was merely an invitation to treat.

Pharmaceutical Society etc. v. *Boots etc.* (1953), C.A.: It was held that the display of goods on the shelves of a self-service store was an invitation to treat. An offer was made by the customer when he presented the goods at the cash desk. The customer's offer could be accepted or rejected by the pharmacist whose duty it was to supervise transactions at the cash desk.

12. A statement of price is not an offer. A mere statement of price will not be construed as an offer to sell.

Harvey v. *Facey* (1893), P.C.: the following telegraph messages passed between the parties:
H: "Will you sell us Bumper Hall Pen? Telegraph lowest cash price."
F: "Lowest cash price for Bumper Hall Pen £900."
H: "We agree to buy Bumper Hall Pen for £900 asked by you."
There was no reply to the last message. H claimed that there was a contract. HELD: "Lowest cash price for Bumper Hall Pen £900" was not an offer: it was merely a statement of the lowest price in the event of a decision to sell. The last message could not, therefore, be regarded as an acceptance.

COMMUNICATION OF THE OFFER

13. Manner of communication. An offer may be communicated in any manner whatsoever. Express words may be used, orally or in writing, or an offer may be implied from conduct. An offer may be partly expressed and partly implied.

14. Necessity of communication. An offer has no validity unless and until it is communicated to the offeree so as to give the opportunity to accept or reject.

Taylor v. *Laird* (1856): T threw up the command of L's ship during the course of a voyage. T then helped to work the ship home. He claimed to be paid for this work. HELD: since T had not communicated his offer to do the work so as to give L the opportunity to accept or reject the offer, there was no contract.

15. Communication may be particular or general. An offer may be communicated to a particular person or group of persons; or it may be communicated generally to the whole world.

(a) *Where an offer is made to a particular person or group of persons*, no valid acceptance may be made by a person who is not an offeree.

> *Boulton* v. *Jones* (1857): B bought a hose-pipe business from X. J, to whom X owed a debt, addressed an order to X for a length of piping. B supplied the piping notwithstanding the fact that the order was not addressed to him. J refused to pay B for the piping. He claimed that he intended to deal with X, and X only, because of his right of set-off against him, which he intended to use. HELD: the offer was made to X and it was not in the power of B to step in and accept.

(b) *Where an offer is made generally to the world at large*, a valid acceptance may be made by any person with notice of the offer: *Carlill* v. *Carbolic Smoke Ball Co.* (1893). It seems that an acceptance is valid even though made for a *motive* which is quite unconnected with the terms of the offer: *Williams* v. *Carwardine*. But it is essential that the person accepting the offer had *notice* of the offer.

ACCEPTANCE MUST BE UNQUALIFIED

16. Unreserved assent. Acceptance must be *unqualified* and must *correspond exactly* with the terms of the offer.

NOTE: Not all transactions lend themselves to an easy analysis into "offer" and "acceptance" yet the court will always examine the communications between the parties to discover whether, at any time, one party may be deemed to have assented to all the terms, express and implied, of a firm offer by the other party. An assent which is qualified in any way does not take effect as an acceptance. For example, where goods are offered at a certain price, an assent coupled with a promise to pay by instalments is not an acceptance.

17. A counter-offer operates as a rejection. Where an offeree makes a counter-offer, the original offer is deemed to have been rejected and cannot be subsequently accepted.

Hyde v. *Wrench* (1840): on 6th June, W offered H a farm for £1000: H made a counter-offer of £950. On 27th June, W rejected the counter-offer. On 29th June, H made a purported acceptance of the offer of 6th June. HELD: the counter-offer operated as a rejection of the original offer. No contract.

NOTE: A mere request for further information does not operate as a rejection of an offer: *Stevenson* v. *McLean* (1880).

18. Tentative assent. Acceptance *subject to contract* is not binding. In sale of land, it is usual to express tentative preliminary agreements to be "subject to contract," so as to give the parties an opportunity to reflect or to seek legal or other advice before entering a binding contract. The expression "subject to contract" and similar expressions have received judicial recognition, and have become a safe formula for this purpose.

But if any other form of wording is used, care must be taken to show clearly that assent is qualified. There is a difference between a tentative agreement (not binding) and a provisional agreement, which may be binding: *Branca* v. *Cobarro* (1947).

Eccles v. *Bryant* (1948): the parties agreed on the sale of certain property "subject to contract." The contract was drawn up and counterparts prepared for each party. The purchaser signed his counterpart and posted it to the vendor, but the vendor did not sign his counterpart. HELD: there was no contract between the parties.

Branca v. *Cobarro* (1947): the parties signed an agreement which ended with the words, "This is a provisional agreement until a fully legalised agreement drawn up by a solicitor and embodying all the conditions herewith stated is signed." HELD: the wording of the agreement showed that the parties intended it to be binding, and that it would remain in force until its provisions were embodied in a formally drawn up document.

ACCEPTANCE OF A TENDER

19. Categories of tender. A tender is an offer and may be either

(a) a definite offer to supply goods or services, or
(b) a standing offer.

(c) not an offer at all.

20. Tender as a definite offer. Where tenders are invited for the supply of *specified goods* or services, each tender submitted is an offer. The party inviting the tenders can accept any tender he chooses, and thus bring about a binding contract. For example if X, who requires a million bricks, invited tenders to supply this quantity, and X in due course accepts Y's tender, there is a contract between X and Y: the terms of the contract are that Y shall supply, and that X shall accept and pay for, one million bricks.

21. Tender as a standing offer. Where tenders are invited to supply goods or services *as and when demanded*, a trader who submits a tender is making a standing offer. "Acceptance" of a standing offer has not the same effect as acceptance of a definite offer. Where a standing offer has been made, there is a separate acceptance each time an order is placed with the person who submitted the tender and, accordingly, a distinct contract is made on each occasion. It also follows that the standing offer can be revoked at any time, except as to goods or services actually ordered, unless there is a binding undertaking to keep the standing offer open for a stipulated period: *i.e.* the standing offer must be under seal or consideration must be given for it, otherwise it can be revoked at any time.

COMMUNICATION OF ACCEPTANCE

22. Acceptance must be communicated. The general rule is that acceptance must be communicated to the offeror. Acceptance speaks from the moment it is communicated. Where the offeree merely intended to accept, but did not communicate his intention to the offeror, there is no contract, *i.e.* mere mental acceptance is not sufficient. Moreover, the offeror may not stipulate that he will take silence to be acceptance, and thus bind the offeree.

Felthouse v. *Bindley* (1863): F offered to buy his nephew's horse for £30 15*s*. In the letter containing the offer, F wrote, "If I hear no more about him, I consider the horse mine at £30 15*s*." The nephew did not reply to this letter. Six weeks later, when the nephew was about to sell his farming stock, he instructed B, an auctioneer, to keep the horse out of the sale as it was already sold. B inadvertently sold the horse. F sued B for conversion. (To succeed in conversion, F would have to show that he had a right to immediate possession of the horse, *i.e.* that there was a contract between himself and his nephew.) HELD: the nephew had not communicated his intention to sell the horse to F, therefore there was no contract, and no property to the horse had ever vested in F.

23. Manner of acceptance. Acceptance may be communicated in any manner. Generally, the offeree may decide for himself the manner of acceptance: but if the offeror prescribes expressly or by implication the mode of acceptance, it seems that communication of acceptance in any other manner will not suffice: *Compagnie de Commerce et Commission S.A.R.L.* v. *Parkinson Stove Co. Ltd* (1953).

(a) *Where performance constitutes acceptance.* Where the offeror is deemed to have included in his offer a term providing that complete performance by the offeree shall be a sufficient acceptance, then communication is not necessary. In such cases, the offeror is bound when the offeree performs whatever act is required of him according to the terms of the offer.

Carlill v. *Carbolic Smoke Ball Co.* (1893): the following advertisement appeared in newspapers: "£100 reward will be paid by the Carbolic Smoke Ball Company to any person who contracts the increasing epidemic influenza, colds, or any other disease caused by taking cold, after having used the ball three times daily for two weeks according to the printed directions supplied with each ball. £1000 is deposited with the Alliance Bank, Regent Street, showing our good faith in the matter." C, in reliance on this advertisement, bought a smoke ball and used it according to the directions but nevertheless suffered an attack of influenza. She claimed £100 from the company. HELD: (*a*) the deposit of £1000 showed that the company intended to create legal relations, (*b*) the advertisement was an offer made to all the world, and a contract was made with that limited portion of the public who came forward and performed the condition on the faith of the advertisement, (*c*) the offer contained an intimation that performance of the condition was sufficient acceptance and that there was no need for notification of acceptance to be given to the offeror.

(b) *Acceptance by post.* Where post is deemed to be the proper means of communicating acceptance, the acceptance takes effect from the moment the letter of acceptance is properly posted. This rule applies even where the acceptance is delayed or lost in the post.

Henthorn v. *Fraser* (1892): It was held that "Where the circumstances are such that it must have been within the contemplation of the parties that, according to the ordinary usages of mankind, the post might be used as a means of communicating the acceptance of an offer, the acceptance is complete as soon as it is posted."

Household Fire Insurance Co. v. *Grant* (1897): G applied for shares in the plaintiff company. The company sent a letter of allotment by post, but it never reached G. The company went into liquidation and the liquidator, on behalf of the company, sued for the balance outstanding on the shares. G contended that he was not bound to pay, since he had not received a reply to his offer to buy the shares. HELD: a contract was made at the moment the letter of allotment (*i.e.* the acceptance) was posted.

REVOCATION

24. Termination of an offer. An offer may come to an end by revocation, lapse, or rejection. In any case, the offer loses its legal effect and becomes incapable of acceptance.

25. When revocation is possible. The offeror may withdraw (*i.e.* revoke) his offer at any time before acceptance: but once a valid acceptance has been made, he is bound by the terms of his offer. An offer cannot be revoked after acceptance.

Payne v. *Cave* (1789): C made the highest bid for P's goods at an auction sale, but he withdrew his bid before the fall of the hammer. P contended that C was bound by the sale. HELD: C's bid was an offer and could be revoked before acceptance, *i.e.* before the fall of the hammer. There was an effective revocation by C.

26. Options. Where the offeror gives an undertaking to keep the offer open for a stipulated period he is not bound by his undertaking unless the offeree gave consideration in return for it. Where the offeree gives consideration to keep the offer open for a period there is a separate binding contract known as an *option*, and revocation within the period will be in breach of contract.

27. Companies Act, 1948, s. 50 (5). An offer to buy shares in or debentures of a company made in pursuance of a prospectus issued generally shall not be revocable until after the expiration of the third day after the time of the opening of the subscription lists.

28. Communication essential. Revocation is effective only upon the actual notice of it reaching the offeree. Where revocation is communicated by post, it takes effect from the moment it is received by the offeree, and not from the time of posting.

> *Byrne* v. *Van Tienhoven* (1880): the following communications passed between the parties:
> 1st Oct: T posted an offer in Cardiff to B in New York.
> 8th Oct: T posted a revocation of the offer.
> 11th Oct: B sent a telegram accepting the offer of 1st Oct.
> 15th Oct: B sent a letter confirming the acceptance.
> 20th Oct: B received the revocation dated 8th Oct.
>
> HELD: T's revocation was inoperative because it did not reach B until after acceptance had been made. A contract was made on 11th October, when B accepted the offer.

LAPSE

29. Lapse of an offer. An offer may lapse, and thus become incapable of acceptance:

(a) by passage of time, or
(b) by the death of one of the parties, or
(c) the non-fulfilment of a condition precedent.

30. Passage of time. An offer will lapse through passage of time in the following circumstances:

(a) Where acceptance is not made within the period prescribed by the offeror.
(b) Where no period is prescribed, and acceptance is not made within a reasonable time. (What is reasonable depends upon the circumstances of the case.)

> *Ramsgate Victoria Hotel Co., Ltd.* v. *Montefiore* (1866): in June, M offered to buy shares from the company. In November, the company allotted shares to M, who refused to take them, contending that his offer had lapsed. HELD: the offer had lapsed through passage of time: acceptance had not been made within a reasonable period.

31. Death of a party. The death of the offeror or offeree sometimes causes the offer to lapse. The position is not free from doubt, and may be summarised as follows:

(a) The offer lapses when the offeree hears of the death of the offerer: *re Whelan* (1897). But whether an acceptance made in ignorance of the offeror's death is effective is a matter of doubt: *Bradbury* v. *Morgan* (1862).

(b) It seems that the death of the offeree will cause the offer to lapse.

REJECTION

32. Rejection: express and implied. An offeree who has rejected an offer cannot subsequently accept it. Rejection may be expressed or implied.

33. Express rejection. Express rejection is effective when notice of it has reached the offeror. But where rejection is made by post it is not clear whether it operates from the moment of posting the letter, or from the moment the letter reaches the offeree. For example, if X posts an offer to Y, and Y posts a letter rejecting the offer, but soon afterwards changes his mind and sends a telegram accepting the offer, what is the position if X receives the telegram before the letter?

It is suggested that a contract is made when X receives the telegram, and that Y's letter has no legal effect.

34. Implied rejection. Rejection is implied by law:

(a) where the offeree makes a counter-offer: *Hyde* v. *Wrench* (1840);

(b) where the offeree makes a conditional acceptance: *Jordan* v. *Norton* (1838).

NOTE: there is no implied rejection of the offer where the offeree makes a request for further information: *Stevenson* v. *Maclean* (1800).

INTENTION TO CREATE LEGAL RELATIONS

35. Intention to be bound is essential. The intention to create legal relations is an essential element in contract. Where no intention to be bound can be attributed to the parties, there is no contract. The test of intention is objective. The courts seek to give effect to the presumed intentions of the parties.

36. Commercial and business agreements. In commercial and business agreements, there is a rebuttable presumption that the parties intended to create legal relations. To rebut the presumption, it must be shown that the parties did not intend to be bound. The parties are not contractually bound where the agreement is expressed to be binding in honour only, or where it is expressed to be subject to contract.

Rose and Frank Co. v. *Crompton Bros.* (1925), H.L.: an agreement was expressed to be "not subject to legal jurisdiction in the law courts." HELD: no binding contract.

Appleson v. *Littlewood Ltd.* (1939), C.A.: A sent in a football pools coupon containing a condition that it "shall not be attended by or give rise to any legal relationship, rights, duties, consequences." HELD: the condition was valid and the agreement was not binding.

37. Social and domestic agreements. In agreements of a social or domestic nature, there is a presumption that the parties did not intend legal relations to arise. But this presumption is rebuttable by evidence to the contrary.

Balfour v. *Balfour* (1919), C.A.: a husband agreed to send his wife £30 a month for her support while he was working abroad. HELD: no contract.

Simpkins v. *Pays* (1955): a lodger and the members of the family with whom he lived agreed to go shares in a newspaper competition. They sent in a winning entry. HELD: there was an intention to be bound. The prize money should be shared according to the agreement.

Jones v. *Padavatton* (1969), C.A.: there was an agreement between a mother and her daughter by which the mother provided the purchase price of £6000 for a house, which was conveyed to the daughter, the mother being abroad. Under the agreement, the daughter was to live in part of the house and let the rest furnished, using the rent to cover expenses. Subsequently, the parties quarrelled and the mother, complaining that she could not get any accounts, brought this action for possession of the house, on the grounds that the agreement between mother and daughter was not made with the intention to create legal relations. HELD: the agreement was lacking in contractual intent and, consequently, the mother was entitled to possession.

PROGRESS TEST 1

1. What are the three fundamental elements of a valid simple contract? **(3)**

2. What do you understand by the expression "breach of contract"? **(8)**

3. What is an invitation to treat? Give examples. **(11)**

4. D goes into a self-service store, takes up a wire basket from the stock provided, and then fills the basket with goods from the shelves. He is about to leave the store, when he remembers that he has forgotten to bring money with him: so he starts to replace the goods on the shelves. The store manager stops him, saying that he has bought these goods and must pay for them. Advise the manager. **(10, 11)**

5. What is the effect of a counter-offer? **(17)**

6. Distinguish between a tentative agreement and a provisional agreement. **(20)**

7. Are there any exceptions to the rule that a contract is not made until acceptance is actually communicated to the offeror? **(22, 23)**

8. May an offeror always revoke before acceptance has taken place? **(25)**

9. Explain how an offer may lapse (*a*) by passage of time, (*b*) by death, and (*c*) by the non-fulfilment of a condition. **(30, 31)**

10. "The intention to create legal relations is an essential element in a binding contract." Explain this statement. **(35–37)**

11. Consider the legal effect of the two following stipulations:

   (a) "This agreement is binding in honour only and is not to give rise to legal rights and obligations."

   (b) "This agreement is outside the jurisdiction of the courts, and the parties hereby agree not to bring any action in the courts on any question arising from this agreement." **(36)**

12 A invited B to his (A's) home for dinner, and B accepted the invitation. In an attempt to impress B, A arranged for a sumptuous and expensive meal to be prepared. B forgot about the invitation and did not arrive. The food was wasted. A now wishes to know whether he has any claim against B. Advise him. **(37)**

CHAPTER II

CONSIDERATION AND TERMS OF CONTRACT

CONSIDERATION

1. A bare promise is not binding. In an action on a *simple* contract, the plaintiff must show that the defendant's promise was *part of a bargain* between the parties. The plaintiff must show that he gave, or promised to give, some advantage to the defendant in return for his promise. This advantage moving from the plaintiff to the defendant is known as consideration.

It is a complete defence for the defendant to show that no consideration was given. A bare promise is not binding, *e.g.* if A promises to make a gift of £5 to B, and subsequently changes his mind, B cannot succeed against A for breach of contract.

2. Definition. A valuable consideration "may consist either in some right, interest, profit, or benefit accruing to the one party, or some forbearance, detriment, loss, or responsibility given, suffered, or undertaken by the other": *Currie* v. *Misa* (1875).

3. Executory and executed consideration. Consideration may be something promised or something done. Regarding a simple contract as a transaction which is essentially a bargain, consideration may be a price promised, or a price paid. ("Price" is used here in the widest sense.)

  (a) *Executory consideration* is the price *promised* by one party in return for the other party's promise.
  (b) *Executed consideration* is the price *paid* by one party in return for the other party's promise.

  NOTE: The party alleging the breach of contract must show that he gave consideration: generally, this is the plaintiff, but where a defendant brings a counter-claim for breach of contract—*i.e.* where he alleges that the plaintiff was in

15

breach of contract—then he must show that he, the defendant, gave consideration.

4. Rules governing consideration. The following rules govern consideration:

(a) Consideration must be real (or sufficient).
(b) Consideration need not be adequate.
(c) Consideration must move from the promisee.
(d) Consideration must not be past.
(e) Consideration must not be illegal.
(f) Consideration must not be vague.
(g) Consideration must be possible of performance.

Rules (a) to (d) above are fundamental to the nature of consideration. Rules (e) to (g) may be regarded as auxiliary.

5. Consideration must be real. Consideration must have *some* value. It matters not how small that value is, so long as it is worth something. Indeed, the word "value" is sometimes used to mean consideration. It follows that where a party performs an act which is merely a discharge of a pre-existing obligation, there is no consideration: but where a party does *more* than he was already bound to do, there may be consideration.

Stilk v. *Myrick* (1809): the captain of a ship promised his crew that, if they shared between them the work of two seamen who had deserted, the wages of the deserters would be shared out between them. HELD: the promise was not binding because the seamen gave no consideration: they were already contractually bound to do any extra work to complete the voyage.

Hartley v. *Ponsonby* (1857): a ship's crew had been seriously depleted by a number of desertions. The captain promised the remaining crew members £40 extra pay if they would complete the voyage. HELD: the promise was binding. It was dangerous to put to sea in a ship so under-manned. The seamen were not obliged to do this under their contracts of service and were, therefore, free to enter into a fresh contract for the remaining part of the voyage.

NOTE: The test is: "*Did the party claiming to have given consideration do any more than he was already bound to do?*"

6. Consideration need not be adequate. It is no part of the court's duty to assess the relative value of each party's contribution to the bargain. Once it is established that a bargain was freely reached, it will be presumed that each party stipulated according to his wishes and intentions at the time. There is no reason, for example, why a party should not be bound by a promise to sell a new Rolls Royce motor car for one penny. If the agreement was freely reached, the inadequacy of the price is immaterial to the existence of a binding contract.

7. Consideration must move from the promisee. No stranger to the consideration may sue on a contract. Any action for breach of contract must be brought by a party who gave consideration. (This rule is related to, but must be distinguished from, the doctrine of privity of contract: *see* VI, **1–4.**)

EXAMPLE: X, Y and Z enter into an agreement under which X promises to do certain work for Y if Y will pay £10 to Z. If X does the work, he can sue Y on his promise; but Z cannot sue, for he gave no consideration to Y.

8. Consideration must not be past. Where one party has performed an act before the other party's promise was made, that act cannot be consideration to support the promise.

Thus A offers to drive B from London to Cambridge in his motor car. On arrival at Cambridge, B promises A to pay 50 pence towards the cost of the petrol. B's promise is not binding because the "consideration" for which it was given was past.

Roscorla v. *Thomas* (1842): at T's request, R bought T's horse for £30. After the sale, T promised R that the horse was sound and free from vice. The horse proved to be vicious. HELD: there was no consideration to support T's promise and he was not bound. The sale itself could not be valuable consideration, for it was completed at the time the promise was given.

9. Bills of Exchange Act, 1882, s. 27 (1). Section 27 (1) of the *Bills of Exchange Act*, 1882, provides an exception to the rule that past consideration is no consideration: *see* XI.

s. 27 (1) "Valuable consideration for a bill may be constituted by:
  (a) Any consideration sufficient to support a simple contract.
  (b) An antecedent debt or liability. Such debt or liability

is deemed valuable consideration whether the bill is payable on demand or at a future time."

WAIVER MUST BE SUPPORTED BY CONSIDERATION

10. Waiver of a contractual right. Where a contracting party waives his rights under the contract, wholly or in part, the waiver is not binding unless consideration is given for it. For example, if X owes Y £100, and Y tells X that he will take £90 in full satisfaction of the debt, X will not be discharged from his obligation to pay the £100. If X pays £90 to Y, he will remain liable to pay to the extent of £10.

11. Consideration makes a waiver binding. Where a debtor gives consideration in return for the waiver, there is accord and satisfaction, and the waiver becomes a part of a new binding contract between the parties.

12. Where payment of a lesser sum discharges an obligation to pay a greater sum. If, at the creditor's request, some new element is introduced, such as payment at a different place, or at a different time, compliance with this request will amount to consideration for the waiver.

Thus if D is under a contractual obligation to pay C the sum of £1000 in London on 28th June, and he (C) requests D to pay £800 in London on 2nd June, saying that he will take the lesser sum in full discharge of the greater, C will have no further claim against D if he complies.

NOTE: There must be some new element introduced at the request of the creditor.

Pinnel's Case (1602): Pinnel sued Cole for a debt of £8 10s. due on 11th November. Cole pleaded that, at Pinnel's request, he had paid £5 2s. 6d. on 1st October, and that this had been accepted by Pinnel in full satisfaction. The court found for the plaintiff Pinnel, on a technical point of pleading, but it was made clear in the judgment that, but for this flaw, the court would have found for the defendant, Cole, because the payment of the lesser sum had been made on an earlier date and at the plaintiff's request.

EQUITABLE ESTOPPEL

13. The doctrine. Consideration must be given to make the waiver of contractual rights binding. But where a party has waived his contractual rights against another, and that other party has changed his position in reliance on the waiver, it would be unjust to allow an action against him on the original contract to succeed. In equity, the party who waived his rights will be estopped from denying that he intended the waiver to be binding: *Central London Property Trust, Ltd.* v. *High Trees House, Ltd.* (1947).

14. What the defendant must prove. In order to raise the defence of equitable estoppel, the following conditions must be satisfied:

(a) There must have been an original agreement between the parties out of which the defendant owed an obligation to the plaintiff.
(b) The plaintiff must have waived, partly or wholly, his rights against the defendant.
(c) The defendant must have given no consideration for the waiver so as to make it binding at law.
(d) The defendant must have altered his position in reliance on the waiver, so that it would be inequitable to allow the plaintiff to insist on the terms of the original agreement.

THE TERMS OF A CONTRACT

15. Terms. The terms of a contract are its contents, and these determine the extent to which the parties may be deemed to be in agreement. Accordingly, the terms of the contract define the rights and obligations arising from the contract. Contractual terms may be expressed or implied.

(a) *Express terms* are express statements made by the parties and by which they intend to be bound.
(b) *Implied terms* are those which have been implied by the law either (i) according to the provisions of a statute, or (ii) to give effect to the presumed intentions of the parties.

16. Statements made during negotiations. Material statements made by the parties during negotiations leading up to a contract can be divided into two groups:

(a) Statements by which the parties intend to be bound. These become terms of the contract.

(b) Statements made, but which the parties did not intend to be binding terms. These statements are mere representations if they helped to induce the making of the contract.

Thus, the parties are bound by statements by which they intended to be bound: where there is no such intention, the parties are not bound. In this connection, the court discovers intention by the application of an objective test. The test question is *"What would a reasonable man understand to be the intention of the parties having regard to all the circumstances?"* In applying the test, the court will take notice of all the circumstances of the negotiations between the parties.

17. Construction of a contract. The court will construe a contract as follows:

(a) Words are presumed to have their *ordinary literal meaning;* but legal technical terms are presumed to have their technical meaning.

(b) *Where a contract is ambiguous,* so that it may have either a legal or an illegal meaning, the legal meaning will be preferred.

(c) *Where the meaning of a word is not clear*, or where two terms conflict, the intention of the parties will prevail. Thus an oral term may prevail over a contradictory written term: *Couchman* v. *Hill* (1947).

(d) The contract will be construed most strongly against the party who drew it up. This is known as the *contra proferentem* rule, and is most important in connection with exemption clauses: *see* **18** *below*.

18. Exemption clauses. An exemption clause is a contractual stipulation purporting to limit or exclude the liability of one of the parties in contract or in tort. Where a standard form contract is used, it is not unusual for the party who drew it up to take advantage of his dominant position by including an exemption clause. Where a case turns on whether an exemption clause is binding, the ordinary rules are followed; *e.g.* the existence of the clause must be communicated to the other party; the circumstances must show an intention to be bound; the clause will be construed most strongly against the party seeking to take advantage of it. (The courts tend to lean against exemption clauses, following the *contra proferentem* rule.)

Chapelton v. *Barry U.D.C.* (1940), C.A.: the Council hired out deck chairs and by the stack of chairs was a notice containing the terms of hire. C hired two chairs, paid his money, and received two tickets which he put in his pocket. When C sat in one of the chairs, it broke and caused him injury. The chair was not fit for use. C sued the Council for negligence and was met with the defence that the words printed on the back of his ticket included "The Council will not be liable for any accident or damage arising from hire of chair." HELD: the terms of the contract of hire were contained in the notice by the stack of chairs. The ticket issued was a mere receipt, therefore the writing on the back of it could not be included in the contract. The Council could not rely on the exemption clause.

19. Construction of exemption clauses. The courts will lean against exemption clauses and will not enforce them unless they are clearly intended to be binding terms. Note:

(a) An exemption clause will not be binding if it was not brought to the attention of the other party before the contract was made: *Olley* v. *Marlborough Court* (1948); *Chapelton* v. *Barry U.D.C.* (1940).

(b) An exemption clause written on a receipt has no validity: *Chapelton* v. *Barry U.D.C.* (1940).

(c) Where the clause was brought to the notice of the other party during previous dealings it may be implied to give effect to the presumed intentions of the parties: *Spurling* v. *Bradshaw* (1956).

(d) Where a party signs a document containing an exemption clause, it is binding even though it may not have been read by that party: *L'Estrange* v. *Graucob* (1934).

(e) Where the party seeking to rely on an exemption clause has misrepresented the extent of the clause, the clause will not be binding: *Curtis* v. *Chemical Cleaning Co.* (1951).

(f) Where a party is entitled to treat a contract as repudiated by fundamental breach, and that party does so, the whole contract is at an end, including any exemption clauses. But if the party affirms the contract, it is a matter of construction whether the exemption clauses continue to operate: *Suisse Atlantique Case* (1966).

Suisse Atlantique Société d'Armament Maritime S.A. v. *N.V. Rotterdamsche Kolen Centrale* (1966), H.L.: The plaintiffs agreed by a charterparty dated December 1956 to charter their ship to the defendants for carrying coal from the U.S.A. to Europe. The charterparty was expressed to remain in force for two years' consecutive voyages between U.S.A. and Europe. By the charterparty if the vessel was delayed beyond the agreed loading time, the defendants were to pay $1000 a day demurrage. Similarly, demurrage was payable if the vessel was delayed beyond the agreed unloading time. In September 1957 the plaintiffs regarded themselves as being entitled to treat the charterparty as repudiated by reason of the defendants' delays in loading and unloading the vessel. The defendants did not accept this intention and it was agreed (without prejudice to this dispute) that the charterparty should be continued. From October 1957 the vessel made eight round voyages under the charter. It was contended by the plaintiffs that each round voyage ought reasonably to have been completed in thirty to thirty-seven days, including loading and unloading. On this basis, the eight voyages which took 511 days should have been completed in 240 or 296 days. From this the plaintiffs argued that they had lost freights which they would have earned on nine or, alternatively, six voyages. The plaintiffs claimed damages of $773,000 or, alternatively, $476,000. The basis of the plaintiffs' contention was that the charterparty gave them a contractual right to the number of voyages which would be made in the event of both parties carrying out their contractual obligations, and that their claim was not limited to their entitlement to demurrage. The plaintiffs, who failed in the High Court and in the Court of Appeal, appealed to the House of Lords. An argument, not advanced in the courts below, was put forward, namely, that if the delays were such as to entitle the appellants to treat the charterparty as repudiated, the demurrage clauses did not apply, and that the appellants would then be entitled to recover their full loss on the bases they claimed. HELD: the appellants, having elected in 1957 to affirm the charterparty, were bound by its provisions, including the demurrage clauses, which operated as agreed damages. The appellants were not entitled to damages for loss of freight, nor would they be so entitled if the respondent's breaches were delivered.

Thornton v. *Shoe Lane Parking, Ltd.* (1971), C.A.: the plaintiff drove his car to a multi-storey automatic car park which he had never used before. On the outside of the park there was a notice under the heading "Shoe Lane Parking." The notice contained the parking charges and other information. At the end of the notice were the following words: "ALL CARS PARKED AT OWNERS RISK." When the plaintiff reached the entrance there was no one in attendance. A traffic light turned from red to green and a ticket was pushed out from a machine. The plaintiff took the ticket and drove into the car park. He left his car there and returned for it several hours later. As he attempted to put his belongings into his car the plaintiff was severely injured. The trial judge held that the accident was half the fault of Shoe Lane Parking, Ltd., and half the fault of the plaintiff himself. The defendants claimed that they were exempted from liability by certain conditions which had become part of the contract. The defendants claimed that the ticket was a contractual document and that it incorporated a condition exempting them from liability. On the ticket appeared the words: "This ticket is issued subject to the conditions of issue as displayed on the premises." The plaintiff, who had looked at the ticket to see the time printed on it, had not read the other printing on the ticket. He did not read the words which provided that the ticket was issued subject to conditions. Nor did he read the conditions which were set out on a pillar opposite the ticket machine. One of these conditions provided that the defendants would not be responsible or liable for injury to the customer occurring when the customer's motor vehicle was in the parking building. It was this condition which the defendants relied upon. HELD: the exempting condition did not bind the plaintiff because he did not know of it and the defendants did not do what was reasonably sufficient to give him notice of it.

IMPLIED TERMS

20. Unexpressed terms. There is a general presumption that the parties have expressed, orally or in writing, every material term which they intend should govern their contract. But there are circumstances where terms which have not been expressed by the parties are inferred by law. An implied term is binding to the same extent as an express term. The courts will infer a term

    (a) to give effect to the presumed intentions of the parties; or
    (b) on the grounds of a statute.

21. Implied terms and presumed intentions. In order to discover the unexpressed intention of the parties, the courts may
take notice of trade customs, the conduct of the parties, or the
need to give "business efficacy" to a contract.

> *The Moorcock* (1889), C.A.: there was a contract between the
> defendants, who owned a Thames-side wharf and jetty, and the
> plaintiff, by which it was provided that the plaintiff's vessel
> *Moorcock* should be unloaded and re-loaded at the defendants'
> wharf. The *Moorcock* was, accordingly, moored alongside the
> wharf, but, as the tide fell, she took to the ground and sus-
> tained damage on account of the unevenness of the river bed
> at that place. The plaintiff brought this action for damages for
> breach of contract. HELD: there was an implied term in the
> contract that the defendants would take reasonable care to see
> that the berth was safe; that both parties must have known at
> the time of the agreement that if the ground were not safe the
> ship would be endangered when the tide ebbed; that there was
> a breach of the implied term.

22. Terms implied on the grounds of a statute. Certain
statutes provide for the implication of terms in contracts.
Students should note that in these circumstances terms may be
implied irrespective of the intentions of the parties, unless the
statutory provision has been clearly excluded. By virtue of
ss. 12–15 of the *Sale of Goods Act*, 1893, in contracts of sale of
goods, there are implied terms which, in effect, reverse the
common law rule of *caveat emptor* (let the buyer beware).
Where the Act applies, it would be more accurate to say "let
the seller beware." Section 55 provides, however, that the
implied terms can be excluded if the parties so intend.

CONDITIONS AND WARRANTIES

23. Conditions and warranties. Each term of a contract,
express or implied, is either a condition or a warranty, depending upon its importance with regard to the purpose of the
contract. Broadly, a term which goes to the essence of the
contract is a condition, and any other term is a warranty.

Since there is, usually, a stronger remedy available for breach
of condition than for breach of warranty, it is not unusual for
the parties to be in dispute as to whether a term is a condition
or a warranty. There is no special test which the courts can
apply to such disputes, for there is no complete definition of

"condition" and "warranty." The courts are forced to treat the distinction generally as resting on the intention of the parties, and to be discovered by an examination of all the outward circumstances of the case.

24. Criticisms. There have been serious criticisms of the use of the words "condition" and "warranty" to mean the two kinds of contractual term. In particular:

(a) The distinction is not significant until there is a breach of contract.

(b) The word "condition" is also used in a different sense in the expressions "condition precedent" and "condition subsequent." This can lead to confusion. (Where an agreement contains a condition precedent, no rights or obligations arise until its fulfilment. Where an agreement contains a condition subsequent, its fulfilment releases all parties from obligations under the agreement.) *See* VII, 8.

(c) In commercial usage, the word "warranty" often denotes a major term of the contract. It matters not whether the parties have called any particular term a condition or a warranty—in the event of a breach, the court will decide according to the intention of the parties.

MATTERS AFFECTING THE VALIDITY OF A CONTRACT

25. Vitiating factors. The validity of a contract may be impaired in any form of the following circumstances:

(a) Where the element of agreement is impaired by;

    (i) *mistake, i.e.* where one party, or both parties, entered the contract under a misapprehension; or,

    (ii) *misrepresentation, i.e.* where one party was induced to enter the agreement party by a false representation of the other party, the false representation not being a term of the contract; or,

    (iii) *duress or undue influence, i.e.* direct or subtle coercion brought to bear on a contracting party: *see* III.

(b) Where one or more of the contracting parties has not full *contractual capacity: see* IV.

(c) Where the contract is illegal: *see* V.

(d) Where the contract is partly or wholly *void under a statute: see* V.
(e) Where a contract is partly or wholly *void at common law* as being against public policy: *see* V.
(f) Where the contract is of a class *requiring formalities*, and these are absent: *see* V.

26. Impaired contracts. Where any vitiating factor is present in a contract, the legal consequences will vary according to the circumstances. It will be seen that a contract may be:

(a) *Void, i.e.* an absolute nullity.
(b) *Voidable, i.e.* a contract which gives rise to legal consequences, but may be set aside, or rescinded.
(c) *Illegal, i.e.* one upon which no action may be taken except in very special circumstances.
(d) *Unenforceable, i.e.* a good contract, but one upon which a plaintiff may not bring an action at law because of the absence of written evidence where this is required, or because of some defect in the contractual capacity of the defendant.

PROGRESS TEST 2

1. Define consideration and distinguish between executory and executed consideration. **(2, 3)**

2. State briefly the rules governing consideration. When, if ever, will past consideration suffice? **(4–9)**

3. Where a party waives a contractual right, is he bound by the waiver? **(10–11)**

4. A is a student at a technical college and promises B, one of the lecturers employed by the college, £10 for a series of private lessons. B gives the lessons as agreed, but A fails his examination and refuses to pay B the money promised on the grounds that B gave no consideration for it. Advise B. **(5)**

5. C's car has broken down on a lonely road. C asks D, a passing motorist, to tow the car to the nearest garage 20 miles away. D agrees and when they arrive at the garage C promises him £5 as payment for his trouble. Is C bound by his promise? **(5; VII, 35)**

6. E, a tailor, contracts to make a suit for F for £35. Later F loses his job and tells E that he cannot afford the agreed price, so F promises to charge no more than £25. If E delivers the suit

and receives £25, can he later claim the further ten pounds of the original price? Would it make any difference to your answers if before the suit was delivered F had obtained a new and highly paid job? (13, 14)

7. "Contractual terms may be expressed or implied." Explain. (15–22)

8. How does the court decide whether a particular statement is contained as a term of a contract? (16)

9. What rules do the courts follow in construing the express terms of a contract? (17)

10. What is the general purpose of exemption clauses in contracts? It is said that the courts lean against exemption clauses: explain this. (18, 19)

11. In what circumstances are terms which are not expressed by the parties nevertheless implied by the court? (20–22)

12. At an auction sale a picture, described in the sale catalogue as a Picasso, was up for sale. Before the bidding started, A asked the auctioneer whether he could confirm that it was a genuine Picasso. The auctioneer replied, "It is definitely a Picasso." The picture was knocked down to A for £750. Seven months later he discovered that it was by an unknown artist, and was almost worthless. Advise A. How would it affect your advice if the printed conditions of sale contained a clause to the effect that the auctioneer would not be liable for errors of description? (15–19)

13. B bought a motor car from C by private sale. C had described the car as being a 1961 model. Three months after the sale, B discovered that it was a 1956 model. Advise B. (15–17)

CHAPTER III

CONTRACTUAL CAPACITY

CAPACITY, PERSONS AND RIGHTS

1. Capacity and persons. In law, persons may be natural or artificial. Natural persons are human beings: artificial persons are corporations. Contractual capacity (or lack of it) is an incident of personality. It is not possible for contractual capacity to attach to animals or inanimate objects.

   (a) *Natural persons.* The general rule is that all natural persons have full contractual capacity. But there are exceptions in the case of infants, drunken persons, insane persons and enemy aliens.
   (b) *Corporations.* The contractual capacity of a corporation depends on the manner in which it was created.

2. Capacity, rights and obligations. In order to benefit from a contractual right, or to incur a contractual obligation, a contracting party must have the appropriate capacity. Rights and obligations can exist only where there is capacity to support them. Incapacity may, therefore, affect the apparent rights and obligations created by a contract.

INFANTS AS CONTRACTING PARTIES

3. Infants' contracts classified. A contract entered into by an infant will fall into one of the four following classes:

   (a) Contracts rendered *void by statute.*
   (b) Contracts *voidable by the infant.*
   (c) Contracts *binding on the infant.*
   (d) Contracts *enforceable by the infant* but not against him.

4. Void contracts. The *Infants' Relief Act,* 1874, *s.* 1, provides that "All contracts, whether by specialty or by simple contract, henceforth entered into by infants:

(a) for the repayment of money lent or to be lent, or
(b) for goods supplied or to be supplied (other than contracts for necessaries), and
(c) all accounts stated with infants,

shall be absolutely void."

NOTE
(i) *An account stated* is an agreed balance payable between parties, often resulting from a series of transactions.
(ii) Where a person of full age agrees to repay a loan contracted during infancy, the agreement is void: *Betting and Loans (Infants) Act*, 1892.

5. Effect of infants' contracts rendered void. Contracts governed by the *Infants' Relief Act*, 1874, and the *Betting and Loans (Infants) Act*, 1892, are void and cannot be enforced in any circumstances.

NOTE
(i) *Where an infant fraudulently states that he is of full age,* so as to induce the other party to enter a void contract, no action in tort will lie against the infant at the suit of the party misled: *Leslie* v. *Sheill* (1914). No action will lie for the recovery of money from the infant.
(ii) *Where an infant has fraudulently obtained goods* under a void contract, although there is no recovery at law, in equity the court may order restitution of the goods.
(iii) *An infant may be liable in tort* for an act quite independent of the contract. This is not considered an indirect way of enforcing the contract. An example would be where an infant bailee parts with hired goods when his contract does not give him the right to part with them: *Ballett* v. *Mingay* (1943).
(iv) The *Infants' Relief Act, s. 1,* will not be construed so as to allow an infant to recover money paid by him for something he has consumed or used: *Valentini* v. *Canali* (1889).

6. Infants' voidable contracts. Where an infant enters a contract of *continuing obligation*, the contract is voidable at the option of the infant before, or within a reasonable time after, reaching his majority.

Contracts in this class include tenancy agreements, partnership agreements, and agreements to take shares which are not fully paid up. Where an infant repudiates a contract during infancy, he may cancel his repudiation and treat it as binding on reaching the age of 21.

7. Effect of repudiation. The general rule is that where an infant repudiates a contract of continuing obligation, he can recover money paid or property transferred only where there has been a complete failure of consideration. Where the infant has received any benefit at all, he cannot recover. In the case of partnership agreements, however, the infant can claim to recover his share of the partnership assets after the payment of partnership debts, *i.e.* he will have to share in the payment of partnership debts.

> *Steinberg* v. *Scala (Leeds) Ltd.* (1923): an infant who had bought partly paid-up shares in a company sought to repudiate the contract and recover her money. HELD: (i) she was entitled to repudiate and have her name removed from the register of members; and (ii) since the shares had some value, there was no failure of consideration, and she could not recover money paid. (But the infant was entitled to repudiate her obligation to pay further calls.)

8. Contracts binding the infant. An infant is bound when he enters contracts of the following kind:

(a) *Contracts for necessaries.* An infant is bound by contracts for necessaries. "Necessaries" are defined in *s.* 2 of the *Sale of Goods Act*, 1893, as "goods suitable to the condition in life of such infant . . . and to his actual requirements at the time of sale and delivery." The section also provides that "where necessaries are sold and delivered to an infant . . . he must pay a reasonable price therefor."

NOTE
  (i) The infant's liability to pay a reasonable price for necessaries is quasi-contractual. He is *not liable on an executory contract for necessaries*. The use of the words "sale or delivery" and "sold and delivered" excludes liability on executory contracts of sale.
  (ii) Although the *Sale of Goods Act* mentions only goods sold and delivered as necessaries, at common law the term "necessaries" includes such things as medical attendance, lodgings, and necessaries for an infant's wife or children.
  (iii) It has been held that a *loan to an infant* to enable him to purchase necessaries from another is recoverable by the lender as if he himself had supplied the necessaries: *Martin* v. *Gale* (1876). It is suggested, however, that the lender would have to show that the infant actually bought, and was supplied with, the necessaries.

(b) *Contracts of education, training, or beneficial service.* An infant is bound by a contract under which he obtains education, or training for a trade or profession, or beneficial experience in a trade or profession. He is bound to pay a reasonable price for training where a price is agreed. The following contracts of service have been held to be beneficial:

   (i) A contract by which an infant boxer undertook to abide by the rules of the British Boxing Board of Control: *Doyle* v. *White City Stadium Ltd.* (1935).

   (ii) A contract by which an infant billiards professional undertook to go on tour with a well-known player: *Roberts* v. *Gray* (1913).

NOTE: Where an infant is engaged in trade, an ordinary trading contract is not binding on him, even though it may be for his benefit: *Mercantile Union Corporation Ltd.* v. *Ball* (1937).

9. Contracts enforceable by the infant but not against him. Infants' contracts which are not void, voidable, or binding form a residual class of contracts which are enforceable by the infant but are not enforceable against him. Infants' contracts to marry fall into this class.

10. Infants' Relief Act, 1847, s. 2. Section 2 of the *I.R.A.,* 1847, provides that "No action shall be brought whereby to charge any person upon any promise made after full age to pay any debt contracted during infancy, or upon any ratification made after full age of any promise or contract made during infancy, whether there shall or shall not be any new consideration for such promise or ratification after full age."

INSANE OR DRUNKEN PERSONS

11. Incapacity through insanity or drunkenness. Where a person who is drunk or insane, and thus does not understand what he is doing, enters into a contract, the contract is voidable at his option, provided that the other party knew of his condition. Points to note are:

   (a) *Mentally unbalanced persons* are bound by contracts made during periods of *lucidity.*

   (b) *Voidable contracts may be ratified* and made binding after the period of incapacity has ended.

(c) Insane and drunken persons are bound to pay a *reasonable price for necessaries* according to the same rules as apply to infants: *Sale of Goods Act*, 1893, *s.* 2.

CORPORATIONS

12. Contractual capacity of corporations. The contractual capacity of a corporation may be determined as follows:

(a) *Chartered corporations.* There are no legal limits to the contractual capacity of a chartered corporation. There are, however, limits imposed by the artificial nature of the corporation, *e.g.* it cannot contract to have its hair cut, or to have its appendix removed. Where a chartered corporation enters into a contract, beyond the powers granted in the charter, the act is valid and binding. But a member of a chartered corporation may apply for an injunction to restrain an act beyond the powers granted in the charter.

(b) *Statutory corporations.* The contractual capacity of a statutory corporation is defined expressly or by implication by the statute under which the corporation was created. Any contract which is beyond the powers conferred by the statute is void.

(c) *Registered corporations.* The contractual capacity of a company registered under the *Companies Act*, 1948, is defined expressly or by implication in the objects clause of the company's memorandum of association. Any act going beyond the capacity as defined in the memorandum is *ultra vires* (beyond the powers) and void. A registered corporation (or company) is bound only by those contracts which are *intra vires* (within the power). *See* XVI, **10.**

PROGRESS TEST 3

1. State and explain the provisions of *s.* 1 of the *Infants' Relief Act*, 1874. **(4, 5)**

2. What kinds of contracts entered into by infants are voidable at the option of the infant? Where an infant exercises his option to repudiate, may he recover money paid to the other party under contract? **(6, 7)**

3. Explain the contractual capacity of insane persons. (11)

4. A, an infant, enters into the following contracts. Explain whether he is bound by them:

  (a) A contract of hire-purchase of a television set.

  (b) A contract of apprenticeship with C, a gardener.

  (c) An account stated with D to the effect that A owes D the sum of £21. (3–10)

5. By representing himself to be over 18, X, an infant, obtained a loan of money from Y, and a car on hire from Z which X later sold for cash to another person. What rights, if any, have Y and Z if X repudiates his contracts with them? (5)

CHAPTER IV

MISTAKE, MISREPRESENTATION AND COERCION

MISTAKE—ITS EFFECT UPON AGREEMENT

1. Agreement affected in two ways. Where there was some kind of misapprehension or misunderstanding as to a material fact at the time of reaching agreement, the factual circumstances will fall into one of the two following classes:

(a) Where agreement has been reached on the basis of a mistake common to both parties.

(b) Where there was a mere appearance of agreement because of mutual or unilateral mistake.

2. Common mistake. Common mistake occurs where both parties to an agreement are suffering from the same misapprehension. Where this kind of mistake occurs, offer and acceptance correspond, *i.e.* there has been agreement between the parties. It is necessary to consider whether the underlying common mistake affects the validity of the contract. An example of common mistake would be where X agrees to sell certain goods to Y, and at the time of the agreement the goods have perished unknown to both parties.

3. Mutual and unilateral mistake.

(a) *Mutual mistake* occurs where the parties have negotiated at cross-purposes, *e.g.* where A agrees to sell a horse to B, and A intended to sell his white horse, while B thought he was agreeing to buy A's grey horse.

(b) *Unilateral mistake* occurs where one party only is mistaken and the other party knows, or is deemed to know, of the mistake. An example would be where C makes an offer to D only and it is accepted by X, who knows that the offer is made to D only: C thinks, mistakenly, that acceptance was made by D.

Where mutual or unilateral mistake has occurred, the acceptance may not correspond with the offer, and there is, consequently, doubt as to the validity of the agreement.

4. Mistake at law and mistake in equity. Lord Denning said in *Solle* v. *Butcher* (1950):

"... mistake is of two kinds: first, mistake which renders the contract void, that is, a nullity from the beginning which is the kind of mistake which was dealt with by the courts of common law, and secondly, mistake which renders the contract not void, but voidable, that is, liable to be set aside on such terms as the court thinks fit, which is the kind of mistake which was dealt with by the courts of equity."

Since 1875 the court has had the power to give equitable relief or legal relief for mistake, according to the circumstances of the case, and according to the kind of relief asked for by the parties.

MISTAKE AT COMMON LAW

5. Operative mistake. Where there is a mistake of fact which *prevents the formation of any contract at all*, the court will declare the contract void. This kind of mistake is known as operative mistake: any other kind of mistake does not affect the contract in the eyes of the common law, *e.g.*

Harrison & Jones, Ltd. v. *Bunton & Lancaster, Ltd.* (1953): there was a contract for the sale of a quantity of Calcutta "Sree" brand kapok. Buyer and seller thought this to be tree kapok, whereas, in fact, it contained an admixture of bush cotton. The true nature of "Sree" brand kapok was generally known in the trade. HELD: goods answering the contract description had been supplied and there was no operative mistake.

6. Examples of operative mistake. Operative mistake may be common, mutual, or unilateral. It must be of such a nature that it cannot be deemed that there was any contract at all.

The circumstances in which operative mistake can occur are as follows:

(a) Common mistake as to the existence of the subject-matter of the contract.

- (b) Common mistake as to a fact fundamental to the entire agreement.
- (c) Mutual mistake as to the identity of the subject-matter of the contract.
- (d) Unilateral mistake as to the identity of the person with whom the contract is made.
- (e) Unilateral mistake by the offeror in expressing his intention, the mistake being known to the offeree.
- (f) Unilateral mistake as to the nature of a document signed or sealed.

NOTE: In all these cases, the mistake is operative only where it prevented the formation of any real agreement between the parties. If any party is under some misapprehension at the time of making the contract, and the mistake is not operative, then the contract is valid at common law in spite of the mistake. The mistaken party is then bound by the contract unless (i) there is fraud or illegality, or (ii) some relief for the mistake, equity: *see* **13** *below.*

7. Common mistake as to the existence of the subject-matter. Where both parties believe the subject-matter of the contract to be in existence, but in fact it is not in existence at the time of making the contract, there is operative mistake and the contract is void.

NOTE: Section 6 of the *Sale of Goods Act*, 1893, provides that: "Where there is a contract for the sale of specific goods, and the goods without the knowledge of the seller have perished at the time when the contract is made, the contract is void." But where the circumstances are such that the seller is deemed to have warranted the existence of the goods, the seller is probably liable to the buyer for breach of contract if the goods are non-existent: *McRae* v. *Commonwealth Disposals Commission* (1951), an Australian case.

8. Common mistake as to a fact fundamental to the agreement. Where the parties have made a contract based on a common misapprehension relating to the fundamental subject-matter of the contract there is operative mistake. In *Bell* v. *Lever Brothers* (1932), Lord Atkin suggested that the test should be: "Does the state of the new facts destroy the identity of the subject-matter as it was in the original state of the facts?"

Galloway v. *Galloway* (1914): the parties, believing themselves to be married, entered into a separation agreement under seal by which the man undertook to make money payments to the woman. It was later discovered that they were not, in fact, married. The woman claimed the promised payments. HELD: the deed was void on the ground of the parties' mistake.

9. Mutual mistake as to the identity of the subject-matter. Where the parties have negotiated completely at cross-purposes, it cannot be said that they were ever in agreement.

Raffles v. *Wichelhaus* (1864): there was a contract for the sale of 125 bales of cotton "to arrive ex *Peerless* from Bombay." It happened that there were two ships named *Peerless* leaving Bombay at about the same time: the buyer meant one and the seller meant the other. HELD: the contract was void for mistakes.

Scriven v. *Hindley* (1913): in an auction sale, the auctioneer was selling tow. X bid for a lot, thinking that he was buying hemp. HELD: no contract.

10. Unilateral mistake as to identity of the person contracted with. Where an offer is made to a particular offeree and to no one else, a purported acceptance by any other person will not be valid: *Boulton* v. *Jones* (1857).

Mistakes as to the identity of the person with whom the contract is made may operate to nullify the contract where:

(a) *the identity is of material importance* to the contract, and
(b) *the mistake is known to the other person*, *i.e.* he knows that is not intended that he should become a party to the contract.

Ingram v. *Little* (1960), C.A.: three ladies, the joint owners of a car, advertised for its sale. A swindler called at their home and agreed to buy the car for £717. He offered a cheque in payment, and this was refused. The swindler then attempted to convince the ladies that he was a Mr Hutchinson of Stanstead Road, Caterham, and one of them checked this name and address in the telephone directory. The ladies then decided to accept the cheque in payment. The cheque was dishonoured and the swindler disappeared (he was not Mr Hutchinson). The swindler had sold the car to L, who bought it in good faith. The ladies sought to recover possession of the car from L. HELD: the offer to sell, with payment to be made by cheque, was made to Hutchinson only. As the swindler knew this, the offer was not one which he could accept. Therefore, there was no contract for the sale of the car, and the plaintiffs were entitled to its return.

In *Lewis* v. *Averay* (1971), Lord Denning said that the title of the ultimate purchaser should not depend on such refinements as whether the original seller was mistaken as to the rogue's identity or merely as to his attributes, for in either case it is the seller who has let the rogue have the goods and thus enabled him to commit the fraud, whereas the ultimate purchaser has acted with complete circumspection and in entire good faith. Accordingly a mistake as to identity does not mean that there is no contract or that the contract is a nullity and void from the beginning; it only means that the contract is voidable.

Lewis v. *Averay* (1971): a rogue introduced himself to the plaintiff, who wished to sell his car, as "Richard Green," making the plaintiff believe that he was the well-known film actor of that name. The rogue wrote out a cheque for £450, the price of the car, but the plaintiff asked for proof of identity. The rogue showed a special admission pass to Pinewood Studios bearing the name "Richard A. Green," and a photograph which was plainly that of the rogue. The plaintiff was then satisfied and let the rogue have the car and log book. A few days later the plaintiff was told by his bank that the cheque was worthless. In the meantime, the rogue sold the car to the defendant, who bought in good faith without any knowledge of the fraud. The plaintiff brought this action for conversion of the car. HELD: (i) a contract was made between the plaintiff and the rogue because there was nothing to rebut the presumption that the plaintiff was dealing with the person present before him, even though the plaintiff thought that he was dealing with another person; (ii) accordingly, the contract was void and not voidable; (iii) the plaintiff had failed to avoid the contract before the rogue parted with the property in the car to the defendant, who, having bought the car *bona fide* and without notice of the fraud, acquired a good title and the plaintiff's action failed.

Phillips v. *Brooks* (1919): the plaintiff was a jeweller. One North entered his shop and asked to see some jewellery. He chose a pearl necklace, price £2550, and a ring, price £450. He then took out his cheque-book and wrote out a cheque for £3000. As he signed the cheque, he said, "You see who I am, I am Sir George Bullough," and gave a London address, which the jeweller checked in a directory. The jeweller then asked whether he would like to take the articles with him, to which North replied that he would like to take the ring. North promptly pledged the ring with the defendant, a pawnbroker, for £350. The cheque was dishonoured and the jeweller claimed to recover the ring from the pawnbroker. HELD: the jeweller intended to contract with the person present in front of him, whoever he was, *i.e.* the mistake as to identity of the man North did not affect the formation of the contract. North got a voidable title to the ring, and since it was not avoided at the time of pledging it, the pawnbroker got a good title.

In the above case, North's title to the ring was voidable because of the fraudulent misrepresentation, but at the time of the pledge, his title was still good, since by then the jeweller had done nothing to avoid his title. In connection with sale under a voidable title, *Sale of Goods Act*, *s.* 23, provides that: "When the seller of goods has a voidable title thereto, but his title has not been avoided at the time of the sale, the buyer acquires a good title to the goods, provided he buys them in good faith and without notice of the seller's defect in title."

Cundy v. *Lindsay* (1878), H.L.: Alfred Blenkarn ordered certain goods from Lindsay & Co., signing the order in such a way as to make it appear to have come from Blenkiron & Co., a respectable firm. The goods were delivered to Blenkarn but he did not pay for them. Blenkarn sold the goods to Cundy's. Lindsay's claimed the recovery of the goods, or their value from Cundy's. HELD: the contract between Blenkarn and Lindsay's was void for mistake; therefore no property passed to Cundy's. Cundy's were liable to Lindsay's for the value of the goods.

11. Unilateral mistake as to the expression of intention.

Where the offeror makes a material mistake in expressing his intention, and the other party knows, or is deemed to know, of the error, the mistake may be operative.

Hartog v. *Colin & Shields* (1939): H claimed damages for breach of contract, alleging that C had agreed to sell him 30,000 Argentinian hare skins and had failed to deliver them. C contended that the offer contained a material mistake and that H was well aware of this mistake when he accepted the offer. The mistake alleged by C was that the skins were offered at certain prices *per pound* instead of *per piece*. In the negotiations preceding the agreement, reference had always been made to prices *per piece*; moreover, this was the custom of the trade. C contended that the contract was void for mistake. HELD: the

contract was void for mistake. H could not reasonably have supposed that the offer expressed C's real intention; H must have
known that it was made under a mistake.

12. Unilateral mistake as to the nature of a document signed.

The general rule is that a person is bound by the terms of any
instrument which he signs or seals even though he did not
read it, or did not understand its contents: *L'Estrange* v.
Graucob (1934). But since the sixteenth century the courts
have allowed, in certain cases, a person who in fact signed a
document to plead that it was not his deed. This plea is called
non est factum. This plea has been allowed in exceptional cases
where the person signing a document was permanently or
temporarily unable, through no fault of his own, to have
without explanation any real understanding of the purport of
the document, whether from defective education, illness or
innate incapacity. A person pleading *non est factum* must
show that he took such precautions as he reasonably could.
Where an innocent third party has relied on the signature on
a document, he will suffer loss if the maker of that document
is allowed to have it declared a nullity on the grounds of *non
est factum*. The courts therefore impose a heavy burden of
proof on any person who pleads *non est factum*. He will be
required to prove all the circumstances necessary to justify the
remedy being granted to him, and that involves his proving
that he took all reasonable precautions in the circumstances.
It will be exceptional for a man of full mental and physical
capacity to plead *non est factum* successfully. The remedy will
not be available where a person signed a document without
reading it because he was too busy to do so or too lazy.

The essence of the plea *non est factum* is that the person
signing a document believed that the document had one
character or one effect whereas, in fact, its character was quite
different, or its effect was quite different. It should be noted
that the person signing the document could not have such a
belief unless he had taken steps or had been given information
to support his belief. The amount of information he must have
and the firmness of belief required must depend on the
circumstances of each case. *Non est factum* is never available
to a person whose mistake was really a mistake as to the legal
effect of the document signed, whether the mistake was his
own or that of his adviser.

Saunders v. *Anglia Building Society* (1970), H.L.: the plaintiff was an elderly widow who had made a will leaving all her possessions to her nephew, Walter Parkin. Her house was leasehold with more than 900 years to go. She gave the deeds of the house to Parkin because she had left it to him in her will, and she knew that he wanted to raise money on it. She was content to allow him to do this provided she was able to remain in the house during her lifetime. When Parkin told his friend, the first defendant, that the plaintiff had left the house to him in her will, they came to an arrangement by which the first defendant, who was heavily in debt, could raise some money. According to the arrangement, a document was drawn up by solicitors by which the plaintiff was to sell the house to the first defendant for £3,000. The understanding between Parkin and the first defendant was that after signature by the plaintiff, no purchase price would be paid over, and the first defendant would then mortgage the property to raise money. The first defendant took the document to the plaintiff, who at that time was 78 years old, to get her signature. She did not read the document because she had broken her spectacles. She asked him what it was for, and he replied, "It is a deed of gift for Wally [Parkin] for the house." She thought at the time that Parkin was going to borrow money on the deeds and that the first defendant was arranging this for him. After the plaintiff had signed the document no money was paid to her, although the document provided that she acknowledged receipt of £300 paid by the first defendant. The first defendant then obtained a loan of £2000 from the second defendant, a building society, on the security of the deeds. For this purpose, Parkin gave a reference to the building society, falsely stating that he was a reliable person. Subsequently, the first defendant defaulted in the instalment payments to the building society, which then sought to recover possession of the house. The plaintiff then brought this action, contending that she was not bound by the assignment on the grounds that it was not her deed. It was held by the trial judge that the assignment was not her deed and the building society was ordered to deliver up the title deeds to the plaintiff. The building society appealed to the Court of Appeal, where it was held that the plea of *non est factum* could not be supported. The plaintiff in the meantime having died, her executrix appealed to the House of Lords. HELD: the plaintiff fell very short of making the clear and satisfactory case which is required of those who seek to have a legal act declared void and of establishing a sufficient discrepancy between her intentions and her act. The plea *non est factum* accordingly failed.

MISTAKE IN EQUITY

13. Equitable relief for mistake. Where a person has entered
a contract under a misapprehension, and the contract is good
at common law (*i.e.* the court has not declared it void for
operative mistake), the mistaken party may, in proper circumstances, obtain equitable relief from his contractual obligations.
The relief afforded by equity is of three kinds:

    (a) Rescission on terms.
    (b) Refusal of specific performance.
    (c) Rectification.

14. Rescission on terms. In order to get rescission on terms,
the claimant must show the court that it would be against
good conscience for the other party to take full advantage of
his contractual rights. In these circumstances, the court has
powers to attach terms to the order that the contract be set
aside. In effect, the original contractual rights and obligations are dissolved and replaced by fresh rights and obligations
based on what the court thinks fair and just: *Solle* v. *Butcher*
(1949); *Grist* v. *Bailey* (1966).

15. Refusal of specific performance. Specific performance is
a discretionary remedy and is not awarded as of right. The
court will not usually award specific performance where the
defendant entered the contract under some material misapprehension and

    (a) it would be unduly harsh to force the defendant to
        comply specifically with the terms of the contract, or
    (b) the mistake was caused by the misrepresentation of the
        plaintiff, or
    (c) the plaintiff knew of the defendant's mistake.

If none of these conditions is satisfied, mistake is no defence
to an action for specific performance.

16. Rectification. Where a written contract does not ac-
curately express the agreement actually reached between the
parties, the court will rectify the written document so as to

bring it into conformity with the actual agreement reached. A party claiming rectification must prove:

(a) that a complete and certain agreement was reached between the parties, and
(b) that the agreement was unchanged at the time it was put into writing, and the writing did not correspond with the agreement reached, *i.e.* there was a mistake in expressing the terms of the agreement.

MISREPRESENTATION: REPRESENTATIONS DISTINGUISHED FROM EXPRESS TERMS

17. Material statements during negotiations. Material statements made during negotiations leading to a contract can be divided into two classes:

(a) Statements by which the parties *intended to be bound*. Such statements form the express terms of the contract.

(b) Statements by which the parties *did not intend to be bound*, but which, nevertheless, helped to *induce* the contract. These statements are known as *mere representations*.

NOTE: Where a mere representation proves to be false, there has been no breach of contract, for representation was not a term.

18. Mere representations. A mere representation is a statement

(a) of material fact;
(b) made by one party to another;
(c) during the negotiations leading to the agreement;
(d) which was intended to operate, and did operate, as an inducement to enter the contract;
(e) but was not intended to be a binding contractual term.

Where a statement of this class proves to be *false*, there is misrepresentation. The remedies available to the party who has been misled may depend on whether the misrepresentation was made fraudulently or innocently.

19. Statement of material fact. A representation is an assertion of the truth that a fact exists or did exist. It can, therefore, have no reference to future events or promises. The assertion must be materially connected to the contract.

POINTS TO NOTE ARE :

(a) *A promise to do something relates to the future.* If it is material to the agreement, it will be a term and not a mere representation.

(b) *A statement as to the state of a man's mind may be a statement of fact: Edgington* v. *Fitzmaurice* (1885). A mis-statement of the state of a man's mind is misrepresentation of fact. A statement as to state of mind may be made with reference to intention or to opinion.

　(i) *An expression of intention* may be a statement of fact.

　(ii) *An expression of opinion* may be a statement of fact. But if it is proved that the expressed opinion was not actually held, there is a misrepresentation. If, however, the expressed opinion was actually held, there is no misrepresentation—even where the opinion was mistakenly held.

Bisset v. *Wilkinson* (1927), P.C.: the vendor of a piece of land in New Zealand told a prospective purchaser that, in his opinion, the land would carry 2000 sheep. In fact, the land would not carry that number of sheep. HELD: there was no misrepresentation, for the statement was one of opinion which was honestly held.

(c) *Simplex commendatio non obligat* ("a simple recommendation does not bind"). The law allows a trader a good deal of latitude in his choice of language when commending his wares. Mere advertisement puff is not misrepresentation, but statements of a specific nature will usually be terms or representations.

(d) *A statement of law must be distinguished from a statement of fact.* If a legal principle is wrongly stated there is no misrepresentation: but a false statement as to the existence of a legal right may be a misrepresentation.

20. Statement by one party to another. A statement made by a person who is not a party to the agreement cannot be a representation unless there is a principal–agent relationship (express or implied) between that person and one of the parties.

21. Statement made in negotiations. Any statement which was not made during the course of negotiations leading to the formation of an agreement cannot be a representation, *e.g.* a statement made after the agreement has been concluded.

22. Inducement to enter the contract. A statement cannot be a representation unless it was intended to be an inducement to the other party to enter the contract, and, in fact, operated as an inducement. There is no misrepresentation, therefore, where:

(a) the statement was not actually communicated to the other party; or

(b) the statement did not affect the other party's decision to enter the contract; or

(c) the statement was known to be untrue by the other party; or

(d) the other party did not believe the statement to be true.

23. No intention to be bound. A mere representation is a statement by which the parties did not intend to be bound. Intention is discovered, in cases of dispute, by the application of an objective test. Where the court finds an intention to be bound, the statement is a contractual term and not a mere representation: *Couchman* v. *Hill* (1947), *see* II, **15.**

MISREPRESENTATION MAY BE INNOCENT OR FRAUDULENT

24. Fraudulent misrepresentation. Where any statement (whether it is a mere representation or not) is made fraudulently there is the tort of deceit, and an action for damages will lie at the suit of the person who has been misled. A statement is fraudulent when it is made "(i) knowingly, or (ii) without belief in its truth, or (iii) recklessly, careless whether it be true or false": *Derry* v. *Peek* (1889).

25. Remedies for fraudulent misrepresentation. A party who has been deceived by fraudulent misrepresentation may sue for *damages in tort for deceit*, and *in addition*, he may either

(a) affirm the contract, or

(b) disaffirm the contract and refuse further performance.

Where a party disaffirms the contract he may either:

(i) *take no legal action*, and plead fraud as a defence and counter-claim for damages in the event of his being sued for breach of contract by the other party; or

(ii) *bring an action* for rescission of the contract.

26. Innocent misrepresentation. Any misrepresentation which is made with an honest belief in its truth is innocent. The test of honesty is a subjective one: the usual objective test of intention is not used in this distinction.

27. Remedies for innocent misrepresentation. A party who has been misled by an innocent misrepresentation may choose from the following alternatives:

(a) He may *affirm* the contract and treat it as binding.

(b) He may *claim for rescission* of the contract. Rescission is an equitable remedy, granted only in the discretion of the court. A person is entitled to rescission even though (i) the misrepresentation has become a term of the contract or (ii) the contract has been performed: *Misrepresentation Act*, 1967, *s*. 1.

(c) He may *sue for damages* under *s*. 2 of the *Misrepresentation Act*, 1967. By section 2(1), where a party has suffered loss as a result of a misrepresentation, the party making the misrepresentation is liable to pay damages unless he proves that he had reasonable ground to believe, and did believe, up to the time the contract was made, that the facts represented were true. Section 2(2) gives the court a discretionary power to award damages in lieu of rescission where it would be equitable to do so.

28. No general duty of disclosure. There is no general duty to disclose material facts during negotiations, *e.g.* in sales of goods the rule is "buyer beware"—the seller is under no duty to reveal unflattering truths about the goods sold. Only in a few contracts does the law impose a duty of disclosure.

> *Hands* v. *Simpson, Fawcett & Co. Ltd.* (1928): a commercial traveller obtained employment without disclosing that he was disqualified from driving a car. The new employer regarded driving as an essential part of his duties, and contended that his silence amounted to misrepresentation. HELD: the traveller was under no duty to volunteer the information. Mere silence cannot be misrepresentation where there is no positive duty to speak.
>
> EXCEPTIONS: *A duty of disclosure* is imposed by the law in the following cases:
> (a) Contracts *uberrimae fidei: see* **30** *below*.
> (b) Where a part-truth amounts to a falsehood.

(c) Where there is a fiduciary element in the relationship between the contracting parties.

(d) Where a statement true when made becomes untrue through a change of circumstances during the negotiations: *Davies* v. *London Provincial* (1878).

(e) Where a party who made a statement in the belief that it was true subsequently discovers that it was false: *With* v. *O'Flanagan* (1936).

29. Uberimma fides (utmost good faith). In contracts of insurance of all kinds, disclosure of all material facts must be made to the insurer. A fact is material if it would affect the judgment of a prudent insurer in deciding whether to accept the risk or in deciding what shall be the premium. It has been held that there was a duty to disclose in the following cases:

(a) Where the insured goods were carried on the deck of a ship instead of in the hold: *Hood* v. *West End Motor Car Packing Co.* (1917).

(b) Where it is not disclosed that a proposal has been refused by another insurance company: *Locker and Woolf, Ltd.* v. *West Australian Insurance Co. Ltd.* (1936).

(c) Where a ship was insured and it was not disclosed that her cargo was insured at a value exceeding the real value: *Ionides* v. *Pender* (1874).

Where there has been a material non-disclosure, the insurer may avoid the contract.

30. Contracts affected by the uberrima fides principle. There are also the following classes of contract in which the principle of *uberrima fides* operates:

(a) *Company prospectuses.* The *Companies Act*, 1948, provides that certain matters shall be included in prospectuses inviting the public to subscribe for shares or debentures. Any person responsible for the non-disclosure of the stipulated matters shall be liable to a fine: *s.* 38. Also, a contract to buy shares is voidable where there is a material non-disclosure in the prospectus.

(b) *Contracts for the sale of land.* The vendor of an estate or interest in land is under a duty to the purchaser to show good title to the estate or interest he has contracted to sell. All defects in *title* must, therefore, be disclosed. This duty does not extend to physical defects in the property itself.

(c) *Family arrangements* are agreements or arrangements between members of a family for the protection or distribution of family property. If any member of the family withholds material information, the agreement or arrangement may be set aside: *Gordon* v. *Gordon* (1821); *Greenwood* v. *Greenwood* (1863).

(d) *A confidential relationship* between the contracting parties gives rise to a duty to disclose material facts. This rule is sometimes known as the equitable doctrine of constructive fraud, and is closely connected with undue influence.

> *Tate* v. *Williamson* (1866): A, who was a young man heavily in debt, sought the advice of B. A was advised by B to sell certain land in order to raise money to repay the debts. B then offered to buy the land for half its real value. Certain facts which were material to the value of the land were known to B and he did not disclose them to A. HELD: The contract could be set aside for constructive fraud.

(e) *Suretyship and partnership contracts*. Contracts of suretyship (guarantee) and contracts of partnership do not require *uberrima fides*: but they do create a relationship between the parties which requires a measure of good faith (*i.e.* disclosure of material facts) in their dealings after the contract has been made.

DURESS AND UNDUE INFLUENCE

31. Duress. Duress at common law occurs where a party enters a contract under violence or threatened violence to himself or his immediate family; or where he is threatened with false imprisonment; or where he is threatened with the dishonour of a member of his family. Coercion of this kind is legal duress when it is exercised by another party to the contract, or by the agent of another party, or by any person to the knowledge of another party. Cases of duress are rare in modern times.

32. Legal effect of duress. Where there is duress, the assent is not freely given, and the contract is *voidable* at the option of the party who has been coerced.

Kaufman v. *Gerson* (1904): G had taken money which K had entrusted with him. K threatened to prosecute G, unless G's wife made good the loss out of her own property. G's wife agreed to do so, in order to save her husband's honour. HELD: G's wife was not bound by her promise. She was entitled to avoid the contract which she entered under duress.

33. Undue influence. Undue influence in equity occurs where a party enters a contract under any kind of influence which prevents him from exercising a free and independent judgment. The courts have always taken care not to define undue influence, for a definition would cramp their equitable jurisdiction in this connection. Where undue influence is alleged, the court regards itself as a court of conscience with full discretion to make its findings accordingly. There is a rebuttable presumption of undue influence where a fiduciary or confidential relationship exists between contracting parties; in all other cases, the onus is on the party alleging undue influence to prove it.

34. Legal effect of undue influence. A contract (or gift under seal) may be set aside at the suit of a party who contracted under influence. This relief is equitable and, therefore, discretionary. It may be disallowed where the plaintiff has delayed making his claim, for *delay defeats the equities: Allcard* v. *Skinner* (1887). Also, it may be disallowed where the plaintiff's conduct has been tricky, for *he who comes to equity must come with clean hands.*

35. Presumed influence. Where the relationship between contracting parties is such that one is entitled to rely upon the confidential advice of the other, undue influence is presumed to have been exercised, until it is proved to the contrary.

The presumption arises where the contracting parties are in any of the following relationships: solicitor and client, trustee and beneficiary, doctor and patient, parent and child, guardian and ward, religious adviser and person over whom religious influence is exercised. It is not clear whether the presumption arises in the case of engaged couples, but it certainly does not arise in the case of husband and wife.

Evidence required to rebut the presumption will vary

according to the circumstances, but it is usually necessary to show:

(a) that the consideration moving from the dominant party was at least adequate;
(b) that the plaintiff had the benefit of competent, independent advice, in the light of a full disclosure of all material facts;
(c) that, in the case of a gift by deed, the gift was made spontaneously.

Inche Noriah v. *Shaik Alli Bin Omar* (1928), P.C.: a nephew was managing the affairs of his aged aunt and persuaded her to give him property by deed of gift. The lawyer who drew up the deed of gift explained to the aunt that it was irrevocable and asked whether she was signing it voluntarily. He did not know that the gift constituted practically the whole of her property, nor did he advise her that she could have left the property to her nephew by will instead of making the gift. HELD: the nephew was unable to rebut the presumption of undue influence and the gift should be set aside.

36. Where undue influence must be proved. Where there is no relationship between the parties giving rise to the presumption of undue influence, a party alleging undue influence must prove that the other party had a dominant influence over his mind so that there was no exercise of independent will in entering the contract. Where the existence of the influence is proved, the court will assume that it was exercised, unless the contrary is proved.

PROGRESS TEST 4

1. Distinguish between common mistake, mutual mistake and unilateral mistake. (2, 3)
2. What is operative mistake? Give examples. (5, 6)
3. Explain fully how mistaken identity may affect a contract. (10)
4. In what circumstances may the defence of *non est factum* be pleaded? (12)
5. What do you understand by "rescission on terms"? Do you consider that an order of rescission on terms is likely to achieve a more just result than a declaration that a contract is void *ab initio*? (13, 14)

6. In what circumstances will common mistake avoid a contract? **(7, 8)**

7. There was a contract of sale between A, the seller, and B, the buyer, for 1000 Japanese cameras, described to be lying in A's warehouse in London. Immediately before the agreement, the cameras were destroyed in a fire in A's warehouse. A did not know about the fire until after the agreement. B, who had planned to make a large profit on a re-sale of the cameras, wishes now to claim damages from A for breach of contract. Advise B. **(7)**

8. E agrees to buy F's horse, Dobbin. At the time of the agreement, F intends to sell his grey horse called Dobbin. He does not know that E thinks he is buying F's white horse, which is also called Dobbin. Is there a binding contract between the parties? **(9)**

9. G advertises in a newspaper for the sale of his motor car. H calls at G's house in response to the advertisement, introducing himself falsely as "Henry Jones." G agrees to sell his car to H and to take a cheque in payment. H drives off in the car, and the cheque is subsequently dishonoured. H sells the car to J, and then disappears. What must G prove in order to be able to recover the car from J? **(10)**

10. Define carefully a "mere representation," distinguishing it from a contractual term. **(17, 18)**

11. How do the courts distinguish between innocent misrepresentation and fraudulent misrepresentation? **(24)**

12. What are the remedies available for

    (a) innocent misrepresentation, and
    (b) fraudulent misrepresentation? **(25–27)**

13. Is there a general duty to disclose material facts during negotiations preceding a contract? **(28)**

14. A, the vendor of a small general store, told B, the purchaser, that he thought trade would double within twelve months because four large blocks of council flats were nearing completion and would soon be occupied. A year after the contract, the trade in B's store had not increased at all. The flat-dwellers, when they arrived, hardly used the store at all. B wishes to know whether he has any claim against A with respect to his statement that trade would double within twelve months. Advise him. **(19)**

15. Distinguish between duress and undue influence and explain the legal effect of each. **(31–35)**

CHAPTER V

ILLEGAL, VOID AND UNENFORCEABLE CONTRACTS

ILLEGALITY GENERALLY

1. Ex turpi causa non oritur actio. It is against public policy, *i.e.* against the policy of the common law, to allow an action on a contract containing an illegal or wrongful element. The maxims upon which this policy is founded are:

(a) *Ex turpi causa non oritur actio:* no action arises from a base cause. (Sometimes expressed as *ex dolo malo non oritur actio.*)

(b) *In pari delicto potior est conditio defendentis:* where there is equal fault, the defendant is in the stronger position.

Lord Mansfield, C.J., said in *Holman* v. *Johnson* (1775), "The objection, that a contract is immoral or illegal as between plaintiff and defendant, sounds at all times very ill in the mouth of the defendant. It is not for his sake, however, that the objection is ever allowed; but it is founded in general principles of policy, which the defendant has the advantage of, contrary to the real justice, as between him and the plaintiff, by accident, if I may say so. The principle of public policy is this: *ex dolo malo non oritur actio.* No court will lend its aid to a man who founds his cause of action upon an immoral or illegal act. If, from the plaintiff's own stating or otherwise, the cause of action appears to arise *ex turpi causa,* or the transgression of a positive law of this country, there the court says he has no right to be assisted. It is upon that ground the court goes; not for the sake of the defendant, but because they will not lend their aid to such a plaintiff."

2. No rights from an illegal contract. Where the plaintiff's cause of action arises from an illegal contract, the general rule is that the court will drive the parties from its presence, recognising no rights or obligations between them, and making no order as to damages or costs. Thus, where a party has paid money under an illegal contract, he is usually unable to recover it: *see* **11** *below*.

SCOPE OF ILLEGALITY IN CONTRACTS

3. Examples of illegal contracts. A contract is illegal if it involves the transgression of a rule of law (statutory or otherwise) or where it is base or immoral. Examples are:

(a) Contracts *prohibited* by statute.
(b) Contracts to defraud the Revenue.
(c) Contracts involving the commission of a crime or tort.
(d) Contracts with a sexually immoral element.
(e) Contracts against the interests of the United Kingdom or a friendly state.
(f) Contracts leading to corruption in public life.
(g) Contracts which interfere with the course of justice.

4. Contracts prohibited by statute. A contract which contravenes the terms or policy of a statute is illegal.

NOTE

(i) There is a distinction between a statutory provision which *prohibits* a contract, and one which merely renders a contract *void*: *see* **13**.
(ii) Where a party to a lawful contract performs his side of the bargain in a manner forbidden by statute, the contract itself does not thereby become illegal: *St John Shipping Corporation* v. *Joseph Rank Ltd.* (1957).

5. Contracts to defraud the Revenue. A contract which is designed to defraud the Revenue is illegal.

Napier v. *National Business Agency Ltd.* (1951), C.A.: N was employed by the company at a salary plus £6 a week for expenses. As both parties knew, N's expenses were never more than £1 a week. The company dismissed N summarily and he claimed his salary for a period in lieu of notice. HELD: the part of the agreement relating to expenses was tax evasion and illegal: the rest of the agreement was tainted with illegality.

6. Contracts to commit a crime or a tort. Where the consideration in, or the purpose of, a contract is criminal or tortious, the contract is illegal.

Beresford v. *Royal Insurance Co. Ltd.* (1938), C.A.: R shot himself a few minutes before his life insurance policy expired. His personal representatives claimed on the policy. HELD: it would be against public policy to allow a man to benefit his estate by committing a crime. The sum assured was not recoverable.

Contracts involving *maintenance or champerty* fall into this class, *i.e.* contracts whereby a person promises to support another improperly in bringing an action at law.

7. Contracts with a sexually immoral element. A contract is illegal for immorality as follows:

(a) Where the consideration is an act of sexual immorality, *e.g.* an agreement for future illicit co-habitation. (NOTE: An agreement with respect to *past* illicit co-habitation is not illegal, and is binding if made under seal.)

(b) Where the purpose of the contract is the furtherance of sexual immorality, and both parties know this.

> *Pearce* v. *Brooks* (1866): there was a contract under which a firm of coachbuilders hired out a carriage to a prostitute. It was known that she intended to use the vehicle as part of her display to attract men. The prostitute fell into arrears with the hire payments, and the coachbuilders claimed the sum due. HELD: the contract was illegal and the sum claimed could not be recovered.

8. Contracts against the interest of the State. Any contract which is detrimental to the interest of the United Kingdom is illegal, *e.g.* a trading contract which would benefit a country at war with the United Kingdom.

The rule also covers agreements which might disturb the friendly relations between the U.K. and other states. Thus the court once refused to recognise an agreement to export whisky to the U.S.A. contrary to the prohibition laws of that country in the 1920s: *Foster* v. *Driscoll* (1929).

9. Contracts leading to corruption in public life. Contracts involving the bribery of officials, or attempts to buy honours, are illegal.

> *Parkinson* v. *College of Ambulance* (1925): P gave the secretary of a charitable organisation £3000 on the understanding that he would secure a knighthood for him. The title was not forth-

coming and P sought to recover his money. HELD: the agreement was illegal, and P could not recover.

10. Contracts which interfere with the course of justice. A contract not to prosecute, or to compromise, in criminal proceedings is illegal, unless the proceedings could have been initiated in the civil courts for tort. Also, a contract under which an accused person indemnifies a person who has gone bail for him is illegal: *Herman* v. *Jeuchner* (1885).

THE CONSEQUENCES OF ILLEGALITY

11. Consequences of illegality. The general rule is that no action can be brought by a party to an illegal contract: *ex turpi causa non oritur actio*. The following points should be noted:

(a) *No action will lie for the recovery of money paid* or property transferred under an illegal contract: *Parkinson's case.*

(b) *No action will lie for breach* of an illegal contract: *Pearce* v. *Brooks; Beresford's case.*

(c) Where part of an illegal contract would have been lawful by itself, *the court will not sever* the good from the bad. The whole contract becomes tainted with illegality: *Napier's case.*

(d) *Any contract which is collateral* to an illegal contract is also tainted with illegality, and is treated as being illegal, even though it would have been lawful by itself.

Fisher v. *Bridges* (1854): there was an illegal contract under which F agreed to sell certain land to B. B paid the purchase price except for £630, and the land was conveyed to him. By a separate deed B promised to pay £630 to F. HELD: the collateral agreement under seal was tainted with the illegality.

12. Exceptions to the general rule of no recovery. A party to an illegal contract may sue to recover money paid or property transferred as follows:

(a) *Where the parties are not in pari delicto, i.e.* not equally at fault, the "innocent" party may recover. This circumstance may arise in two ways:

(i) Where the contract is prohibited by statute in order to protect the class of person to which the plaintiff belongs.

(ii) Where a party has been induced to enter an illegal contract by fraudulent misrepresentation, or where an ignorant man enters an illegal contract under the influence of a cleverer man: *Hughes* v. *Liverpool Friendly Soc.* (1916).

(b) *Where no substantial part of the illegal act has been performed*, a party who is truly repentant may recover. In this way, the law encourages repentance. But a party seeking to take advantage of this rule must show that his repentance is genuine, and that he is not repudiating the contract for mere reasons of convenience: *Bigos* v. *Bousted* (1951).

(c) Where a contract is lawful in its actual formation, but there is an *illegal purpose known to one party* and not to the other, the innocent party may recover: *Cowan* v. *Milbourn* (1867). But a contract which is *ex facie* lawful will be treated as illegal if both parties knew of the illegal purpose: *Pearce* v. *Brooks* (1866).

(d) Where a party to an illegal contract is *able to frame his action so as not to depend on contract*, he may succeed in recovering property: *Bowmakers Ltd.* v. *Barnet Instruments Ltd.* (1944); *Sajan Singh* v. *Sardara Ali* (1959).

VOID CONTRACTS GENERALLY

13. Distinction between void and illegal contracts. A contract which is void does not give rise to rights and obligations, but the full consequences of illegality are not present. A contract may be void in any of the following circumstances:

(a) Where a *statute* renders contracts of that class void.

(b) Where the contract is void at *common law* as being against public policy.

(c) Where the *Restrictive Trade Practices Court* declares that the contract is against the public interest.

(d) Where the contract is *void at common law generally, e.g.* for operative mistake, or for lack of capacity of one of the parties.

CONTRACTS MADE VOID BY STATUTE

14. Examples of contracts in this class.

(a) *Assignments of retired pay* by officers of the army, navy, or air force. Also, assignments of pensions by teachers, policemen and old age pensioners.

(b) Infants' contracts rendered void by *s.* 1 of the *Infants' Relief Act,* 1874.

(c) *Wagering contracts.* Under the *Gaming Act,* 1845, all contracts by way of gaming or wagering are null and void.

(d) Contracts made void by the *Resale Prices Act,* 1964: *see* 33 *below.*

15. Consequences where a contract is void by statute. No enforceable rights arise from a void contract. However, the transaction may not be entirely without legal effect. For example, a contract by an infant to repay money lent to him is "absolutely void," but the legal effect is that the lender is unable to recover his loan. Similarly, money paid under a wagering contract cannot be recovered.

CONTRACTS VOID AT COMMON LAW AS BEING AGAINST PUBLIC POLICY

16. Contracts offending public policy. Most contracts which offend against public policy are illegal, and have been dealt with above. There are, however, certain remaining contracts against public policy which have escaped the full stigma of illegality. These contracts are void, but only so far as they are against public policy. They are:

(a) Contracts to oust the courts from their jurisdiction.

(b) Contracts striking at the sanctity of marriage.

(c) Contracts impeding parental duties.

(d) Contracts in restraint of trade.

17. Contracts to oust the jurisdiction. The court is the final arbiter on questions of law, and this jurisdiction cannot be ousted by any agreement between the parties. Thus, although a party may bind himself to submit to the findings of fact by a competent arbitrator or domestic tribunal, he cannot bind himself to refrain from submitting questions of law to the courts: *Lee* v. *Showmen's Guild* (1952). Similarly void is an agreement not to refer to the court a dispute over the meaning of words in a contract document: *Baker* v. *Jones* (1954). *See* XIV.

18. Contracts striking at the sanctity of marriage. The institution of marriage is protected by the policy of the courts. Contracts in undue restraint of marriage, contracts which impede a party in his marital duties, and marriage brokage contracts are void.

EXAMPLES

   (i) A contract by which a party undertakes not to marry at all is void. A partial restraint is not necessarily void, *e.g.* where X contracts not to marry Y, the restraint does not necessarily make the contract void; but where X promises not to marry at all, the contract is void. A contract not to marry for six years has been held to be void.

  (ii) A contract between husband and wife for a definite or possible *future* separation is void. But a contract between husband and wife for an *immediate* separation is valid.

 (iii) Where a party whose present spouse is still alive contracts to marry another, the contract is void, *e.g.* X, who is married to Y, contracts with Z that he will marry her after the death of Y—the contract is void. But a contract to marry entered into after a decree nisi and before the decree absolute of divorce is not void.

19. Contracts impeding parental duties. A contract by which a party deprives himself of the custody of his child is void. But note that a court order to the same effect is binding.

20. Contracts in restraint of trade. A contract in restraint of trade is one whereby a party undertakes to suffer some restriction as to carrying on his trade or profession. There is an agreement in restraint of trade:

  (a) Where an employee, apprentice, or articled clerk undertakes not to set up in business, or enter the service of another, within a specified area.

  (b) Where the vendor of the goodwill of a business undertakes not to compete with the purchaser.

  (c) Where merchants or manufacturers give mutual under-

takings for the regulation of their business relations: *e.g.*
by agreeing (i) to regulate the output of any commodity,
or (ii) to control prices.

21. Contracts in restraint of trade are prima facie void. A
contract in restraint of trade is *prima facie* void, but it will
be upheld by the court if it can be shown that the restraint is:

(a) *reasonable as between the parties*; in particular, the restraint must be no wider than is necessary to protect the
proper interests of the person whom it is designed to
benefit; *and also*
(b) *reasonable as regards the interests of the public, i.e.* not
injurious to the public.

"Restraints of trade and interference with individual liberty
of action, may be justified by the special circumstances of a
particular case. It is a sufficient justification, and indeed it is
the only justification, if the restriction is reasonable—reasonable, that is, in reference to the interests of the parties concerned and reasonable in reference to the interests of the
public, so framed and so guarded as to afford adequate protection to the party in whose favour it is imposed, while at the
same time it is in no way injurious to the public": *per* Lord
Macnaghten in the *Nordenfelt* case.

22. Reasonableness in contracts in restraint of trade. The
question of whether a restraint is reasonable is decided by the
judge. The duty of the jury is to find any facts which are
necessary to the judge's decision. The concept of *reasonableness* should be considered separately with reference to restraints
in contracts of (*a*) employment, (*b*) sale of goodwill and (*c*)
trading agreements.

23. Reasonableness in contracts of employment. An employer is entitled to the benefit of a restraint clause protecting
confidential information or a proprietary interest, *e.g.* goodwill
or trade secrets. Where an employer can show that the restraint is no wider than this, the presumption that the contract
is void is rebutted.

But a restraint clause which purports to restrict an employee from using his *skill* in competition with his master

(after leaving his master's employment) is always void, even where the skill was acquired in the master's service: *Morris* v. *Saxelby* (1916). In deciding whether a restraint is reasonable, the courts will consider the following factors:

(a) The nature of the employer's business.
(b) The status of the employee.
(c) The geographical area covered by the restraint clause.
(d) The duration of the restraint clause in time.

Fitch v. *Dewes* (1921), H.L.: F entered a contract of employment with D as a solicitor's managing clerk. The contract provided that after the expiration of F's term of service, he should never be concerned in a solicitor's business within seven miles of D's office. HELD: (i) the restraint was reasonable to give D the protection he was entitled to, even though it was unlimited as to time, and (ii) the restraint was not against the public interest.

Mason v. *Provident Clothing Co. Ltd.* (1913), H.L.: a canvasser contracted not to be employed in any business similar to his employer's within 25 miles of London within three years of the termination of his employment. HELD: the restriction was wider than reasonably necessary, and, therefore, void.

Home Counties Dairies Ltd. v. *Skilton* (1970), C.A.: a milk roundsman was employed under a contract which provided that he would not at any time within one year after the determination of his employment sell milk to, or solicit orders for milk from, any customer of the employer who was served by the roundsman in the course of his employment. The employer sold the goodwill of his business to a company which agreed to take over all employees. Soon afterwards, the roundsman gave notice to end his employment. He then entered into employment with another dairyman and immediately began to serve the same milk round that he had worked during the course of his previous employment. The company which had bought the goodwill of his original employers brought this action to enforce the restraint in the original contract. HELD: the agreement, on its true construction, was an agreement not to serve another employer as milk roundsman calling on the customers of the old milk round. The restraint was not unreasonable and was, accordingly, binding.

24. Reasonableness in sale of goodwill. Where the vendor of the goodwill of a business undertakes not to compete with the purchaser, the courts are more likely to uphold the restraint than in the case of the restraint imposed on an employee. Nevertheless, restraints of this class are void unless they protect a definite proprietary interest.

NOTE
 (i) There must be a genuine sale of a business: *Vancouver Brewery case* (1934).
 (ii) The restraint must relate to the actual business sold and to no others: *British Reinforced Concrete Co.* v. *Schelff* (1921).

25. Reasonableness in contracts regulating trade. At common law, agreements between merchants and manufacturers to regulate trade in any way are reasonable with regard to the public interest if they are reasonable as between the parties. The common law position has, however, been altered by the *Restrictive Trade Practices Act,* 1956, and the *Resale Prices Act,* 1964.

CONSEQUENCES WHERE A CONTRACT IS VOID AS BEING AGAINST PUBLIC POLICY

26. General consequences. Contracts to oust jurisdiction, or which are prejudicial to marriage, or which impede parental duties, or which are in restraint of trade, *are not illegal in the full sense*: they are merely void in so far as public policy is contravened. Contracts of this kind are binding except as to clauses which do not satisfy public policy.

NOTE
 (i) Such contracts are severable: *see below.*
 (ii) Collateral transactions are not necessarily void: contrast illegal contracts.
 (iii) Money paid or property transferred is generally recoverable: *Hermann* v. *Charlesworth* (1905).

27. Severance. Contracts in this class are said to be severable, *i.e.* the void part (if any) is rejected and the rest of the contract is valid and enforceable. But note *Attwood* v. *Lamont* (1920), *below.*

Attwood v. *Lamont* (1920), c.a.: L, who was a tailor's cutter, entered a contract of employment as head of the tailoring department of A's general outfitting shop. Under the contract, L covenanted not to engage in "the trade of a tailor, dressmaker, general draper, milliner, hatter, haberdasher, gentlemen's, ladies' or children's outfitter at any place within a radius of 10 miles of [A's] place of business." HELD: (i) no part of this clause could be severed because it constituted a single covenant for the protection of A's entire business. It must stand or fall in its entire form; (ii) the clause as a whole was wider than necessary in the circumstances and was void.

NOTE: Contracts which are void by statute are also severable, but contracts *illegal* at common law are not severable.

28. Collateral transactions. Where a contract is void, in part or in whole, as being against public policy, collateral transactions remain unaffected.

29. Recovery of money. In *Hermann* v. *Charlesworth* (1905) it was held that money paid under a marriage brokage contract was recoverable upon total failure of consideration. It would seem to follow that money paid, or property transferred, under a contract merely *void* as contravening public policy, is always recoverable.

RESTRICTIVE TRADE PRACTICES

30. The Restrictive Trade Practices Act, 1956. The main provisions of the Act are:

(a) The creation of the Restrictive Practices Court.

(b) That certain restrictive agreements shall be registered.

(c) That the Restrictive Practices Court shall have jurisdiction to decide whether registrable agreements are contrary to the public interest.

(d) That restrictive contracts shall be void as far as they are declared to be against the public interest.

(e) That agreements for the collective enforcement of resale prices shall be prohibited.

(f) That, subject to conditions, the individual enforcement of resale price agreements shall be lawful (*see* XV).

31. The duty to register. Where two or more parties carrying on business in the United Kingdom agree to restrictions on any of the following matters, the agreement must be registered with the Registrar of Restrictive Trading Agreements:

(a) The prices to be charged for goods or the process of manufacture of goods.

(b) The conditions on which goods are supplied or processed.

(c) The quantities or descriptions of goods to be produced or acquired or supplied.

(d) Persons with whom, or areas with which, trade is to be done.

32. The jurisdiction of the Restrictive Practices Court. The Court has power to declare whether any registered agreement is contrary to the public interest, and consequently void. For the purposes of any proceedings before the Court, a restriction shall be deemed to be contrary to the public interest unless the Court is satisfied as to certain specified circumstances: *s.* 21 (1).

33. The Resale Prices Act, 1964. Section 1 of the *Resale Prices Act*, 1964, provides that any term of a contract for the sale of goods by a supplier to a dealer shall be void in so far as it purports to establish *minimum* prices to be charged on the re-sale of the goods. The section is, however, subject to the following provisos:

(a) The Restrictive Practices Court has power to exempt any *class* of goods from the provisions of the Act.

(b) Contracts of sale of goods which are of a class registered for exemption are not affected by the provisions of *s.* 1 until the Court refuses to make an exemption order with respect to that class of goods.

(c) The Act does not apply to any agreement which is made under statutory authority.

NOTE: The *Resale Prices Act*, 1964, does not apply to contracts to fix the *maximum* resale price of goods.

UNENFORCEABLE CONTRACTS

34. Unenforceable contracts. Certain contracts are not enforceable unless the plaintiff can produce a *sufficient note or memorandum* in writing of the agreement. The note must be signed by the defendant or his agent.

The contracts in this class are:

(a) Contracts of guarantee: *s.* 4 *Statute of Frauds*, 1677.

(b) Contracts for the sale or other disposition of land or any interest in land: *s.* 40 *Law of Property Act*, 1925.

35. Contracts of guarantee. A contract of guarantee is made where one party, the guarantor, promises to answer for the "debt, default or miscarriage" of another person. The expression "debt, default or miscarriage" is taken from *s.* 4 of the *Statute of Frauds*, 1677, and covers the guarantee of a contractual liability or a tortious liability. In most cases, however, the liability guaranteed is a contractual debt.

NOTE: Contracts of guarantee are sometimes called contracts of suretyship; a guarantor is sometimes called a surety.

36. Nature of guarantee. In any contract of guarantee, there is a principal creditor, a principal debtor and a guarantor. Thus, where G guarantees D's debt to C, there is a triangular relationship in which three collateral contracts may be distinguished:

(a) *As between C and D* there is a contract out of which the guaranteed debt arises.
(b) *As between G and C* there is the contract by which G makes himself secondarily liable to pay D's debt. G promises that he will pay D's debt in the event of D's default.
(c) *As between G and D* there is always a contract by which D indemnifies G. Thus, if G pays C according to the guarantee, then D will be liable to G. This contract is always implied if it is not expressed between the parties.

NOTE: It is the contract between the guarantor and the principal creditor which includes the promise to answer for the debt, default or miscarriage of another. But there must always be the other two contracts collateral.

37. Indemnity distinguished from guarantee. A contract of indemnity must be distinguished from a contract of guarantee. There are the following points of difference:

(a) A guarantor makes himself *secondarily* liable.
(b) A person giving an indemnity makes himself *primarily* liable.

Whether a contract is a guarantee or an indemnity contract depends entirely upon the intention of the parties.

38. The note or memorandum. In connection with the

"sufficiency" of the memorandum, the following should be noted:

(a) *The memorandum need not be in any special form.* It may consist of several documents provided there is evidence to connect them. The memorandum may have been made at any time after the contract was made.

(b) The memorandum must be *signed by the defendant* or his agent.

(c) The memorandum must contain the *material terms* of the agreement. These include: (i) *the parties:* the parties must be named or described sufficiently in the note, and (ii) *the subject-matter of the agreement, e.g.* in the case of a lease—the address of the premises, the duration of the lease, the rent to be paid.

NOTE: In the case of contracts of guarantee, the consideration need not appear in the memorandum: *Mercantile Law Amendment Act,* 1856; but there must be consideration.

39. Absence of sufficient memorandum. Where a party cannot produce in evidence a sufficient note or memorandum, the agreement is *unenforceable* at his suit. The legal consequences of unenforceability should be viewed from the standpoint of a party who cannot produce the memorandum:

(a) No action can be brought for damages at common law for breach of contract.

(b) No action can be brought for specific performance of the contract in equity, unless there is a sufficient act of *part performance.*

(c) All rights which do not require action in the courts are retained, *e.g.* where the purchaser is in breach of an unenforceable contract for the sale of land, the vendor may keep the deposit: *Thomas* v. *Brown* (1876).

40. Part performance. The *Statute of Frauds,* 1677, and *s.* 40 of the *Law of Property Act,* 1925, were designed to prevent fraud. Therefore, where a party to an unenforceable contract has partly, or wholly, performed his side of the agreement, trusting the other party to do the same, the court has a discretion to order specific performance of the contract, notwithstanding the absence of a memorandum.

The court will make the order on the grounds that, in these

circumstances, the defendant's breach of the unenforceable contract is fraudulent, and equity will not allow a statute to be used as an engine of fraud. The court will not make the order unless the following conditions are satisfied:

(a) The contract must be one for which *specific performance* would be a proper remedy apart from the matter of the absence of the memorandum: *see* VII, **41, 42.**

(b) The act of part performance must have been *performed by the plaintiff.*

(c) The act of part performance must be *exclusively referable to the unenforceable contract.* This means that the act must be such as could not have been done with any other purpose in view.

(d) The defendant's refusal to perform his side of the agreement must amount to fraud, bearing in view the plaintiff's act of part performance in reliance on the agreement: *Dickinson* v. *Barrow* (1904); *Rawlinson* v. *Ames* (1925).

(e) There must be sufficient oral or other evidence of the material terms of the agreement.

NOTE: The mere payment of money is never a sufficient act of part performance because it is an act which is not unequivocally referable to any particular agreement.

THE HIRE-PURCHASE ACT, 1965

41. Statutory requirements. The *Hire-Purchase Act,* 1965, provides that certain contracts for the disposition of goods are *unenforceable* unless certain requirements are complied with. The contracts affected by the Acts are:

(a) hire-purchase contracts;
(b) conditional sale agreements; and
(c) credit-sale agreements.

42. Hire-purchase and conditional sales. A hire-purchase agreement is not enforceable by the owner, and a conditional sale agreement is not enforceable by the seller, unless the agreement is *signed by the hirer or the buyer,* as the case may be, *and by all other parties: see* XIII.

43. Credit-sale agreements. A credit-sale agreement is not

enforceable by the seller unless the agreement is signed by
the buyer and by or on behalf of the seller: *see* XIII.

PROGRESS TEST 5

1. Explain the maxims *ex turpi causa non oritur actio* and *in pari
delicto potior est conditio defendentis*. (1, 2)

2. Give some examples of the kinds of contract which are
illegal. (3)

3. The general rule is that there is no recovery of money paid
or property transferred under an illegal contract. Give a careful
account of the exceptions to this rule. (12)

4. A entered a contract of service with an employer, B. According to the terms of the contract, B agreed to pay A £18 a
week salary and £10 a week by way of expenses. The agreement
was designed to defraud the Revenue, for it was never envisaged
that A should require more than £2 a week as expenses. B has
just dismissed A summarily, giving no reason for doing so. A
seeks your advice as to whether he can claim three weeks' arrears
of salary and expenses. Advise him. (5)

5. C agrees to let D have the use of C's motor yacht for a week.
C knew at the time of the agreement that D intended to use the
yacht for smuggling dope into England. D paid C £2000 deposit
before going aboard the yacht, and when he got aboard, he found
that C had removed some vital parts of the engine, so that it was
impossible to put to sea. Advise D as to whether he can recover
the £2000. (6, 11)

6. K enters a contract with L for the purchase of 100 packets
of cigarettes which he knows that L has recently stolen. K pays
£5 to L under the agreement, but when, later, L tried to deliver
the cigarettes, K refused to accept them. K's refusal was due to
a sudden fear that the cigarettes would be traced to him. L now
refuses to return the £5. Will K be able to recover the money?
Would your answer be different if K's refusal had been out of
true repentance? (11, 12)

7. Which kinds of contract are void at common law as being
against public policy? (16)

8. In what circumstances will a contract in restraint of trade
be upheld by the court? (20–25)

9. Consider the concept of "reasonableness" in connection with
a restraint clause in a contract between employer and employee.
(23)

10. L entered into a contract under seal whereby he (L) became articled to M, a chartered accountant. There was a clause
in the agreement by which L covenanted not to be concerned in

any chartered accountant's business within six miles of M's office during his (L's) lifetime. L wishes to know whether the restraint is binding on him. Advise him.   (23)

11. N sold his tobacconist retail shop to Universal Tobaccos Ltd., a company owning a chain of tobacco shops throughout the country. In the agreement of sale, N covenanted not to engage in the trade of tobacconist within ten miles of any of the branch shops of Universal Tobaccos Ltd. N has opened a new tobacco shop a hundred miles from the one he sold to the company, but within ten miles of one of their numerous branches. The company now wish to take action against N to enforce the restraint. Advise the company.   (24)

12. Distinguish between the legal consequences of (a) a contract which is void as being against public policy, and (b) an illegal contract.   (11, 26)

13. Which contracts are unenforceable unless the plaintiff can produce a sufficient note or memorandum of the contract?   (34)

14. Describe fully a contract of guarantee. How does a contract of indemnity differ from a contract of guarantee?   (35–37)

15. In a guarantee what are the requirements of a "sufficient note or memorandum"? Is consideration necessary?   (38)

16. Explain and illustrate the equitable doctrine of part performance. Is the payment of money ever an act of part performance?   (40)

17. A agreed orally to buy Blackacre from B, and following the agreement he paid to B £700, being 10% of the purchase price agreed on. A has now informed B that he does not want Blackacre after all. Advise the parties:

(a) Whether B can bring an action to claim specific performance of the contract.

(b) Whether A can recover the £700.   (40)

CHAPTER VI

PRIVITY AND ASSIGNMENT

PRIVITY OF CONTRACT

1. The doctrine of privity. A contract creates right and obligations *between the parties to it*. A contract does not generally confer rights on a stranger, nor does it impose obligations on a stranger. The general rule is, therefore, that no person can sue or be sued on a contract unless he is a party to it.

Per Lord Haldane in *Dunlop* v. *Selfridge* (1915): "In the law of England certain principles are fundamental. One is that only a person who is a party to a contract can sue on it."

Scruttons, Ltd. v. *Midland Silicones, Ltd.* (1962), H.L.: there was a contract between X and Y for the carriage of a cargo of goods belonging to Y. There was another contract between X and Z for the unloading of the goods from X's ship. The goods were damaged through Z's negligence during unloading. Y claimed damages from Z. Z relied on an exemption clause in the contract between X and Y. HELD: Z was a stranger to the contract between X and Y, and could not rely on the exemption clause.

2. Third-party benefits. Although a contract cannot confer a substantive right upon a stranger, it is possible for a contract to confer a benefit on him. In these circumstances it has been held that the stranger cannot sue in the event of his not receiving the benefit: *Tweddle* v. *Atkinson* (1861). The House of Lords decision in *Beswick* v. *Beswick* (1967) confirms that there is no general rule allowing third parties to sue for a benefit conferred by contract.

NOTE: Exceptions to the doctrine of privity of contract are to be found in (i) The *Restrictive Trade Practices Act, s.* 25, *see* XV, **10**; (ii) Agency law, *see* IX; (iii) Negotiable instruments, *see* XI; (iv) Assignment of contractual rights, *see* **3–11** below.

ASSIGNMENT OF CONTRACTUAL RIGHTS

3. Contractual rights as a form of property. A right under a contract has a certain economic value and may, therefore, be regarded as a personal right of property. In property law, contractual rights belong to a class known as *choses in action* or things in action.

4. Choses in action. "Chose in action" has been defined as "an expression used to describe all personal rights of property which can only be claimed or enforced by action, and not by taking physical possession": *per* Channell, J., in *Torkington* v. *Magee* (1903). Choses in action may be legal or equitable according to whether they are founded on legal or equitable rules.

(a) *Legal choses in action* include debts and other contractual rights, company shares, insurance policies, bills of lading, patents, and copyrights.

(b) *Equitable choses in action* include rights under a trust and legacies.

5. Assignment of choses in action. A valid assignment of a chose in action may take place in one of three ways:

(a) Statutory (or legal) assignment: *see* **6** *below.*
(b) Equitable assignment: *see* **8–10** *below.*
(c) Assignment by operation of the law: *see* **11** *below.*

6. Statutory assignment: L.P.A., s. 136. Statutory assignments are sometimes called *legal assignments*.

Section 136 provides that:

"Any absolute assignment by writing under the hand of the assignor (not purporting to be by way of charge only) of any debt or other legal thing in action, of which express notice in writing has been given to the debtor, trustee, or other person from whom the assignor would have been entitled to claim such debt or thing in action, is effectual in law (subject to equities having priority over the right of the assignee) to pass and transfer from the date of such notice:

(a) the legal right to such debt or thing in action;
(b) the legal and other remedies for the same; and

(c) the power to give a good discharge for the same without the concurrence of the assignor."

7. Analysis of s. 136. In order to comply with *s.* 136, the assignment must

(a) be in *writing;*
(b) be *signed* by the assignor;
(c) be *absolute, i.e.* the entire chose must be assigned and not merely a part of it;
(d) *not purport to be by way of charge only;* and
(e) be accompanied or followed by *express notice in writing* to the debtor or other person from whom the assignor would have been entitled to claim the chose in action.

Further points to notice when considering the analysis of *s.* 136 are:

(a) The expression *legal thing in action* in its context in *s.* 136 means lawful thing in action. Thus, the section applies to equitable as well as to legal choses in action.
(b) It is not necessary that the assignee should have given consideration to the assignor.
(c) The assignment takes effect from the date when written notice was given to the debtor.
(d) Statutory assignments are subject to the equities (as indeed are equitable assignments). This means that:

　(i) Any defence or counter-claim which would have been available to the debtor against the assignor at the time of notice of the assignment is available against the assignee.
　(ii) If there have been two or more assignments of the same chose in action, the rights of the second and subsequent assignees are postponed to the first.

8. Equitable assignment. If, in any transaction, there was an intent to assign a chose in action, but *s.* 136 was not complied with, there may be a valid assignment in equity.

NOTE: There is no statutory assignment, *e.g.* where the assignment is not in writing, or where the assignment is not signed by the assignor, or where the assignment is of part only of a chose in action, or where no written notice was given to the debtor. In all these circumstances there may be a valid equitable assignment.

9. Equitable assignments of equitable choses in action.
Equity has always allowed the assignment of equitable choses in action so that the assignee can bring an action in his own name without joining the assignor.

NOTE
 (i) The assignment is *subject to the equities*. Thus, although notice to the person liable is not essential, it is highly desirable, for where there are two or more assignees, they take priority each according to the date on which notice was given.
(ii) *Consideration is necessary unless* the assignment is complete and perfect, *i.e.* unless all necessary formalities are completed according to the equitable right assigned.

10. Equitable assignments of legal choses in action. Provided the assignee can show that there was an intention to assign a legal chose in action, there may be a good equitable assignment.

NOTE
  (i) The assignment is subject to the equities.
 (ii) The assignee must join the assignor in any action he takes against the debtor. (If the assignor refuses to be co-plaintiff, he will be made a co-defendant.)
(iii) The assignee must show that he gave consideration to the assignor.

11. Assignment by operation of law.

(a) *Automatic assignment.* An involuntary assignment of choses in action will take place automatically on the death or bankruptcy of the owner.

(b) *Assignment on death.* The general rule is that all contractual rights and obligations pass to the personal representatives of a party who dies. Thus, the personal representatives may sue or be sued on a contract to which the deceased was privy. The rule does not, however, apply to contracts of personal services.

(c) *Assignment on bankruptcy.* The principal aim of bankruptcy law is to provide for a fair distribution of the debtor's property between the creditors. When a debtor has been adjudicated bankrupt, his property vests in the trustee in bankruptcy and becomes divisible between the creditors.

ASSIGNMENT OF CONTRACTUAL OBLIGATIONS

12. Obligations cannot be assigned. There can be no effective assignment at common law or in equity or contractual obligations without the creditor's consent. The need for the creditor's consent means, in effect, that the assignment may be achieved only through a new contract. This process is known as *novation*.

For example, a partner in a firm will usually wish to assign his liabilities to the firm as newly constituted on his retirement. Any such assignment of a liability is ineffective unless the creditor is a party. Novation is a tri-partite agreement.

13. Vicarious performance. Where A is under a contractual obligation to perform services of a personal nature for B, A cannot be discharged if the services are vicariously performed by C. B is entitled to the personal performance by A.

Robson and Sharpe v. *Drummond* (1831): a coachbuilder contracted to hire out, maintain, and repaint a carriage. He purported to assign this contractual obligation. HELD: there could be no vicarious performance of this obligation. The other party was entitled to the taste and judgment of the coachbuilder.

Where, however, the obligation does not involve a personal element, the law permits vicarious performance on the principle that *qui facit per alium facit per se* ("he who does anything by another does it himself"): *British Waggon Co.* v. *Lea* (1880).

NOTE: Where a party arranges for his obligations to be vicariously performed, he is not thereby discharged. He remains liable until the vicarious performance is complete. For example, where X is under an obligation to Y, and X arranges with Z for Z to perform the obligation, X is not discharged merely because Z had promised performance. He remains liable until Z's performance is complete.

NEGOTIABLE INSTRUMENTS

14. Negotiability. Negotiability is a characteristic which should be distinguished from assignability. It is a characteristic which has been conferred on certain instruments, mainly bills of exchange and promissory notes. (For a fuller treatment of negotiability *see* XI.)

The following definitions are taken from the *Bills of Exchange Act*, 1882:

(a) *"A bill of exchange* is an unconditional order in writing, addressed by one person to another, signed by the person giving it, requiring the person to whom it is addressed to pay on demand or at a fixed or determinable future date a sum certain in money to or to the order of a specified person, or to bearer": *s.* 3 (1).

(b) *"A cheque* is a bill of exchange drawn on a banker payable on demand": *s.* 73.

(c) *"A promissory note* is an unconditional promise in writing made by one person to another signed by the maker, engaging to pay, on demand or at a fixed or determinable future time, a sum certain in money, to, or to the order of, a specified person or to bearer": *s.* 83 (1).

15. Meaning of negotiability. The special legal qualities of a negotiable instrument are as follows:

(a) *Transfer of ownership:* the rights of ownership of the instrument are transfered thus:

   (i) Where the instrument is drawn payable to order, or is specially indorsed, ownership is transferred by indorsement and delivery to the transferee.

   (ii) Where the instrument is payable to bearer or indorsed in blank, ownership is transferred by mere delivery.

(b) *Free from the equities:* where an instrument is negotiated, the transferee takes the rights of ownership free from the equities, provided he is a holder in due course.

(c) *Holder may sue in own name:* the holder of a negotiable instrument may, in the event of dishonour, sue all prior parties to the instrument, *i.e.* the drawer, the acceptor, and all persons who transferred the instrument by indorsement and delivery.

16. Holder in due course. "A holder in due course is a holder who has taken the bill, complete and regular on the face of it, under the following conditions, namely:

(a) that he became the holder of it before it was overdue,

and without notice that it had been previously dishonoured, if such was the fact;

(b) that he took the bill in good faith and for value, and that
at the time the bill was negotiated to him he had no
notice of any defect in the title of the person who negotiated it": *Bills of Exchange Act*, 1882, *s.* 29 (1).

PROGRESS TEST 6

1. State simply the doctrine of privity of contract, and mention
some exceptions to the doctrine. (1–11)

2. A contract was made between A and B. One of the terms
of the contract was that B should pay £100 to C. B now refuses
to pay C, and A declines to sue B. Advise C as to whether he can
claim against B. (1, 2)

3. What is a chose in action, and how may it be assigned?
(4–10)

4. What are the requirements of a statutory assignment of a
contractual right? Is consideration necessary? (5–7)

5. How may an equitable assignment of a chose in action
take place? (8–10)

6. Is it possible to assign a contractual obligation? (12, 13)

7. Define a bill of exchange. (14)

8. What are the main characteristics of a negotiable instrument? (15)

9. What is a holder in due course? (16)

10. A owes B the sum of £50. B owes A the sum of £20. B
assigns his right to the £50 to C, and the assignment satisfies the
requirements of *s.* 136 of the *Law of Property Act*, 1925. Comment on C's rights against A. (6, 7)

11. D owes E the sum of £100. E assigns his rights against D
to F by way of gift. The assignment is in writing, but E has not
signed it. Written notice has been given to D. F wishes to know
whether he can claim against D for the £100. Advise him. (8, 10)

CHAPTER VII

DISCHARGE AND BREACH

THE END OF A CONTRACT

1. Discharge of obligations. Every contractual obligation gives rise to a corresponding contractual right. Thus, where the obligation of one party is discharged, the corresponding right of the other party is extinguished. Where all obligations which arose under the contract are discharged—and all rights are thus extinguished—the contract is said to be discharged.

2. Ways in which a contract may be discharged. A contract may be discharged in any of the following ways:

    (a) Performance.
    (b) Agreement.
    (c) Acceptance of breach.
    (d) Frustration.

DISCHARGE BY PERFORMANCE

3. Performance must be complete. A contractual obligation is discharged by a complete performance of the undertaking. The promisee is entitled to the benefit of complete performance exactly according to the promisor's undertaking. Where the promisor is unable or unwilling to give more than a partial performance, the general rule is that there is no discharge.

Cutter v. *Powell* (1795): a seaman promised to proceed, continue and do his duty as second mate on a certain voyage. In return, he was promised the sum of £30. The seaman died shortly before the end of the voyage, and his widow (as his personal representative) claimed a proportion of the £30. HELD: the seaman's obligation remained undischarged and no proportion of the £30 was payable.

NOTE: The rule in *Cutter* v. *Powell* is the general rule, in spite of its apparent injustice in the particular case. There are, however, certain exceptions to the general rule.

4. Exceptions to the rule in Cutter v. Powell. The following exceptions exist to the rule that performance must be complete and total:

(a) *Divisible contracts:* where the parties are deemed to have intended their contract to be divided into two or more separate contracts, then each separated contract is discharged separately, *e.g.* where there is a contract for the delivery of goods by instalment, payment is due from the buyer upon the delivery of each instalment. The buyer cannot defer payment until all the instalments have been delivered, unless there is a term of the contract to that effect.

NOTE: The question as to whether a contract is divisible or entire depends upon the intention of the parties. Divisible contracts are sometimes called severable contracts.

(b) *Substantial performance:* according to the doctrine of substantial performance, a promisor who has substantially done what he promised to do can sue on the contract. His right to sue will be subject to a claim for damages by the promisee in respect of that part of the contract remaining unperformed: *Hoenig* v. *Isaacs* (1952), C.A.

(c) *Prevention of performance:* where a party is prevented from completing his undertaking because of some act or omission of the other party, it would be unjust to apply the rule in *Cutter* v. *Powell.* In these circumstances, the party who has been prevented from performance may sue either for damages or on a *quantum meruit* ("as much as he has earned").

5. Tender of performance. In an action for breach of contract, it is a good defence for the defendant to prove that he tendered performance, *i.e.* that he offered to perform his side of the bargain, and that the plaintiff refused to accept this. In these circumstances, the defendant is discharged from all liability under the contract. But note that:

(a) The tender of performance must be exactly in accordance with the terms of contract.

(b) Where tender of performance took the form of an offer to make a money payment

(i) the amount tendered must have been the exact amount due, and in the form required by the *Currency and Bank Notes Act*, 1928, and the *Coinage Act*, 1971, and

(ii) the defence of tender must be accompanied by payment into court of the amount due.

Silver coins of denominations of more than 10p are legal tender for payments not exceeding £10; silver of denominations of not more than 10p are legal tender for payments not exceeding £5.

DISCHARGE BY AGREEMENT

6. Eodem modo quo quid constituitur, eodem modo destruitur ("a thing may be destroyed in the same manner in which it is constituted"). A contractual obligation may be discharged by agreement as follows:

(a) A contractual obligation may be discharged by a subsequent binding contract between the parties.

(b) A contractual obligation may be discharged by the operation of one of the terms of the contract itself.

7. Discharge by subsequent binding contract. Discharge by subsequent agreement (which must be binding) may occur in any of the following ways:

(a) *Where the contract is wholly executory, i.e.* where neither party has completed his undertaking:

(i) *Waiver:* a contract may be discharged by mutual waiver. In effect, there is a new contract under which each party agrees to waive his rights under the old contract in consideration of being released from his obligations under the old contract.

(ii) *Waiver plus new rights and obligations:* a subsequent agreement between the parties may be to waive the old agreement and substitute an entirely new contract.

(b) *Where the contract is partially executory, i.e.* where one party only has completed his undertaking, and something remains to be done by the other party:

(i) *Release:* the party to whom the obligation is owed may release the other party by a subsequent agreement under seal.

NOTE: Such a promise must be under seal because it is given for no consideration.

(ii) *Accord and satisfaction:* the party to whom the obligation is owed <u>may agree</u> with the other party to accept something different in place of the former obligation. The subsequent agreement is the accord, and the new consideration is the satisfaction. Where there has been accord and satisfaction, the former obligation is discharged. But the accord must be reached without duress, *i.e.* it must be true accord: *D. & C. Builders Ltd.* v. *Rees* (1966), C.A.

8. Discharge by the operation of a term in the contract. There is no reason why a contract should not contain a term providing for the discharge of obligations arising from the contract. Such a term may be either a *condition precedent* or a *condition subsequent*, or it may be a term giving one or both parties the right to end the agreement by giving notice to the other party.

(a) *A condition precedent* is a condition which must be satisfied before a contract becomes binding. Where a condition precedent is not fulfilled, there is no true discharge because the rights and obligations never came into existence.

(b) A *condition subsequent* is a term providing for the discharge of obligations outstanding under the contract, in the event of a specific occurrence.

(c) A *party's right to end the agreement.* A contract may contain a term providing that one or both parties may bring the agreement to an end by giving notice to that effect. This provision is quite usual in contracts of employment.

DISCHARGE BY FRUSTRATION

9. Supervening impossibility. It is a basic common law rule that a party is *not* discharged from his contractual obligations merely because performance has become more onerous or impossible because of some unforeseen event. The general rule is that a contractual obligation is absolute, and if a party wishes to protect himself against subsequent difficulties in performance, he should stipulate for that protection. The doctrine of frustration has, however, developed a number of exceptions to this general rule of absolute contractual liability.

10. The doctrine of frustration. Under the doctrine of frustration, a contract will be discharged and the parties released from a further obligation where the following conditions are satisfied:

(a) That the contract does not contain an *absolute undertaking*, express or implied, which precludes frustration.

(b) That due to some event *the fundamental purpose of the contract became frustrated*, or rendered impossible of performance; so that any attempted performance would amount to something quite different from what must have been contemplated by the parties when they entered the contract. It is not sufficient that an event makes an obligation more onerous: *Tsakiroglou & Co. Ltd.* v. *Noblee Thorl GmbH* (1962); *Davis Contractors* v. *Fareham U.D.C.* (1956).

(c) That the event causing the frustration was *not* one which the parties could be deemed to have *contemplated* at the time of making the contract.

(d) That the event causing the frustration was *not induced by one of the parties*.

NOTE: It seems that the doctrine does not apply to leases. The point remains to be settled by a House of Lords decision or by legislation.

11. Factual circumstances in which a contract may be frustrated. Decisions show that the doctrine of frustration may be invoked in circumstances such as the following:

(a) *Where there is a total or partial destruction* of some object necessary to the performance of the contract.

   In *Taylor* v. *Caldwell* (1863), a music hall was burnt down before it could be used for certain performances under a contract. In *Nickoll* v. *Ashton* (1901), a ship was so damaged as to render the unloading of the cargo impossible according to the contract.

(b) *Where a change in the law* renders any attempted performance illegal.

   In *Baily* v. *de Crespigny* (1869), statutory powers conferred on a railway company frustrated the performance of a covenant in a lease.

(c) *Where death or illness* prevents a party from performing an obligation of a personal nature.

In *Robinson* v. *Davison* (1871), a pianist was discharged from a contractual obligation to give a performance on a specified day.

(d) *Where an event which is fundamental* to the contract does not occur: *but there must be an absolute non-occurrence.*

Krell v. *Henry* (1903), C.A.: there was a contract under which K licensed H to use a room on two specified dates. The flat overlooked the route of a proposed coronation procession, and the dates were the dates of this procession, but this was not mentioned in the contract. The procession was abandoned. HELD: the contract was discharged.

Herne Bay Steamboat Co. v. *Hutton* (1903), C.A.: there was a contract for the use of a boat on a specified date "for the purpose of viewing the naval review and for a day's cruise round the fleet." The review was cancelled *but the fleet remained to be seen.* HELD: the contract was not discharged.

12. Payment, retention and recovery of money after frustration. Where a contract is terminated by the doctrine of frustration, there can be no liability on damages for acts or omissions after the date of the frustration. Notice that the contract is terminated by the frustrating event: *it is not rendered void.* At common law, money paid under a frustrated contract can be recovered in quasi-contract: the *Fibrosa Case*, (1943), H.L. This common law rule works unfairly where one party has been put to considerable expenditure before frustration occurs. For this reason, the common law rule has been much modified by the *Law Reform (Frustrated Contracts) Act*, 1943.

13. The Frustrated Contracts Act. Section 2 of the *Law Reform (Frustrated Contracts) Act*, 1943, provides that: "All sums paid or payable to any party in pursuance of the [frustrated] contract . . . shall, in the case of sums paid, be recoverable from him as money received by him to the use of the party by whom the sums were paid, and, in the case of the sums payable, cease to be so payable: Provided that, if the party to whom the sums were so paid or payable incurred expenses before the time of discharge in, or for the purpose of, the performance of the contract, the court may, if it considers it just to do so having regard to all the circumstances of the case, allow him to retain or, as the case may be, recover the whole or any part of the sums so paid or payable, not being an amount in excess of the expenses so incurred." Section **3** provides further that: "Where any party to the contract has, by reason of anything done by any other party theretoin, or for the purpose of the performance of the contract, obtained a valuable benefit. . . before the time of discharge, there shall be recoverable from him by the said other party such sum, . . . not exceeding the value of the said benefit to the party obtaining it, as the court considers just, having regard to all the circumstances of the case . . ."

NOTE

    (i) The Act does not apply to voyage charterparties, insurance contracts, or to contracts to which the *Sale of Goods Act*, 1893, *s.* 7 applies (*s.* 7 of the *S.G.A.* provides that where there is an agreement to sell specific goods, and subsequently the goods, without any fault on the part of the seller or buyer, perish before the risk passes to the buyer, the agreement is thereby avoided).

    (ii) In effect, the *Frustrated Contracts Act* provides that the court may order payment, retention or recovery of money as it thinks just, having regard to the circumstances of each case.

DISCHARGE BY ACCEPTANCE OF BREACH

14. Breach of contract. Breach occurs where a party fails to perform his contractual obligations, or where he repudiates his obligations, expressly or implied, without justification. A party not in breach always has an action for damages against the party in breach, and in certain circumstances *he may treat the contract as repudiated by the party in breach and refuse further performance*. That is to say, breach by one party may enable the other party to become discharged from further liability.

15. Breach does not always cause a contract to become discharged. A contract is not always discharged by breach unless the party not in breach elects to treat the breach as repudiation of the contract.

NOTE: The party not in breach may, if he wishes, give the other party an opportunity to change his mind and perform his contractual obligations. In these circumstances, the right to treat the contract as repudiated by breach will be lost if the contract is discharged in some other manner: *Avery* v. *Bowden* (1855).

16. When may a breach be treated as a repudiation? Not every breach may be treated as a repudiation of the contract. The party not in breach may treat the contract as repudiated in the following circumstances:

(a) *Contracts generally:* where the breach is of such a nature as to render further performance of the contract purposeless the law will not force the party not in breach to complete his side of the bargain.

Ellen v. *Topp* (1851): T was apprenticed to E to learn three trades, *viz.* auctioneer, appraiser, and corn factor. During the contract period, E gave up trading as a corn factor. T refused further performances. HELD: T was discharged from further liability on the contract of apprenticeship because E's act had rendered the real purpose of the contract unattainable.

(b) *Contracts of sale of goods:* where there has been a breach of *condition* by the seller of the goods, the buyer may treat the contract as repudiated, and refuse further performance. But the buyer may elect, or be compelled, to treat the breach of condition as a breach of warranty giving rise to an action for damages only. Where a condition sinks to the level of a warranty in this way, the breach is known as a breach of warranty *ex post facto*. These rules apply equally to express conditions and to implied conditions.

REMEDIES FOR BREACH OF CONTRACT

17. Ubi jus ibi remedium ("where there is a right, there is a remedy"). A right would be of little value if there were no remedy available in the event of an infringement. A remedy is the means given by law for the enforcement of a right, or for the recovery of pecuniary compensation in lieu of performance. A breach of contract by one party necessarily causes an infringement of the contractual rights of the other party. A breach of contract usually, but not always, causes a loss: in any event, there is a right of action against the contract-breaker.

18. Breach of contract. There is a breach of contract where

a party fails to perform his contractual obligations, or where
he repudiates his obligations, expressly or by implication.

19. Repudiation before performance is due. Where a party
repudiates his contractual obligations before the time for performance, a right of action for damages will *immediately* accrue
to the other contracting party. Repudiation before performance
is due is known as *anticipatory* breach.

Notice that, in theory, there is no breach, for the time of
performance has not arrived, yet a right of action exists as if
there were a breach.

Where, however, the party who has committed an anticipatory breach becomes subsequently entitled under the terms
of the contract to determine that contract, the other party will
not succeed in an action for damages for the anticipatory breach:
Maredelanto Compania Naviera S.A. v. *Bergbau-Handel
GmbH; The Mihalis Angelos* (1970) C.A.

20. Remedies for breach of contract. There are various
remedies for breach of contract. The appropriate remedy in
any case will depend on the subject-matter of the contract and
the nature of the breach. In certain circumstances there may
be a plurality of remedies available, either together or in the
alternative. In all cases the plaintiff must state in his plead-
ings the remedy (or remedies) that he desires: he may

(a) sue for *unliquidated damages*;
(b) sue for *liquidated damages*;
(c) sue for *damages by way of recovery* of a specific sum of
     money owed under a contract, *e.g.* for the agreed price
     of goods, or for the agreed remuneration for services;
(d) sue on a *quantum meruit*;
(e) sue for a *reasonable price for goods* where the price is not
     determined in accordance with *s.* 8 (1) of the *S.G.A.*;
(f) sue for a decree of *specific performance*;
(g) sue for an *injunction* to restrain the breach of a negative
     term.

These various remedies should each be considered separately.

UNLIQUIDATED DAMAGES

21. Compensation, not punishment, is the object. Where a plaintiff claims damages for breach of contract, it is the function of the court to assess the money value of the loss suffered, and to award this sum as *damages*. In effect, this is an order to the party in breach to pay the sum fixed by the court as compensation to the other party. Notice that damages is a remedy to the injured party: punishment of the contract-breaker is *not* the object of damages.

Unliquidated damages may be:

(a) *Substantial damages, i.e.* pecuniary compensation to put the plaintiff in the position he would have enjoyed had the contract been performed.

(b) *Nominal damages, i.e.* a small token award where there has been an infringement of a contractual right, but no actual loss has been suffered.

(c) *Exemplary damages, i.e.* a sum awarded beyond the pecuniary loss sustained by the plaintiff. Exemplary damages are awarded only where a banker improperly dishonours a trader's cheque.

22. The measure of damages. In its endeavours to assess the loss suffered by the injured party for which damages should be awarded, the court will consider the following questions:

(a) Was the loss caused by the breach?

(b) Is any part of this loss too remote (in terms of causation) from the breach to be the proper subject of compensation?

(c) Could the loss have been mitigated in any way by any reasonable act on the part of the injured party?

23. Victoria Laundry, Ltd. v. Newman Industries, Ltd. (1949). In this case before the Court of Appeal there was a single judgment which contained a summary of the law relating to causation and remoteness of loss. The summary took the form of six propositions:

(a) *The governing purpose of damages* is to put the party

whose rights have been violated in the same position, so far as money can do so, as if his rights had been observed.

(b) The aggrieved party is entitled to recover only such part of the loss actually resulting as was at the time of the contract *reasonably foreseeable* as liable to result from the breach.

(c) *What is reasonably foreseeable* depends on the knowledge possessed by the parties.

(d) *Knowledge "possessed"* is of two kinds:

  (i) *Imputed knowledge:* everyone is taken to know the ordinary course of things and what loss is liable to result from a breach of that ordinary course.

  (ii) *Actual knowledge:* an actual knowledge of special circumstances may make an additional loss also recoverable.

(e) It is not necessary that the contract-breaker should actually have asked himself what loss is liable to result from the breach.

(f) *If, on the given state of knowledge of the contract-breaker, a reasonable man could foresee that a loss was on the cards, the contract-breaker is liable to that extent.* The given state of knowledge = (actual + imputed) knowledge.

In the *Heron II, Koufos* v. *Czarnikow, Ltd.* (1967), Lord Upjohn pointed out that in the *Victoria Laundry case* the words "likely to result" were used as being synonymous with a serious possibility or a real danger, which was equated with the expression "on the cards." Lord Upjohn, together with all the judges in this House of Lords case, deprecated the use of the phrase "on the cards" as being far too imprecise. Lord Upjohn went on to say: "It is clear that on the one hand the test of foreseeability as laid down in the case of tort is not the test for breach of contract: nor on the other hand must the loser establish that the loss is a near certainty or an odds-on probability. I am content to adopt as the test a 'real danger' or a 'serious possiblity.' There may be a shade of difference between these two phrases, but the assessment of damages is not an exact science and what to one judge or jury will appear a real danger may appear to another judge or jury to be a serious possibility."

24. The duty to mitigate the loss. Where one party has suffered loss resulting from the other party's breach of contract, the injured party should take reasonable steps to minimise the effect of the breach. Any failure to mitigate the loss will be taken into account by the court in its assessment of damages, and the injured party will be penalised to that extent. But the duty to mitigate does not preclude a party from performing his side of the contract after the other party has wrongfully repudiated the contract.

LIQUIDATED DAMAGES

25. Pre-assessment of loss. Where contracting parties make a *genuine pre-assessment* of the loss that would flow from any particular breach, and stipulate accordingly in their contract that this sum shall be payable in the event of a breach, the sum payable is *liquidated damages*. A clause stipulating for liquidated damages must be distinguished from a penalty clause.

26. Penalty clauses. Where a contract contains a term providing for the payment of money in the event of a breach, the sum fixed being as *in terrorem* of the party in breach, the term is a penalty clause. The aim of a penalty clause is to compel performance of the contract.

27. Effect of liquidated damages and penalties compared.

(a) *A liquidated damages clause* is binding on the parties. In the event of a breach, the sum fixed and no more and no less can be claimed. No action for unliquidated damages is allowed.

(b) *A penalty clause* is void. In the event of a breach, the injured party may bring an action for unliquidated damages. The penalty clause is disregarded.

28. Penalty or liquidated damages? It occasionally happens that contracting parties are in dispute as to whether a sum stipulated is a penalty or liquidated damages. In these circumstances it is the duty of the court to decide the issue in the light of the rules given by Lord Dunedin in *Dunlop Tyre Co.* v. *New Garage Co.* (1914), a House of Lords case:

(a) The use by the parties of the words "penalty" or "liquidated damages" is not conclusive.

(b) The essence of a penalty is a payment stipulated as *in terrorem* of the offending party: the essence of liquidated damages is a genuine pre-estimate of loss.

(c) *The issue is one of construction of each particular contract*, judged at the time of making the contract and not at the time of the breach. In construing the contract, the following tests may be used:

   (i) If the sum stipulated is extravagant or unconscionable in amount compared with the greatest loss which could conceivably be proved to have followed from the breach, it is a penalty.

  (ii) If the breach consists only of the non-payment of money, and the sum stipulated is greater, it is a penalty.

 (iii) Where a single lump sum is payable on the occurrence of one or more of several events, some of which may occasion serious and others but trifling loss, there is a *presumption* that it is a penalty.

 (iv) It is no obstacle to the sum stipulated being a genuine pre-estimate of loss that the consequences of the breach are such as to make precise pre-estimation almost an impossibility.

29. Examples.

(a) Where a wholesaler was in breach of his agreement not to sell tyres below the manufacturer's list prices, the sum of £5 payable for each breach was held to be liquidated damages: *Dunlop* v. *New Garage* (1914), H.L.

(b) Where the hirer of a juke box under a hire-purchase contract terminated the agreement and returned the juke-box a reasonable sum stipulated to be payable by way of depreciation was held to be liquidated damages: *Phonographic Equipment Ltd.* v. *Muslu* (1961), C.A. But where a depreciation clause in a hire-purchase contract of a motor-car bore no relation to the actual depreciation in value of the car, but was intended only to ensure a certain financial return to the owner, the clause was held to be a penalty clause: *Bridge* v. *Campbell Discount Co., Ltd.* (1962), H.L.

CLAIM FOR A SPECIFIC SUM AS DAMAGES

30. Non-payment as a breach of contract. Where one party is under a contractual obligation to pay a specific sum of money to the other party, and there is a total or partial failure to pay according to the contract, there is a breach of contract.

31. Liquidated demands. In a case of breach by non-payment of a specific sum of money, it is advantageous to the plaintiff to make a liquidated demand rather than to claim unliquidated damages. A liquidated demand is a claim that the defendant owes the plaintiff a certain sum of money.

NOTE: Under Order 14 of the Rules of the Supreme Court, an expeditious procedure is available for the recovery of a specific sum of money under a liquidated demand.

32. Actions for the contractual price of goods. The *Sale of Goods Act*, 1893, *s.* 49, provides that where, under a contract of sale, the buyer wrongfully neglects or refuses to pay for the goods according to the terms of the contract, the seller may maintain an action against him for the price of the goods. Section 8 (1) of the Act provides that the price in a contract of sale may be fixed by the contract, or may be fixed in a manner thereby agreed, or may be determined by a course of dealing between the parties. An action for the price of goods where the price is determined in accordance with *s.* 8 (1) will take the form of a liquidated demand.

33. Damages in addition to a liquidated demand. Where a plaintiff has suffered some loss in addition to the non-payment of money, he may also claim for unliquidated damages. Damages may be claimed in the same action as the liquidated demand, or in an action subsequently brought: *Yeomen Credit Ltd.* v. *Waragowski* (1961); *Overstone* v. *Shipway* (1962).

Overstone, Ltd. v. *Shipway* (1962), C.A.: the plaintiff finance company had entered a contract of hire-purchase of a motor car with S, the defendant. S fell into arrears with his hire instalments and the company took the car from him and recovered the arrears of instalments on a liquidated demand. In the present action, the company claimed damages with respect to the loss incurred on the re-sale of the car. HELD: the claim for damages should succeed as it was quite distinct from the liquidated demand in the earlier action. *Per* Holroyd Pearce, L.J., "In my judgment, it is impossible to hold that a claim for sums due under the hiring is the same cause of action as a claim for damages for breach."

QUANTUM MERUIT AS A REMEDY FOR BREACH

34. The quantum meruit claim. Where a plaintiff sues to recover an *unliquidated* sum by way of payment for services rendered, he is said to claim on a *quantum meruit* ("as much as he has earned"). The distinction between a *quantum meruit* claim and a claim for damages is that the former is a claim for reasonable remuneration, while the latter is a claim for compensation for a loss. Both are claims for an unliquidated sum. It is usually a matter of procedural tactics whether a plaintiff claims on a *quantum meruit* in preference to a claim for damages.

35. Circumstances where a quantum meruit is appropriate.

(a) *Where there is an express or implied contract to render services, but no agreement as to remuneration*, reasonable remuneration is payable. The court decides what is reasonable. The reasonable remuneration is the *quantum meruit*.

Upton R.D.C. v. *Powell* (1942), C.A.: there was an implied contract between P and the Upton fire brigade for the services of the brigade. HELD: reasonable remuneration was payable by P for the services he had received.

(b) Where, from the circumstances of the case and the conduct of the parties, *a new contract is implied*, taking the place of their original contract, an action in a *quantum meruit* is available to a party who has performed his obligations under the fresh implied contract.

Steven v. *Bromley* (1919): there was a contract between S, a ship-owner, and B, a charterer, for the carriage of a certain consignment of steel, at an agreed rate of freight. The goods actually delivered to S for shipment consisted partly of steel and partly of general merchandise, for which the freight rates were higher than for steel. S accepted the goods entirely and they were stowed on the ship. S claimed freight in excess of that agreed under the contract. HELD: a new contract could be implied from the facts, and the higher freight could be claimed as reasonable remuneration, *i.e.* on a *quantum meruit*.

(c) Where a contracting party has *elected to treat the contract as discharged* by the breach of the other party, he may bring an action on a *quantum meruit*. Similarly, where one party prevents the other party from performing his obligations under a contract, that other party may sue on a *quantum meruit*.

De Bernady v. *Harding* (1853): a principal wrongfully revoked his agent's authority before the agent had completed his duties. HELD: the agent could recover on a *quantum meruit* for the work he had done and the expenses he had incurred in the course of his duties. See also *Planché* v. *Colburn* (1831).

NOTE: (a), (b) and (c) above are examples of *quantum meruit* as a remedy for breach of contract. The remedy is also available in certain circumstances where there has been *no* breach of contract, *i.e.* in quasi-contractual actions.

RECOVERY OF A REASONABLE PRICE FOR GOODS

36. The price of goods. Where, under a contract of sale, the buyer wrongfully neglects or refuses to pay for the goods according to the terms of the contract, the seller may maintain an action against him for the price of the goods: *Sale of Goods Act*, 1893, *s.* 49. Where the price is ascertainable in a manner provided in *s.* 8 (1) of the Act, the appropriate claim is a liquidated demand: the remedy is the award of the liquidated sum. But where the price is not determined in accordance with *s.* 8 (1), the buyer must pay a *reasonable price*. What is reasonable is a question of fact dependent on the circumstances of each particular case: *s.* 8 (2). (As to *s.* 8 (1), *see* **19** *above.*)

37. The action for a reasonable price. The action for a reasonable price for goods is a claim for an unliquidated sum. The remedy is the award of whatever sum the court (or the jury, if there is one) considers reasonable in the circumstances.

38. Quantum valebant. Before 1894, when the *Sale of Goods Act* came into operation, an action for the reasonable price of goods under a contract of sale took the form of a claim on a *quantum valebant* ("as much as they are worth"). This common law action is comparable to the *quantum meruit* in the case of services rendered. A claim on a *quantum valebant* may still be available today in cases where there has been no breach of contract. Such a claim would arise *quasi ex contractu*.

LIMITATION ACT 1939

39. Limitation of actions on simple contract. Section 2(1) of the Act provides that an action founded on simple contract shall not be brought after the expiration of six years from the date on which the cause of action accrued.

40. Limitation of actions on specialties. Section 2 (3) of the Act provides that an action upon a specialty shall not be brought after the expiration of twelve years from the date on which the cause of action accrued.

SPECIFIC PERFORMANCE

41. An equitable remedy. A decree of specific performance is issued by the court to the defendant, requiring him to carry out his undertaking exactly according to the terms of the contract. Specific performance is an equitable remedy and is available only where there is no adequate remedy at common law or under a statute. Generally, this means that specific performance is available only where the payment of a sum of money would not be an adequate remedy. Specific performance is, therefore, an approporiate remedy in cases of breach of contract for the sale or lease of land, or of breach of contract for the sale of something which is not available on the market, *e.g.* a rare book.

42. The court's discretion. The granting or withholding of a decree of specific performance is in the discretion of the court. The discretion is, however, exercised on certain well-established principles:

(a) Specific performance will never be granted where *damages* or a liquidated demand is appropriate and *adequate*.

(b) The court will take into account the conduct of the plaintiff, for *he who comes to equity must come with clean hands.*

(c) The action must be brought with *reasonable promptness, for delay defeats the equities.* Undue delay sufficient to cause the court to withhold an equitable remedy is known as *laches.*

(d) Specific performance will not be awarded where it would cause *undue hardship* on the defendant.

(e) A promise given for *no consideration* is not specifically enforceable, even if made under seal.

(f) Specific performance will not be awarded for breach of a contract of *personal services, e.g.* in *Lumley* v. *Wagner* (1852) the court refused to order specific performance of a contract to sing in a theatre.

(g) Specific performance will not be awarded for breach of an obligation to perform a series of acts which would need the *constant supervision* of the court. Thus building contracts are specifically enforceable only in certain special circumstances.

(h) Specific performance will not be awarded for breach of a *contract wanting in mutuality, i.e.* a contract which is not binding on both parties. Thus where a contract is voidable at the option of one party, he will not get specific performance against the other. This rule is of particular importance in connection with infants' voidable contracts.

INJUNCTION

43. Injunctions to restrain breach of contract. Where a contracting party is in breach of a *negative term* of the contract (*i.e.* where he is doing something which he promised not to do), the appropriate remedy may be an injunction. Where this remedy is awarded, the court issues an order to the defendant restraining him from doing what he promised not to do. In *Lumley* v. *Wagner* (1852) the court refused to order a performer to sing according to the contract, but the court did grant an injunction to restrain the singer from singing elsewhere, in breach of a negative term of the contract.

Injunction, like specific performance, is an equitable remedy, and is granted in the discretion of the court. An injunction will not be granted where damages would be adequate, or where the plaintiff has not come with clean hands, or where there is *laches*, or where undue hardship would be caused to the defendant.

Ehrman v. *Bartholomew* (1898): an employee contracted to serve his employer for ten years and during that period not engage in any other business. The employee left his employment in breach of the positive term, and obtained other employment in breach of the negative term. HELD: an injunction would not be granted to restrain the breach of the negative term because, in the circumstances of the case, it would inflict undue hardship on the defendant (*i.e.* an injunction would force the defendant to choose between starvation or returning to his former employer.)

Warner Brothers v. *Nelson* (1937): N, a film actress, contracted to give her services as an actress exclusively to the plaintiffs, and not to engage in any other occupation without the consent of the plaintiffs. In breach of the contract, N undertook to work for another film producer during the period of the contract with the plaintiffs. HELD: an injunction would be awarded to restrain the negative part of the contract, but the injunction would be limited in area, to the jurisdiction of the court, and, in time, to three years.

PROGRESS TEST 7

1. What exceptions are there to the rule in *Cutter* v. *Powell*? (4)

2. "In an action for breach of contract, it is a good defence for the defendant to prove that he tendered performance." Comment on this statement. (5)

③ Explain how a contract may be discharged by agreement. (6–8)

4. "It is a basic common law rule that a party is not discharged from his contractual obligations merely because performance has become more onerous or impossible owing to some unforeseen event." Explain the doctrine of frustration as an exception to this rule. (9–11)

5. Outline the provisions of the *Law Reform (Frustrated Contracts) Act*, 1943. (13)

⑥ A, an American exporter, contracted to sell to B, a British importer, 5000 tins of cooked ham, to be packed in cases of 50 tins. When the ham was tendered to B, he discovered that about a third of the cases contained only 25 tins, but the total consignment was 5000 tins. B thereupon refused to take delivery of the ham. A wishes to know whether he can claim against B. Advise him. (16)

7. C agrees to coach D for an examination. Shortly before the date of the first lesson, C falls seriously ill, and is unable to give any lessons at all. D cannot find another tutor, and he fails the examination. Consider the legal position. **(11)**

8. What is an anticipatory breach of contract? **(17)**

9. Outline the various remedies available for breach of contract. **(20)**

10. "Where one party is in breach of contract, there is a duty on the other to mitigate the loss occasioned by the breach." Explain this statement. **(24)**

11. What is a penalty clause? How does a penalty differ from liquidated damages? **(25–29)**

12. Distinguish between a *quantum meruit* claim and a claim for damages. In what circumstances is a *quantum meruit* claim appropriate? **(34, 35)**

13. Explain how the *Limitation Act*, 1939, fixes the period within which an action must be brought. **(39, 40)**

14. What is specific performance? Explain the principles on which the court awards or withholds the remedy. **(41, 42)**

15. In what circumstances is an injunction the appropriate remedy for breach of contract? **(43)**

CHAPTER VIII

QUASI-CONTRACT

THE MEANING OF QUASI-CONTRACT

1. The circumstances generally. Where, in all justice, one person should be held accountable to another for a sum of money, and no action lies for its recovery in contract or in tort, the law will, in certain circumstances, allow an action in so-called *quasi-contract*. Also, an action in quasi-contract will sometimes lie as an alternative to damages for breach of contract.

2. The characteristics of quasi-contract. Although this part of the law is called quasi-contract, there is a sharp division of opinion as to whether it has any real connection with contract at all. The characteristics of a quasi-contractual right are:

(a) *It is always a right to claim a sum of money:* usually, but not always, a liquidated claim.

(b) Unlike a contractual right, a quasi-contractual right *does not stem from agreement:* quasi-contractual rights and obligations are, as in tort, imposed by the general law.

(c) Quasi-contractual rights and obligations *exist between specific persons*, as in contract: in tort, on the other hand, rights exist against the whole world.

3. The basis of quasi-contract. *There is no generally accepted juridical theory of quasi-contract* into which all the cases can be neatly fitted. There are two conflicting theories to be considered:

(a) That quasi-contract is a *form of implied contract*, and that a quasi-contractual right will exist only according to usual rules of implied terms in contracts.

(b) That the courts have a jurisdiction, quite apart from

implied contract, to recognise claims where one person should, in justice, account to another for a sum of money. That is to say, a claim may be made in any case of *unjust enrichment*. There is considerable judicial support for this theory: *The Fibrosa Case* (1943); *Nelson* v. *Larholt* (1948).

ACTIONS IN QUASI-CONTRACT

4. The particular circumstances. An action in quasi-contract may be allowed in any of the following circumstances:

(a) Where the plaintiff has paid money to a third person to the defendant's use.

(b) Where the plaintiff has paid money to the defendant under a mistake of fact.

(c) Where the plaintiff has paid money to the defendant and the consideration moving from the defendant has totally failed.

(d) Where the plaintiff claims on an account stated with the defendant.

(e) Where the plaintiff claims on a *quantum meruit* not based on a contract with the defendant.

5. Money paid to the defendant's use. The plaintiff has a quasi-contractual claim where he has paid a sum of money *to a third person* to the use of the defendant. This may happen in one of two ways:

(a) Where the defendant expressly requests or allows the plaintiff to make a payment or incur an obligation on his behalf. It seems here that the basis of the action is the implied promise by the defendant to re-imburse the plaintiff, *e.g.* the implied indemnity given by a principal debtor to a guarantor.

(b) Where the plaintiff is *compelled* to make a payment to a third party, and the payment discharges the defendant's obligation to that third party.

Brooks Wharf v. *Goodman Bros.* (1937): the defendant stored a consignment of imported skins, on which he was liable to pay customs duty, in the plaintiff's bonded warehouse. The skins were stolen before the defendants had paid the duty. The plaintiff was, consequently, under a statutory obligation to pay the customs duty to the authorities. The plaintiff paid the duty and then, in this action, claimed the amount from the defendants. HELD: the sum paid was recoverable.

6. Money paid under a mistake of fact.

Where the plaintiff was induced to pay money to the defendant by a mistake of *fact* (not law), the sum paid is recoverable.

Larner v. *L.C.C.* (1949): L, who was in the employment of the L.C.C., was called up for military service. Now the L.C.C. had resolved to pay its employees who went on military service the difference between their service pay and their former civilian pay. In order to benefit from this resolution, employees had to undertake to notify the L.C.C. of any change in their service pay. L did not notify the L.C.C. of his increase in service pay, and, in consequence, he was overpaid by the Council. HELD: the amount overpaid was recoverable.

NOTE: But where overpayment is made on a misconstruction of regulations, and the payee does not know of the mistake, the mistake is regarded as one of law, and recovery is not permitted: *Holt* v. *Markham* (1923).

7. Money paid on a total failure of consideration.

Where the plaintiff has paid money to the defendant under a valid contract, and the defendant *totally* fails to perform his contractual duty, the plaintiff may elect to bring his action in contract or quasi-contract. In quasi-contract, the amount recoverable is limited to the sum paid: in contract, the rules relating to the measure of damages apply.

8. Account stated.

Where there has been a series of transactions between the parties, followed by an agreed balance payable by one party to the other, the agreed balance is known as an account stated. It may be regarded as an admission of indebtedness by the party owing. Where an action is brought on an account stated, it is not necessary to prove the series of transactions: it is necessary to prove the account stated only.

Thus, if X sells to Y £300 worth of goods; then Y sells to X £100 worth of goods; then Y supplies to X £50 worth of services; then the parties agree in writing that, on balance, Y owes X £150, that is an account stated.

9. Quantum meruit.

The *quantum meruit* claim as a remedy for breach of contract has already been considered. The claim is also available where there is no contract between the parties, and yet, in justice, reasonable remuneration should be paid. These circumstances may arise where work has been done under a void contract, or where the courts cannot infer a contract between the parties.

Craven-Ellis v. *Canons, Ltd.* (1936): C-E rendered services to the company as managing director. The contract under which he was appointed was void. C-E sought to recover remuneration (i) by way of damages on a liquidated demand, and (ii) in the alternative, on a *quantum meruit*. HELD: the claim for damages failed because the contract was void *ab initio*; the claim on the *quantum meruit* should succeed.

PROGRESS TEST 8

1. What are the characteristics of a quasi-contractual right? (2)
2. In what circumstances will the court allow an action in quasi-contract? Give examples. (4–9)
3. A took a lease of B's house. C took a sub-lease from A. A had fallen into arrears with rent payable to B, who is threatening to re-enter the property. C, therefore, pays A's arrears of rent to B. C now brings an action against A to recover the sum paid. Will he succeed? Give reasons for your answer. (5)
4. D has worked for the XYZ Company as a factory manager for three months. He has just been informed that his appointment was void as it was not made in a manner required by the memorandum of association. D has not yet received any remuneration from the XYZ Company. On what grounds can he claim payment? (9)

PART TWO

COMMERCIAL LAW

CHAPTER IX

AGENCY

THE PRINCIPAL–AGENT RELATIONSHIP

1. The essential characteristic. The essential characteristic of an agent is that he is invested with a legal power to establish contractual relations between his principal and third parties.

2. The creation of the relationship. The relationship of principal and agent may be created in the following ways:

(a) *By express appointment.*
(b) *By implication of the law,* which may arise

    (i) from the conduct of the parties, *i.e.* agency by estoppel, or

    (ii) from the necessity of the case, *i.e.* agency of necessity.

(c) *By subsequent ratification* of an authorised act.
(d) *By statute. See* X, **10**; XIII, **9**.

3. Express appointment. Where the principal expressly appoints his agent, and the agent accepts the appointment, the relationship is based on contract and is sometimes known as contractual agency. No particular form of appointment is needed unless the agent is required to enter into contracts under seal, in which case the authority must be given under seal. (An authority given under seal is known as a *power of attorney.*)

4. Contractual capacity of an agent. Usually, though not always, the agent incurs no contractual obligations towards the third party. Thus the general rule is that an agent *need not* have contractual capacity, although, of course, the principal *must* have capacity.

5. Kinds of appointed agents. Appointed agents may be divided into three classes:

(a) *Special agents*, who are appointed to perform a particular act, after which their authority comes to an end.
(b) *General agents*, who have a continuous authority to act in some particular trade or business.
(c) *Universal agents*, who have unlimited authority to act for their principals.

6. Implication of law. The law may infer an agency from the conduct of the parties or from the necessity of the case. The former gives rise to agency by estoppel and the latter to agency of necessity.

7. Agency by estoppel. Consider the following generalised example: as a result of X's conduct, Y appears to be X's agent, and on the faith of this appearance Z contracts with Y and suffers consequent loss. If Z has a cause of action arising from the contract, he may sue X, who will be estopped from denying that Y is his agent and may thus be liable.

Agency by estoppel sometimes arises after the actual authority of an agent has been *determined*—for if a former agent continues to deal with third parties who believe the agency to be afoot, the former principal will be estopped from denying that he is the principal. Thus a principal should be careful to give notice of the determination of his agent's authority to all possible third parties.

Trueman v. *Loder* (1840): A dealt with T on behalf of his principal, P. The agency was determined but notice of this was not given to T. A subsequently dealt with T in his own name. T suffered loss as a result of A's breach of contract and he sued P. HELD: P was estopped from denying that A was still his agent. Damages awarded against P.

8. Agency of necessity. An authority may be conferred by law in circumstances where property is in jeopardy, and, at the time of the emergency, the instructions of the owner cannot be obtained. In such cases, there is a legal implication that the owner has consented to the creation of an agency, or to the extension of an existing authority. It may be regarded as yet another example of the law giving effect to the presumed intentions of the parties.

An agency of necessity arises when all the following conditions are satisfied:

(a) The person claiming to be an agent of necessity must have been driven by a *real emergency*, and not by mere convenience: *Prager* v. *Blatspiel* (1924).

(b) It must be *practically impossible to obtain fresh instructions* from the owner: *Springer* v. *Great Western Rly.* (1921).

(c) An agent of necessity must act *bona fide* in the interests of all concerned: if he does not, he will be personally liable for his action.

9. Ratification of an unauthorised act. Where A acts in the name of, or professedly on behalf of, B, without B's authority, B may ratify the act and make it as valid as if it had been done with his authority. The result is the same whether A had no authority at all to act for B, or whether A merely acted in excess of an authority conferred by B. Ratification is effective only subject to the following conditions:

(a) *The only person having power to ratify* is the person on whose behalf the act was done: and this person must then: (i) have existed, (ii) have been named or described, (iii) have been competent, and must have remained competent to be principal.

(b) There must have been an *act capable of ratification*.

(c) Ratification must take place within a *reasonable time*.

(d) The person ratifying must have *full knowledge* of all material facts, or be prepared to ratify in any event.

NOTE: Ratification is an expression of intention, and may be express or implied from conduct.

POSITION OF PRINCIPAL AND AGENT WITH REGARD TO THIRD PARTIES

10. Three possible circumstances. Here it is necessary to consider whether a third party (with whom the agent has con-

tracted) is capable of suing, or of being sued by, the agent or
the principal. On the footing that the agent was authorised to
enter the contract, there are three circumstances to examine:

(a) Where both the fact of agency and the name or description of the principal are disclosed to the third party.
(b) Where the agent discloses the existence of the principal, but not his name or description.
(c) Where the existence of the principal is not disclosed.

11. Where the name of the principal is disclosed. Where the
agent discloses the fact of the agency and the name or description of the principal to the third party, the general rule is that
the agent incurs no rights or obligations. The contract is made
between the principal and the third party, and it is between
these that the rights and obligations are created. The legal
effect is the same as if the principal had contracted directly
with the third party.

NOTE: This general rule will be modified by any term, express or
implied, to the effect that the agent is to be liable to the third
party or to the principal. In particular:

(i) The agent is always liable on a deed executed in his own name.
(ii) The agent is always liable on a bill of exchange signed in his own name, without any words showing that he signed as agent.
(iii) The agent is liable where he is made so by custom of a trade, *e.g.* in a contract of marine insurance, the broker is liable to the insurer for the amount of the premium.

**12. Where the existence but not the name of the principal is
disclosed.** Where the agent clearly contracts as agent, but does
not disclose the name or sufficient description of his principal,
the third party and the principal are contractually bound. The
legal position is the same as where the principal is named. The
agent normally drops out when the contract is made unless
there is a term, express or implied, to the effect that he undertakes liability.

13. Where the principal is undisclosed. Where a principal has
conferred authority on an agent and the agent subsequently
contracts with a third party, but does not disclose the fact
of the agency, so that the third party does not know of the

existence of the principal, the doctrine of the undisclosed principal will apply. According to this doctrine, the parties have rights as follows:

(a) *If a cause of action accrues to the third party*, he may *elect* to sue either the agent or the undisclosed principal, if he can find him. A judgment against one is a bar to action against the other.

(b) *If a cause of action accrues to the undisclosed principal* against the third party, his rights will be subject to the following limitations:

    (i) The agent's authority must have existed at the time of the contract with the third party.

    (ii) The agent must not have contracted in terms incompatible with agency, *e.g.* in a contract of sale or hire, he must not have described himself as "owner": *Humble* v. *Hunter* (1848).

If conditions (i) and (ii) are not satisfied, the undisclosed principal cannot intervene.

(c) Only a principal whose existence has been disclosed can ratify: *Keighley Maxsted* v. *Durant* (1901).

POSITION AS BETWEEN PRINCIPAL AND AGENT

14. General. The relationship between a principal and his agent is partly contractual and partly fiduciary. The fiduciary element is important. There are always certain rights and obligations existing between principal and agent, apart from those which clearly stem from their contractual relationship. It must be remembered that the relationship is essentially a confidential one.

15. Obligations of the agent. In addition to his express contractual obligations, an agent is always under the following duties to his principal. These may, of course, be regarded as giving corresponding rights to the principal, who may sue for damages in the event of a breach of duty by the agent:

(a) *To exercise diligence and whatever skill is professed*, *e.g.* a salesman must sell his principal's property at the best possible price: *Keppel* v. *Wheeler* (1927).

(b) *To render accounts* to the principal as required.

(c) *Not to let his own interests conflict* with his obligations to the principal, *e.g.* an agent must not become principal as against his own principal.

(d) *Not to disclose confidential information* obtained during the course of his duties as agent.

(e) *Not to take any secret profit* or bribe from any party with whom he deals on behalf of the principal. Where this occurs to the knowledge of the third party, the contract is voidable at the option of the principal.

(f) *Not to delegate his duties* to a sub-agent without authority, expressed or implied: *delegatus non potest delegare* ("a delegate has no authority to delegate").

(g) *To comply with his principal's instructions* and to notify him when compliance becomes impossible.

16. Obligations of the principal. The principal has always the following duties towards his agent. From these duties the agent derives corresponding rights which he can enforce against his principal:

(a) *To pay remuneration and expenses* as agreed; or, failing agreement, as is customary; or, failing a custom, to pay what is reasonable.

(b) *To indemnify* the agent against *losses* arising from the execution of his authority.

(c) *To indemnify* the agent against *losses* and liabilities arising out of an unauthorised act subsequently *ratified*.

(d) *An agent has a lien* on goods of his principal lawfully in his possession where the principal has not paid remuneration or expenses properly due.

NOTE: An agent is not entitled to be indemnified against the consequences of his own negligence, default or breach of duty; nor is he entitled to be indemnified against the consequences of an unlawful act except where he is entitled to a contribution towards damages in cases of his liability in tort towards a third party.

BREACH OF WARRANTY OF AUTHORITY

17. The warranty of authority. A person who purports to act as an agent is deemed to warrant that he has his principal's

authority. Where a person contracts as agent without any
authority, or where an agent contracts in excess of his
authority, there is a breach of warranty of authority.

18. Who may bring the action? Any person who has relied
on the warranty of authority and has acted upon that reliance
and has thereby suffered loss may bring an action for damages
against the agent. But no person who knew of the agent's lack
of authority, or did not believe him to be an agent, may sue.

NOTE: *It is no defence* for the agent to plead that he acted in
good faith and that he did not know his authority to be at an
end. The agent's liability arises independent of fraud or negligence, but where this is present, the party who has suffered
loss may bring his action for breach of warranty and also in tort
in the alternative.

TERMINATION OF THE AGENCY RELATIONSHIP

19. Ways in which authority may be ended. The relationship
of principal and agent may be terminated by act of the parties
or by operation of law as follows:

(a) *By notice of revocation* given by the principal to the agent.
(b) *By notice of renunciation* given to the principal by the
agent.
(c) *By the completion of the transaction,* where the authority
was given for that transaction only, *i.e.* in the case of a
special agency.
(d) *By the expiration of the period* stipulated in the contract
of agency.
(e) *By mutual agreement,* by which the principal discharges
the agent from further liability, and duty in consideration for a reciprocal discharge from the agent.
(f) Generally, by *death, lunacy, or bankruptcy* of the principal or agent.
(g) *By dissolution,* where the principal is a corporation
(probably also, where the agent is a corporation).
(h) *By the destruction of the subject-matter* of the agency.
(i) *By the contract becoming unlawful.*

20. Unilateral termination of agency. Where there is a contract of agency, summary unilateral termination, unless within

the terms of the contract, will be in breach of contract, and damages may be awarded against the party revoking or renouncing. However, if there is no period of notice stipulated in the contract of agency, either party may give reasonable notice at any time.

NOTE: Although the general rule is that an agency agreement is always revocable and will not be specifically enforced, where the agency is coupled with an interest, the authority is irrevocable; *e.g.* if A owes money to B and subsequently gives him power of attorney to sell certain property and to discharge the debt from the purchase money, the power is coupled with an interest and is, therefore, irrevocable: *Gaussen* v. *Morton* (1830).

21. Ostensible authority. The termination of an agent's actual authority does not necessarily mean that the principal is not bound by future acts of the former agent. Where notice of revocation has not been given to third parties, they may still regard the former agent as having actual authority to enter contracts for the former principal. If such a third party enters a contract with a former agent, on the faith of his ostensible authority, the former principal will be liable if a cause of action accrues to the third party: *Trueman* v. *Loder* (1840). A prudent principal will therefore give notice of the termination of agency to all who have dealt with his former agent as agent.

PARTICULAR CLASSES OF AGENTS

22. Mercantile agents. A mercantile agent is one "having, in the customary course of his business as such agent, authority either to sell goods, or to consign goods for the purpose of sale, or to buy goods, or to raise money on the security of goods": *Factors Act,* 1889, *s.* 1. This definition covers factors, brokers, auctioneers and dealers on commission: but it does not cover clerks and servants. Where a mercantile agent sells goods without authority, the buyer gets good title to the goods. This is a statutory exception to the common law principle *nemo dat quod non habet: see* XII, **14.**

23. Factors. A factor is a mercantile agent employed to sell goods which have been placed in his possession or control. He is the apparent owner of the goods in his custody and can sell in his own name. A factor has, in the absence of agreement to the contrary, a lien over his principal's goods in respect of any claim he may have arising out of the agency.

24. Brokers. A broker is an agent employed to make bargains and contracts in matters of trade, commerce, and navigation between other parties for a compensation commonly called brokerage. A broker is distinguished from a factor in the matter of possession of goods. A broker does not take his principal's goods into his possession, whereas a factor does. Also, a broker cannot sue third parties in his own name, whereas a factor may always sue third parties if they are in breach. Finally, a broker may not buy and sell in his own name unless permitted by a custom of his particular branch of trade: a factor may always buy and sell in his own name. Where a broker makes a contract between buyer and seller, he enters the terms into his book and signs it. He then sends a memorandum of the contract to each party—a *bought note* to the buyer and a *sold note* to the seller. He is thus an agent for both the buyer and the seller.

25. Auctioneers. An auctioneer is an agent whose ordinary course of business is to sell goods or real property by public auction. An auctioneer must (a) disclose his principal, (b) sell to a third person, (c) accept the highest bid made at the sale, unless there is a reserve price which is not reached. Until the fall of the hammer, the auctioneer is the agent of the vendor, but he becomes the agent of the purchaser for the purpose of signing the memorandum of sale.

26. Del credere agents. A *del credere* agent is a mercantile agent who earns an extra commission (*del credere* commission) in return for giving an undertaking to his principal that third parties shall pay the sums due on their contracts. In the event of default by a third party, the *del credere* agent is bound to pay his principal the sum owed by the third party. (The agent may, of course, sue the third party.) A *del credere* agency may be implied on the grounds of a custom of a trade. A *del credere* agent's undertaking is incidental to the contract between the principal and the third party. It is, therefore, not a guarantee within the meaning of *s.* 4 of the *Statute of Frauds*.

27. Partners. In a partnership firm every partner is an agent of the firm and his other partners for the purpose of the business of the partnership: *Partnership Act*, 1890, *s*. 5.

PROGRESS TEST 9

1. What is the essential characteristic of an agent? **(1)**

2. Explain the different ways in which the relationship of principal and agent may be created. **(2–9)**

3. A dealt with B in the course of his (A's) duties as C's agent. The agency relationship has now been brought to an end, but A continues to deal with B. A has always used his own name in his dealings with B, but B knew that he was acting as C's agent. B has not yet been informed of the termination of A's agency. Advise C as to his liabilities towards B. **(7)**

4. D, a carrier, discovers that a consignment of tomatoes owned by E has deteriorated badly before the destination has been reached. He therefore sells the consignment for what he can get: this is about a third of the market price for good tomatoes. E has now brought an action against D for damages. D wishes to know whether he can claim that he was an agent of necessity. Advise him. **(8)**

5. In what circumstances does an agent who has contracted within his authority remain liable on the contract? **(11)**

6. Explain the doctrine of the undisclosed principal. **(13)**

7. What rights and duties exist between principal and agent? **(15, 16)**

8. In what circumstances may an action be brought for breach of warranty of authority? Who may bring the action? **(17, 18)**

9. In what ways may the principal–agent relationship be terminated? **(19, 20)**

10. Distinguish between the actual authority and the ostensible authority of an agent. **(7, 21)**

11. Define a "mercantile agent." **(22)**

12. What special rules apply to (a) factors, (b) brokers, and (c) *del credere* agents? **(23–26)**

CHAPTER X

THE LAW OF PARTNERSHIP

NATURE OF A PARTNERSHIP

1. Sources of partnership law. The law of partnership was amended and declared in the *Partnership Act*, 1890. Any study of partnership must, therefore, be based on the Act; but the rules of common law, particularly contract and agency, continue to apply except where the Act provides to the contrary.

2. Definition. "Partnership is the relation which subsists between persons carrying on a business in common with a view of profit": *P.A.*, 1890, *s.* 1(1).

3. Formation of partnerships. Partnership agreements may be made with or without formality. They may be oral or written, and may or may not be under seal. The ordinary rules of contract are applied to test whether agreement has been reached. Where a partnership agreement is in writing, the document is called the *articles of partnership*. Partnership agreements may be varied by subsequent agreement, *express or implied*, between the partners.

4. Testing the existence of partnership. Where there is a dispute as to whether a partnership exists the point must be decided in order to know whether the *Partnership Act* applies. First, the definition in *s.* 1(1) must be used as a test. Further, the Act provides certain rules which must be used where applicable to determine whether or not a partnership exists:

(a) *Co-ownership of property* does not of itself create a partnership whether or not the co-owners share any profits made by the use of the property.

(b) *The sharing of gross returns* does not of itself create a partnership, whether the persons sharing such returns have or have not a joint or common right or interest in any property from which the returns are derived.

(c) *The receipt by a person of a share of the profits* of a business is *prima facie* evidence that he is a partner in the business. But this evidence may be rebutted where it can be shown that the purpose of the share of the profits was any of the following:

    (i) The payment of a *debt* by fixed instalments.
    (ii) *The remuneration* of an employee of the business.
    (iii) Payment made to the *widow* or *child* of a deceased partner.
    (iv) Payments to the previous owner of a business who has *sold the goodwill, i.e.* where the consideration for the goodwill is a share in subsequent profits.
    (v) Payments by way of *interest on a loan* advanced for use in the business.

5. The firm and the firm-name. Persons who have entered into a partnership with one another are called collectively a *firm*. The name under which the business is carried on is the *firm-name*. A firm is *not* a distinct legal entity and must be clearly distinguished from a corporation. Where partners contract in the firm-name, the contract will take effect as if the names of each and every partner were substituted in the contract for the firm-name. Similarly, partners may sue or be sued in the firm-name.

6. Choice of firm-name. The general rule is that partners may carry on their business under any firm-name they choose. But this rule is subject to the following provisos:

(a) *The firm-name must not be such* as to raise the implication that the business is connected with another with which it is in competition.

(b) The requirements of the *Registration of Business Names Act*, 1916, must be satisfied. This Act provides that where the firm-name does not consist of the true names of *all* the partners, the following particulars must be registered:

    (i) The firm-name.
    (ii) The nature and place of the business.
    (iii) The present forename and surname of each partner.

(iv) Any former Christian name and surname held by any partner.
(v) The usual residence of each partner.
(vi) The nationality of each partner.
(vii) Any other business occupation of any partner.

These particulars must be registered within *fourteen days* of commencement of business. Where any particular becomes altered, the alteration must be registered within fourteen days. Failure to register renders the persons concerned liable to a fine, and, moreover, they may not be able to enforce any contract made. It should be noticed that the purpose of registration is to give *publicity of the identity of partners*, thus reducing the possibility of fraud.

(c) *The word "limited"* must not be used in a firm-name.

7. Number of partners. The *Companies Act*, 1948, provides that no banking partnership consisting of more than ten members may be formed, and that, in the case of any other kind of partnership, the maximum shall be twenty: *ss*. 429 and 434. This provision has now been amended by the *Companies Act*, 1967. Section 119 of the 1967 Act provides that banking partnerships may consist of not more than twenty persons each of whom is authorised by the Department of Trade and Industry to be a member of such a partnership. Section 120 of the 1967 Act provides that partnerships of more than twenty persons may be formed in the case of solicitors, accountants and stockbrokers.

RELATIONSHIP BETWEEN PARTNERS

8. Partners' rights and duties. The mutual rights and duties between partners are ascertained by:

(a) the express and implied terms of the partnership agreement; and
(b) the provisions of the *Partnership Act*.

In either case, the rights and duties may be varied by the consent of all the partners of a firm. Such consent may be express or may be implied from a course of dealing. In ascertaining the terms of the partnership agreement, the ordinary rules of contract apply. In practice, the articles of partnership

usually contain detailed terms which determine the mutual
rights and obligations of the partners.

9. P.A., Section 24. This important section of the *P.A.*
provides a set of rules which apply subject to any agreement,
express or implied, between the partners.

Section 24 provides that unless it is otherwise agreed:

(a) *Equal shares.* All the partners are entitled to share
equally in the capital and profits of the business, and
must contribute equally towards the losses whether of
capital or otherwise sustained by the firm.

(b) *Indemnity.* The firm must indemnify every partner in
respect of payments made and personal liabilities incurred by him:

    (i) in the ordinary and proper conduct of the business of
the firm; or

    (ii) in or about anything necessarily done for the preserva-
tion of the business or property of the firm.

(c) *Interest on advances.* A partner, making, for the purpose
of the partnership, any actual payment or advance
beyond the amount of capital which he has agreed to
subscribe, is entitled to interest at the rate of 5% per
annum from the date of the payment or advance.

(d) *Interest on capital.* A partner is not entitled, before the
ascertainment of profits, to interest on the capital subscribed by him.

(e) *Management.* Every partner may take part in the
management of the partnership business.

(f) *Remuneration.* No partner shall be entitled to remuneration for acting in the partnership business.

(g) *Introduction of partners.* No person shall be introduced
as a partner without the consent of all existing partners.

(h) *Internal disputes.* Any difference arising as to the
ordinary matters connected with the partnership business may be decided by a majority of the partners, but
no change may be made in the nature of the partnership
business without the consent of all existing partners.

(i) *Books.* The partnership books are to be kept at the
place of business of the partnership (or the principal
place, if there is more than one), and every partner may,

when he thinks fit, have access to and inspect and copy any of them.

10. Partners as agents. Every partner is an agent of the firm and his other partners for the purpose of the business of the partnership: *P.A.*, *s.* 5. Thus the general law of agency is incorporated into the law of partnership, and, in this connection, the Act makes specific provision for the following duties:

(a) *Uberrima fides.* Partners are bound to render true accounts and full information of all things affecting the partnership to any partner or his legal representative: *s.* 28.

(b) *No secret profits.* Every partner must account to the firm for any benefit derived by him without the consent of the other partners from any transaction concerning the partnership, or from any use by him of the partnership property name or business connection: *s.* 29.

(c) *No competition.* If a partner, without the consent of the other partners, carries on any business of the same nature as, and competing with, that of the firm, he must account for and pay over to the firm all profits made by him in that business: *s.* 30.

11. Partnership property. Partnership property includes:

(a) Property originally brought into the partnership stock: *s.* 20.

(b) Property acquired on account of the firm for the purposes of the partnership business: *s.* 20. Unless the contrary intention appears, property bought with money belonging to the firm is deemed to have been bought on account of the firm: *s.* 21.

Partnership property must be held and applied by the partners exclusively for the purposes of the partnership and *in accordance with the partnership agreement*: *s.* 20.

RELATIONS OF PARTNERS AND THIRD PARTIES

12. Partnership contracts with third parties. Partnership firms enter into contracts with third parties through the agency of one or more of the partners. Every partner is an agent of the firm and his other partners for the purpose of the business of the partnership. And the acts of every partner who does any act for carrying on, in the usual way, business of the kind carried on by the firm are binding on the firm unless:

(a) the partner so acting has in fact no authority to act in the particular matter, *and*

(b) the person with whom he is dealing either

(i) knows that he has no authority to act in the particular matter, *or*

(ii) does not know or believe him to be a partner: *s.* 5.

13. A partner's authority. Where a partner enters into a contract with a third party on behalf of his firm, the partner is an agent and the firm (including the partner himself) is the principal. As in the case of any other agent, the partner can bind his principal only to the *limit of his actual or apparent authority*. An act is within a partner's apparent authority if it is "for carrying on in the usual way business of the kind carried on by the firm." For example, a partner in a firm of house builders will have an apparent authority to enter a contract for the purchase of a quantity of bricks. A partner's apparent authority thus depends upon the nature of the business of his firm.

In the case of a *trading partnership* (*i.e.* one in which the principal operations are buying and selling), a partner has the apparent authority to bind his firm in the following kinds of transaction:

(a) *Pledging* the partnership goods: *Butchart* v. *Dresser* (1853).

(b) *Selling* the partnership goods: *Dore* v. *Wilkinson* (1817).

(c) *Buying* goods on the firm's account: *Bond* v. *Gibson* (1808).

(d) *Borrowing money* on behalf of the firm.

(e) *Paying the firm's debts* so as to give a good discharge to the debtor.

(f) Drawing, accepting, indorsing of *negotiable instruments*.

(g) *Engaging employees* for the firm.

NOTE: The apparent authority of a partner in a *non-trading* firm is considerably narrower than in the case of a trading firm:

in particular, he cannot draw, accept or indorse negotiable instruments so as to bind the firm (except ordinary cheques).

The apparent authority of a partner (whether of a trading or a non-trading firm) does not extend to any of the following: (i) giving a guarantee, unless this is within the usual business of the firm or there is a trade custom permitting it; (ii) submission of a dispute with a third party to arbitration; (iii) the execution of a deed on behalf of the firm unless under a power of attorney.

14. Contractual liability of partners to third parties. Every partner in a firm is liable *jointly* with the other partners for all debts and obligations of the firm incurred while he is a partner: s. 9.

Accordingly, a firm's creditor may sue any or all of the partners; he may not bring a fresh action against the remaining partners in the event of judgment being unsatisfied. In practice, it is advisable to bring an action against the firm in the firm-name, for this has the same effect as if the action were brought against each and every partner.

15. Liability of the firm for torts. Where a partner commits a tort while acting in the ordinary course of the partnership business, the firm is vicariously liable. The firm is similarly liable where a partner commits a tort with the authority of his co-partners. The firm's liability in tort is *joint and several*. This means that an unsatisfied judgment against one or some of the partners is *not* a bar to a further action against the remaining partners.

16. Liability of new partners. The general rule is that an incoming partner is not liable for the firm's debts incurred before he became a partner: s. 17. The incoming partner can, however, assume liability by *novation*. Novation in this case is a tripartite agreement between (a) a creditor of the firm, (b) the partners existing at the time the debt was incurred, and (c) the incoming partner.

17. Liability of retiring partners. A retiring partner's liability to the firm's creditors depends primarily upon whether the debt was incurred before or after the retirement.

(a) *Debts incurred before retirement.* A partner who retires from a firm does not thereby cease to be liable for partnership debts or obligations incurred before his retirement: *s.* 17. The only way in which an outgoing partner can be discharged from liability to the firm's creditors is by *novation*: in this case the parties are (i) the retiring partner, (ii) the firm as newly constituted after the retirement, and (iii) the creditor.

(b) *Debts incurred after retirement.* Where a person deals with a firm after a change in its constitution he is entitled to treat all apparent members of the old firm as still being members of the firm until he has notice of the change: *P.A., s.* 36. A retiring partner must therefore ensure that all persons who deal with the firm are given notice of the retirement, or he will be liable to them for debts incurred after he has left the firm. An advertisement in the *London Gazette* is sufficient notice of the retirement as to persons who had no dealings with the firm before the retirement.

18. Death or bankruptcy. The estate of a partner who dies, or who becomes bankrupt, or of a partner who, not having been known to the person dealing with the firm to be a partner, retires from the firm, is not liable for partnership debts contracted after the date of the death, bankruptcy, or retirement respectively: *P.A., s.* 36.

19. Holding out. Any person who represents himself, or allows himself to be represented, as a partner of a particular firm, is liable as a partner to any person who gives credit to the firm on the faith of the representation, *P.A., s.* 14. This is a form of agency by estoppel.

20. Guarantees. A *continuing* guarantee given either:

(a) to a firm, or

(b) to a third person in respect of the transactions of a firm, is, in the absence of agreement to the contrary, revoked as to future transactions by any change in the constitution of the firm to which, or of the firm in respect of the transactions of which the guarantee was given: *P.A., s.* 18. A guarantee given *by* a firm is not affected by subsequent changes in the constitution of that firm.

DISSOLUTION OF PARTNERSHIP

21. How a partnership may be dissolved. A partnership may come to an end in any of the following ways:

(a) By expiration or notice.
(b) By bankruptcy, death or charge.
(c) By illegality.
(d) By decree of the court.

22. Expiration or notice. Subject to any agreement between the partners, a partnership is dissolved

(a) If entered into for a *fixed term*, by the expiration of that term.
(b) If entered into for a *single adventure* or undertaking, by the termination of that adventure or undertaking.
(c) If entered into for an *undefined time*, by any partner giving notice to the other or others of his intention to dissolve the partnership: *P.A.*, s. 32.

23. Bankruptcy or death. *Subject to any agreement* between the partners, every partnership is dissolved as regards all the partners by the death or bankruptcy of any partner: *P.A.*, s. 33. It is not usual, however, for a partnership business to come to an end because of the death or bankruptcy of one of the partners. The business is usually continued by the remaining partners. The agreement to continue may be contained in the articles, or the remaining partners may by fresh agreement, express or implied, continue the partnership business.

24. Charge. A partnership may, at the option of the other partners, be dissolved if any partner suffers his share of the partnership property to be charged under the *Partnership Act* for his separate debt: *P.A.*, s. 33. The charge referred to here is that provided for by s. 23 of the *Partnership Act*, whereby the court may make an order charging the interest of any partner in the partnership property for the payment of a judgment debt. This provision (a) recognises the undesirability of a partner who cannot pay his judgment debts, and (b) allows the other partners to get rid of him.

25. Illegality. A partnership is in every case dissolved by the happening of any event which makes it unlawful for the business of the firm to be carried on, or for the members of the firm to carry it on in partnership: *s.* 34.

26. Decree of the court. *On application by a partner* the court may decree a dissolution of the partnership in any of the following cases:

(a) When a partner is found *lunatic by inquisition,* or is shown to the satisfaction of the court to be of permanently unsound mind. (In this case the application may be made on behalf of the lunatic partner by his committee or next friend.)

(b) When a partner, other than the partner suing, becomes in any other way *permanently incapable* of performing his part of the partnership contract.

(c) When a partner, other than the partner suing, has been *guilty of such conduct* as, in the opinion of the court, regard being had to the nature of the business, is calculated to affect prejudicially the carrying on of the business.

(d) When a partner, other than the partner suing, *wilfully or persistently commits a breach* of the partnership agreement, or otherwise so conducts himself in matters relating to the partnership business that it is not reasonably practicable for the other partner or partners to carry on the business in partnership with him.

(e) When the business of the partnership can only be *carried on at a loss*.

(f) Whenever in any case circumstances have arisen which, in the opinion of the court, render it *just and equitable* that the partnership be dissolved: *P.A., s.* 35.

27. Settlement of accounts on dissolution. It is provided by the *Partnership Act,* 1890, that in settling accounts between the partners after a dissolution of partnership, the following rules shall, *subject to any agreement*, be observed:

(a) *Losses*, including losses and deficiencies of capital, must be paid first out of profits, next out of capital, and lastly if necessary, by the partners individually in the proportion in which they were entitled to share profits.

(b) *The assets* of the firm, including the sums, if any, contributed by the partners to make up losses or deficiencies of capital, must be applied in the following manner and order:

(i) In paying the debts and liabilities of the firm to persons who are not partners therein.

(ii) In paying to each partner rateably what is due from the firm to him for advances as distinguished from capital.

(iii) In paying to each partner rateably what is due from the firm to him in respect of capital.

(iv) The ultimate residue, if any, shall be divided among the partners in the proportion in which profits are divisible: *P.A., s.* 44.

28. Remaining deficiencies of capital. Where there remains insufficient capital to repay all the partners in full, the general rule (as above) is that the partners are paid rateably each according to his share in the capital. Where, however, the deficiency of capital is attributable to the insolvency of one of the partners, that deficiency must be borne by the other partners in the proportion of their last agreed shares in the capital. This is known as the rule in *Garner* v. *Murray* (1904).

29. Goodwill. The goodwill of a partnership is an asset, which, if it exists, should be sold on dissolution as in the case of any other asset. Goodwill is that approbation which has been earned by a business over a period of time. It usually involves the acquisition of a number of regular customers or clients who will remain after a change in the constitution of the firm, or even in the event of the business being sold as a going concern. It has been said that goodwill is merely the *probability that the old customers will resort to the old place.* The rights of the vendor and purchaser of goodwill may be defined as follows

(a) *Purchaser's rights.* On the sale of goodwill the purchaser may, unless the terms of the contract of sale provide otherwise:

(i) represent himself as continuing the business;

(ii) maintain the exclusive rights to the use of the firm-name; and

(iii) solicit former customers of the business and restrain the vendors from doing so.

(b) *Vendor's rights.* The vendor may enter into competition with the purchaser unless he is prevented by a valid restraint clause in the contract of sale: *see* V, **16**.

LIMITED PARTNERSHIPS

30. The Limited Partnerships Act, 1907. Partnerships with limited liability were made possible by the Act of 1907. There are, however, very few limited partnerships in existence today because the advantages accorded to this kind of partnership are more conveniently gained by operating the business in the form of a registered company. The *Limited Partnerships Act, 1907*, contains a number of far-reaching modifications to the general law of partnership.

31. Constitution and registration. The Act of 1907 provides as follows:

(a) *Number of partners.* A limited partnership must not consist of more than twenty members or ten in the case of a banking partnership. This provision does not apply in the case of solicitors, stockbrokers or accountants: *Companies Act, 1967, s.* 121.

(b) *General and limited partners.* Every limited partnership must include at least one general partner and at least one limited partner.

- (i) *General partners* are liable for all debts and obligations of the firm and are entitled to take part in the management of the firm.
- (ii) *Limited partners* contribute capital or property valued at a stated amount, and are not liable for the debts of the firm beyond that amount.
  This contribution may not be withdrawn except in the event of dissolution. Limited partners have no rights to share in the management of the firm, nor are they deemed to be the agents of the firm.

(c) *Registration.* Every limited partnership must be registered by sending to the Registrar of Joint Stock Companies a statement signed by the partners containing the following particulars:

- (i) The firm-name.
- (ii) The general nature of the business.
- (iii) The principal place of business.

(iv) The full name of each of the partners.
 (v) The term, if any, for which the partnership is entered into and the date of its commencement.
(vi) A statement that the partnership is limited, and the description of every limited partner as such.
(vii) The sum contributed by each limited partner, and whether paid in cash or how otherwise.

If default is made in registration, the partnership will be deemed a general partnership, and the limited partners will lose the advantage of limited liability and be fully liable for the firm's debts.

PROGRESS TEST 10

1. Define "partnership" and comment on your definition. What restrictions are there on the choice of a firm-name?   **(1, 5, 6)**

2. Explain fully the legal relationship existing between partners. **(8, 9, 10)**

3. In what circumstances may a partner bind his firm in dealing with a third party?   **(10, 12–14)**

4. Explain the liability of (a) new and (b) retiring partners. **(16, 17)**

5. How may a partnership be dissolved?   **(21–26)**

6. What are the rules as to settlement of accounts on the dissolution of a partnership?   **(27)**

7. Outline the provisions of the *Limited Partnerships Act*, 1907. **(31)**

CHAPTER XI

NEGOTIABLE INSTRUMENTS

BILLS OF EXCHANGE

1. Characteristics of negotiable instruments. Certain instruments have the special quality of negotiability. Instruments may be made negotiable by statute (*e.g.* bills of exchange and promissory notes) or by mercantile custom judicially recognised (*e.g.* bearer debentures and Exchequer bills). Any negotiable instrument has the following characteristics which should be carefully compared with assignment of an ordinary chose in action: *see* VI, **5–11.**

(a) Title to a negotiable instrument passes either by (i) mere delivery, or by (ii) delivery together with indorsement, *i.e.* signature of the transferor.

(b) No notice of the transfer of title is required to be given to any person liable on the instrument.

(c) The holder of a negotiable instrument may sue in his own name.

(d) The transferee of a negotiable instrument takes free from the equities, *i.e.* free from any right of counterclaim or set-off which any person might have against the transferor.

2. The Bills of Exchange Act, 1882. This Act, together with the *Cheques Act*, 1957, codifies the law relating to bills of exchange (including cheques) and promissory notes.

3. Bills of exchange. A bill of exchange is an unconditional order in writing, addressed by one person to another, signed by the person giving it, requiring the person to whom it is addressed to pay on demand or at a fixed or determinable future time a sum certain in money to or to the order of a specified person, or to bearer: *B.E.A.*, *s.* 3. Any instrument which does not comply with this definition, or which orders any act to be done in addition to the payment of money, is not a bill of exchange.

NOTE
  (i) A bill is an *order* and not a request. But the use of the word "please" as a form of courtesy will not prevent an instrument from being an order.
 (ii) The order must be: (*a*) unconditional, (*b*) in writing, (*c*) addressed by one person (the drawer) to another (the drawee), (*d*) signed by the person giving the order (the drawer).
(iii) The order must require the drawee to pay a sum certain in money: (*a*) on demand, or (*b*) at a fixed or determinable future time.
 (iv) The order must require the drawee to make payment: (*a*) to a specified person (the payee), (*b*) to the order of the payee, or (*c*) to bearer.
  (v) A bill is not invalid by any of the following reasons: (*a*) that it is not dated; (*b*) that it does not specify the value given, or that any value has been given for it; (*c*) that it does not specify the place where it is drawn or the place where it is payable; (*d*) that it is ante-dated or post-dated, or that it bears the date of a Sunday.

4. Inland and foreign bills. An *inland bill* is a bill which is or on the face of it purports to be:

  (a) both drawn and payable within the British Islands, or
  (b) both drawn and payable within the British Islands upon some person resident therein: *B.E.A.*, *s*. 4.

Any other bill is a *foreign* bill: *B.E.A.*, *s*. 4.

5. Demand bills. A bill is payable on demand which is expressed to be payable on demand, or at sight, or on presentation; or in which no time for payment is expressed. Such bills become payable when presented to the drawee for payment: *B.E.A.*, *s*. 10.

6. Bills payable at a future time. A bill is payable at a determinable future time which is expressed to be payable (*a*) at a fixed period after date or sight, or (*b*) on or at a fixed period after the occurrence of a specified event which is certain to happen, though the time of happening may be uncertain: *B.E.A.*, *s*. 11.

NOTE

(i) An instrument expressed to be *payable on a contingency* is not a bill, and the happening of the event does not cure the defect.

(ii) Where a bill expressed to be payable at a *fixed period after date* is issued, or where the acceptance of a bill payable at a fixed period after sight is undated, any holder may insert therein the true date of issue or acceptance, and the bill shall be payable accordingly.

(iii) *Sight* refers to the first sighting of the bill by the drawee.

7. Time of payment. Where a bill is not payable on demand, the day on which it falls due is determined as follows:

(a) *Three days,* called *days of grace,* are in every case where the bill itself does not otherwise provide, added to the time of payment as fixed by the bill, and the bill is due and payable on the last day of grace: provided that:

(i) When the last day of grace falls on a Sunday, Christmas Day or Good Friday, the bill is due and payable on the preceding business day.

(ii) When the last day of grace is a bank holiday (other than Christmas Day or Good Friday) or when the last day of grace is a Sunday and the second day of grace is a bank holiday, the bill is due and payable on the *succeeding* business day.

(b) *Where a bill is payable at a fixed period after date,* after sight, or after the happening of a specified event, the time of payment is determined by excluding the day from which the time is to begin to run and by including the day of payment.

(c) *Where a bill is payable at a fixed period after sight,* the time begins to run from the date of acceptance if the bill is accepted, and from the date of noting or protest if the bill be noted or protested for non-acceptance, or for non-delivery.

ACCEPTANCE OF A BILL

8. Definition. The *acceptance* of a bill is the signification by the drawee of his assent to the order of the drawer: *B.E.A., s.* 17.

NOTE

(i) The acceptance must be *written on the bill and signed* by the drawee. But the mere signature of the drawee is sufficient.

(ii) *It must not express that* the drawee will perform his promise by any means other than the payment of money.

(iii) Acceptance is incomplete and revocable until the bill is *delivered by the drawee* to the holder. Upon delivery the drawee becomes liable on the bill, and is then called the *acceptor*.

9. General acceptance. A general acceptance assents without qualification to the order to the drawer: *B.E.A.*, *s.* 19.

NOTE

(i) An acceptance to pay at a particular place is a general acceptance, unless it expressly states that the bill is to be paid there *only* and not elsewhere.

(ii) *The mere signature* of the drawee on the face of the bill constitutes a general acceptance.

(iii) In addition to the signature, there may also be written the word "accepted," and/or the date, and/or a statement as to where the bill is payable.

10. Qualified acceptance. An acceptance is qualified which is

(a) *Conditional*, *i.e.* where payment by the acceptor is expressed to be dependent on the fulfilment of a stated condition.

(b) *Partial*, *i.e.* an acceptance to pay part only of the amount for which the bill is drawn.

(c) *Local*, *i.e.* an acceptance to pay at a particular specified place *only*.

(d) *Qualified as to time*, *e.g.* where the acceptor of a bill drawn as payable one month after date qualifies his acceptance with the words "payable three months after date."

(e) *By some, but not all, of the drawees* where there is more than one drawee: *B.E.A.*, *s.* 19.

11. The effect of acceptance. The drawee is not liable on the bill unless and until he accepts it. By accepting the bill, he engages that he will pay it according to the tenor of his acceptance. If it is a general acceptance, he is fully liable to pay according to the order of the drawer. If it is qualified acceptance, he is liable to pay according to the order of the drawer as qualified by the acceptance.

NOTE

(i) *The holder of a bill may refuse to take a qualified acceptance.* If he does not get a general acceptance, he may treat the bill as dishonoured.

(ii) *Where a qualified acceptance is taken,* and the drawer or an indorser (a transferor who has signed his name on the back of the bill) has not authorised the qualified acceptance, or does not subsequently give his assent to it, such drawer or indorser is discharged from liability on the bill. (This provision does not apply to a partial acceptance provided due notice is given by the holder.)

(iii) *When the drawer or indorser of a bill receives notice of a qualified acceptance,* and does not within a reasonable time express his dissent to the holder, he is deemed to have assented to it.

12. Presentment for acceptance. A bill must be presented for acceptance in the following cases:

(a) *Where a bill is payable after sight,* presentment for acceptance is necessary in order to fix the maturity date of the instrument. A holder of such a bill must present it for acceptance or negotiate it within a reasonable time.

(b) *Where a bill expressly stipulates* that it shall be presented for acceptance, it must be presented for acceptance before it can be presented for payment.

(c) *Where a bill is drawn payable elsewhere than at the residence or place of business of the drawee,* it must be presented for acceptance before it can be presented for payment: *B.E.A., s.* 39.

In no other case is presentment for acceptance necessary in order to render liable any party to the bill. In particular, there is no need to present for acceptance bills drawn payable (*a*) on sight, on demand or on presentation, or (*b*) after date.

13. Rules as to presentment for acceptance. A bill is duly presented for acceptance if it is presented according to the following rules:

(a) Presentment must be made *by the holder* (or his agent) to the drawee (or his agent) at a reasonable hour on a business day before the bill is overdue.

(b) Where a bill is addressed to *two or more drawees,* who are not partners, presentment must be made to them all, unless one has authority to accept for all, when presentment may be made to him only.

(c) *Where the drawee is dead*, presentment may be made to his personal representative.

(d) *Where the drawee is bankrupt*, presentment may be made to him or to his trustee.

(e) Where authorised by agreement or usage, a *presentment through the Post Office* is sufficient: *B.E.A.*, *s.* 41.

14. Excuses for non-presentment. Presentment for acceptance according to the rules is excused, and the bill may be treated as dishonoured by non-acceptance in the following circumstances:

(a) *Where the drawee is dead or bankrupt*, or is a fictitious person or a person not having capacity to contract by bill.

(b) Where, after the exercise of reasonable diligence, *presentment cannot be effected*.

(c) Where, although presentment has been irregular, *acceptance has been refused on some other ground*: *B.E.A.*, *s.* 41.

15. Dishonour by non-acceptance. A bill is dishonoured by non-acceptance

(a) when it is duly presented for acceptance, and acceptance is refused or cannot be obtained; or

(b) when presentment for acceptance is excused: *B.E.A.*, *s.* 43.

NEGOTIATION OF A BILL

16. Definition. A bill is negotiated when it is transferred from one person to another in such a manner as to constitute the transferee the holder of the bill: *B.E.A.*, *s.* 31.

NOTE

(i) The holder of a bill is either (*a*) the payee or indorsee in possession, or (*b*) the bearer.

(ii) A bill payable to bearer is negotiated by delivery.

(iii) A bill payable to order is negotiated by the indorsement of the holder completed by delivery.

17. Indorsements. When a holder places his signature on the back of the bill, he is said to *indorse* the bill. There are several kinds of indorsements:

(a) *Indorsement in blank.* This kind of indorsement specifies no indorsee, *i.e.* it is no more than the signature of the holder as transferor. *A bill so indorsed becomes payable to bearer,* i.e. it becomes transferable by mere delivery.

(b) *Special indorsement.* A special indorsement specifies the person to whom, or to whose order, the bill is to be payable. A bill so indorsed is further negotiated by indorsement completed by delivery.

(c) *Restrictive indorsement.* An indorsement is restrictive which prohibits the further negotiation of the bill or which expresses that it is a mere authority to deal with the bill as directed, and not a transfer of ownership of it, *e.g.* "Pay D only," or "Pay D for the account of X," or "Pay D or order for collection."

(d) *Conditional indorsement.* An indorsement may purport to make payment or transfer subject to some condition. In such cases the condition may be disregarded by the payer, and payment to the indorsee is valid whether the condition has been fulfilled or not.

(e) *Indorsement sans recours.* Where the holder of a bill indorses it *Sans recours* or "Without recourse to me," he negatives his own liability on the bill. A transferee can, of course, refuse to take a bill indorsed in this way.

18. Transfer by delivery. A bill payable to bearer is negotiated by delivery and no indorsement is necessary. In this case, the transferor is called a *transferor by delivery*; and since he does not sign the bill, he is not subsequently liable as a party to it: *B.E.A., s.* 58.

NOTE: A bill is payable to bearer in the following circumstances:
  (i) Where it is expressed to be payable to bearer.
  (ii) Where the last indorsement is in blank.
  (iii) Where it is payable to a fictitious person.

In all other cases, an indorsement is necessary to negotiate the bill.

PAYMENT OF A BILL

19. Presentment for payment. A bill must be duly presented for payment according to the following rules, otherwise the drawer and indorsers are discharged: *B.E.A., s.* 45.

(a) Where the bill is not payable on demand, presentment must be made on the day it falls due.

(b) Where the bill is payable on demand, presentment must be made within a reasonable time.

(c) Presentment must be made by the holder (or his agent) to drawee named on the bill (or his agent).

(d) Presentment must be made at the proper place.

(e) Where authorised by agreement or usage a presentment through the Post Office is sufficient.

20. Excuses for delay or non-presentment. Delay in presentment for payment is excused when caused by circumstances beyond the control of the holder, and not due to his negligence. Presentment for payment is dispensed with in the following circumstances:

(a) Where, after the exercise of reasonable diligence, presentment cannot be effected.

(b) Where the drawee is fictitious.

(c) *As regards the drawer* where the drawee or acceptor is not bound, as between himself and the drawer, to accept or pay the bill, and the drawer has no reason to believe that the bill would be paid if presented.

(d) *As regards an indorser* where the bill was accepted or made for the accommodation of that indorser and he has no reason to expect that the bill would be paid if presented.

(e) By waiver of presentment by a person entitled to notice of dishonour: *B.E.A.*, *s.* 46.

21. Dishonour by non-payment. A bill is dishonoured by non-payment:

(a) when it is duly presented for payment and payment is refused or cannot be obtained, or

(b) when presentment is excused: *B.E.A. s.* 47.

When a bill is dishonoured by non-payment, an immediate right of recourse against the drawer and indorsers accrues to the holder: *B.E.A.*, *s.* 47.

22. Notice of dishonour. When a bill has been dishonoured by *non-acceptance* or *non-payment*, notice of dishonour must be given to the drawer and each indorser, and any drawer or indorser to whom notice is not given is discharged; provided that:

(a) Where a bill is dishonoured by non-acceptance, and notice of dishonour is not given, the rights of a holder in due course subsequent to the omission are not affected.

(b) Where a bill is dishonoured by non-acceptance and notice of dishonour is given, it is not necessary to give notice of a subsequent dishonour by non-payment unless the bill in the meantime has been accepted: *B.E.A.*, *s.* 48.

NOTE: Notice of dishonour must be given to *prior parties* to the bill by the holder of the dishonoured bill, or by any indorser who is liable on the bill. In practice, it is usual for each party to the bill to claim against the party immediately before him (usually his own transferor), so that a chain of notice-giving takes place from the holder, through each indorser, ultimately reaching the drawer. *Notice may take any form, i.e.* it may be oral or in unsigned writing, or it may take the form of the return of the dishonoured bill.

23. Excuses for non-notice and delay. Delay in giving notice of dishonour is excused where the delay is not caused by default or negligence. Notice of dishonour is dispensed with in the following circumstances:

(a) When, after the exercise of reasonable diligence, notice cannot be given or does not reach the drawer or indorser sought to be charged.

(b) By waiver by a person entitled to receive notice.

(c) *As regards the drawer* in the following cases:

  (i) Where drawer and drawee are the same person.
  (ii) Where the drawee is a fictitious person or has no contractual capacity.
  (iii) Where the drawer is the person to whom the bill is presented for payment.
  (iv) Where the drawee or acceptor is as between himself and the drawer under no obligation to accept or pay the bill.
  (v) Where the drawer has countermanded payment.

(d) *As regards the indorser* in the following cases:

  (i) Where the drawee is a fictitious person or has no contractual capacity, and the indorser was aware of the fact at the time of indorsing.

(ii) Where the indorser is the person to whom the bill is presented for payment.

(iii) Where the bill was accepted or made for his accommodation: *B.E.A. s.* 50.

24. Noting and protesting. These are two methods of obtaining formal evidence of the dishonour of a bill.

(a) *Noting.* A dishonoured bill is *noted* by a notary public, who must re-present the bill, and then write on the face of the bill that it was dishonoured. The holder of an *inland bill* which has been dishonoured may arrange for the bill to be noted, but this procedure is not necessary to preserve the recourse against prior parties.

(b) *Protesting.* In this case, the notary re-presents the bill, and then makes out a formal certificate of dishonour (the protest) containing a copy of the bill. Where the services of a notary cannot be obtained, a householder may sign a certificate attesting the dishonour of the bill: two witnesses must also sign. *A foreign bill must be protested for dishonour by non-acceptance or by non-payment.* If it is not protested, the drawer and indorsers are discharged: *B.E.A., s.* 51.

CONSIDERATION FOR A BILL: HOLDERS

25. What constitutes consideration. Section 27 of The *Bills of Exchange Act*, 1882, provides that valuable consideration for a bill may be constituted by:

(a) Any consideration sufficient to support a simple contract.

(b) An antecedent debt or liability (but the antecedent debt must be owed by the negotiator or drawer of the bill): *Oliver* v. *Davis* (1949).

26. Holder for value. Where value has been given *at any time* for a bill, the holder is deemed to be a holder for value as regards the acceptor and all parties to the bill who became parties prior to such time.

27. Holder in due course. A holder in due course is a holder who has taken a bill, complete and regular on the face of it, under the following conditions:

(a) That he became the holder of it before it was overdue,

and without notice that it had been previously dishonoured, if such was the fact.

(b) That he took the bill in good faith and for value, and that at the time the bill was negotiated to him he had no notice of any defect in the title of the person who negotiated it: *B.E.A.*, *s.* 29.

28. Presumption of value and good faith. In the case of bills of exchange, the following two presumptions exist:

(a) *Consideration.* Every party whose signature appears on a bill is *prima facie* deemed to have become a party for value.

(b) Every holder of a bill is *prima facie* deemed to be a holder in due course: *B.E.A.*, *s.* 30.

29. Holder's rights. The rights and powers of a holder of a bill are as follows:

(a) He may sue on the bill in his own name.

(b) *Where he is a holder in due course,* he holds the bill free from any defect of title of prior parties, as well as from mere personal defences available to prior parties among themselves, and may enforce payment against all parties liable on the bill.

(c) Where his title is defective:

   (i) if he negotiates the bill to a holder in due course, that holder obtains a good and complete title to the bill, and

   (ii) if he obtains payment of the bill, the person who pays him in due course gets a valid discharge for the bill: *B.E.A.*, *s.* 38.

30. Holder's duties. The general duties of the holder of a bill are as follows:

(a) To present the bill for acceptance where necessary according to the rules.

(b) To present the bill for payment according to the rules.

(c) To give notice of dishonour for non-acceptance or non-payment.

(d) In the case of a dishonoured foreign bill, to obtain a protest.

LIABILITY OF PARTIES: DISCHARGE

31. Drawee/acceptor. The *drawee* of a bill who does not accept it is not liable on the instrument: *B.E.A., s.* 53. The *acceptor* engaged that he will pay the bill according to the tenor of his acceptance and is precluded from denying to a holder in due course the existence of the drawer and the genuineness of his signature: *B.E.A., s.* 54.

32. The drawer. The drawer of a bill:

(a) engages that on due presentment it shall be accepted and paid, and that, if it be dishonoured, he will compensate any party who is compelled to pay it, provided the requisite proceedings on dishonour be taken;

(b) is precluded from denying to a holder in due course the existence of the payee: *B.E.A., s.* 55.

33. The indorser. The indorser of a bill:

(a) engages that on due presentment it shall be accepted and paid, and that, if it be dishonoured, he will compensate any subsequent party who is compelled to pay it, provided the requisite proceedings on dishonour be taken;

(b) is precluded from denying to a holder in due course the genuineness of the drawer's signature and all previous indorsements;

(c) is precluded from denying to any subsequent indorsee that he had a good title to it: *B.E.A., s.* 55.

34. Transferor by delivery. A transferor by delivery, *i.e.* one who negotiates the bill without indorsing it, is not liable on the instrument: *B.E.A., s.* 58. A transferor by delivery warrants to his immediate transferee, being a holder for value, that the bill is what it purports to be, that he has a right to transfer it, and that at the time of transfer he is not aware of any fact which renders it valueless: *B.E.A., s.* 58.

NOTE: Although a transferor by delivery will not be liable on the bill, he will be liable for breach of contract *to his immediate transferor* in the event of the bill being dishonoured.

35. Forged signatures. The general rule is that a forged signature on a bill is *totally inoperative: B.E.A., s.* 24. The effect of the forgery depends upon which signature has been forged, *i.e.* whether it is the drawer's, acceptor's or indorser's.

(a) *Where the drawer's signature is forged* the instrument does not satisfy the definition in *s.* 3 of the Act, and it therefore cannot be a bill of exchange. However, the indorsers of such an instrument will be liable as between each other as if the instrument were a valid bill by reason of the rule of statutory estoppel in *s.* 55. Also, if the instrument has been accepted, the acceptor is likewise estopped from denying to a holder in due course the genuineness of the drawer's signature: *B.E.A.*, *s.* 54.

(b) *Where an indorsement is forged*, the rights of the parties to the bill prior to the forgery are not affected, but those taking the bill after the forgery will have rights *as between one another* as if the bill were valid for them. This is the effect of the rule of statutory estoppel in *s.* 55:

> Consider this example: A draws a bill on B payable to C; then C indorses this bill specially to D, who indorses the bill specially to E; then X steals the bill from E and forges E's signature to a special indorsement to F; then F indorses the bill specially to G, who indorses the bill specially to H. Applying the rule in *s.* 24, that the forged signature is totally inoperative, it is clear that the bill remained the property of E after the forgery and that no title to the bill passed to F, G and H. The *forgery caused a break in the chain of transference of title.* But H can claim against G or F, who will not be allowed to set up the forgery (*s.* 55). If H claims against G, then G in his turn will be able to claim similarly against F. F will not be able to claim against any of the parties prior to the forgery: his only recourse will be against X, if he can find him.

(c) *Where the acceptance is forged.* A forged acceptance is by virtue of *s.* 24 totally inoperative. The instrument remains a good bill whose legal effect is that of a bill which has not been accepted. The drawer and indorsers are liable according to the usual rules.

36. Discharge of a bill. A bill is discharged when no rights and obligations attach to it. A party to a bill is discharged when he is no longer liable on it.

Discharge may occur in any of the following ways:

(a) *Payment in due course, i.e.* payment made at or after maturity to the holder in good faith: *B.E.A.*, *s.* 59.

(b) *Merger*, *i.e.* when the acceptor is the holder at or after maturity: *B.E.A.*, *s.* 61.

(c) *Waiver*, *i.e.* when the holder at or after maturity renounces his rights against the acceptor: *B.E.A.*, *s.* 62.

(d) *Intentional cancellation* of the bill by the holder: *B.E.A.*, *s.* 63.

(e) *Material alteration* without the consent of all parties liable. In this case, the bill is avoided except as against any party who has himself made or assented to the alteration and subsequent indorsers. But where a bill has been materially altered, but the alteration is not apparent, and the bill is in the hands of a holder in due course, such holder may avail himself of the bill as if it had not been altered, and may enforce payment of it *according to its original tenor: B.E.A.*, *s.* 64.

CHEQUES

37. Definition. A cheque is a bill of exchange drawn on a banker and payable on demand: *B.E.A.*, *s.* 73. A cheque is a particular kind of bill of exchange to which certain special rules apply. These rules are to be found in Part III of the *Bills of Exchange Act*, 1882, and the *Cheques Act*, 1957. The two Acts must be construed as one.

38. Banker and customer. The relationship between banker and customer is a contractual one under which the banker is under a general duty to pay cheques drawn by the customer, provided there is a sufficient credit balance in the customer's account. For this purpose, the banker may be regarded as the customer's agent, with authority to pay the cheques drawn.

The duty and authority of a banker to pay a cheque drawn on him by his customer are *terminated* by:

(a) *Countermand of payment: B.E.A.*, *s.* 75. This may be written or oral; but an oral countermand should, in practice, be confirmed in writing.

(b) *Notice* of the customer's *death*: *B.E.A.*, *s.* 75.

(c) *Notice* of the customer's *lunacy*.

(d) *Notice* of the presentment of a *bankruptcy petition* against the customer.

(e) *The making of a receiving order* against the customer.

(f) *The assignment* of the customer's credit balance to a third party.

(g) The service of a *garnishee order* attaching to the customer's account, *i.e.* an order forbidding the bank to pay the moneys attached to the customer.

(h) Where the account contains *trust funds,* notice that the customer is in *breach of trust.*

(i) Where the credit balance is *not sufficient* to cover the cheque.

(j) Where the cheque is *not signed* with the customer's usual signature.

39. Paying banker and collecting banker. Where a customer draws a cheque on his banker, that banker is known as the *paying banker* with respect to that cheque. Where the holder of a cheque presents it to his banker for credit to his account, the banker's duty is to collect the amount from the drawer's banker (*i.e.* the paying banker): the holder's banker is known as the *collecting banker* with respect to that cheque.

40. Crossed cheques. The practice of crossing cheques is intended to reduce the possibility of the wrong person being paid.

Crossings may be *general* or *special* and, in either case, may or may not include the words "not negotiable": *B.E.A., s.* 76.

(a) *A general crossing* is constituted by two parallel transverse lines on the face of the cheque, with or without "& Co." between them. This crossing is a direction to the *paying* banker to pay only to a collecting banker, *i.e. not* to pay across the counter.

(b) *A special crossing* is constituted by the addition across the face of a cheque of the name of a banker. Transverse lines are not essential to a special crossing, but they are usual. This crossing is a direction to the *paying* banker to pay only to the collecting banker named in the crossing.

(c) *"Not negotiable."* Where a cheque bears these words, it is not a negotiable instrument and the payee or any transferee takes it subject to the equities, *i.e.* the instrument is assignable but not negotiable: *B.E.A., s.* 81.

(d) *"Account payee."* These words written across the face of a cheque constitute a direction to the *collecting* banker to collect for the account of the named payee only. If the cheque has been negotiated, so that the holder is not the payee named, the collecting banker is put on enquiry when the cheque is presented for payment. This crossing originated in banker's custom and is now recognised judicially.

41. Protection of the paying banker. The drawee banker has the benefit of statutory protection which is not accorded to other drawees of bills of exchange. The purpose is to allow bankers to carry out their commercial functions as unhampered as possible. Statutory protection is accorded to a banker who pays a cheque in any of the following circumstances:

(a) *Forged indorsement.* Where a banker pays a cheque: (i) in good faith, and (ii) in the ordinary course of business, he is deemed to have paid the cheque in due course (*i.e.* he is discharged) even though an indorsement has been forged: *B.E.A., s.* 60. (Any other kind of drawee of a bill would remain liable to the true owner in these circumstances.)

(b) *Crossed cheques.* Where a banker on whom a crossed cheque is drawn pays it: (i) in good faith, and (ii) without negligence, and (iii) according to the crossing, he is not liable if payment is made to a person other than the true owner of the cheque: *B.E.A., s.* 80.

(c) *No indorsement/irregular indorsement.* Where a banker: (i) in good faith, and (ii) in the ordinary course of business, pays a cheque drawn on him which is not indorsed or irregularly indorsed, he is deemed to have paid it in due course: *Cheques Act, 1957, s.* 1. *This provision does not give the banker the intended amount of protection, since the Committee of London Clearing Bankers have ruled that banking practice (i.e. the ordinary course of business) requires all cheques to be indorsed except where the account of the payee is credited.*

42. Protection of the collecting banker. Where a banker: (*a*) in good faith, and (*b*) without negligence, receives payment of a cheque for a *customer* with no title or a defective title, he is not liable to the true owner of the cheque: *Cheques Act*, 1957, *s*. 4. (This section applies also to certain instruments analogous to cheques.)

43. Collecting banker's inquiries. In order to benefit from the *Cheques Act*, 1957, *s*. 4, the collecting banker must not have been negligent. The banker is not expected to be abnormally and perpetually suspicious, but *he is expected to be reasonably prudent in circumstances where he is to put on inquiry*. In particular, he may be negligent if he does not make inquiries when collecting payment in the following circumstances:

(a) Where a customer presents a cheque for the credit of his private account, but drawn in favour of his employer.

(b) Where a customer presents a cheque drawn in favour of him *in his official capacity* for the credit of his private account.

(c) Where a customer presents a cheque for the credit of his own account, but drawn in favour of his principal or where the cheque is drawn by the customer on behalf of his principal, but in favour of the customer (the agent) personally.

(d) Where a customer presents a cheque crossed "Account payee" and he is not the payee named.

PROMISSORY NOTES

44. Definition. A promissory note is an unconditional promise in writing made by one person to another signed by the maker, engaging to pay, on demand or at a fixed or determinable future time, a sum certain in money, to, or to the order of, a specified person or to bearer: *B.E.A.*, *s*. 83.

NOTE: The fundamental difference between a bill of exchange and a promissory note is that the bill is an *order* to pay, and a note is a *promise* to pay.

45. I.O.U.s. An I.O.U. is merely a written admission of indebtedness: it is not a promissory note and is not negotiable.

46. Inland and foreign notes. A note which is, or on the face of it purports to be, both made and payable within the British

C.I.L—F

Islands is an *inland note*. Any other note is a *foreign note*: *B.E.A.*, *s.* 83.

When a foreign note is dishonoured, there is no need for it to be protested as in the case of foreign bills: *B.E.A.*, *s.* 89.

47. Application of B.E.A. to notes. In applying the provisions of the *Bills of Exchange Act*, 1882, to promissory notes, the *maker* corresponds with the acceptor of the bill, and the *first indorser of a note* corresponds with the *drawer of an accepted bill payable to drawer's order*. But the provisions relating to acceptance of a bill do not apply to notes: *B.E.A.*, *s.* 89. Where, in a bill, the drawer and drawee are the same person, or where the drawee is a fictitious person or a person without contractual capacity, the holder may treat the instrument, at his option, either as a bill or a note: *B.E.A.*, *s.* 5.

In particular, a note, like a bill, is incomplete and revocable until it has been delivered to the payee or bearer: *B.E.A.*, *ss.* 5 and 84.

PROGRESS TEST 11

1. Compare negotiability with assignability. **(1; VI, 5–11)**
2. Analyse the statutory definition of a bill of exchange. What is the difference between an inland bill and a foreign bill? **(3, 4)**
3. What are the rules as to time of payment of a bill? **(7)**
4. Distinguish between general and qualified acceptance. What is the effect of acceptance? **(8–11)**
5. When must a bill be presented for acceptance? What are the rules as to presentment for acceptance? **(12–14)**
6. Explain fully how a bill may be negotiated. **(16)**
7. What are the rules as to presentment for payment of a bill? **(19, 20)**
8. When must notice of dishonour be given? What do you understand by (a) noting, and (b) protesting a bill? **(21–24)**
9. What constitutes consideration for a bill of exchange? What presumptions are made in connection with consideration? **(25, 28)**
10. Define "holder in due course." What are the rights and duties of a holder of a bill? **(27, 29, 30)**
11. What are the liabilities of (a) the drawer, (b) an indorser, of a bill of exchange? In what way do the liabilities of a transferor by delivery differ from those of an indorser? **(31–34)**
12. Explain the effect of a forged signature to a bill. **(35)**
13. In what ways may a bill be discharged? **(36)**

14. Define a cheque. In what ways may a cheque be crossed? (Explain the legal effect of the different kinds of crossing.) (37, 40)

15. What is the usual relationship between banker and customer? When is the banker's duty and authority to pay a cheque drawn on him terminated? (38)

16. What is the difference between a paying banker and a collecting banker? Outline the statutory provisions designed for the protection of bankers. (39, 41–43)

17. Define a promissory note and compare it with a bill of exchange. (44–47)

CHAPTER XII

SALE OF GOODS

THE CONTRACT OF SALE

1. Definition. A contract of sale of goods is a contract whereby the seller transfers or agrees to transfer the property in goods to the buyer for a money consideration, called the price: *Sale of Goods Act*, 1893, *s*. 1.

2. Goods. "Goods" includes all *chattels personal* other than things in action and money. The term includes emblements (annual agricultural crops), industrial growing crops, and things attached to or forming part of the land which are agreed to be severed before sale or under the contract of sale.

"*Future goods*" are goods to be manufactured or acquired by the seller after the making of the contract of sale.

"*Specific goods*" are goods identified and agreed on at the time the contract is made.

3. Sale and agreement to sell. Where under a contract of sale the property in the goods is transferred from the seller to the buyer, the contract is called a sale; but where the transfer of the property in the goods is to take place *at a future time or subject to some condition* thereafter to be fulfilled, the contract is called an agreement to sell.

4. Conditional sale and credit-sale. Certain conditional sale agreements and credit-sale agreements are affected by the provisions of the *Hire-Purchase Acts*, 1965.

Conditional sale agreements affected by the Acts are those under which the purchase price or part of it is payable by instalments and the total purchase price does not exceed two thousand pounds; and the property in the goods is to remain in the seller (notwithstanding that the buyer is to be in possession of the goods) until such conditions as to the payment of instalments or otherwise as may be specified in the agreement are fulfilled; and the purchaser is not a body corporate.

Credit-sale agreements affected by the Acts are those where the purchase price is payable by five or more instalments; and the total purchase price exceeds thirty pounds but does not exceed two thousand pounds; and the purchaser is not a body corporate; and the agreement is not a conditional sale agreement as defined above.

5. Capacity to buy and sell. Capacity to buy and sell is regulated by the general law concerning capacity to contract and to transfer and acquire property. But where necessaries are sold and delivered to an infant or to a person who by reason of mental incapacity or drunkenness is incompetent to contract, he must pay a reasonable price for the goods. Necessaries are goods suitable to the condition in life of such infant or other person and to his actual requirements at the time of sale and delivery.

6. Goods which perish. Where goods which are the subject of a sale perish, the following rules apply:

(a) Where there is a contract for the sale of specific goods and the goods, without the knowledge of the seller, have perished at the time when the contract is made, the contract is void.

(b) Where there is an agreement to sell specific goods, and subsequently the goods, without any fault on the part of the seller or buyer, perish before the risk passes to the buyer, the agreement is thereby avoided.

7. Contracts for work and materials. Where the substance of the contract is an undertaking to use skill in producing a particular article, the contract may be one for work and materials and not a contract for the sale of goods. The *Sale of Goods Act* does not apply to contracts for work and materials.

(a) A contract to paint a portrait has been held to be a contract for the exercise of skill and not a contract of sale of goods: *Robinson* v. *Graves* (1935).

(b) A contract to make and supply a set of false teeth has been held to be a contract of sale of goods: *Lee* v. *Griffin* (1861). Similarly, a contract to make and supply ship's propellers has been held to be a contract of sale of goods, in spite of the skill involved: *Cammell Laird & Co. Ltd.* v. *Manganese Bronze Co. Ltd.* (1934).

DUTIES OF SELLER AND BUYER

8. The duty to deliver the goods. It is the duty of the seller to deliver the goods in accordance with the terms of the contract of sale. Whether it is for the buyer to take possession of the goods or for the seller to send them to the buyer is a question depending in each case on the contract between the parties. Apart from any such contract, express or implied, *the place of delivery* is the seller's place of business, if he has one, and if not, his residence.

NOTE
  (i) *The time of delivery* is the time, if any, fixed in the contract of sale. But where, under the contract of sale, the seller is bound to send the goods to the buyer, but no time for sending them is fixed, the seller is bound to send them within a *reasonable* time.
 (ii) Unless otherwise agreed, delivery of the goods and payment of the price are *concurrent conditions*, that is to say, the seller must be ready and willing to give possession of the goods to the buyer in exchange for the price.

9. The duty to pass good title. Under a contract of sale, the seller transfers, or agrees to transfer, the property in goods to the buyer.

The seller's right to sell: unless the circumstances show a different intention, there is:

  (a) *An implied condition* on the part of the seller that in the case of a sale he has a *right to sell* the goods, and that in the case of an agreement to sell he will have a right to sell the goods at the time when the property is to pass: *S.G.A., s.* 12(1).
  (b) *An implied warranty* that the buyer shall have and enjoy *quiet possession* of the goods: *s.* 12(2).
  (c) *An implied warranty* that the goods shall be *free from any charge or encumbrance* in favour of any third party, not declared or known to the buyer before or at the time when the contract is made: *s.* 12(3).

Rowland v. *Divall* (1923): R bought a motor car from D for £334. Two months after the sale, R, who was a motor dealer, sold the car to X for £400. Some two months later, the police took the car from X, as it had been stolen before it came into D's possession. R refunded the £400 to X, and then brought this action to recover the £334 from D. HELD: D was in breach of the condition implied in *s.* 12(1). There was a total failure of consideration, and R was entitled to recover all the money he had paid. It was immaterial (i) that R had possession of the car for two months, and (ii) that *restitutio* was not possible.

10. The duty to deliver goods of the right kind. It is the duty of the seller to deliver to the buyer goods which accord with the terms of the contract. Where there are no express or implied terms describing the goods, *caveat emptor* ("let the buyer beware") applies.

Unless otherwise agreed, the following implied conditions will apply to contracts of sale of goods:

(a) *Correspondence with description.* Where there is a contract for the sale of goods by description, there is an implied condition that the goods shall correspond with the description: *S.G.A., s.* 13.

Varley v. *Whipp* (1900): V contracted to sell to W a second-hand reaping machine. W had not seen the machine, and V described it as being new the previous year, and that it had been used to cut about 50 or 60 acres only. When the machine was delivered, W discovered that it was a very old machine, so he returned it to V. V brought this action against W for the price of the machine. HELD: there was a contract of sale by description and there was a breach of the implied condition as to correspondence with description in *s.* 13.

(b) *Fitness for a particular purpose.* There is no implied term as to the fitness for any particular purpose except: (i) where there is a statutory provision as to fitness for purpose, or (ii) where the buyer, expressly or by implication, *makes known to the seller the particular purpose for which the goods are required*, so as to show that the buyer relies on the seller's skill or judgment, and the goods are of a description which it is in the course of the seller's business to supply, there is an implied condition that the goods shall be reasonably fit for such purpose: *S.G.A., s.* 14(1). It is provided, however, that in the case of a contract for the sale of a specified article under its patent or other trade name, there is no implied condition as to its fitness for any particular purpose: s. 14(3).

Where goods have a self-evident purpose there is no need for the buyer to make known to the seller expressly the purpose for which the goods are required: the seller will be deemed to know by implication.

Frost v. *Aylesbury Dairy Co. Ltd.* (1905): the defendant dairy company supplied the plaintiff with milk for the consumption of his family. The book used to record the amount supplied to the plaintiff contained a notice in which the dairy company stated the precautions taken to ensure that the milk supplied was pure. The plaintiff's wife died as a result of being infected with typhoid by milk supplied by the defendants. The plaintiff claimed damages under s. 14(1). HELD: the defendants knew, by implication, the purpose for which the plaintiff bought the milk, *i.e.* for domestic consumption. The plaintiff had relied on the skill of the defendants. As the milk was not reasonably fit for domestic consumption, the defendants were in breach of the implied condition in s. 14(1).

Kendall v. *Lillico & Sons, Ltd.* (1968), H.L.: G bought ground nuts from K. G's purpose was to re-sell in smaller quantities for compounding as food for cattle and poultry—this purpose being known to K. The nuts were in fact toxic and unfit for poultry. G sold some of the nuts to S, knowing that S required them for compounding into food for pigs and poultry. S compounded the nuts into food which was then bought by H, who fed it to his pheasants, which consequently died. S (who admitted liability to H) sued G, who sued K. The claim was for breach of the implied condition of fitness for purpose under s. 14(1) and of merchantable quality under s. 14(2). HELD: (i) *As between G and S.* The compounding into foodstuffs was a "particular purpose" within s. 14(1) and S had relied on G's skill or judgment. G was liable to S. (ii) *As between K and G.* The purpose for which G required the goods was sufficiently "particular" to be within s. 14(1) and K was liable for breach of the implied condition of fitness for purpose.

Ashington Piggeries v. *Christopher Hill* (1971), H.L.: the defendants were two mink companies concerned with the breeding of mink and with the supply of equipment and foodstuffs to other mink breeders. The plaintiffs, who manufactured compounds for animal feeding, entered an agreement with the defendants for the manufacture of a mink food to be called King Size. The formula was supplied by the defendants, and the plaintiffs had made it clear that they knew nothing about the nutritional requirements of mink. The plaintiffs did, however, suggest, as a variation in the formula, the substitution of herringmeal for fishmeal. For about a year King Size was used by about 100 mink farms without complaint. But in March, 1961, the plaintiffs bought a large consignment of herringmeal which had been contaminated by a chemical known as D.M.N.A., toxic to mink, but harmless to other animals. The inclusion of contaminated herringmeal in the manufacture of King Size resulted in serious losses on some mink farms. The plaintiffs claimed payment for King Size containing the contaminated meal and the defendants counterclaimed for damages for breach of contract. HELD: (i) there was a breach of the condition implied by *s.* 14(1) of the *Sale of Goods Act*, 1893, that the goods were reasonably fit for their purpose, the buyers having relied on the skill and judgment of the sellers, even though that reliance was only partial; (ii) the sellers were also in breach of the condition implied by *s.* 14(2) that the goods were of merchantable quality.

(c) *Quality of the goods.* There is no implied term as to the quality of the goods supplied under a contract of sale except (i) where there is a statutory provision as to quality, and (ii) where goods are bought by description from a seller who deals in goods of that description, there is an implied condition that the goods shall be of merchantable quality; provided that if the buyer has examined the goods, there shall be no implied condition as regards defects which such examination ought to have revealed: *s.* 14(2).

An article is not merchantable "if it has defects unfitting it for its only proper use but not apparent on ordinary examination": *Grant* v. *Australian Knitting Mills* (1936).

Wilson v. *Rickett, Cockerell & Co.* (1954): W bought from the defendant coal merchants "a ton of 'Coalite'." When part of the consignment was being burned in the grate, there was an explosion which caused damage to W's goods in the room. The explosive substance was not "Coalite", but some foreign matter which had got mixed with the "Coalite." W claimed damages under *s.* 14. HELD: (i) *s.* 14(1) did not apply because the "Coalite" was bought under its trade name; (ii) but there was a breach of the implied condition as to merchantability under *s.* 14(2).

Brown & Son, Ltd. v. *Craiks, Ltd.* (1970), H.L.: B gave two orders to C for the manufacture of large quantities of rayon cloth to a detailed specification. The buyer intended to use the cloth for making dresses and the seller *bona fide* thought it was for industrial use. Both orders were accepted and the agreed price was 36·25d. per yard. B, on discovering subsequently that the cloth was not suitable for dressmaking, wrote to C cancelling the contract. Both parties were left with a considerable amount of cloth on their hands which was eventually sold, C obtaining 30d. per yard and B only 15d. per yard. B brought this action against C, claiming that the goods were not of merchantable quality, basing his case on s. 14(2). B claimed: (i) that there was only one normal use for such cloth at the time of delivery, namely dressmaking, and that there was not any normal use of the cloth of the description ordered for industrial purposes, and (ii) that the discrepancy between the contract price (36·25d. per yard) and the price at which C subsequently sold the remaining cloth (30d. per yard) showed that the goods were not of merchantable quality. HELD: (i) the cloth was reasonably capable of being used, was saleable for a number of industrial purposes and was merchantable for these purposes, and (ii) there was not a sufficient abatement in price as to lead to the conclusion that the cloth was not of merchantable quality.

(d) *Sale by sample.* In the case of a contract for sale by sample, there is (i) an implied condition that the bulk shall correspond with the sample in quality, and (ii) an implied condition that the buyer shall have a reasonable opportunity of comparing the bulk with the sample, and (iii) an implied condition that the goods shall be free from any defect, rendering them unmerchantable, which would not be apparent on reasonable examination of the sample: *S.G.A.*, s. 15. Also, where there is a contract for the sale of goods by sample, as well as by description, it is not sufficient that the bulk of the goods do not also correspond with the description: there is an implied condition that the goods shall correspond with the description: s. 13.

NOTE: *Exclusion of implied conditions and warranties.* It is possible for the parties to a contract of sale of goods to exclude all implied conditions and warranties arising under the Act: s. 55.

11. The duty to deliver the right quantity. It is the duty of the seller to deliver the quantity of goods he agreed to sell to the buyer. A stipulated quantity is part of the description of the goods. There is, therefore, an implied condition that the quantity delivered corresponds with the quantity contracted for.

(a) *Delivery of too little.* Where the seller delivers to the buyer a quantity of goods less than he contracted to sell, the buyer may reject them, but if the buyer accepts the goods as delivered, he must pay for them at the contract rate: *S.G.A.*, *s.* 30(1).

(b) *Delivery of too much.* Where the seller delivers to the buyer a quantity of goods larger than he contracted to sell, the buyer may accept the goods included in the contract and reject the rest, or he may reject the whole. If the buyer accepts the whole of the goods so delivered, he must pay for them at the contract rate: *s.* 30(2).

(c) *Delivery of mixed goods.* Where the seller delivers to the buyer the goods he contracted to sell mixed with goods of a different description, not included in the contract, the buyer may accept the goods which are in accordance with the contract, and reject the rest, or he may reject the whole: *s.* 30(3).

12. Buyer's duties.

(a) *Duty to accept the goods.* It is the duty of the buyer to accept the goods in accordance with the terms of the contract of sale. The buyer is deemed to have accepted the goods when he intimates to the seller that he has accepted them, or when after the lapse of a reasonable time, he retains the goods without intimating to the seller that he has rejected them.

NOTE: Where goods are delivered to the buyer, which he has not previously examined, he is not deemed to have accepted them unless and until he has had a reasonable opportunity of examining them for the purpose of ascertaining whether they are in conformity with the contract.

(b) *Duty to pay the price.* It is the duty of the buyer to pay for the goods according to the terms of the contract. The price in a contract for sale may be fixed by the contract, or may be left to be fixed in a manner thereby agreed, or may be determined by the course of dealing between the parties. Where the price cannot be determined in this way, the buyer must pay a reasonable price.

TRANSFER OF OWNERSHIP

13. Transfer of property. Where there is a contract for the sale of unascertained goods, no property in the goods is transferred to the buyer unless and until the goods are ascertained: *s.* 16. *Unascertained goods* are goods of a specified class, but which have not yet become identified as the goods which are to pass under the contract: *re Wait* (1926).

Otherwise, the general rule is that property passes when the parties *intend that it shall pass*: for the purpose of ascertaining the intention of the parties, regard shall be had to the terms of the contract, the conduct of the parties, and the circumstances of the case: *S.G.A., s.* 17.

In cases where it is not possible to acertain the intention of the parties in this way, the rules set out in *s.* 18 should be applied. These are:

Rule 1. Where there is an unconditional contract for the sale of specific goods, in a deliverable state, the property in the goods passes to the buyer when the contract is made, and it is immaterial whether the time of payment or the time of delivery, or both, be postponed.

Rule 2. Where there is a contract for the sale of specific goods and the seller is bound to do something to the goods, for the purpose of putting them into a deliverable state, the property does not pass until such thing be done, and the buyer has notice thereof.

Rule 3. Where there is a contract for the sale of specific goods in a deliverable state, but the seller is bound to weigh, measure, test, or do some other act or thing with reference to the goods for the purpose of ascertaining the price, the property does not pass until such act or thing be done, and the buyer has notice thereof.

Rule 4. When goods are delivered to the buyer on approval or "on sale or return" or other similar terms the property therein passes to the buyer:

(a) When he signifies his approval or acceptance to the seller or does any other act adopting the transaction.

(b) If he does not signify his approval or acceptance to the seller but retains the goods without giving notice of rejection, then, if a time has been fixed for the return of the goods, on the expiration of such time, and, if no time has been fixed, on the expiration of a reasonable time. What is a reasonable time is a question of fact.

Rule 5. (1) Where there is a contract for the sale of unascertained or future goods by description, and goods of that description and in a deliverable state are unconditionally appropriated to the contract, either by the seller with the assent of the buyer, or by the buyer with the assent of the seller, the property in the goods thereupon passes to the buyer. Such assent may be expressed or implied, and may be given either before or after the appropriation is made.

(2) Where, in pursuance of the contract, the seller delivers the goods to the buyer or to a carrier or other bailee (whether named by the buyer or not) for the purpose of transmission to the buyer, and does not reserve the right of disposal, he is deemed to have unconditionally appropriated the goods to the contract.

NOTE: *The passing of risk.* Unless otherwise agreed, the goods remain at the seller's risk until the property therein is transferred to the buyer, but when the property therein is transferred to the buyer, the goods are at the buyer's risk.

14. Transfer of title. Title to goods is the *right* of ownership with respect to them. As to the passing of title from buyer to seller, the general rule is that where goods are sold by a person who is not the owner thereof, the buyer acquires no better title to the goods than the seller had: *s.* 21. This principle is often expressed by use of the maxim *nemo dat quod non habet.*

EXCEPTIONS

(a) *Sale by an agent.* Where goods are sold by a person who is not the owner thereof, and who sells them under the authority or with the consent of the owner, the buyer acquires good title to the goods: *s.* 21.

(b) *Sale by a mercantile agent without authority.* Where a mercantile agent is, with the consent of the owner, in possession of goods or of the documents of title to goods, any sale, or other disposition of the goods, made by him when acting in the ordinary course of business of a mercantile agent, shall be as valid as if he were expressly authorised by the owner to make the same: *Factors Act,* 1889, *s.* 2.

(c) *Sale in market overt.* Where goods are sold in market overt, according to the usage of the market, the buyer acquires good title to the goods, provided he buys them in good faith and without notice of any defect or want of title on the part of the seller: *s.* 22(1). Market overt obtains in all shops in the City of London, and in all markets where the usage is established. A sale in a shop in the City of London is deemed to be a sale in market overt when (i) the sale takes place in business hours on a business day, and (ii) the entire transaction takes place in the part of the shop which is open to the public, and (iii) the goods are of a class usually sold in that shop, and (iv) the shopkeeper is the seller, *i.e.* he must not be the buyer.

(d) *Sale under a voidable title.* When the seller of goods has a voidable title thereto, but his title has not been avoided at the time of the sale, the buyer acquires a good title to the goods, provided he buys them in good faith and without notice of the seller's defect of title: *s.* 23. The same rule applies where there is any other kind of disposition of goods under a voidable title, *e.g.* where goods are pawned: *see* IV, **10.**

(e) *Seller in possession after the sale.* Where a person having sold goods continues or is in possession of the goods, or of the documents of title to the goods, the delivery or transfer by that person, or by a mercantile agent acting for him, of the goods and/or documents of title under any sale, pledge or other disposition thereof, to any person receiving the same in good faith and without notice of the previous sale, shall have the same effect as if the person making the delivery or transfer were expressly authorised by the owner of the goods to make the same: *s.* 25(1). According to this rule, if X sells goods to Y, so that Y has the property in the goods but the actual possession is retained by X, and X sells and delivers the same goods to Z, who takes them in good faith, Z gets good title. Y will be left with an action for damages against X, for he cannot recover the goods from Z.

(f) *Buyer in possession after the sale.* Where a person having bought or agreed to buy goods obtains, with the consent of the seller, possession of the goods or the documents of title to the goods, the delivery or transfer by that person, or by a mercantile agent acting for him, of the goods or documents of title, under any sale, pledge, or other disposition thereof, to any person receiving the same in good faith and without notice of any lien or other right of the original seller in respect of the goods, shall have the same effect as if the person making the delivery or transfer were a mercantile agent in possession of the goods or documents of title with the consent of the owner: *s.* 25(2).

(g) *Sale under a court order or special power.* Where a contract of sale of goods is made under any special common law or statutory power of sale, or under the order of a court, the buyer acquires a good title to the goods: *s.* 21(2)(b). An example of a common law power is that of a pledgee (other than a pawnbroker) to sell goods pledged if the loan is not repaid according to the agreement. An example of a statutory power is that of a trustee in bankruptcy to sell the goods of the debtor under the *Bankruptcy Act,* 1914.

RIGHTS OF UNPAID SELLER AGAINST THE GOODS

15. Unpaid seller's rights. Notwithstanding that the property in the goods may have passed to the buyer, the unpaid seller of goods, as such, has by implication of law the following rights:

- (a) *A lien* on goods for the price while he is in possession of them.
- (b) In case of the insolvency of the buyer, a right of *stopping the goods in transit* after he has parted with possession of them.
- (c) *A right of re-sale: s.* 39.

16. Unpaid seller's lien. The unpaid seller of goods who is in possession of them is entitled to retain possession of them until payment or tender of the price in the following cases, namely:

- (a) Where the goods have been sold without any stipulation as to credit.
- (b) Where the goods have been sold on credit, but the term of credit has expired.
- (c) Where the buyer becomes insolvent: *s.* 41.

NOTE: *The seller loses his lien* (i) when he delivers the goods to a carrier or other bailee for the purpose of transmission to the buyer without reserving the right of disposal of the goods; or (ii) when the buyer or his agent lawfully obtains possession of the goods; or (iii) by waiver: *s.* 43(1). Also, the seller ceases to have a right of lien when the price is paid or tendered.

17. Stoppage in transit. When the buyer of goods becomes insolvent, the unpaid seller who has parted with the possession of the goods has the right of stopping them in transit, that is to say, he may resume possession of the goods so long as they are in the course of transit, and may retain them until payment or tender of the price: *s.* 44.

NOTE
- (i) *Documents of title.* The right of stoppage will be defeated by the prior right of a person to whom the buyer transferred documents of title relating to the goods, provided they were received in good faith and for value: *ss.* 47 and 25(2).

(ii) *Duration of transit.* Goods are deemed to be in course of transit from the time when they are delivered to a carrier or other bailee for the purpose of transmission to the buyer, until the buyer or his agent takes delivery of them from such carrier or other bailee: *s.* 45. There is no right of stoppage after transit is at an end.

(iii) *How stoppage is effected.* The unpaid seller may exercise his right of stoppage in transit either: (a) by taking actual possession of the goods, or (b) by giving notice of his claim to the carrier or other bailee in whose possession the goods are: *s.* 46(1).

18. Right of re-sale. An unpaid seller's right to re-sale may arise either from an express contractual reservation, or from the provisions of the *Sale of Goods Act*, 1893, or from the common law generally.

(a) *Express reservation.* Where the seller expressly reserves a right of re-sale in case the buyer should make default, the seller may re-sell the goods. Where the seller exercises this right, the original contract is rescinded but he is not deprived of any claim for damages he may have against the original buyer: *s.* 48(4).

(b) *Statutory right of re-sale.* The Act provides that an unpaid seller may re-sell the goods:

(i) where the goods are of a perishable nature; or
(ii) where the unpaid seller gives notice to the buyer of his intention to re-sell, and the buyer does not, within a reasonable time, pay or tender the price: *s.* 48(3).

Where the seller exercises his statutory right of re-sale, the original contract is not thereby rescinded: *Gallagher* v. *Shilcock* (1949).

(c) *Re-sale at common law.* Where the buyer has repudiated the contract of sale, the unpaid seller may have a right of re-sale. This right arises because a repudiation by one party has the effect of allowing the other party to elect to treat himself as discharged from further liability.

SELLER'S PERSONAL REMEDIES

19. Seller's remedies. Where the buyer is in breach of contract, the seller may bring either:

(a) an action for the price of the goods, or

(b) an action for damages for non-acceptance, according to the nature of the breach.

20. Action for the price. The seller's right to action arises in either of the following circumstances:

(a) Where, under a contract of sale, the property in the goods has passed to the buyer, and the buyer *wrongfully* neglects or refuses to pay for the goods according to the terms of the contract.
(b) Where, under a contract of sale, the price is payable on a certain day irrespective of delivery, and the buyer *wrongfully* neglects or refuses to pay such price: *s.* 49.

21. Ascertainment of price. The price of goods may be:

(a) fixed by the contract; or
(b) left to be fixed in a manner agreed between the parties; or
(c) determined by the course of dealing between the parties; or
(d) a reasonable price, which is payable:

    (i) when the price is not fixed by the contract, or in a manner agreed between the parties; or
    (ii) where there is an agreement to sell at a valuation, and no valuation is made, and the goods have been delivered to, and appropriated by, the buyer: *ss.* 8 and 9.

22. Damages for non-acceptance. Where the buyer *wrongfully* neglects or refuses to accept and pay for the goods, the seller may maintain an action against him for damages for non-acceptance: *s.* 50(1). The measure of damages for non-acceptance is:

(a) the estimated loss directly and naturally resulting, in the ordinary course of events, from the buyer's breach of contract: *s.* 50(2); and
(b) any further loss due to special circumstances outside the ordinary course of events, but which the buyer had knowledge of, actual or imputed: *s.* 54 (see also *Victoria Laundry* v. *Newman* (1949)).

NOTE: The seller should take reasonable steps to mitigate the loss. Usually he will sell the goods to a third person.

23. The prima facie rule. Where there is an available market for the goods in question, the measure of damages is, *prima facie*, to be ascertained by the difference between the contract price, and the market or current price at the time or times when the goods ought to have been accepted or, if no time was fixed for acceptance, then at the time of refusal to accept: *s.* 50(3). This means that the seller should sell the goods for what he can get and then claim for damages to recover the difference between the market price and the contract price. The court may disregard this rule wherever it would not produce a just result: *Thompson, Ltd.* v. *Robinson, Ltd.* (1955).

Campbell Mostyn v. *Barnett* (1954): the buyer agreed to buy 500 tons of tinned ham, and when the seller attempted to deliver 350 tons, the buyer refused to accept. The seller then resold the 350 tons at a price higher than the original contract price. But at the date of the original buyer's refusal to accept delivery, the market price was below the contract price. The seller brought the action against the buyer for damages for non-acceptance. HELD: the measure of damages should be the difference between the contract price and the market price at the time of the refusal to accept. *The subsequent rising of the market price was immaterial.*

Charter v. *Sullivan* (1957): the buyer agreed to buy a Hillman "Minx" motor car, and later wrote to the seller telling him that he no longer intended to complete the sale. A few days later, the seller sold the car to another buyer, for at the time he could sell all Hillman "Minx" cars he could get. HELD: the seller was entitled to nominal damages only.

BUYER'S PERSONAL REMEDIES

24. Buyer's remedies. Where the seller is in breach of contract, one or more of a number of remedies may be available to the buyer. The remedies are:

(a) An action for damages for non-delivery.
(b) To reject the goods and treat the contract as repudiated.
(c) An action for damages for breach of warranty.
(d) To set up breach of warranty as a defence to an action for the price.
(e) An action for money paid on a consideration which has wholly failed.

(f) An action for specific performance.

The remedies available in any case will depend upon the circumstances.

25. Damages for non-delivery. Where the seller *wrongfully* neglects or refuses to deliver the goods to the buyer, the buyer may maintain an action against the seller for damages for non-delivery: *s.* 51(1). The measure of damages for non-delivery is:

(a) the estimated loss directly and naturally resulting, in the ordinary course of events, from the seller's breach of contract: *s.* 51(2); and

(b) Any further loss due to special circumstances outside the ordinary course of events, of which the seller had knowledge, actual or imputed: *s.* 54 and *Victoria Laundry* v. *Newman* (1949).

NOTE: *Mitigation of loss.* The buyer should take reasonable steps to mitigate the loss. Generally, this means that he should buy similar goods from a third person.

26. The prima facie rule. Where there is an available market for the goods in question, the measure of damages is, *prima facie*, to be ascertained by the difference between the contract price and the market or current price of the goods to the time or times when they ought to have been delivered, or, if no time was fixed, then at the time of refusal to deliver: *s.* 51(3). This means that the buyer should buy similar goods at the current price obtaining, and claim damages to recover the difference between the current price and the contract price. This is a *prima facie* rule, and the court may disregard it where it so wishes.

27. Right to treat the contract as repudiated. Where the seller is in breach of a *condition*, express or implied, the buyer may reject the goods and treat the contract as repudiated: *s.* 11.

NOTE

(i) The Act does not define "condition." But a condition is generally regarded as being a term of contract which is identified with the main purpose of the contract.

"Warranty" is defined in *s.* 62(1) as being *collateral* to the main purpose of a contract.

(ii) The buyer loses the right of rejection where the contract is not severable and he has accepted the goods, or part of them. By *s.* 35, as amended by the *Misrepresentation Act*, 1967, the buyer is deemed to have accepted the goods when he intimates to the seller that he has accepted them, or, except where *s.* 34 applies (buyer's right of examining the goods), when the goods have been delivered to him, and he does any act in relation to them which is inconsistent with the ownership of the seller, or when, after the lapse of a reasonable time, he retains the goods without intimating to the seller that he has rejected them.

(iii) It was originally provided by *s.* 11(1)(c) that the buyer's right of rejection was lost where the property in specific goods had passed to him. This provision is now omitted by virtue of the amendment contained in *s.* 4(1) of the *Misrepresentation Act*, 1967. The result is that the buyer of specific goods is not compelled to treat a breach of condition as a breach of warranty merely because property in those goods has passed to him.

28. Damages for breach of warranty. Where there is a breach of *warranty* by the seller, or where the buyer elects, or is compelled, to treat any breach of condition on the part of the seller as a breach of warranty, the buyer may maintain an action for damages for the breach of warranty: *s.* 53.

NOTE

(i) *Definition.* Warranty means an agreement with reference to goods which are the subject of a contract of sale, but *collateral to the main purpose of such contract.* But whether a term in a contract of sale is a condition or a warranty depends in each case on the construction of the contract.

(ii) *Breach of warranty ex post facto.* The buyer may elect to treat the seller's breach of condition as a breach of warranty, *i.e.* he may waive his right to treat the contract as repudiated, accept delivery of the goods, and bring an action for damages for breach of warranty *ex post facto.* Also, where a contract of sale is not severable, and the buyer has accepted the goods, or part of them, or where the contract is for specific goods, the property in which has passed to the buyer, the breach of any condition by the seller can only be treated as a breach of warranty, and not as a ground for rejecting the goods and treating the contract as repudiated, unless there is a term of the contract to that effect.

(iii) *Measure of damages.* The measure of damages for breach of warranty is:

    (a) the estimated loss directly and naturally resulting in the ordinary course of events, from the breach of warranty: *s.* 53(2); and

    (b) any further loss due to special circumstances outside the ordinary course of events, of which the seller had knowledge, actual or imputed: *s.* 54 and *Victoria Laundry* v. *Newman* (1949).

AUCTION SALES

29. The fall of the hammer. A sale by auction is complete when the auctioneer announces its completion by the fall of the hammer, or in other customary manner. Until such announcement is made, any bidder may retract his bid: *s.* 58(2).

30. Seller's right to bid. A right to bid may be expressly reserved by or on behalf of the seller. Where a right to bid is expressly reserved, but not otherwise, the seller, or any *one* person on his behalf, may bid at the auction: *s.* 58.

31. Reserve price. A sale by auction may be notified to be subject to a reserve price: *s.* 58(4). Where there is such notification, every bid is a "conditional offer subject to its being up to the reserve price," and where an auctioneer inadvertently knocks down to a bidder who has bid less than the reserve price, there is no contract of sale: *McManus* v. *Fortescue* (1907).

32. Illegal bidding agreements. A knockout, *i.e.* an agreement by which an intending bidder undertakes to abstain from bidding, is not illegal at common law, but the position is altered by the *Auctions (Bidding Agreements) Act,* 1927. This Act provides that if any dealer agrees to give, or gives, or offers any gift or consideration to any other person as an inducement or reward for abstaining from bidding at a sale by auction, or if any person agrees to accept any such gift or consideration, he is guilty of a criminal offence.

INTERNATIONAL TRADING CONTRACTS

33. Commercial practice. The expressions c.i.f. (cost, in-surance, freight), f.o.b. (free on board) and f.a.s. (free alongside ship), are generally used in commerce, and are useful in that they give a general indication of the terms of the contracts they describe. The expressions do not, however, indicate with pre-cision the details of the contract. In order to avoid confusion, many traders made use of "incoterms 1953" which are standardised interpretations of these expressions.

34. C.i.f. contracts. The duties of the parties under a c.i.f. contract are usually as follows:

(a) *Seller's duties*

    (i) To obtain any export licence required.
    (ii) To arrange for the carriage of the goods to the port of destination and to pay the freight charges.
    (iii) To arrange the loading of the goods at the port of shipment.
    (iv) To procure a policy of insurance to cover the goods during transit for the benefit of the buyer.
    (v) To furnish the buyer with a bill of lading, the invoice of the goods, and the insurance policy.

(b) *Buyer's duties*

    (i) To pay the contract price on delivery of the documents.
    (ii) To pay all unloading, lighterage and wharfage charges at the port of destination.
    (iii) To pay all customs and import duties.

35. F.o.b. contracts. The duties of the parties under an f.o.b. contract are usually as follows:

(a) *Seller's duties*

    (i) To deliver the goods on board the ship named by the buyer.
    (ii) To notify the buyer immediately the goods have been delivered on board.

(b) *Buyer's duties*

    (i) To arrange for the contract of affreightment.
    (ii) To give the seller sufficient notice of the name of the

ship, its loading berth, and the time for delivery to the ship.

(iii) To pay all charges and to bear all risks from the time the goods have passed the ship's rail.

36. F.a.s. contracts. The duties of the parties under an f.a.s. contract are usually as follows:

(a) *Seller's duties*

(i) To deliver the goods alongside the ship.
(ii) To notify the buyer immediately the goods have been delivered alongside.

(b) *Buyer's duties*

(i) To arrange for the contract of affreightment.
(ii) To give the seller sufficient notice of the name of the ship, its loading berth, and the time for delivery alongside.
(iii) To pay all charges and to bear all risks from the time the goods are delivered alongside.

PROGRESS TEST 12

1. Define a contract of sale of goods. What do you understand by the expression *goods*? What is an *agreement to sell goods*? (**1–3**)

2. What rules are applied where the goods which are the subject of a sale perish? (**6**)

3. Distinguish between a contract for work and materials and a contract of sale of goods. (**7**)

4. Outline the duties of the seller under a contract of sale of goods. Which of these duties arise by virtue of an implied contractual term? May the parties, by their agreement, exclude or modify the implied terms? (**8–11**)

5. Estimate the commercial significance of *ss.* 12–15 of the *Sale of Goods Act*, 1893. (**9–11**)

6. What are the main duties of the buyer under a contract of sale of goods? (**12**)

7. Summarise the law relating to the transfer of ownership of goods under a contract of sale. (**13**)

8. The general rule is that where goods are sold by a person who is not the owner of them, the buyer acquires no better title than the seller had (*nemo dat quod non habet*). State six exceptions to this general rule. (**14**)

9. Explain the rights of an unpaid seller *against the goods*. (15–18)

10. In what circumstances may a seller sue the buyer for the *price of goods*? How is the price ascertained? (20, 21)

11. In what circumstances may a seller sue the buyer for *damages*? What is the measure of damages? (22)

12. List the remedies available to the buyer in the event of the seller's breach. Explain how damages are assessed. Mention the circumstances in which the buyer may treat the contract as repudiated and, accordingly, reject the goods. (24–28)

13. What special rules are applicable to sales of goods by auction? (29–31)

14. Outline the duties of the parties under c.i.f., f.o.b. and f.a.s. contracts. (34–36)

CHAPTER XIII

HIRE-PURCHASE AND CONDITIONAL SALE AGREEMENTS

HIRE-PURCHASE AT COMMON LAW

1. The nature of hire-purchase. A contract of hire-purchase is a bailment of goods coupled with an option to purchase. The option to purchase may or may not be exercised, and there is no contract of sale unless and until the option is exercised. The hirer is not a person who has agreed to buy goods and the *Sale of Goods Act,* 1893, does not apply: thus the hirer cannot pass title to a third party under *s.* 25. Moreover, in case of bankruptcy of the hirer, the owner can recover the goods.

2. The parties. The parties to a contract of hire-purchase are:

(a) *The owner,* who undertakes to let out the goods on hire with an option to purchase when all payments have been made; and

(b) *The hirer,* who undertakes to pay the hire-purchase charges according to the agreement.

The usual commercial procedure is for the dealer to sell the goods to a finance company which then enters the hire-purchase agreement with the customer. The finance company is the owner of the goods and the customer is the hirer. The dealer or shopkeeper is not usually a party to any contract with the hirer at common law, although he may be bound by an express undertaking given to the hirer: *Andrews* v. *Hopkinson* (1957).

3. The dealer as agent. Disputes have occurred as to the extent of the authority of the dealer as agent of the finance company. The position is often complicated by the insertion in the contract of hire-purchase of a clause to the effect that the dealer is *not* an agent of the company.

In *Financings Ltd.* v. *Stimson* (1962), Lord Denning, M.R., said that "if we take, as we should, a realistic view of the position, the dealer is in many respects, and for many purposes, the agent of the finance company. I am aware, of course, that the finance companies often put clauses into their forms in which they say that the dealer is not their agent. But these clauses are often not worth the paper they are written on. Nobody can make an assertion of that kind in an agreement so as to bind the courts if it is contrary to the facts of the case."

The agency of the dealer must be decided on the facts of each case. (But where the contract of hire-purchase is governed by the *Hire-Purchase Acts*, 1938–64, the dealer is deemed to be the agent of the owner: *see* **9** *below*.)

THE HIRE-PURCHASE ACT, 1965

4. The purpose of the Act. The Act of 1965, which consolidates previous enactments, is designed to protect the interests of the hirer under a hire-purchase agreement and the buyer under a credit-sale agreement. The Act applies to:

(a) hire-purchase agreements,
(b) conditional sale agreements, and
(c) credit-sale agreements,

under which the hire-purchase price, or total purchase price, as the case may be, does not exceed two thousand pounds. The Act does not apply to contracts in which the hirer or buyer is a body corporate.

5. The agreements defined. For the purposes of the Act, the agreements covered are defined as follows:

(a) *Hire-purchase agreement* means an agreement for the bailment of goods under which the bailee may buy the goods or under which the property in the goods will or may pass to the bailee.
(b) *Conditional sale agreement* means an agreement for the sale of goods under which:

(i) the purchase price is payable by instalments, and

(ii) the property in the goods is to remain in the seller (notwithstanding that the buyer is to be in possession of the goods) until such conditions as to the payment of instalments or otherwise as may be specified in the agreement are fulfilled.

(c) *Credit-sale agreement* means an agreement for the sale of goods, *not being a conditional sale agreement*, under which the purchase price exceeds thirty pounds and is payable by five or more instalments.

6. Statutory requirements: hire-purchase and conditional sales. The Act provides as follows:

(a) *Statement of cash price.* Before any hire-purchase agreement (or conditional sale agreement) is entered into the owner (or the seller) must state in writing the cash price. It is sufficient if the hirer (or buyer) has seen the cash price on a price ticket or in a catalogue.

(b) *Written agreement.* A hire-purchase agreement (or conditional sales agreement) is unenforceable by the owner (or seller) unless the agreement is signed by the hirer (or buyer) and by or on behalf of all other parties. The agreement must contain:

   (i) A statement of the hire-purchase price (or total purchase price) and the cash price and the amount of each instalment and when payable.

   (ii) A list of the goods.

   (iii) A copy of the statutory notice setting out the hirer's (or buyer's) rights under the contract.

7. Statutory requirements: credit-sales. The Act provides as follows:

(a) *Statement of cash price.* Before making any credit-sale agreement the seller must state in writing to the prospective buyer the cash price of the goods. It is sufficient if the buyer has seen the cash price on a price ticket or in a catalogue.

(b) *Written agreement.* A credit-sale agreement is not enforceable by the seller unless the agreement is signed by the buyer and by or on behalf of the seller.

8. The right of cancellation. Where a person signs a hire-purchase agreement, a conditional sale agreement, or a credit-sale agreement and the document is signed at a place other than appropriate trade premises, a right to serve notice of cancellation arises in favour of the hirer or buyer. Notice of cancellation operates to rescind the agreement, which is then deemed never to have had effect.

NOTE
(i) *Appropriate trade premises* means premises at which either the owner or seller normally carries on a business, or goods of the description to which the agreement relates are normally offered for sale in the course of a business carried on at these premises.

(ii) *Time limit.* The right of cancellation may be exercised at any time between signing the agreement and the end of the period of four days beginning with the day on which the hirer (or buyer) receives the second statutory copy of the agreement.

9. The dealer as agent. The 1965 Act has clarified the position of the dealer as agent: *see* **3** *above.* The Act provides that where a dealer makes any representations to the hirer (or buyer) with respect to goods to which a hire-purchase, conditional sale or credit-sale agreement relates, such representations shall be deemed to have been made by him as agent of the owner or seller. It is provided that *representations* includes any statement or undertaking whether constituting a condition or a warranty or not. The dealer is also deemed to be an agent for the purpose of receiving notice of cancellation.

10. Implied terms: hire-purchase and conditional sales. The Act provides for the following implied terms in hire-purchase and conditional sale agreements for the benefit of the hirer, or buyer, as the case may be.

(a) *Title and quiet possession.* A condition on the part of the owner (or seller) that he will have a right to sell the goods at the time when property is to pass; a warranty that the hirer (or buyer) will have and enjoy quiet possession of the goods; and a warranty that the goods shall be free from any charge or encumbrance in favour of any third party at the time when the property is to pass. The condition and these warranties cannot be excluded

and will be implied notwithstanding any agreement to
the contrary.
(b) *Merchantable quality*. A condition that the goods are of
merchantable quality. (But where the hirer (or buyer)
has examined the goods, or a sample of them, the condition will not be implied in respect of defects which the
examination ought to have revealed. Where the goods
are second-hand and the agreement contains a statement
to that effect which is brought to the attention of the
hirer (or buyer) and its effect made clear to him, the
condition may be excluded. Where defects are specified
in the agreement and before the contract was made, and
those defects were brought to the notice of the hirer (or
buyer) and an exclusionary clause specifying the defects and its effect was made clear to him, the condition
will not be implied in respect to those defects.)
(c) *Fitness for purpose*. Where the hirer (or buyer), whether
expressly or by implication: (i) has made known to the
owner or seller, or to a servant or agent of the owner or
seller, the particular purpose for which the goods are
required, or (ii) in the course of any antecedent negotiations has made that purpose known to any other
person by whom those negotiations were conducted, or
to a servant or agent of such a person, there is implied a
condition that the goods will be reasonably fit for the
purpose. This implied condition may be excluded by
an exclusionary clause, but the owner (or seller) may
not rely on such a clause unless he proves that, before the
agreement was made, the clause was brought to the
attention of the hirer (or buyer) and its effects made
clear to him.
(d) *Correspondence with description*. Where goods are let
(or agreed to be sold) by description, there is implied in
the agreement a condition that the goods will correspond
to the description. Any provision which purports to
exclude or modify this condition is void.
(e) *Sample*. Where goods are let (or agreed to be sold) by
reference to a sample, there is implied in the agreement:
(i) a condition that the bulk will correspond with the
sample in quality; and (ii) a condition that the hirer
(or buyer) will have a reasonable opportunity of comparing the bulk with the sample. If the goods are let or

agreed to be sold under the agreement by reference to a sample, as well as by description, it will not be sufficient if the bulk of the goods corresponds with the sample if the goods do not also correspond with the description.

11. Right to end the agreement. A hirer is, at any time, entitled to determine the agreement by giving notice of termination in writing to any person entitled, or authorised to receive the sum payable. Where a hirer terminates the agreement, he is liable to pay the amount, if any, by which *one-half of the hire-purchase price exceeds the total of the sums paid and the sums due* in respect of the hire-purchase price immediately before the termination, or such less amount as may be specified in the agreement.

The buyer under a *conditional sale agreement* has a similar right to end the agreement.

PROGRESS TEST 13

1. Explain the nature of hire-purchase.   (1–3)

2. Define (a) the conditional sale agreements and (b) the credit-sale agreements to which the *Hire-Purchase Act*, 1965, applies. (4, 5)

3. In what circumstances are contracts rendered unenforceable by one of the parties under the *Hire-Purchase Acts*?   (6, 7)

4. Compare the implied terms under the *Sale of Goods Act*, 1893, with those under the *Hire-Purchase Act*, 1965.   (10; XII, 9–11)

CHAPTER XIV

COMMERCIAL ARBITRATION

REFERENCE TO ARBITRATION

1. Settlement of disputes. Arbitration is the inquiry into, and settlement of, disputes otherwise than in a court of law. The inquiry is conducted and the award made by one or more arbitrators, an umpire or an official or special referee, according to the circumstances. The reference of a dispute to arbitration may be made:

(a) by order of the court;
(b) by the provisions of an Act of Parliament; or
(c) by consent out of court.

2. Order of the court. The Rules of the Supreme Court give the court authority to refer matters arising from any hearing to an *official* or *special* referee. The matter referred may be the entire dispute or a specific issue within it.

(a) *Official referees.* An official referee is an officer of the court to whom matters are referred which require a prolonged investigation into books of account or other documents.
(b) *Special referees.* A special referee is one whom the parties to the dispute have agreed to, and who is remunerated by the parties at a rate determined by the court. The court may refer an issue to a special referee in cases where a special technical or local knowledge is required.

3. Statutory arbitration. An Act of Parliament may provide that specified kinds of disputes must be determined by some particular arbitral tribunal. Where this occurs, the arbitral tribunal has exclusive jurisdiction.

EXAMPLES
(a) *The Electricity Act,* 1947. Under this Act, the Electricity Arbitration Tribunal was set up and authorised to determine

any disputes arising out of the nationalisation of the various electricity supply undertakings. The Act contains a code of procedure which must be followed in all hearings by the tribunal.

(b) *National Insurance.* Tribunals have been set up under the *National Insurance Act,* 1965, and the *National Insurance (Industrial Injuries) Act,* 1965, to determine disputes over claims for benefits under the Acts.

4. Consent out of court. Where two or more parties are in dispute, *e.g.* as to whether there has been a breach of contract, they may agree to refer their dispute to an arbitrator. This is an alternative to litigation. The agreement to refer to arbitration is called an *arbitration agreement,* and it may be oral or in writing. In cases of disputes over a contract, the arbitration agreement may have been incorporated into the original contract, or it may be made after the dispute has arisen.

NOTE

(i) *Written agreements.* Where the arbitration agreement is in writing, the *Arbitration Act,* 1950, applies: *see below.*

(ii) *Oral agreements.* Where the arbitration agreement is oral, the Act applies only if the parties have agreed that it shall apply.

(iii) *Valuation distinguished.* An arbitration agreement by consent out of court is not the same as a *valuation.* Where parties agree to appoint a valuer and to accept his valuation, the purpose is to *avoid* a dispute. When the valuer makes his valuation, there is no question of dispute between the parties. On the other hand, an arbitration is always concerned with a dispute between the parties.

5. Advantages of arbitration. Business men often prefer to settle their disputes by arbitration rather than in open court. This is because the following advantages are often to be gained:

(a) Arbitration may be *quicker* and lead to an earlier settlement of the dispute.

(b) Arbitration may be *less expensive* than litigation.

(c) The parties may have their dispute settled by a person with *knowledge* of some special branch of commerce.

(d) Arbitration proceedings may always be conducted in *private hearings,* thus avoiding the publicity of open court.

ARBITRATION AGREEMENTS

6. Effect of an arbitration agreement. Here, it is necessary to consider the extent to which a party is bound by his agreement to submit to arbitration. In particular, it is necessary to consider whether a party to an arbitration agreement can bring a dispute before the court, notwithstanding the agreement.

7. Legal proceedings. A party to an arbitration agreement may always commence legal proceedings in spite of the arbitration agreement. But the other party may ask the court to *stay* the proceedings so that the dispute may be heard by an arbitrator according to the agreement. The court will then decide whether or not to grant the stay. A stay will be granted:

(a) If the matter in dispute is within the scope of the arbitration agreement.
(b) If the applicant for the stay has delivered no defence, nor taken any other step in the legal proceedings.
(c) If the applicant has always been ready and willing to do everything necessary for the proper conduct of the arbitration according to the agreement.
(d) If there is no sufficient reason why the dispute should not be referred to the arbitrator.

8. The court's discretion. It is within the discretion of the court to grant or refuse a stay. In any case, the court will look to the party opposing the stay to show some good reason why arbitration should not take place according to the agreement. The court may refuse a stay:

(a) If there is reason to suspect that the appointed arbitrator may be biased.
(b) If the question of fraud has arisen. (The court will wish to determine whether any party has been fraudulent.)
(c) If the only issue in dispute is a point of law.

9. Validity of the arbitration agreement. The validity of an arbitration agreement is determined according to the general rules of contract. Where the arbitration agreement is a clause operating within a contract between the parties, the dispute may be either:

- (a) as to whether the contract is binding (in which case the arbitrator has no power to determine the issue), or
- (b) as to whether there is a breach of contract, the parties agreeing that their contract is binding (in which case the arbitrator has power to determine the case, subject to the discretion of the court.)

10. Implied terms in arbitration agreements. In every arbitration agreement which is governed by the *Arbitration Act*, 1950, the following terms are implied unless expressly excluded:

- (a) Reference shall be made to a single arbitrator.
- (b) Where reference is to two arbitrators, that they shall appoint an umpire.
- (c) Where the arbitrators cannot agree, the umpire shall enter on the reference.
- (d) The parties must submit to examination on oath and produce all documents called for by the arbitrator(s).
- (e) The award shall be final and binding.

11. Arbitrator's duties. It is the duty of the arbitrator to make an inquiry into the dispute and then to make an *award*. The arbitrator should fix the time and place for the hearing and give due notice to the parties and witnesses. He is entitled to use his own knowledge of any commercial matter in connection with the dispute.

12. The award. Where the point at issue is mainly one of law, the arbitrator will usually make his award in the form of a *case stated* for the opinion of the court. In these circumstances the award will take the form of a statement of the facts found by the arbitrator, together with the questions of law arising out of those facts. The statement of facts and the questions of law should be complete so that by answering the questions of law the court determines the dispute between the parties and no further reference is needed. (An arbitrator may, if necessary, state a *special case* for the opinion of the court during the course of the hearing, and before the award is made.)

An award is valid, final and binding on the parties if it satisfies the following conditions:

(a) It must decide a matter within the arbitration agreement and not something outside its scope.
(b) It must be certain.
(c) It must be reasonable and possible, *e.g.* must not order a party to do something which is clearly beyond his ability or power.
(d) It must dispose of *every* matter referred.

13. Enforcement of an award. Where a party is reluctant to comply with the order of the arbitrator in the award, the other party may seek to enforce the award in one of two ways:

(a) *As a judgment.* With the leave of the court, which is usually granted, the award may be enforced in the same way as a judgment.
(b) *Action.* An award may be enforced by bringing an action on it. The action is in the nature of an action for breach of contract, since it is founded on the agreement to comply with the award.

14. Remission to arbitrator. The court has power to remit an award for the reconsideration of the arbitrator in any of the following circumstances:

(a) Where there is misconduct on the part of the arbitrator, *e.g.* where he refused to state his case.
(b) Where evidence concerning the dispute has come to light after the making of the award.
(c) Where the arbitrator has acted under a mistake, *e.g.* where he inadvertently exceeds his powers.

15. Setting an award aside. The court has power to set an award aside in any of the following circumstances:

(a) Where there has been *misconduct* of the arbitrator, *e.g.* where there has been an irregularity of proceedings, or where the arbitrator was biased.
(b) Where the award is *uncertain* in its terms.
(c) Where the contract on which the award was made was illegal or void.

PROGRESS TEST 14

1. Define "arbitration." Explain how a reference to arbitration may be made (a) by order of the court, (b) under the provisions of a statute, and (c) by consent out of court.   (1–4)

2. What are the advantages of arbitration?   (5)

3. In what circumstances will the court grant a stay when legal proceedings have been commenced by a party to an arbitration agreement?   (6–8)

4. How is the validity of an arbitration agreement determined? (9)

5. In what circumstances are there implied terms in an arbitration agreement? What are these implied terms?   (4, 10)

6. What are the duties of an arbitrator? When is the award of an arbitrator binding on the parties?   (11, 12)

7. How may an arbitrator's award be enforced?   (13)

8. Explain the court's power of (a) remission, and (b) setting the award aside.   (14, 15)

CHAPTER XV

RESTRICTIVE TRADE PRACTICES

RESTRICTIVE AGREEMENTS GENERALLY

1. Registrable agreements. The *Restrictive Trade Practices Act*, 1956, created the office of Registrar of Restrictive Trading Agreements whose duties are (a) to keep a register of certain kinds of restrictive agreements, and (b) to bring these agreements before the Restrictive Practices Court.

By *s.* 6, the registrable agreements are those which contain any of the following restrictions:

(a) As to prices to be charged for goods, or for the process of manufacture of goods.

(b) As to the conditions on which goods are supplied or processed.

(c) As to the quantities or descriptions of goods to be produced, supplied or acquired.

(d) As to processes of manufacture of goods.

(e) As to persons with whom, or areas with which, trade is to be done with goods.

By *s.* 6(3) of the *Restrictive Trade Practices Act*, 1956, "agreement" includes any agreement or arrangement, whether or not it is intended to be enforceable by legal proceedings. It has been held that the word "arrangement" is to be broadly construed and will cover the bilateral situation where each party intentionally arouses in the other the expectation that he will act in a particular way: *Re British Basic Slag Ltd.'s Agreement* (1963) C.A.

2. Excepted agreements. Certain specified kinds of restrictive agreement need not be registered under the *Restrictive Trade Practices Act*. These kinds of agreement are set out in *s.* 8, the most important of which are as follows:

(a) Agreements expressly authorised by Act of Parliament or by Statutory Instrument.

(b) Certain agreements between two persons only, neither of whom is a trade association, for the supply of goods.
(c) Certain agreements between two persons only, neither of whom is a trade association, for the exchange of information relating to the operation of processes of manufacture.
(d) Agreements whose restrictions relate exclusively

    (i) to the supply of goods by export from the United Kingdom;
   (ii) to the production of goods, or the application of any process of manufacture to goods, outside the United Kingdom;
  (iii) to the acquisition of goods to be delivered outside the United Kingdom and not imported into the United Kingdom for entry for home use; or
  (iv) to the supply of goods to be delivered outside the United Kingdom otherwise than by export from the United Kingdom.

For the purposes of these exemption provisions, two or more companies within the same group will be treated as a single person. Similarly, two or more individuals in partnership with each other will be treated as a single person.

Further exempting provisions are included in the *Restrictive Trade Practices Act*, 1968. By *s.* 1 of the 1968 Act, certain agreements which are of importance to the national economy, or which are designed to promote efficiency in a trade or industry, are exempted from registration. Section 2 of the 1968 Act examples any agreement which relates exclusively to the prices to be charged in connection with transactions of any description and which is designed either to prevent or restrict increases or to secure reductions in those prices.

3. The Restrictive Practices Court. The *Restrictive Trade Practices Act*, 1956, set up the Restrictive Practices Court. The Court is a superior court of record, *i.e.* it has the status of the High Court. It consists of five judges assisted by up to ten lay members. When the Court sits, it usually does so in divisions consisting of one judge assisted by two lay members. The lay members have equal voice with the judge in questions of fact, but on questions of law the opinion of the judge prevails.

4. The eight gateways. The Court considers agreements which have been placed on the register kept by the Registrar of Restrictive Trade Agreements. In any hearing, the onus is on the parties to the agreement to satisfy the Court that the agreement is not contrary to the public interest.

By *s.* 21, as amended by the 1968 Act, a restrictive agreement is deemed to be against the public interest unless the Court is satisfied of any *one or more* of the following eight circumstances (sometimes known as "the eight gateways"):

(a) that the restriction is reasonably necessary, having regard to the character of the goods to which it applies, to protect the public against injury (whether to persons or to premises) in connection with the consumption, installation or use of those goods;

(b) that the removal of the restriction would deny to the public as purchasers, consumers or users of any goods other specific and substantial benefits or advantages enjoyed or likely to be enjoyed by them as such, whether by virtue of the restriction itself or of any arrangements or operations resulting therefrom;

(c) that the restriction is reasonably necessary to counteract measures taken by any one person not party to the agreement with a view to preventing or restricting competition in or in relation to the trade or business in which the persons party thereto are engaged;

(d) that the restriction is reasonably necessary to enable the persons party to the agreement to negotiate fair terms of the supply of goods to, or the acquisition of goods from, any one person not party thereto who controls a preponderant part of the trade or business of acquiring or supplying such goods, or for the supply of goods to any person not party to the agreement and not carrying on such a trade or business who, either alone or in combination with any other such person, controls a preponderant part of the market for such goods;

(e) that, having regard to the conditions actually obtaining or reasonably foreseen at the time of the application, the removal of the restriction would be likely to have a serious and persistent adverse effect on the general level of unemployment in an area, or in areas taken together, in which a substantial proportion of the trade or industry to which the agreement relates is situated;

(f) that, having regard to the conditions actually obtaining or reasonably foreseen at the time of the application, the removal of the restriction would be likely to cause a reduction in the volume of earnings of the export business which is substantial either in relation to the whole export business of the United Kingdom or in relation to the whole business of the said trade or industry;

(g) that the restriction is reasonably required for purposes connected with the maintenance of any other restriction accepted by the parties, whether under the same agreement or under any other agreement between them, being a restriction which is found by the Court not to be contrary to the public interest; or

(h) that the restriction does not directly or indirectly restrict or discourage competition to any material degree in any relevant trade or industry and is not likely to do so.

The Court must be further satisfied that the restriction is not unreasonable having regard to the balance between those circumstances and any detrimental to the public, or to persons not parties to the agreement, resulting or likely to result from the operation of the restriction.

5. Failure to register. The consequences of failure to register a restrictive agreement within the time stipulated by the 1968 Act are that:

(a) the agreement is void,

(b) it is unlawful for a party to give effect to or enforce the agreement,

(c) any party who enforces or gives effect to a restriction is liable in damages at the suit of anyone suffering a consequential loss and

(d) the Court may make an order in the nature of an injunction restraining any party from giving effect to or enforcing the restriction: *s.* 7 of the 1968 Act.

RESALE PRICE MAINTENANCE

6. Price maintenance of goods. Resale price maintenance agreements are those by which manufacturers of goods seek to control the retail prices of their manufactured goods. Such agreements are usually made between manufacturer and whole-saler, the wholesaler giving an undertaking not to sell to a retailer except upon the undertaking by the retailer not to sell below the manufacturer's list prices. At common law, this kind of agreement was not enforceable by the manufacturer against the retailer on grounds of privity of contract.

> *Dunlop* v. *Selfridge & Co. Ltd*. (1915): D sold motor tyres to X, a wholesaler, on terms that X would not sell the tyres to a retailer except under a contract whereby the retailer promised to sell at D's list prices. X sold some of these tyres to S who undertook not to sell below D's list prices. Subsequently, S sold tyres below the list prices. D brought this action against S claiming an injunction and damages. HELD by the House of Lords: there was no contract betwen D and S. S's contract was with X, and D was a stranger to this contract, and the action failed.

The common law doctrine of privity of contract as applied to resale price maintenance is now affected by the *Restrictive Trade Practices Act*, 1956, *ss*. 24 and 25, and the *Resale Prices Act*, 1964.

7. Collective enforcement. Section 24 of the *Restrictive Trade Practices Act*, 1956, provides that it is *unlawful* for two or more persons carrying on business as *suppliers* of goods to make an agreement by which they undertake

(a) to withhold supplies of goods for delivery from dealers who resell in breach of any condition as to the price at which those goods may be resold;

(b) to refuse to supply goods for delivery to such dealers except on terms less favourable than those applicable to other dealers; or

(c) to supply goods only to persons who undertake to with-hold supplies of goods from dealers who resell in breach of any conditions as to the price at which the goods may be resold.

8. Individual enforcement. While *s*. 24 prohibits the col-lective enforcement of resale price maintenance, the *individual* enforcement is permitted by *s*. 25, as an exception to the doctrine of privity of contract. Section 25 of the *Restrictive Trade Practices Act*, 1956, provides that where goods are sold by a supplier subject to a condition as to the price at which those goods may be resold, either generally or by or to a specified class or person, that condition may be enforced by the supplier against any person not party to the sale who subsequently acquires the goods with notice of the condition as if he had been a party thereto. In other words, *s.* 25 reverses the rule in *Dunlop* v. *Selfridge* so far as price maintenance is concerned. Section 25 has now been much modified in its effect by the *Resale Prices Act*, 1964.

9. The Resale Prices Act, 1964. Section 1 of the Act provides that any stipulation purporting to establish a *minimum* resale price of goods shall be *void*. The Act further prohibits indirect methods of maintaining minimum resale prices, *e.g.* the withholding of supplies or the refusal to supply goods.

The Restrictive Practices Court may, however, on a reference made by the Registrar of Restrictive Trading Agreements, by order direct that goods of any class shall be exempt from the provisions of the *Resale Prices Act*, 1964. The Court may make an exemption order for any class of goods if it appears that in default of a system of maintained minimum resale prices:

(a) the quality or varieties available for sale would be substantially reduced; or

(b) the number of establishments in which the goods are sold by retail would be substantially reduced; or

(c) the prices would, in the long run, be increased; or

(d) the goods would be sold by retail under conditions likely to cause danger to health in consequence of their misuse by the public; or

(e) any necessary services actually provided in connection with or after sale would cease,

and in any case that the resulting detriment to the public would outweigh any detriment resulting from minimum resale price maintenance: *s.* 5.

PROGRESS TEST 15

1. In what circumstances, if at all, is a contract in restraint of trade valid and binding at common law? (V, 21)

2. What kinds of restrictive agreements are registrable under the *Restrictive Trade Practices Act*, 1956? (1)

3. Are export agreements registrable? (2)

4. What is the status and jurisdiction of the Restrictive Practices Court? What are the eight "gateways"? (3, 4)

5. Is a restriction contained in a "gentleman's agreement" registrable? (1)

6. What was the significance of the decision in *Dunlop* v. *Selfridge* (1915)? Which statute altered the legal effect of this decision? (6, 8)

7. Distinguish between (a) collective enforcement, and (b) the individual enforcement, of resale price maintenance agreements. (7, 8)

8. What is the main provision of the *Resale Prices Act*, 1964? In what circumstances may the Court make an exemption order under this Act? (9)

PART THREE
COMPANY LAW

CHAPTER XVI

FORMATION OF COMPANIES

NATURE AND FORMATION OF COMPANIES

1. Definition. A company is a *legal person* (*i.e.* capable of undertaking legal obligations and exercising legal rights) with an existence quite distinct and separate from the co-existing individuals who compose it from time to time. A company is thus distinct from its directors and shareholders.

> *Salomon* v. *Salomon & Co Ltd.* (1897): S, who had for some years owned a boot manufacturing business, formed a company with himself, his wife and children as members. S then sold his business to the company for fully paid shares and debentures, the debentures being secured on the assets. The company subsequently went into liquidation and the assets were sufficient to discharge the debentures issued to S in full, but were not sufficient to pay the unsecured creditors. The liquidator sought to have the debentures issued to S set aside on the ground that the company was merely his agent. HELD: The company had a legal existence distinct from S and, therefore, the grant of debentures to S was valid.

2. Advantages of incorporation. Where a business is owned by a company there are considerable commercial advantages:

(a) *The company continues to exist* in spite of the death, bankruptcy or lunacy of any of its shareholders.
(b) The capital used by the company is its permanent *joint stock*. This is the capital contributed by the shareholders. It is permanent because it cannot be withdrawn.
(c) Although the capital cannot be withdrawn by the share-

holders, it may nevertheless be *transferred, i.e.* a share-holder may sell his shares in the capital of a company.

(d) *The liability of a shareholder* for the debts and other obligations incurred by the company may be *limited* either to the extent of any amount still unpaid on his shares, or to the amount he has guaranteed (in the case of a company limited by guarantee).

(e) Members, as members, have *no power to bind the company.* The company may only act through its properly appointed agents.

(f) The extent to which *legal obligations* may be incurred is governed by the *constitution of the company,* mainly in the objects clause of the memorandum of association.

3. The Companies Acts. The *Companies Act,* 1948, consolidates the law relating to companies. The Act governs companies whether formed under the 1948 Act or under previous *Companies Acts.* A company which is registered under any *Companies Act* is known as a *registered company.* Registration is effected by the depositing of specified documents with an official known as the Registrar of Companies at Companies House in London.

The *Companies Act,* 1967, makes various amendments mainly concerning directors, auditors, accounts, exempt private companies and the power of the Department of Trade and Industry, formerly the Board of Trade, to investigate companies.

In this Part all references are to sections of the 1948 Act unless otherwise stated.

4. Kinds of company. Registered companies may be classified into the following groups:

(a) *Limited companies.* These are companies for which the liability of members for the debts of the company is limited. Thus, where a company has not sufficient assets to meet its liabilities, the creditors of the company cannot look to the members for payment of the debts, *i.e.* not beyond the limited liability undertaken by the members. The liability of members for the debts of the company may be limited in one of two ways:

(i) *In a company limited by shares,* no member (*i.e.* shareholder) is liable to contribute to the company any more than the amount (if any) unpaid on his shares.

(ii) *In a company limited by guarantee,* no member is liable to contribute to the company more than the amount he has guaranteed. A company limited by guarantee may also have a share capital.

(b) *Unlimited companies.* It is possible, but rare, for a company to be composed of mèmbers with unlimited liability for the company's debts and obligations. Such a company may or may not have a share capital.

Limited companies are now all obliged to file accounts with the Registrar of Companies, but an unlimited company need not do so provided it satisfies the stringent conditions laid down in *s. 47, Companies Act,* 1967.

5. Private and public companies. Registered companies are either private or public. Private companies (the majority of those registered) have certain advantages not enjoyed by public companies.

(a) *A public company* is one having not less than 7 members, and whose shares are usually freely transferable, *e.g.* on the stock exchange. It can offer its shares or debentures to the general public: *C.A.,* 1948, *s.* 1.

(b) *A private company* is one having not less than 2 members which, by its Articles, restricts the right to transfer its shares, limits the number of its members to 50 (not including past and present employees), and prohibits any invitation to the public to subscribe for its shares or debentures.

An exempt private company was one having certain special privileges which it obtained by satisfying the conditions laid down in *s.* 129 and the 7th Schedule. The most important of these privileges was the exemption from filing accounts with the Registrar of Companies.

The status of exempt private company was abolished by the 1967 Act, which repealed *s.* 129 and the 7th Schedule.

6. Formation of registered companies. The promoters of a company must obtain the necessary minimum of subscribers (two for a private, seven for a public company) and get them to sign the Memorandum of Association of the proposed company.

The following documents are then filed with the Registrar of Companies, who, when satisfied that the requirements of the

Companies Act have been complied with, issues a *certificate of incorporation* (which brings the company into existence as a legal person): *C.A.*, *s.* 15.

DOCUMENTS TO BE FILED

(a) *Memorandum of Association*, signed by the first members and containing a statement of the objects of the company, its name, location of the registered office (whether in England or in Scotland), nominal capital and whether liability of members is limited: *see* **9** *below.*

(b) *Articles of Association* (if any): *see* **11** *below.* These contain the regulations governing the relations of the members among themselves, and of the company to the members.

(c) *Statutory declaration* that the requirements of the *C.A.*, 1948, have been complied with: *s.* 15.

(d) *A statement of nominal capital* (if it is a limited company having a share capital).

And, except in the case of a private company or a company not having a share capital:

(e) *A list of persons* who have consented to be directors, and the *written consent* of such persons to act: *C.A.*, *s.* 181.

(f) *A written undertaking* from such directors to take and pay for qualification shares, if any: *s.* 181.

NOTE: The grant of the Certificate of Incorporation permits a private company (or any company not having a share capital) to commence business immediately: *C.A.*, *s.* 109. But a public company cannot commence business until it has obtained a trading certificate: *see* **7** *below.*

The company must also file notice of the situation of the *registered office* within 14 days of incorporation: *s.* 107. In practice this is usually filed at the same time as the Memorandum, etc.

7. Public companies: trading certificates.

(a) *Where it is intended to obtain capital from the general public* a prospectus must be issued complying with the strict requirements of the *Companies Act*. In these circumstances, a trading certificate will not be issued until a *statutory declaration* signed by a director or the secretary has been deposited with the Registrar. The statutory declaration must state that:

(i) An amount not less than the *minimum subscription* has been raised. (The minimum subscription, which must be stated in the prospectus, is the amount considered necessary to provide for the purchase of property, preliminary expenses and working capital.)

(ii) *Every director has paid* on the shares he has contracted to take, and for which he must pay in cash, a proportion equal to that payable by other members.

(iii) *No cash is repayable* by reason of the company failing to obtain *permission to deal* in shares or debentures on any stock exchange.

(b) *Where it is not intended to obtain capital from the general public*, *i.e.* where it is intended that persons shall take shares or debentures by private agreement, a prospectus need not be issued. There must, however, be a *statement in lieu of prospectus* containing broadly the same detailed information as a prospectus, but without a statement of a minimum subscription. In these circumstances, a trading certificate will not be issued until the following documents have been deposited with the Registrar:

(i) *The statement in lieu of prospectus;* and

(ii) *A statutory declaration* that every director has paid on the shares he has contracted to take, and for which he must pay in cash, a proportion equal to that payable by other members.

NOTE: Contracts entered into by a public company after incorporation but before issue of the trading certificate are *provisional* only, and do not become fully binding on the company until the certificate is issued.

8. Promoters. Persons who undertake to form a company and set it going are called promoters: *Twycross* v. *Grant* (1877). But agents who merely give professional assistance to the promoters are not themselves promoters, *e.g.* solicitors who advise on requirements of registration: *s.* 43. The distinction is important, since promoters are in a fiduciary relation to the company they promote: *see* (c) *below*.

(a) *Preliminary contracts*. A promoter often undertakes to make preliminary contracts and obtain property for the company to be formed. If he does so before incorporation he may be personally liable on such contracts, and the company cannot ratify the transactions so as to accept liability itself: *Kelner* v. *Baxter* (1866). Therefore such preliminary contracts usually *contain a clause* stating that: (i) after incorporation the company can adopt the contract as a *novation* and so release the promoter from liability, and (ii) if the company fails to adopt the contract within a specified time, the promoter or the other party may determine the contract. Clause 9(2) of the *European Communities Bill*, 1972, will make the promoter personally liable on a preliminary contract unless a contrary agreement is made.

(b) *Remuneration.* Promoters are not automatically entitled to remuneration for their services, but the company may pay them if it chooses (usually by granting them shares treated as fully paid for.)

(c) *Secret profits.* Like other agents, promoters who make any secret profit from their office can be compelled to surrender it to the company: *Gluckstein* v. *Barnes* (1900), and *see* IX, **15**.

9. Memorandum of Association.

(a) *Contents:* (i) The name of the company, with "Limited" as the last word, if it is a limited company; (ii) The country in which the registered office will be situated; (iii) The company's objects; (iv) A statement that the liability of members is limited, if such be the case; (v) The proposed share capital, and its division into shares of fixed amounts: *C.A.*, *s.* 2.

(b) *Alteration of the Memorandum* is permitted for the following purposes: (i) To change the name, with the approval of the Department of Trade and Industry; (ii) To change the objects; (iii) To change the liability of the members from limited to unlimited, and vice versa; (iv) To increase or to reduce share capital, if authorised to do so by the Articles; (v) To change any clause which could properly have been included in the Articles.

(c) *Name.* A company cannot be registered with a name which is undesirable in the opinion of the Department of Trade and Industry, *e.g.* because it is too like the name of an existing company, or misleading as to the nature of the company's activities, and might lead to deception of the public: *C.A.*, 1948, *ss.* 17 and 18 and *s.* 46, *C.A.*, 1967.

NOTE

(i) A company may *change its name* by special resolution and the written consent of the Department of Trade and Industry:

C.A., *s.* 18. The name must be placed conspicuously on the outside of all business premises, engraved on the company's seal, and mentioned in all letters, circulars, invoices, catalogues, bills of exchange, etc., issued by the company: *s.* 108.

(ii) The *Registration of Business Names Act*, 1916, applies to companies as well as to partnerships: *see* X, 6 *above*. Thus if a company trades under a name other than its registered name, it must register the trade name under the *R.B.N. Act.*

10. The company's objects.

(a) *The objects clause.* A registered company must state its objects clearly in the Memorandum, and they must be lawful. The company must have a main object, and may in addition have many subsidiary objects.

(b) *Express and implied powers.* The company's legal capacity is restricted to the powers stated or implied by the objects clause. These may be stated expressly, but the company also has such implied powers as will be reasonably incidental to the achievement of its objects, *e.g.* a trading company has implied power to borrow money.

(c) *Ultra vires.* Any transaction entered into by the company beyond its powers (*ultra vires*) is *void*, and cannot be ratified in any circumstances, *e.g.* by altering the Memorandum retrospectively in an attempt to validate the transaction: *Ashbury Carriage Co.* v. *Riche* (1875).

(d) *Failure of main object.* If the company achieves its main object, or if it becomes impossible to achieve, the company must be wound up even though some subsidiary objects are still attainable: *re German Date Coffee Co.* (1882).

(e) *Alteration of the objects clause* is allowed (*C.A.*, *s.* 5) by *special resolution* of the members, for the following purposes:

  (i) Increased economy or efficiency.
  (ii) Attaining its main purpose by new or improved means.
  (iii) Enlarging the area of operations.
  (iv) To include a convenient side-line business.
  (v) Restricting or abandoning any objects.
  (vi) Disposing of some or all of the business.
  (vii) Amalgamating with some other company.

NOTE: The holders of *not less than* 15% of the company's shares may apply to the court within 21 days for the alteration to be cancelled: *s.* 5. The court may cancel or confirm the alteration in whole or in part, or adjourn the matter so that an arrangement may be made for the purchase of the dissentients' shares, or make such other order as seems just.

11. The Articles of Association. These are regulations governing (*a*) the internal management of the company, and (*b*) the relationship of the company to the members and of the members among themselves. (Many companies adopt the draft Articles contained in Table A of the *Companies Act*, modified as appropriate to the company's requirements.)

- (a) *Contents:* (i) The issue of shares, class rights, and methods of altering them; (ii) Issue of share certificates, calls on partly paid shares, forfeitures, etc.; (iii) Transfer and transmission of shares; (iv) Provisions as to audits, accounts, etc.; (v) Provisions as to notice and procedure at general meetings; (vi) Appointment and duties of directors and secretary.
- (b) *Alteration of Articles* is by *special resolution* at a general meeting: *s.* 10. Any alteration must be lawful and consistent with the Memorandum, and must not amount to a fraud on or oppression of a minority of members.

  An alteration can be made which affects existing rights so that persons dealing with the company may find that it involves a breach of their contract with the company. They may then sue the company for breach of contract, but they cannot attack the validity of the alteration: *Southern Foundries Ltd.* v. *Shirlaw* (1940).
- (c) *Copies of the Articles* (and of the Memorandum) must be made available to members on request, a payment of not more than 5p being charged in most cases: *C.A., s.* 24.

12. Effect of Memorandum and Articles.

- (a) *Contract between company and members.* The Memorandum and Articles operate as a sealed contract between the company and the members, and among the members *inter se*, as though each had signed the document: *C.A., s.* 20.

BUT NOTE

   (i) *The Articles cannot constitute a contract between the company and a member in a capacity other than that of member, e.g.* where articles state that X is to be managing director, this clause does not constitute a contract between the company and X, even if X is a member: *Eley* v. *Positive Life Assurance Co.* (1876).

   (ii) *The Articles do not constitute a contract between the company and outsiders, e.g.* where they provide that payments are to be made to X as promoter, X cannot sue the company in reliance on the Articles. But the Articles may give directors authority to pay promoters' expenses: *re Rotherham Chemical Co.* (1883).

(b) *Notice to outsiders.* The Memorandum and Articles are *public documents* available for inspection by any member of the public at the office of the Registrar, and they constitute notice of their contents to all such persons. Thus if the company is about to make an *ultra vires* contract with X, X should find out that the contract is beyond the powers of the company by consulting the Memorandum; if he fails to do so, he has no remedy against the company.

By the *rule in Turquand's Case* (*see* XVII, **24** *below*). a person dealing with a company whose contract is consistent with the Memorandum and Articles is entitled to enforce the contract against the company even though it may be inconsistent with some internal regulation, non-compliance with which is not apparent on inspection of the public documents: *Royal British Bank* v. *Turquand* (1856).

NOTE: Clause 9 (1) of the *European Communities Bill*, 1972, will modify these rules in favour of a person dealing with a company in good faith.

SHARES

13. Share capital. A share has been defined judicially as "the interest of a shareholder in the company measured by a sum of money, for the purpose of liability in the first place, and of interest in the second, but also consisting of a series of mutual covenants entered into by all the shareholders *inter se* in accordance with *C.A.*, *s.* 20. The contract contained in the

Articles of Association is one of the original incidents of the share. A share is not a sum of money, but is an interest measured by a sum of money and made up of various rights contained in the contract, including the right to a sum of money of a more or less amount."

The words "share capital" may be used in any of the following ways:

(a) *Nominal or authorised capital.* The nominal value of the total shares which any company is authorised to issue.

(b) *Issued capital.* Nominal capital which has been actually issued to shareholders.

(c) *Subscribed capital.* Issued capital for which the shareholders have paid cash.

(d) *Called-up capital.* The amount actually called up on the shares issued. Any remaining amount is the *uncalled capital* of the company.

(e) *Paid-up capital.* The amount of called-up capital which has actually been paid to the company.

(f) *Reserve capital.* The part, if any, of the uncalled capital which cannot be called up except in the case of the company's being wound up.

NOTE: The word *capital* may also be used in the following senses:

(i) *Capital assets.* The property of a company, including fixed assets acquired for retention and use, or circulating assets held temporarily prior to disposal. Examples of fixed capital are factories and installed machinery. Examples of circulating capital are raw materials to be used for manufacture, and finished goods to be sold.

(ii) *Debenture capital* (sometimes called *loan capital.*) Money raised by a company by borrowing on the security of debentures.

(iii) *Equity capital.* That part of the issued capital whose shareholders may participate *fully* in any distribution of dividends, or of assets in a winding up. Equity capital, therefore, usually comprises the capital represented by ordinary shares.

14. Classes of shares and shareholders. A company may issue shares of different classes, *i.e.* the rights of a shareholder against the company vary according to the class of shares held. To discover the rights attaching to each class of shares it is necessary to look at the Articles of Association or the terms on which the shares were issued. The most common classes are as follows:

(a) *Preference shares.* Holders of preference shares are entitled to preference in the payment of dividends. Preference shareholders are paid dividends at the fixed stipulated rate for the class before any dividend is allocated to ordinary shareholders. Unless otherwise stipulated, preference shares are *cumulative, i.e.* in the event of the company being unable to pay the full dividend in one year, the arrears will be carried forward, and may become payable in a subsequent year. Preference shares are usually *non-participating, i.e.* they do not entitle the holders to participate in surplus profits. But a company may issue *participating preference shares* wherever this is desirable.

(b) *Ordinary shares.* Holders of ordinary shares are entitled to receive such dividends as are declared from time to time, and to receive a share of the surplus assets in the event of the company's being wound up. Holders of ordinary shares are usually entitled to vote at meetings, but sometimes non-voting ordinary shares are issued.

15. Redeemable preference shares. A company may, if authorised by its Articles, issue preference shares which are to be redeemed, or which are, at the option of the company, liable to be redeemed. Provided that:

(a) *No such shares can be redeemed except out of profits* of the company which would otherwise be available for dividend, or out of the proceeds of a fresh issue of shares made for the purpose of the redemption.
(b) No such shares can be redeemed unless they are *fully paid up*.
(c) *The premium,* if any, *payable on redemption,* must have been provided for out of the profits of the company or out of the company's share premium account before the shares are redeemed.
(d) Where any such shares are redeemed otherwise than out of the proceeds of a fresh issue, there shall out of profits which would otherwise have been available for dividend be transferred to the *capital redemption reserve fund* a

sum equal to the nominal amount of the shares redeemed: *C.A.*, *s.* 58.

16. Alteration of capital. A company limited by shares or
having a share capital, if authorised by its Articles, may alter
the conditions of its Memorandum as follows:

(a) *It may increase* its share capital by new shares of such
amount as it thinks expedient.

(b) *It may consolidate and divide* all or any of its share
capital into shares of larger amount than its existing
shares.

(c) *It may convert* all or any of its paid-up shares *into stock*,
and reconvert that stock into paid-up shares of any
denomination.

(d) *It may subdivide its shares*, or any of them, into shares of
smaller amount than is fixed by the Memorandum, so
that in the subdivision the proportion between the
amount paid and the amount, if any, unpaid on each
reduced share becomes the same as it was in the case of
the share from which the reduced share is derived.

(e) *It may cancel shares* which, at the date of the passing of
the resolution in that behalf, have not been taken or
agreed to be taken by any person, and diminish the
amount of its share capital by the amount of the shares
so cancelled. (A cancellation of shares is not deemed to
be a reduction of share capital.)

(f) It may, if authorised by its Articles, by *special resolution
for reducing share capital* reduce its share capital in any
way. The company may, if and so far as is necessary,
alter its Memorandum by reducing the amount of its
share capital and of its shares accordingly. Reduction
of share capital is always subject to the confirmation of
the court.

17. Transfer of shares. A share represents the interest of the
shareholder in the company measured by a sum of money. A
shareholder may transfer his shares unless the Articles provide
otherwise. (The Articles of a private company restrict the
freedom of each shareholder to transfer his shares.) Where
shares are to be transferred, an instrument of transfer is signed
by the transferor. The instrument is then sent to the company

together with the transferor's *share certificate*. The register of shareholders is then amended, and a fresh share certificate is sent to the transferee. A share certificate is *prima facie* evidence of the holder's title to the shares specified in the certificate.

NOTE: The transfer of shares is simplified where a *share warrant* has been issued to replace a share certificate. A public company may, if authorised by its Articles, issue a share warrant in respect of fully-paid shares at the request of the shareholder, who must surrender his share certificate. On the issue of a share warrant, the register is amended by removing the holder's name with respect to the shares covered by the warrant. Share warrants are negotiable instruments, and are transferable by mere delivery. The bearer of a share warrant may surrender it for cancellation and have his name entered in the register of members. Although the holder of a share warrant is not a member of the company, he may, subject to the Articles, be deemed to be a member either to the full extent, or for any purposes defined in the Articles. Private companies may not issue share warrants.

18. The rule in Trevor v. Whitworth. In *Trevor* v. *Whitworth* (1887) it was held unlawful for a company to buy its own shares, since this would be a reduction of its share capital.

This rule is extended by *s*. 54, which prohibits a company from providing financial assistance of any kind to enable any person to purchase shares in itself, or, if it is a subsidiary company, in its holding company (*see* XVII, 16).

The section does not apply, however, to loans made in the ordinary course of business by companies whose ordinary business includes the lending of money, nor to financial assistance given to employees of the company to enable them to acquire shares in the company, whether under a scheme or otherwise.

19. Dividends. *The payment of dividends* to the members of any company is governed by the Articles of Association. But no dividend is due until it has been duly declared. Dividends may be paid out of profits, but not out of capital: but the *capital* of a company is not always clearly definable for this purpose. *The rules relating to the payment of dividends* may be summarised as follows:

(a) The payment of dividends is governed by the *Memorandum and Articles*, but a company cannot be authorised to pay dividends out of capital.

(b) Dividends may be paid only where the company is *solvent*.

(c) *It is not necessary* for a company to allow for the *depreciation of fixed assets* before payment of dividends.

(d) Provided a company is solvent, *revenue losses of past years need not be made good* before payment of dividends in any year in which a profit has been made. Each year is treated separately for this purpose, losses in past years having the effect of reducing the capital fund.

(e) Subject to the Articles, dividends may be paid out of a *realised profit* on the sale of a fixed asset.

(f) Subject to the Articles, dividends may be paid out of the *unrealised profits* where a revaluation shows an increase in value of fixed assets. Accounting practice requires a revaluation of *all* the company's fixed assets before a dividend may be paid from this unrealised profit.

(g) The directors may pay such *interim dividends* as they consider to be justified by the profits.

(h) No dividend may exceed the *amount recommended* by the directors.

(i) The directors may *transfer to reserve* any sum they consider desirable before payment of dividends.

PROGRESS TEST 16

1. Summarise the advantages of incorporating a business as a registered company. **(2)**

2. Explain the distinctions between (a) limited and unlimited companies, (b) private and public companies. **(4, 5)**

3. How is a registered company formed? **(6)**

4. When can a public registered company commence business? **(7)**

5. What is a promoter? Explain the position of promoters with regard to contracts made by them on behalf of a company. **(8)**

6. Summarise the contents of the Memorandum and Articles of Association of a registered company, and explain how each can be altered. **(9–11)**

7. Explain briefly the *ultra vires* doctrine, and the significance of the objects clause of a Memorandum of Association. **(10)**

8. What are the effects of the Memorandum and Articles of Association of a registered company? **(12)**

9. Explain the distinctions between: capital assets, debenture capital, and equity capital.   (13)

10. Distinguish between ordinary and preference shares and explain what is meant by redeemable preference shares.   (14, 15)

11. In what circumstances may a company alter its capital? (16)

12. Summarise the rules relating to the payment of dividends. (19)

CHAPTER XVII

THE OPERATION OF COMPANIES

DIRECTORS

1. Directors and secretary. Every company must have a
secretary. Every *public* company must have at least two
directors and every *private* company must have at least one
director: *C.A.*, *ss.* 176, 177.

2. Appointment and registration. The Articles of Association
usually contain provision for the method of appointment of
directors. It is often provided that directors shall retire and
stand for re-election in rotation. Every company must keep
at its registered office a register of its directors and secretaries:
C.A., *s.* 200. This register must contain the following particulars with respect to each director: name, address, nationality, business occupation and other directorships held. There
must also be kept a register showing the shares and debentures
held by each director and his or her spouse or infant child:
s. 29, *C.A.*, 1967.

3. Remuneration of directors. A director is not entitled to
be remunerated except in accordance with an agreement between himself and the company: this is usually provided for in
the Articles of Association. If he has a service contract with
the company, *s.* 26 of the *Companies Act*, 1967 requires the
company to keep a copy of it, the copy being open to the
inspection of any member. Section 6 of the 1967 Act requires
the accounts to disclose the emoluments of the chairman, and
of the most highly paid director if he is paid more than the
chairman.

4. Authority of directors. The executive authority of a
director is derived from the Articles of Association. Also, a
director has implied authority to appoint secretaries, employees
and agents for the company. In the exercise of their express

or implied authority, the directors are the agents through whom the company acts and, in order to bind the company, must act collectively as a board. But an *individual* director may be given actual or ostensible authority.

5. Duties of directors. A director is employed by the company and it is to the company that he owes his duties. He does not owe duties to shareholders as individuals. Directors are in a fiduciary position and must act with loyalty and good faith in much the same way as a trustee. As *quasi trustees*, they must act for the general advantage of the company and must not make secret profits for themselves. In addition to his fiduciary duties, a director must exercise care and skill. The duties of a director were summarised in *re City Equitable Fire Insurance Co.* (1925) as follows:

(a) *A director need not exhibit* in the performance of his duties a greater degree of skill than may reasonably be expected from a person of his knowledge and experience.

(b) A director is *not bound to give continuous attention* to the affairs of his company and he is not bound to attend all board meetings.

(c) In respect of duties that, having regard to the exigencies of business and the Articles of Association, may properly be left to some other official, a director is, in the absence of grounds for suspicion, justified in trusting that official to perform such duties honestly.

The *Companies Act*, 1967, *s.* 25, prohibits a director and his or her spouse or infant child from dealing in options regarding quoted shares or debentures of the company. The 1967 Act also contains stringent provisions regarding the contents of the directors' report to the members.

MEETINGS

6. The purpose of meetings. In theory, the members (*i.e.* the shareholders) of a company are entitled to control the company and to exercise its powers. In practice, however, most of this power is exercised by the directors at board meetings in accordance with the authority conferred by the Articles.

But any powers which are not delegated to the directors may be exercised by the members at company meetings.

7. The statutory meeting. Every *public* company limited by shares and every company limited by guarantee and having a share capital must hold a general meeting of its members within a period of not less than one month nor more than three months from the date at which the company is entitled to commence business. This meeting is called the statutory meeting: *C.A.*, *s.* 130. At this early meeting, the shareholders have an opportunity to discuss and dispute with the directors any matter arising out of the formation and initial business life of the company.

The directors must send to each member (and to the company auditors) a copy of the *statutory report* at least fourteen days before the day on which the statutory meeting is held. The statutory report must be certified by not less than two directors and must state:

(a) *The total number of shares allotted,* distinguishing shares allotted as fully or partly paid up otherwise than in cash, and stating in the case of shares partly paid up the extent to which they are paid up, and in either case, the consideration for which they were allotted.

(b) *The total amount of cash received* by the company in respect of all the shares allotted distinguishing as in (a) above.

(c) *An abstract of the receipts and payments* of the company, up to a date within seven days of the date of the report, and an account or estimate of the preliminary expenses of the company.

(d) *The names, addresses and descriptions* of the directors, auditors, if any, managers, if any, and secretary of the company.

(e) *The particulars of any contract,* the modification of which is to be submitted to the meeting for its approval, together with the particulars of the modification or proposed modification: *s.* 130.

8. The annual general meeting. Every company must hold in each year its annual general meeting in addition to any other meetings. Not more than fifteen months must elapse between

the date of one annual general meeting and the next: provided
that, so long as a company holds its first annual general meeting within eighteen months of its incorporation, it need not
hold it in the year of its incorporation or in the following year.
If default is made in holding an annual general meeting the
Department of Trade and Industry may, on the application of
any member of the company, call, or direct the calling of, a
general meeting and give such ancillary or consequential
directions as the Department may think expedient. These may
include directions modifying or supplementing (in relation to
the calling, holding and conducting of the meeting) the operation of the company's Articles: *s.* 131.

NOTE: The business transacted at an annual general meeting is
either *ordinary business* or *special business*. All business is presumed to be special business unless the Articles (or Table A,
where it applies) provide otherwise. Ordinary business is
usually specified as (i) the declaring of a dividend, (ii) the consideration of the accounts, balance sheets, and the reports of the
directors and auditors, (iii) the election of directors in the place
of those retiring, and (iv) the appointment of, and the fixing of
the remuneration of, the auditors. In the notice convening the
general meeting, ordinary business need not be specified in
detail, but all *special business must be specified in detail or it
cannot be validly transacted at the meeting*.

9. Extraordinary general meetings. Apart from the statutory
general meeting and the annual general meetings, the directors:

(a) are usually empowered by the Articles to call a general
    meeting whenever they wish; and

(b) *must*, by *C.A.*, *s.* 132, convene a general meeting on the
    requisition of members holding not less than one-tenth
    of such of the paid-up capital of the company as carries
    the right of voting at general meetings (or, in the case
    of a company not having a share capital, members
    representing not less than one-tenth of the total voting
    rights at general meeting).

Such meetings are called *extraordinary general meetings*, and
their purpose is to permit the discussion and transaction of
business which cannot properly be postponed until the next
annual general meeting. All business transacted at an extraordinary general meeting is treated as special business and
must be specified in the notice calling the meeting.

10. Resolutions. At company meetings, the resolutions passed may be ordinary, extraordinary or special.

(a) *Ordinary resolutions.* An ordinary resolution is one which is passed by a simple majority of those voting. Any business may be validly transacted by ordinary resolution unless the Act or the Articles provide that a special or extraordinary resolution is necessary for that particular business.

(b) *Extraordinary resolutions.* An extraordinary resolution is one which has been passed by a majority of not less than three-fourths of such members as, being entitled to do so, vote in person or, where proxies are allowed, by proxy, at a general meeting for which notice specifying the intention to propose the resolution as an extraordinary resolution has been duly given: *C.A.*, *s.* 141. The notice must contain the exact wording of the resolution. Extraordinary resolutions are necessary for the voluntary winding up of an insolvent company.

(c) *Special resolutions.* A special resolution is one which has been passed by the same majority as is required for an extraordinary resolution (*see* (b) *above*) and at a general meeting of which not less than 21 days' notice has been duly given: *C.A.*, *s.* 141. The notice must specify the wording of the resolution. Special resolutions are required to change the name of the company, to alter the objects clause or the Articles, and to reduce the capital of the company.

11. Minute books. Every company must keep minute books in which must be entered the proceedings of general meetings: *C.A.*, *s.* 145. These books must be kept in the registered office of the company, and must be open to the inspection of any member for a specified period of at least two hours on each business day during business hours. No charge may be made for inspection.

COMPANY ACCOUNTS

12. Books of account. Every company must keep proper books of account with respect to:

(a) All sums of money received and 'expended by the company and the matters in respect of which the receipt and expenditure takes place.

(b) All sales and purchases of goods by the company.

(c) The assets and liabilities of the company: *C.A.*, *s.* 147.

These books must give a fair view of the state of the company's affairs and must explain its transactions. The books must be kept at the registered office or at such other place as the directors think fit, and must be at all times open to inspection by the directors.

13. Profit and loss account. The directors must, not later than eighteen months after the incorporation of the company and subsequently once at least in every calendar year, lay before the company in general meeting a profit and loss account or, in the case of a company not trading for profit, an income and expenditure account. The period is, in the case of the first account, since the incorporation of the company, and, in any other case, since the preceding account, made up to a date not earlier than the date of the meeting by more than nine months, or, in the case of a company carrying on business or having interests abroad, by more than twelve months. But the Department of Trade and Industry may, for any special reason, extend these specified periods of account: *C.A.*, *s.* 148.

14. Balance sheet. The directors must cause to be made out in every calendar year, and to be laid before the company in general meeting, a balance sheet as at the date to which the profit and loss account or the income and expenditure account, as the case may be, is made up: *C.A.*, *s.* 148.

15. Group accounts. Where at the end of its financial year a company has subsidiaries, group accounts dealing with the state of affairs and profit or loss of the company and the subsidiaries must be laid before the company in general meeting when the company's own balance sheet and profit and loss accounts are so laid: *C.A.*, *s.* 150.

(a) *Group accounts are not required* where the company is at the end of its financial year the wholly owned subsidiary of another body corporate incorporated in Great Britain; and

(b) *Group accounts need not deal* with a subsidiary of the company if the directors are of the opinion that:

(i) it is impracticable, or would be of no real value to members of the company, in view of the insignificant amounts involved, or would involve expense or delay out of proportion to the value to members of the company; or

(ii) the result would be misleading, or harmful to the business of the company or any of its subsidiaries; or

(iii) the business of the holding company and that of the subsidiary are so different that they cannot reasonably be treated as a single undertaking;

and if the directors are of such opinion about each of the company's subsidiaries, group accounts are not required: *C.A.*, *s.* 150. But the approval of the Department of Trade and Industry is required for not dealing in group accounts with a subsidiary on the ground that the result would be harmful or on the ground of the difference between the business of the holding company and that of the subsidiary.

16. Holding companies and subsidiaries. Section 154 provides the test to be applied to discover whether any two companies are in the "holding company" and "subsidiary company" relationship.

By *s.* 154, ABC Ltd. is deemed to be a subsidiary of XYZ Ltd. if *either* (a) XYZ Ltd. is a member of ABC Ltd. and controls the composition of its board of directors; *or* (b) XYZ Ltd. holds more than half (in nominal value) of its equity share capital.

Further, ABC Ltd. is deemed to be a subsidiary of XYZ Ltd. if ABC Ltd. is a subsidiary of any company which is the subsidiary of XYZ Ltd.

NOTE: By *s.* 154(5), "*equity share capital*" means a company's issued share capital excluding any part thereof which, neither as respects dividends nor as respects capital, carries any right to participate beyond a specified amount in a distribution.

In other words, a company's equity share capital is that part of its issued share capital on which there is no ultimate limit specified on the amount payable to shareholders (a) by way of dividend, or (b) by way of distribution in a winding up.

17. Liability for non-compliance. If a director fails to take all reasonable steps to secure compliance with the statutory requirements relating to accounts, he is liable on summary conviction to a term of imprisonment not exceeding six months, or to a fine not exceeding two hundred pounds. But it is a good defence for a director to prove that he had reasonable grounds to believe, and did believe, that a competent and reliable person was charged with the duty of seeing that the statutory requirements were complied with, and was in a position to discharge that duty. A director will not be imprisoned under these provisions unless the offence was committed wilfully: *C.A.*, *ss.* 147–150.

18. Appointment of first auditors. The professional audit of company accounts is compulsory, and the auditors are given important powers by the Act. The first auditors of a company may be appointed by the directors at any time before the first annual general meeting, and the auditors so appointed hold office until the conclusion of that meeting. But the company in general meeting may:

(a) remove any such auditors and appoint in their place any other persons who have been nominated for appointment by any member of the company and of whose nomination notice has been given to the members of the company not less than fourteen days before the date of the meeting; and

(b) appoint the first auditors if the directors fail to exercise their power of appointment: *C.A.*, *s.* 159.

19. Subsequent appointments. Every company must at each annual general meeting appoint an auditor or auditors to hold office from the conclusion of that, until the conclusion of the next, annual general meeting.

At any annual general meeting a retiring auditor, however appointed, shall be reappointed without any resolution being passed unless:

(a) he is not qualified for reappointment; or
(b) a resolution has been passed at that meeting appointing somebody instead of him or providing expressly that he shall not be reappointed; or
(c) he has given the company notice in writing of his unwillingness to be reappointed.

But where notice is given of an intended resolution to appoint some other person or persons in place of a retiring auditor, and by reason of the death, incapacity or disqualification of that person or of all those persons, as the case may be, the resolution cannot be proceeded with, the retiring auditor shall not be automatically reappointed: *C.A.*, *s.* 159.

Where at an annual general meeting no auditors are appointed or reappointed, the Department of Trade and Industry may appoint a person to fill the vacancy. But the directors have power to fill any casual vacancy in the office of auditor.

20. Qualification of auditors. A person is not qualified for appointment as auditor unless he is a member of a body of accountants established in the United Kingdom and recognised by the Department of Trade and Industry. (In exceptional cases, a person may be authorised by the Department to be appointed as a company auditor on the ground of appropriate experience or similar qualifications obtained outside the United Kingdom.)

Also, none of the following persons is qualified for appointment as auditor of a company:

(a) An officer or servant of the company.
(b) A person who is a partner of or in the employment of an officer or servant of the company.
(c) A body corporate.

21. Auditors' report. The auditors must make a report to the members of the company on the accounts examined by them, and on every balance sheet, every profit and loss account and all group accounts laid before the company in general meeting during their tenure of office: *C.A.*, 1967, *s.* 14. The following matters must be *expressly stated* by auditors in their report:

(a) Whether in the auditors' opinion the company's balance sheet, profit and loss account and group accounts, if any, have been properly prepared, and a true and fair view given of the state of the company's affairs and its profit or loss for the financial year.
(b) That proper books of account have not been kept, and that adequate returns have not been received from the branches visited by them, *if this is the case.*
(c) That the balance sheet and profit and loss account do not

agree with the books of account and returns, *if this is the case.*

NOTE: *An auditor must exercise reasonable skill and care* in the performance of his duties. Unless his suspicions are aroused, he may accept the statements of trusted officials and servants of the company, except where there is a conflict between their duty to the company and their own interests. In short, the auditor does not guarantee that the books of account show the true state of the company's affairs.

CONTRACTUAL CAPACITY OF COMPANIES

22. Memorandum and Articles. The objects clause of the Memorandum of a company sets limits to the contractual capacity of that company. Generally, a company is bound by any contractual undertaking which is within its powers, but an undertaking which is beyond its powers (*i.e. ultra vires*) is void; in these circumstances, the other contracting party has no remedy against the company.

23. The company's agents. A company is an artificial person and can, therefore, only enter into contracts through its agents. Accordingly, the law of agency should be carefully considered in its relationship with company law. The actual and ostensible authority of the company's agents must be seen against the background of the limited contractual capacity of the company itself.

The *authority* of the company's agents is defined by the Articles of Association.

24. The rule in Turquand's case. This rule protects persons when the Memorandum and Articles contain nothing inconsistent with the proposed contract that they intend to make with the company. They are not bound to make further enquiries as to the regularity of the transaction, and are entitled to assume that any internal formalities have been complied with.

If internal formalities have *not* been complied with, the contract will nevertheless be binding on the company (unless the other party knew of the irregularity): *Royal British Bank* v. *Turquand* (1856).

The rule in Turquand's case provides no protection where:

(a) *The outsider knows* that the proposed contract is irregular.
(b) The transaction requires to be validated by the passing of an *extraordinary or special resolution* (since copies of such resolutions are filed with the Registrar and available for inspection with the articles).
(c) *The document relied on is a forgery.*
(d) *The circumstances are so unusual* that the outsider should have been put on his guard, *e.g.* where a junior clerk purports to have authority to borrow on behalf of the company, and relies on a clause in the Articles authorising directors to delegate borrowing power to subordinates: *Houghton* v. *Nothard, Lowe & Wills Ltd.* (1927).

CONTRACTS TO BORROW MONEY

25. The capacity to borrow. All trading companies have, by implication, the capacity to borrow money, although the power to borrow is often expressly conferred by the Memorandum. In the case of non-trading companies, there is no power to borrow unless it is conferred by the Memorandum. Where a company has the power to borrow, it may give security to the lender. The most common form of security given by a company is a fixed or floating charge on its assets.

26. Borrowing ultra vires the company. Where a company borrows money and the amount borrowed is *ultra vires* the company, or the purpose for which the money is borrowed is, to the knowledge of the lender, *ultra vires* the company, the lender has no remedy against the company for breach of contract in the event of non-repayment. In these circumstances, the company is under no legal obligation to repay the lender, and any security given is void. The lender, may, however, by prompt action, obtain an *injunction* restraining the company from parting with the money thus improperly obtained. He can then, in equity, follow and recover his money if it is still separately identifiable; or if it has been used to purchase identifiable assets he may claim those assets. Where the money has been used to pay a specific debt of the company, he can be subrogated to the rights of the creditor, *i.e.* he can bring an action as if he were the creditor.

27. Unauthorised borrowing. Where the borrowing is *intra vires* the company but outside the authority of the directors, the lender may be able to enforce the contract if he can rely on the rule in *Turquand's case*, or if the company is willing to ratify the transaction by resolution in general meeting.

28. Debentures. A debenture may be defined as the instrument containing the company's acknowledgment of indebtedness. It is the written contract containing the express terms by which the company (*a*) gives security to the lender, (*b*) undertakes to pay interest on the loan, and (*c*) undertakes to repay the loan. Debentures may be secured or unsecured, single or in series, registered or bearer, perpetual or redeemable, according to written terms contained in the instrument.

(*a*) *Secured and unsecured.* A debenture is usually secured by a charge on the property of the company. The charge may be *fixed* or *floating*. Where the lender takes no security for his loan, the debenture will be unsecured.

(*b*) *Single and series.* A written contract between a company and a lender whereby the company raises a single loan is known as a single debenture. It is usual, however, for a company to raise the sum needed by offering to the public a large number of debentures in series. Each debenture of a series is issued on the same terms, and they rank *pari passu* among themselves.

(*c*) *Registered and bearer.* Debentures are usually issued and registered in the names of the debenture holders. Thus it is possible to register transfers in the same way as transfers of shares held by members. But where a company issues a debenture payable to bearer, the instrument is negotiable, *i.e.* transferable by mere delivery.

(*d*) *Perpetual and redeemable.* A perpetual debenture is issued on terms that the debt becomes repayable by the company only in the event of its being wound up. A redeemable debenture is issued on terms that the company will repay the debt on or before a stipulated date.

29. Charges on the company's assets. Where secured debentures are issued, the company's assets will be charged by either (*a*) a fixed charge, or (*b*) a floating charge, or (*c*) a combination of fixed and floating charges.

(a) *A fixed charge* is one which attaches to specific property belonging to the company. Where this kind of charge is formally expressed by way of deed, it is a *legal mortgage*, and the debenture holder has the rights of a legal mortgagee. Where the charge is informally created, *e.g.* by the mere deposit of title deeds with the lender, the mortgage is *equitable*. The rights of an equitable mortgagee may be postponed to those of a *bona fide* purchaser of the legal estate in the property mortgaged. An equitable mortgage is thus a less valuable security than a legal mortgage.

(b) *A floating charge* is one which attaches to all or any specified part of the undertaking of the company and its fluctuating assets. A floating charge is usually expressed to become crystallised in the event of the debenture holders taking steps to enforce their security. In any event, a floating charge becomes crystallised if the company commences winding up. Where a floating charge becomes crystallised, it becomes, in effect, a fixed charge thereafter.

The commercial advantage of a floating charge is that it does not prevent the company from using the property thus charged, *i.e.* it can carry on its business unhampered by the charge: whereas, in the case of a fixed charge, a company is restricted in its dealings with the property charged.

NOTE: A floating charge may be impaired or deferred in the following circumstances:
  (i) *If it is not registered* with the Registrar of Companies within twenty-one days of its creation, it will be *void*.
  (ii) *If the company winds up within twelve months* of the creation of the charge, it will be *invalid* if the charge relates to past debts and the company was insolvent at that time.
  (iii) *If the company commences winding up within six months* of the creation of the charge, it may be invalidated as a *fraudulent preference*.
  (iv) *The following claims have priority* over a floating charge: fixed charges, garnishee orders, and preferential debts in a winding up.

30. Remedies of debenture holders. The remedies available to a debenture holder will vary according to whether the debenture is secured or unsecured.

(a) *Unsecured debentures.* The holder of an unsecured debenture is in the position of an ordinary creditor without security. In the event of default in repayment of principal or interest, the debenture holder may either:

(i) bring an action against the company for breach of contract, or
(ii) petition for the winding up of the company by the court; and prove in the winding up of the company.

(b) *Secured debentures*. In the event of default by the company the holder of a secured debenture may have any of the following remedies. He may:

(i) bring an action against the company for breach of contract, claiming the principal and/or interest owed; or
(ii) petition for the winding up of the company by the court; or
(iii) exercise any power conferred by the debenture in the event of the company's default, *e.g.* to sell the property, or to appoint a receiver; or
(iv) apply to the court for an order for sale of the property comprising the security, or foreclosure, or for the appointment of a receiver.

PROGRESS TEST 17

1. What are the rules as to the appointment, registration and remuneration of directors?   (1–3)

2. What are the broad principles governing the authority and duty of directors?   (4, 5)

3. State the purpose and contents of a company's statutory report.   (7)

4. What rules are applicable to the holding of the annual general meeting? What business is transacted at such a meeting? (8)

5. What is an extraordinary general meeting?   (9)

6. What is (a) an ordinary resolution, (b) an extraordinary resolution and (c) a special resolution?   (10)

7. Outline the rules relating to the keeping of company accounts. What additional rules govern group accounts?   (12–17)

8. How are auditors appointed? Are there any rules relating to the qualification of auditors?   (18–20)

9. What matters must be expressly stated in the auditors' report?   (21)

10. State and explain the rule in *Turquand's case*.   (24)

11. Distinguish between borrowings which are *ultra vires* a com-

pany, and those which are merely *ultra vires* the company's agents. (26, 27)

12. Summarise the different kinds of debenture. How does a fixed charge differ from a floating charge?   (28, 29)

13. Summarise the remedies of a debenture holder.   (30)

CHAPTER XVIII

WINDING UP OF COMPANIES

WINDING UP

1. Purpose of winding up. Winding up (or liquidation) is the usual process by which the legal personality of a company is brought to an end. It follows that a company loses its contractual capacity at the completion of winding up. During the course of winding up the company's property is distributed between creditors and members.

As alternatives to winding up, dissolution may also occur in the following ways:

(a) *Improper registration.* Where registration has been improperly permitted, it may be cancelled at the instance of the Crown, *e.g.* where after registration it is discovered that the objects of the company are illegal.

(b) *Defunct companies* can be removed from the register.

2. Kinds of winding up. Winding up may be either: (a) *compulsory* (*i.e.* by order of the court), or (b) *voluntary: see below.*

COMPULSORY WINDING UP

3. Winding up by the court. An application for the winding up of a company may be made to the court by petition, which must be presented by either (a) the company, (b) any creditor or creditors, (c) any contributory or contributories (*see* **16** *below*), or (d) any of these parties together or separately: *C.A., s.* 224.

After hearing the petition, the court may make an order for the winding up of the company in any of the following circumstances:

(a) Where the company has by *special resolution* resolved that the company be wound up by the court.

(b) Where default is made in delivering the *statutory report* to the registrar or in holding the *statutory meeting*.

(c) Where the company *does not commence its business* within a year from its incorporation or suspends its business for a whole year.

(d) Where the *number of members* is reduced, in the case of a private company, below two, or, in the case of any other company, below seven.

(e) Where the company is *unable to pay its debts*.

(f) Where the court is of opinion that it is *just and equitable* that the company should be wound up: *s. 222.*

4. The statement of affairs. When a winding-up order has been made, a statement of the company's affairs must be prepared and submitted to the official receiver (an official of the Department of Trade and Industry attached to the court) by one or more of the directors and the secretary of the company.

It must be submitted within 14 days, and must show the company's assets and liabilities, its creditors, and any securities which the creditors hold.

5. Official receiver's report. As soon as practicable after he has received the statement of affairs, the official receiver must submit to the court a preliminary report containing the following:

(a) The amount of capital issued, subscribed and paid up, and the estimated amount of assets and liabilities.

(b) The causes of the company's failure, where this has occurred.

(c) The official receiver's opinion as to whether further enquiry is desirable as to any matter relating to the promotion, formation or failure of the company or the conduct of its business.

The official receiver may also, if he thinks fit, make a further report stating whether, in his opinion, fraud has been committed. Where such further report is made, the court has powers publicly to examine any promoter or officer of the company who is stated to have committed the fraud.

6. Liquidators. The court may appoint a liquidator (or liquidators) for the purpose of conducting the proceedings in winding up a company. But the official receiver is the provisional liquidator until an appointment is made. The liquidator must take into his custody or under his control all the property and things in action to which the company is or appears to be entitled.

7. Liquidator's powers. The liquidator in a winding up by the court has the following powers:

(a) *Sale.* To sell the real and personal property of the company by public auction or private contract.

(b) *Execution of deeds and documents.* To do all acts and to execute, in the name of the company, all deeds, receipts and other documents.

(c) *Bankruptcy.* To prove, rank and claim in the bankruptcy of any contributory.

(d) *Negotiable instruments.* To draw, accept, make and indorse any bill of exchange or promissory note in the name of the company.

(e) *Borrowing.* To raise on the security of the assets of the company any money requisite.

(f) *Death.* To take out letters of administration to a deceased contributory.

(g) *Agents.* To appoint an agent to do any business which the liquidator is unable to do himself.

(h) *General.* To do all such things as may be necessary for the winding up.

8. Extraordinary powers of liquidator. With the sanction of the court or the committee of inspection, the liquidator also has the following powers:

(a) *Legal proceedings.* To bring or defend any action in the name of the company.

(b) *Carrying on business.* To carry on the business of the company so far as may be necessary for its beneficial winding up.

(c) *Solicitor.* To appoint a solicitor to assist him in the performance of his duties.

(d) *Payment of creditors.* To pay any classes of creditors in full.

(e) *Compromises.* To make any compromise or arrangement with creditors or other persons claiming against the company: and, similarly, to compromise in the case of claims *by* the company.

9. Oppression of minorities. Where there is oppression, *s.* 210 gives an alternative remedy to a winding-up order.

Any member of the company or the Department of Trade and Industry may petition the court for relief in the event of the oppressive conduct of the company's business.

The petitioner must show:

(a) an oppressive course of conduct; and
(b) that the facts justify a winding-up order on the grounds that it would be just and equitable to wind the company up (*see* **3**(f) *above*), but that a winding-up order would be prejudicial to the oppressed persons.

The court may then make such order as it thinks fit.

VOLUNTARY WINDING UP

10. The circumstances. A company may be wound up voluntarily in the following circumstances:

(a) when the period, if any, fixed for the *duration of the company* expires, or the event, if any, occurs, on the occurrence of which the company is by its Articles to be dissolved, and the company in general meeting has passed a resolution requiring the company to be wound up voluntarily;
(b) if the company resolves by *special resolution* that the company be wound up voluntarily;
(c) if the company resolves by *extraordinary resolution* to the effect that it cannot by reason of its liabilities continue its business, and that it is advisable to wind up: *C.A.*, *s.* 278.

A voluntary winding up will be controlled by either the members or the creditors, according to whether the directors are able to make the declaration of solvency. The process of winding up is, in either case, carried out without reference to the court, unless any matter is properly referred to the court.

11. The declaration of solvency. This is a statutory declaration made at a board meeting by the directors or, if more than two, the majority of them, that they have formed the opinion that the company will be able to pay its debts in full within a specified period not exceeding twelve months.

It must be made within the five weeks preceding the date of the passing of the resolution for winding up, and delivered to the Registrar of Companies before that date. It must contain a statement of the company's assets and liabilities at the latest practicable date.

If this declaration is made, the winding up proceeds as a members' voluntary winding up. If it is not made, the winding up proceeds as a creditors' voluntary winding up.

12. Consequences of voluntary winding up. A company must cease to carry on its business (except so far as may be required for the beneficial winding up) from the commencement of the winding up. The corporate powers continue to exist until the company is finally dissolved. But any transfer of shares not made with the sanction of the liquidator, and any alteration in the status of members of the company, will be void.

13. Members' voluntary winding up. The company appoints one or more liquidators in general meeting, and may fix their remuneration. On the appointment of a liquidator, all the powers of the directors cease, except so far as the company in general meeting, or the liquidator, sanctions their continuance.

14. Liquidators. The liquidator of a company is responsible for the process of winding up. In particular, he must ensure that the property of the company is applied in satisfaction of its liabilities. When all liabilities have been satisfied, he must ensure the distribution of the company's property among the members according to their rights and interests. In a members' voluntary winding up, the liquidator has the following powers and duties:

(a) *Payment of creditors.* With the sanction of an *extraordinary resolution* he may pay any class of creditors in full: *s*. 303.

(b) *Compromises.* With the sanction of an *extraordinary resolution*, he may compromise in the case of claims by or against the company: *C.A.*, *s*. 303.

(c) *General.* Without sanction he may exercise any of the powers of the liquidator in a winding up by order of the court, except as to (a) and (b) above: *s*. 303.

(d) *Contributories.* He may settle lists of contributories.

(e) *Calls.* He may make calls on members for amounts unpaid on their shares.

(f) *General meetings.* He may summon general meetings for the purpose of obtaining the extraordinary or special resolutions mentioned in (a), (b) and (g) of this paragraph or for any other purpose he may think fit: *s.* 303. In the event of the winding up continuing for more than one year, the liquidator *must* summon a general meeting at the end of the first year from the commencement of the winding up, and of each succeeding year, and he must lay before the meeting an account of the winding up during the preceding year: *s.* 290.

(g) *Transfer of property to another company.* Where the business of the company being wound up is to be transferred or sold to another company, the liquidator, with the sanction of a special resolution, may receive for the transfer or sale, shares, policies, or other like interests in that other company: *C.A.*, *s.* 287.

(h) *Creditors' meeting.* Where the liquidator is of opinion that the company will not be able to pay its debts within the period specified in the declaration of solvency he must summon a meeting of creditors and must lay before the meeting a statement of the assets and liabilities of the company: *s.* 288.

(i) *Final meeting.* As soon as the affairs of the company are fully wound up, the liquidator must make up an account of the winding up, showing how the winding up has been conducted and how the property of the company has been disposed of. He must then call a general meeting of the company and lay before it, and explain, the account: *s.* 290.

15. Creditors' voluntary winding up. As stated above, where the directors are unable to make the declaration of solvency the winding up will be controlled by the creditors. In these circumstances, the company must cause a meeting of the creditors to be summoned for the day, or the next following day, on which there is to be held the meeting at which the resolution for voluntary winding up is to be proposed. The directors must appoint one of their number to preside over the meeting of creditors, and must lay before this meeting a full statement of the position of the company's affairs. The creditors may appoint a liquidator and a committee of inspection.

CONTRIBUTORIES AND CREDITORS

16. Contributories. The contributories in a winding up are those members who may be liable to contribute towards the discharge of the liabilities of the company. The position of contributories may be summarised as follows:

(a) *Unlimited companies.* In the case of the winding up of an unlimited company, the members are liable to contribute, in proportion to their holdings, to the entire debts and obligations of the company.

(b) *Companies limited by shares:*

 (i) *Fully paid shares.* Members holding fully paid shares are not liable as contributories.

 (ii) *Partly paid shares.* Members holding partly paid shares are liable to the amount unpaid on their shares. Those persons who are members holding partly paid shares at the commencement of winding up are placed on the "A" list of contributories. Those persons who were members and transferred their shares within a year before the commencement of winding up are placed on the "B" list of contributories. A "B" list contributory is called upon only where the present holder defaulted in payment of his call. But a "B" list contributory cannot be made liable in respect of the company's debts incurred after he ceased to be a member.

(c) *Companies limited by guarantee.* In the case of companies limited by guarantee, the members are liable on their guarantees. Contributories are placed on either the "A" list or the "B" list, as in the case of companies limited by shares.

17. Creditors. The position of the company's creditors may be summarised as follows:

(a) *All kinds of debts may be proved.* All debts payable on a contingency, and all claims against the company, present or future, certain or contingent, may be proved against the company. Where the claim does not bear a certain value, a just estimate must be made.

(b) *Preferential payments.* The following debts are paid in priority to all other debts:

 (i) One year's payment of local rates, land tax, income tax, profits tax and purchase tax.

 (ii) Wages and salaries of company servants for services

rendered during the period of four months before the commencement of winding up.

(iii) Accrued holiday remuneration payable to any company servant.

18. Invalid transactions. Winding up affects the validity of certain transactions as follows:

(a) Any disposition of property during the six-month period before the commencement of winding up is *void* if there was the intention to prefer one creditor to another: *C.A., s.* 320.

(b) Any conveyance or assignment by the company of all its property to trustees for the benefit of all its creditors is *void: s.* 320.

(c) A floating charge created within twelve months of the commencement of the winding up to secure past debts is invalid unless it is proved that the company was solvent at the time of its creation: *s.* 322.

(d) The liquidator, with the leave of the court, may disclaim onerous property. Any person suffering loss in connection with a disclaimer may prove in the winding up as if he were a creditor.

19. Distribution of the company's assets. After realising the company's assets, the liquidator must apply the moneys raised as follows:

(a) The payment of secured creditors with fixed charges, unless they have sold the security and paid themselves.

(b) The costs of winding up, including the liquidator's remuneration.

(c) The payment of preferred debts.

(d) The payment of creditors with floating charges.

(e) The payment of unsecured creditors.

(f) The payment of debts due to members as members.

(g) Repayment of money invested in the company by its members.

(h) Where there is any surplus, it is distributed proportionately among the members.

RECONSTRUCTION AND AMALGAMATION

20. Reconstruction and amalgamation. A company may sometimes desire to reorganise its structure, or to amalgamate with another company. (The term "reconstruction" is sometimes used to cover both processes.)

Reconstruction may take the forms set out below.

21. Reconstruction under s. 287. Where a company is being wound up voluntarily, the liquidator may be authorised (by special resolution) to sell the business in return for shares in another company. Such shares are then distributed among the members of the company being wound up.

If the winding up is a creditors' voluntary winding up, such scheme requires the sanction of the court, or committee of inspection.

Dissenting members may within seven days of the resolution require the liquidator to abandon the scheme or to purchase their shares.

NOTE: Where a substantial reorganisation of a company's business is desired, this method may be chosen by the directors who will therefore recommend the members to vote for winding up and to instruct the liquidator to execute the scheme outlined by the directors. The directors will then promote a new company, which will contract with the liquidator to buy the business of the old company and to pay for it with an issue of shares.

22. Schemes of arrangement under C.A., ss. 206 to 208. Where a company wishes to compromise with creditors, or to vary the rights of a class of shareholders, it may apply to the court for assistance. The court may then direct that a meeting of the creditors or members concerned be held and that if a majority in number representing three-fourths in value of those present and voting approve, the scheme shall become binding.

NOTE: This scheme can be used for total reconstruction of the company, *e.g.* where the court orders dissolution (without winding up) of an existing company and transfers its undertaking to a new company, in which members and creditors shall have such rights as are agreed and sanctioned by the court.

23. Amalgamation by share purchase. One company may make a take-over bid for another, offering to buy all the shares of members in the company to be taken over. Where such offer is accepted by the holders of 90% in value within four months, the purchaser may serve a notice on the holders of the remaining shares, who are then compelled to sell: *C.A.*, *s.* 209.

PROGRESS TEST 18

1. What is the purpose of winding up? In what ways, other than winding up, may a company be dissolved? **(1)**

2. In what circumstances will the court make an order for the winding up of a company? **(3)**

3. What are the duties and powers of (*a*) the official reciever and (*b*) the liquidator, in a compulsory winding up? **(5–8)**

4. What action can be taken by an oppressed minority of shareholders who do not want the company to be wound up? **(9)**

5. What is the importance of (*a*) the statement of affairs, and (*b*) the declaration of solvency? **(4, 11)**

6. In what circumstances may a company be wound up voluntarily? **(10)**

7. What are the powers and duties of a liquidator in a voluntary winding up? **(14)**

8. Explain the position of contributories and creditors in a winding up. **(16, 17)**

9. In what order should the company's assets be distributed after realisation? **(19)**

10. Summarise the ways in which reconstruction of a company can be effected. **(20–23)**

PART FOUR

INDUSTRIAL LAW

CHAPTER XIX

THE LAW OF MASTER AND SERVANT

THE CONTRACT OF SERVICE

1. The relationship of master and servant. The relationship between master and servant or, to use the modern terminology, employer and employee, is entirely voluntary. In *Nokes* v. *Doncaster Amalgamated Collieries, Ltd.* (1940), it was argued that a statute gave a power to transfer the employees of one company into the service of another company without any need to obtain the consent of the employees affected. In firmly rejecting this argument, Lord Atkin said: "I confess it appears to me astonishing that apart from over-riding questions of public welfare, power should be given to a court or to anyone else to transfer a man without his knowledge and possibly against his will, from the service of one person to the service of another. I had fancied that ingrained in the personal status of a citizen under our laws was the right to choose for himself whom he would serve and that this right of choice constituted the main difference between a servant and a serf." The voluntary nature of the relationship between master and servant keeps it within the scope of the general law of contract, the agreement being called the *contract of service*.

The essential characteristic of a contract of service is the consideration given by the employee, namely a promise to give service. The concept of service must not be confused with that of work. It is necessary to look at the terms of the contract to discover what is involved by the employee's promise to give service. In *Gorse* v. *Durham County Council* (1971), it was held that a schoolteacher was entitled to his salary for the three and a half days during which he was under temporary suspension from work.

2. The "control" test.

It sometimes becomes necessary to determine the question whether a contract is one of service or for services. This reflects the distinction between the servant and the independent contractor. The distinction is always important, because the legal incidents to the contract of service are quite different from the incidents to the contract for services. Usually it is not difficult to say whether a particular contract to do work is a contract of service or a contract for services, but sometimes it is difficult.

In *Yewens* v. *Nokes* (1880), Bramwell, L. J., said that: "A servant is a person subject to the command of his master as to the manner in which he shall do his work." This statement indicates that the control test is decisive as to whether a person is a servant or an independent contractor. This test is, however, difficult to apply in cases where the servant is a highly-qualified professional man, or in other cases where the employer has little or no power to control the manner in which the work is done. Nevertheless, in these circumstances, the relationship may still be one of master and servant.

Morren v. *Swinton B. C.* (1965): a local authority, wishing to have certain sewerage works carried out, appointed an independent consultant engineer to supervise the execution of the works. The agreement between the local authority and the consultant engineer provided that the local authority should appoint and pay a resident engineer, to be approved by the consultant, to supervise the works under the consultant's instructions. Accordingly, the local authority, with the approval of the consultant, appointed a resident engineer at a salary. The local authority had the right to dismiss him, he was paid subsistence allowance, he was paid for holidays, employer's national insurance contributions were paid in regard to him and there was a provision for a one-month period of notice. HELD: the resident engineer was employed by the local authority under a contract of service (not a contract for services) notwithstanding that his instructions were given to him by the consultant engineer.

Ready Mixed Concrete, Ltd. v. *Minister of Pensions and National Insurance* (1968): a company, whose business was the making and selling of concrete, operated a system of delivery by owner-drivers. In May, 1965, one Latimer entered into a contract with the company for the carriage of concrete. He obtained his lorry by means of a hire-purchase agreement and arranged for it to be painted in the company's colours. The contract between the company and Latimer contained a declaration that Latimer was an independent contractor and provided as follows: (i) that the lorry was to be available exclusively to the company at all times; (ii) that the company could require Latimer to drive the lorry himself for the maximum hours permitted by law; (iii) that Latimer had a restricted right to employ relief drivers; (iv) that Latimer should maintain the lorry and pay all running costs; (v) that the company should pay Latimer at fixed rates for the concrete carried subject to a fixed minimum annual total; (vi) that Latimer should wear the company's uniform and (vii) that he should carry out all reasonable instructions "as if he were an employee of the company." HELD: the contract was one of carriage and not of service.

In *Morren* v. *Swinton B. C.*, Lord Parker, C.J., said: "The cases have over and over again stressed the importance of the factor of superintendence and control, but that it is not the determining test is quite clear. In *Cassidy* v. *Minister of Health*, Somervell, L.J., referred to this matter, and instanced as did Denning, L.J., in the later case of *Stevenson, Jordan & Harrison, Ltd.* v. *Macdonald & Evans*, that clearly superintendence and control cannot be the decisive test when one is dealing with a professional man, or a man of some particular skill and experience. Incidences of that have been given in the form of a master of a ship, an engine driver, a professional architect or, as in this case, a consulting engineer. In such cases there can be no question of the employer telling him how to do the work; therefore, the absence of control and direction in that sense can be of little, if any, use as a test." But when a professional man in private practice agrees to give his professional services, the relation between him and his client is not one of servant and master: *Clayton* v. *Woodman, Ltd.* (1962).

In *Cassidy* v. *Minister of Health* (1951), a patient went into hospital for surgical treatment to cure the stiffness of his third and fourth fingers of his left hand. After the operation he came away with four stiff fingers, his hand being practically useless. It was held by the Court of Appeal that the *prima facie* case of negligence on the part of the surgeons and nurses had not been rebutted and that the defendant was liable. Somervell and Singleton, L.JJ., decided on the footing of vicarious liability flowing from the fact that there was a contract of service between each of the surgeons and each of the nurses, on the one hand, and the hospital authority on the other. (Denning, L.J., was in agreement with the other two judges, but he based his decision on other grounds.)

3. Attributes other than "control." Since the control test is sometimes of little or no value, it becomes necessary to inquire further into the nature of the master and servant relationship to discover whether there are any other attributes besides control which are peculiar to the contract of service and may, accordingly, provide a more satisfactory test. In this connection, there are two valuable decisions of Dixon, J., the distinguished Australian judge, which were both cited with approval by MacKenna, J., in *Ready Mixed Concrete, Ltd.* v. *Minister of Pensions* (1968).

The first of these cases is *Queensland Stations Pty., Ltd.* v. *Federal Comr. of Taxation* (1945), where a drover was employed under a written contract to drive 317 cattle to a destination. By this contract, he was obliged to obey and carry out all lawful instructions and to use the whole of his time, his energy and ability, in the careful driving of the animals, that he should provide at his own expense all men, plant and horses required for the operation, and that he should be paid at a rate per head of cattle delivered safely. It was held that the drover was an independent contractor. Dixon, J., said: "There is, of course, nothing to prevent a drover and his client forming the relation of employee and employer. But whether they do so must depend on the facts. In considering the facts it is a mistake to treat as decisive a reservation of control over the manner in which the droving is performed and the cattle are handled. For instance in the present case the circumstances that the drover agrees to obey and carry out all lawful instructions cannot outweigh the countervailling considerations which are found in the employment by him of servants of his own, the provision of horses, equipment, plant, rations, and a remuneration at a rate per head delivered."

The second Australian case approved by MacKenna, J., in the *Ready Mixed Concrete* case is *Humberstone* v. *Northern Timber Mills* (1949). In this case, the court had to decide whether the owner-driver of a truck was a servant under a contract of service or whether he was an independent contractor. For some years, the truck driver had taken his truck at about the same time each day to a factory, where he had been given goods to carry away and deliver to various customers. He carried on delivering goods each day until about the same time in the evening when he finished work. He maintained the truck himself and supplied the fuel, and was paid for goods carried at a rate per car-mile. It was held that the truck owner-driver was an independent contractor. Dixon, J., said: "The question is not whether in practice the work was in fact done subject to a direction and control exercised by an actual supervision or whether an actual supervision was possible but whether ultimate authority over the man in the performance of his work resided in the employer so that he was subject to the latter's order and directions. In the present case the contract by the deceased was to provide not merely his own labour but the use of heavy mechanised transport, driven by power, which he maintained and fuelled for the purpose. The most important part of the work to be performed by his own labour consisted in the operation of his own motor truck and the essential part of the service for which the respondents contracted was the transportation of their goods by the mechanical means he thus supplied. The essence of a contract of service is the supply of the work and skill of a man. But the emphasis in the case of the present contract is on mechanical traction. This was to be done by his own property in his own possession and control. There is no ground for imputing to the parties a common intention that in all the management and control of his own vehicle, in all the ways in which he used it for the purpose of carrying their goods, he should be subject to the commands of the respondents. In essence it appears to me to have been an independent contract."

In the *Macdonald & Evans case*, Denning, L. J., said: "One feature which seems to run through the instances is that, under a contract of service, a man is employed as part of the business, and his work is done as an integral part of the business; whereas, under a contract for services, his work, although done for the business, is not integrated into it but is only accessory to it." In a more recent case, Lord Denning said that "the test of being a servant does not rest nowadays on submission to orders. It depends on whether the person is part and parcel of the organisation": *Bank voor Handel en Scheepvaart N.V.* v. *Slatford* (1953).

Perhaps the best comment is that of Atiyah in a passage in

his *Vicarious Liability in the Law of Torts*, which was cited with approval in *C.I.T.B.* v. *Labour Force, Ltd.* (1970). He said that it is not possible to lay down "a number of conditions which are both necessary to, and sufficient for, the existence of a contract of service. The most that can profitably be done is to examine all the possible factors which have been referred to in these cases as bearing on the nature of the relationship between the parties concerned. Clearly not all of these factors will be relevant in all cases, or have the same weight in all cases. Equally clearly no magic formula can be propounded for determining which factors should, in any given case, be treated as the determining ones. The plain fact is that in a large number of cases the court can only perform a balancing operation, weighing up the factors which point in one direction and balancing them against those pointing in the opposite direction. In the nature of things it is not to be expected that this operation can be performed with scientific accuracy."

4. Terms of the contract of service. The parties to a contract of service seldom express completely the terms of their contract at the time they make it. The common law therefore implies into every contract of service a number of duties, for example, the duty of competence, the duty of obedience and the duty not to break confidence, on the part of the servant. These implied duties are probably best regarded as various aspects, conveniently separated, of a general duty of fidelity owed to the master.

The vast majority of contracts of employment are affected by collective agreements between workers' associations and employers. The relevant details from the collective agreement are incorporated into the individual contracts of employment of all employees concerned: *National Coal Board* v. *Galley* (1958).

Rights and duties under a contract of service may be ascertained from the terms, express or implied, of the contract. The terms relating to the particular nature of the work involved will usually be express and, in addition to these, there are other terms which will always be implied at common law in the absence of agreement to the contrary. Further, the agreement as reached by the parties is subject to certain important statutory controls.

DUTIES OF THE EMPLOYER

5. Remuneration. It is the duty of the employer to pay his employee according to the terms of the contract of service. But the following statutes are designed to protect the interests of employees.

(a) The *Truck Acts*, 1831–1940. These Acts apply to *workmen* only, *i.e.* servants engaged in *manual* labour. The *Truck Acts* provide that a contract of service between an employer and a workman is *illegal* and null where there is a term to the effect that wages shall be paid otherwise than in current coin of the realm (including banknotes), and where there is a term purporting to govern the manner in which wages shall be spent. In other words, it is an employer's statutory duty to pay his workmen fully in cash. He may not even deduct previous overpayments of wages.

EXCEPTIONS
  (i) *The 1831 Act* permits an employer to deduct the cost of food supplied and eaten on his premises, medical attention, tools used by miners and the rent of dwellings occupied by the workman.
 (ii) *Statutory deductions.* An employer must deduct income tax and National Insurance contributions.
(iii) *Independent contract.* There is nothing to prevent employer and employee from entering a separate contract whereby the workman undertakes to pay the employer for services or goods, provided that the amount is not directly deducted, but is paid by the workman from his full pay.
 (iv) *Debts to third parties.* An employer may, *at the request of the workman*, deduct from wages a debt to a third party owed by the workman. The maximum deductible is one-third of the wages. Thus, where there is a contributory pension or sick fund, the employer may deduct from wages provided payment is made to a third party, *e.g.* a trustee, and the workman has agreed to the deduction.
  (v) *Fines.* An employer may deduct a fair and reasonable amount where there has been some act or omission on the part of the workman likely to cause loss to the employer. But this is permitted only where provision for the fine is made in a *contract in writing* signed by the workman or where there is a notice to this effect in some prominent and easily accessible place. Similar provisions may be made

where a workman spoils materials or goods by bad work-
manship.

(b) The *Payment of Wages Act*, 1960, amends the *Truck
Acts* by providing that, in certain specified circumstances,
payments of wages to a *workman* may be made (i) into the
workman's bank account, (ii) by money order, (iii) by postal
order, (iv) by cheque drawn by the employer.

But payment in these four ways may be made only in the
circumstances provided in the Act of 1960, in particular:

(i) The workman must make a *written request* for payment to
be made in one of these ways and the employer must have
expressed his agreement to the request.

(ii) The employer must give with each payment a *written
notice* setting out any deductions that have been made.

(iii) *No charge or deduction* may be made where payment is
made as allowed by the Act.

(The Act also provides that where a workman is absent from
his usual place of work and the employer believes that this is
due to sickness or that the workman is away on some duty,
payment may be made by postal order unless the workman
objects in writing.)

(c) The *Wages Councils Act*, 1959, consolidates the law
relating to wages councils. The Secretary of State may, by a
wages council order, establish a wages council in any particular
trade or industry where there is no adequate regulation of the
payment of workers. The Secretary of State may decide to
make a wages council order on his own initiative, or he may do
so on the recommendation of a Commission of Inquiry.

It is the *function* of a wages council to make proposals to the
Secretary of State regarding remuneration (including holiday
pay) of the workers of the particular trade or industry with
which it is concerned. The Secretary of State is empowered to
make an order in the terms of any proposal of a wages council,
fixing wages or holidays for a particular trade or industry:
where such an order is made, employers are bound by it, and,
in the event of default, will be liable (i) to a fine and (ii) to pay
workers the amount by which they have been underpaid.

6. Written statement of terms. Although the contract of
employment is not required to be in writing at the time
of making it, by the *Contracts of Employment Act*, 1963, the

employer is under a duty to provide his employee with written particulars of certain of the more important terms of the contract. Section 4, as amended by the *Industrial Relations Act*, 1971, provides as follows.

Not later than 30 weeks after the beginning of an employee's period of employment with an employer, the employer must give to the employee a written statement identifying the parties, specifying the date when the employment began, and giving the following particulars of the terms of employment as at a specified date not more than one week before the statement is given, that is:

(a) the scale or rate of remuneration, or the method of calculating remuneration;

(b) the intervals at which the remuneration is paid;

(c) any terms and conditions relating to hours of work;

(d) any terms and conditions relating to: (i) entitlement to holidays, including public holidays, and holiday pay, (ii) incapacity for work due to sickness or injury, including any provisions for sick pay, (iii) pensions and pension schemes; and

(e) the length of notice which the employee is obliged to give and entitled to receive to determine his contract of employment.

(Section 4 of the 1963 Act is set out in amended form in Schedule 2 of the *Industrial Relations Act*, 1971.)

By *s.* 20(2) of the *Industrial Relations Act*, 1971, it is provided that every statement of terms of employment given to an employee under *s.* 4 of the 1963 Act must include a note:

(a) indicating the nature of the employee's rights under *s.* 5 of the 1971 Act, including where an agency shop agreement or an approved closed shop agreement is in force which applies to him, the effect of that agreement on those rights (*s.* 5 provides that every worker shall, as between himself and his employer, have the following rights: (i) the right to be a member of the trade union of his choice; (ii) subject to the provisions of an agency shop or an approved closed shop, the right if he so desires to be a member of no trade union or to refuse to be a member of any particular trade union; (iii) where he is a member of a trade union, the right at any appropriate

time, to take part in the activities of the trade union and
the right to hold office in the union); and
- (b) specifying by description or otherwise a person to whom
the employee can apply for the purpose of seeking re-
dress of any grievance relating to his employment, and
the manner in which any such application should be
made; and
- (c) either explaining the steps consequent upon any such
application or referring to a document which is reasonably accessible to the employee and which explains
those steps.

7. The provision of work. Provided an employer continues
to pay his employee, he is not generally bound to provide work
for him: *Turner* v. *Sawdon* (1901).

EXCEPTIONS
- (a) *Commission.* Where payment is made on a commission
basis, there is usually an implied term to the effect that the
employer will provide work to enable the employee to earn
payment: *Turner* v. *Goldsmith* (1891).
- (b) *Professional reputation.* Where an employee needs to be
engaged in work in order to maintain or build a reputation,
the employer will be bound to provide suitable work if the
contract provides for payment to be made by way of *salary*.
This rule applies, for example, to journalists and actors.
See *Clayton and Waller* v. *Oliver* (1930).

8. Indemnity. The employee is entitled to be indemnified
by his employer against expenses and liabilities incurred in the
proper course of the employment. But where an employee
incurs liability for an unlawful act he will be liable if he knew
that the act was unlawful.

9. Insurance: statutory duties. The employer must pay his
own and his employee's contributions under the *National
Insurance Act*, 1965, and the *National Insurance (Industrial
Injuries) Act*, 1966. The employer pays the contributions and
is then entitled to recover the employee's contribution by
deduction from pay. *See* XXI, XXII.

10. Safe system of work. The employer has a common
law duty to make *reasonable* provision for the safety of his
employees. Where an employer fails in this duty and, as a
result, the employee is injured, the employer will have com-

mitted the tort of *negligence*. In *Wilson's and Clyde Coal Co. Ltd.* v. *English*, a House of Lords case, this duty was explained by Lord Wright as: "*a duty which rests on the employer and which is personal to the employer, to take reasonable care for the safety of his workmen, whether the employer be an individual, a firm, or a company, and whether or not the employer takes any share in the conduct of operations.*"

In the same speech it was said that the duty is threefold: the provision of (a) a competent staff, (b) adequate material, and (c) a proper system and effective supervision. These three aspects should now be considered separately.

(a) *The duty to provide a competent staff.* An employer should not employ (or continue to employ) a person at a particular task for which he is not qualified or insufficiently experienced where to do so would possibly endanger his fellow employees, *e.g.* to employ a colliery manager who has no knowledge of the dangers of carbon monoxide has been held to be a breach of this duty: *Black* v. *Fife Coal Co. Ltd.* (1912). There was also a breach of this duty where there was continued employment of a workman who habitually indulged in horseplay: *Hudson* v. *Ridge Manufacturing Co. Ltd.* (1957).

(b) *The duty to provide adequate material, premises and plant.* Where an employee is injured because of some defect in materials, equipment or plant in circumstances where the employer did not take reasonable care to make these things safe, the employee will have an action in negligence against the employer. Similarly, the employer will be liable if injury is caused by some defect in his premises, provided it is shown that he did not take *reasonable* care, *e.g.* where a factory was flooded and the subsiding waters left an oily film over the floors, and the employer ordered sand and sawdust to be spread, it was held that there was no breach of the duty of care when an employee slipped and fell on an untreated part of the floor: *Latimer* v. *A.E.C. Ltd.* (1959).

(c) *The duty to provide a proper system and effective supervision.* A system of work is a practice which is permanent and continuous and not merely a method which is casual and emerging in the day's work. It may include the physical lay-out of the job, the sequence in which the work is carried out, the provisions of warnings and notices, and the issue of special instructions. An employer's duty under this head is to take reasonable care for the safety of his employees. In order to discover whether reasonable care was or was not taken in any case, the court will consider all the relevant facts.

Clifford v. *Challen & Son Ltd*. (1951): the work in which an employee was engaged involved sticking pieces of wool together with a synthetic glue. It was well known that this glue would cause dermatitis if allowed to dry on the skin. A Government notice was displayed in the workshop warning of the danger and setting out the precautionary measures that were necessary, *i.e.* the use of a protective cream. The employer kept a stock of this cream in the store to which the men had access but none in the workshop, but the foreman did nothing to encourage or enforce the use of the cream. An employee contracted dermatitis through using the glue. HELD: the protective cream should have been provided in the workshop itself, and an effective system established to ensure the use of it. The employer was, therefore, in breach of his duty to the employee. But the employee was guilty of contributory negligence, and the amount of damages awarded was a half of the full measure.

General Cleaning Contractors Ltd. v. *Christmas* (1952): an employee of the company was a window cleaner of considerable experience. The employer made safety belts available, but the employee did not use these while cleaning the windows of the Caledonian Club because there were no fittings to which they could be attached. In consequence, the employee fell and was injured when a sash fell on his hand. HELD: the employer should have provided wedges to prevent sashes from falling, and should have instructed the employee how to test for dangerously loose sashes. The employer was, therefore, in breach of his duty to provide a safe system of work.

11. References. An employer is *not* under a duty to provide his employee with a reference or testimonial *unless* there is a term in the contract of service that this should be done. Thus, where an employer refuses to give a reference or testimonial, the employee usually has no remedy.

Where, however, an employer does give a reference or testimonial, he has a duty not to defame his employee. This duty arises out of the law of tort regarding libel and slander. The test as to whether a statement is defamatory is *whether the words tend to lower the plaintiff in the estimation of right-thinking members of society generally*. Where a defamatory statement is oral, it is *slander*, and where it is made in writing, it is *libel*. If a reference or testimonial contains a defamatory statement, the employee to whom it refers will succeed against the employer in an action for the tort of defamation (libel or slander) unless the employer can raise one of the following defences:

(a) *Justification.* This defence succeeds if the employer can prove that the statement was substantially true.

(b) *Qualified privilege.* Where an employer gives a reference or testimonial to another person who has a proper interest in the contents, *e.g.* a potential employer of the employee concerned, the statement is subject to what is known as *qualified privilege.* This means that the employer will not be in breach of his duty to the employee if the statement is not entirely true provided it was not made with *malice.* Malice will be proved (i) where the employer did not believe that the statement was true, or (ii) where the employer made a false statement with ill-will, or (iii) where the employer published the statement to a person with no justifiable interest in it.

DUTIES OF THE EMPLOYEE

12. Personal service. The employee's duty is to render *personal* service according to the terms of the contract. He may not delegate his duty without the consent of the employer.

13. Obedience. It is the duty of the employee to obey his employer's lawful orders. Lawful orders are those orders given by the employer within the terms of the contract of employment and which are neither illegal nor contrary to public policy. Where an employer gives an order which is outside the scope of the contract, the employee is entitled to refuse to obey. In *Pryce* v. *Mouat* (1862) it was held that a sales representative who had been ordered to take part in the manufacturing process of his employer's goods was entitled to refuse.

Where an employee's refusal to obey a lawful order indicates an intention on his part to abandon the contract, the employer will be entitled to dismiss him without notice. Where, however, the refusal to obey does not constitute abandonment of contract, the employer will not be entitled to dismiss the employee summarily: *Laws* v. *London Chronicle* (1959).

14. Confidential information. The skills and abilities of the employee are his exclusive property to use as and where he wishes. Even the employer who has given an employee his training, or the necessary experience to acquire and develop skills, has no special claim to the benefit of those skills. But, on the other hand, there are special circumstances where particular aspects of the employee's skill and knowledge may be said to belong to the employer. For example, where the employee possesses information connected with the employer's trade secrets or lists of customers, the employee may not use this information freely. The employee has a duty to respect his employer's confidential information. This duty continues after the contract of service has been discharged; indeed, it is usually only at this stage that the employee may be tempted to make use of the confidential information.

Cranleigh v. *Bryant* (1964): the defendant was the managing director of a company engaged in the manufacture of swimming pools. The defendant designed swimming pools for his employer and, during the course of this work, he had learnt of a foreign patent but had not passed this information to his employer. Instead, he set up a company of his own to exploit the foreign patent, advertising a swimming pool which incorporated certain design features of the pool manufactured by the employer. HELD: the employee was in breach of his duty of confidence in making use of the design features already used by the employer and also he was in breach of his duty of confidence in buying and exploiting the foreign patent without informing the employer. The court took the view that it was not relevant that the design features of the employer's pool were very simple and that the foreign patent was available to any member of the public who cared to look for it at the Patent Office. The defendant was in a special position in that he knew how best to use the design features involved, and where to buy suitable materials for the manufacture of pools of this type. These pieces of information were the trade secrets of the employer and the employee was not entitled to make use of them for his own purposes.

Hivac v. *Park Royal Scientific Instruments, Ltd.* (1946): Hivac had a monopoly in the manufacture of miniature valves for hearing aids and Park Royal began to manufacture them also. Park Royal persuaded some of Hivac's employees to come over to work for them in their free time. The effect of this part-time work was to destroy Hivac's monopoly. Hivac accordingly applied for an injunction to restrain Park Royal from inducing their employees to break their contracts of employment. HELD: Hivac were entitled to the injunction.

15. General duty of fidelity. There is a general duty of fidelity imposed on the employee, and this duty will be extended by the courts to meet the circumstances of any case. In *Sinclair* v. *Neighbour* (1967), for example, the manager of a betting shop took £15 from the till to pay for his own gambling, having left his wallet at home. He put an I.O.U. into the till and replaced the money the next day. It was held that the employee's action was in breach of his contract of employment even though he had not been expressly forbidden to borrow from the till. The main point was that he knew that his employer would not approve.

16. Patents, inventions and copyrights. Where a patent, an invention or a copyright represents work done by an employee under a contract of employment, then the patent, invention or copyright is industrial information, the property of the employer. It does not belong to the employee in these circumstances. Where, under his contract of employment, an employee is required to engage in scientific research or creative writing, there should be a clause in the contract to govern the ownership of patents, inventions or copyright arising out of the employee's work. Failing such a clause, the property in an invention or copyright usually passes to the employer if it is connected with the employee's employment. The question whether the employee may use his invention or copyright without being in breach of confidence depends upon the wording of any specific clause governing the matter. In *British Celanese* v. *Moncrieff* (1948), the Court of Appeal upheld a clause in a contract of service by which the employee undertook to pass on all his discoveries to his employer, who could then use these discoveries making no further payment to the employee.

Where an employee makes a technical or scientific discovery in circumstances where the contract of employment does not require him to do the work involved, there is no hard-and-fast rule as to whether the invention belongs to the employer or the employee. The court will approach such problems on the general basis of the employee's duty of good faith. In *British Syphon Co., Ltd.* v. *Homewood* (1956), an employee invented a new kind of low-pressure syphon. Although the contract did not require him to do the research work involved, he was engaged as a technical adviser. The test question propounded by Roxburgh, J., was: "Would it be consistent with good faith, as between master and servant, that he should in that position be entitled to make some invention in relation to a matter concerning a part of the plaintiff's business and either keep it from his employer or even sell it to a rival?" It was held that the invention belonged to the employer. In *Triplex Safety Glass Co.* v. *Scorah* (1938), the employee had been specifically requested to make a particular invention as part of his duties under his contract of employment. It was held that any invention made by the employee should belong to the employer.

17. Indemnity. Where a servant, in the normal course of his duties, causes injury or loss to a third person through want of care in the performance of his duties, the master will usually be vicariously liable. Where the third party succeeds against the master, the servant is under a duty to give an indemnity. In practice, the employee is seldom sued personally on the indemnity for he is seldom a substantial defendant. A prudent employer will insure against this kind of vicarious liability.

DISCHARGE OF CONTRACT OF SERVICE

18. General law. The rights and obligations under a contract of service may be brought to an end in the same ways as in the case of any other kind of contract: *see* VII. It is necessary, however, to examine the application of the general law of discharge of contracts to this particular class of contract.

19. Notice. A contract of service may be terminated by either party giving due notice to the other. The *Contracts of Employment Act*, 1963, lays down certain minimum periods of notice, but the parties may, by express or implied term in the contract of employment, provide for a longer period. The Act provides that no contractual term can take effect to reduce the statutory minimum period of notice, but an employee may accept payment in lieu of notice. The 1963 Act, as amended by the *Industrial Relations Act*, 1971, requires employers to give the following *minimum* periods of notice to employees who have been continuously employed for thirteen weeks or more:

(a) not less than one week's notice if the period of continuous employment is less than two years, and

  (b) not less than two weeks' notice if the period of continuous
employment is two years or more but less than five
years, and

  (c) not less than four weeks' notice if the period of continuous employment is five years or more but less than
ten years, and

  (d) not less than six weeks' notice if the period of continuous employment is ten years or more but less than
fifteen years, and

  (e) not less than eight weeks' notice if the period of continuous employment is fifteen years or more.

It is also provided that the notice to be given by an employee
who has been continuously employed for thirteen weeks or
more to terminate his contract of employment must not be less
than one week.

NOTE: Any contractual term, express or implied, which does not
contravene the *Contracts of Employment Act*, 1963, will be binding. Where there is no express term as to notice, there may be
an implied term arising from the circumstances of the case, *i.e.*
the status of the employee, the custom of the trade or profession, the manner in which payment was made. An employer
may always choose to give his employee wages (or salary) in
lieu of notice.

20. Termination without notice. Summary dismissal of the
employee or summary departure on the part of the employee
will bring the contract to an end. This holds true whether or
not the dismissal or departure in any case is in breach of
contract. Where there is a breach, the remedy available to the
innocent party is damages only. Where summary dismissal or
summary departure is in breach of contract, there has been an
abandonment of contract, which gives the other party the right
to elect to treat the contract at an end. In *Marriott* v. *Oxford &
District Co-operative Society* (1969), Lord Parker, C. J., applying
the general law of contract, said that unlawful dismissal (*i.e.*
summary dismissal in breach of contract) "would not automatically determine the contract of employment, though it
would be determination as soon as the employee accepted that
repudiation." The House of Lords took a similar view in
General Billposting Co. v. *Atkinson* (1909), in which it was held
that the unlawful dismissal of an employee entitled that
employee to treat the contract as being at an end and, ac-

cordingly, the restrictive promises given in the contract were no longer effective. Where, however, the employer is justified in dismissing his employee without notice, no breach of contract is involved.

Pepper v. *Webb* (1969): in January 1967, the wife of a house owner engaged a gardener on behalf of her husband. The gardener's hours of work on Saturdays were from 8 a.m. to 12 noon. The gardener was paid weekly and provided with a rent-free cottage. At first, the employer and his wife were pleased with the gardener's work, but soon after being engaged he ceased to give satisfaction. On Saturday, 10 June, 1967, between 9 a.m. and 10 a.m., the gardener was told by the employer's wife to put in some plants. She said that if he did not put them in at once they would die. The gardener replied, "I am leaving at 12 o'clock; you can do what you like about them. If you don't like it you can give me notice." Just before 12 noon the employer spoke to the gardener saying that the job would only take half an hour. The gardener replied, "I couldn't care less about your bloody greenhouse and your sodding garden," and walked off. The employer then dismissed the gardener immediately, without notice or wages in lieu. The gardener brought this action for damages for wrongful dismissal. HELD: the employee had repudiated his contract of service by his refusal to obey the lawful and reasonable order to put in the plants, by his statement that he did not care about the grounds and greenhouse, and by his insolence to the employer.

21. Remedies. The remedies for breach of contract of employment are, generally, damages at common law and, in appropriate circumstances, injunction in equity. These two types of remedy should be considered separately.

(a) *Common law remedies:* the right to treat the contract of employment as repudiated in cases where the breach is, in effect, an abandonment of contract, has been discussed above (VII, **14–16**) but whether the breach leads to the discharge of contract or not, the party not in breach may always bring an action for damages. Where a contract of employment has been broken the usual rules for measure of damages are applied VII, **22–24**. The *Contracts of Employment Act*, 1963, *s.* 3., effectively incorporates the statutory minimum periods of notice into each contract of service and will, accordingly, be taken into account when damages for breach of contract against an employer are assessed.

Where an employee absents himself from his place of work in breach of contract, the measure of damages against him will be the cost of paying a substitute—not the commercial loss caused by his absence: *National Coal Board* v. *Galley* (1958).

(b) *Equitable remedies:* the court will never award specific performance against an employee who is in breach of his contract of employment. In proper circumstances, however, an injunction may be awarded to restrain the breach of a negative term, usually where the employee promises not to work for another employer during a specified period. *See* VII, **43.**

Page One Records, Ltd. v. *Britton* (1967): in 1966 a pop group known as The Troggs entered into a written agreement with the plaintiffs by which the plaintiffs agreed to manage the affairs of the group for a term of five years. It was a term of this agreement that The Troggs would not engage any other person to act as manager or agent for them and that they would not themselves act in such a capacity. In 1967, The Troggs claimed to be entitled to determine the contract on the grounds of breach by the plaintiffs. The court found, on the evidence, that The Troggs had not made out a *prima facie* case to justify their treating the agreement as repudiated. The plaintiffs brought this action, claiming an interlocutory injunction to restrain The Troggs from engaging another manager. HELD: the effect of an interlocutory injunction would be to compel The Troggs to continue to employ the plaintiffs and would be equivalent to enforcing the performance of a contract for personal services; accordingly, the interlocutory injunction was refused.

UNFAIR DISMISSAL

22. A new concept. A concept known as unfair dismissal has been introduced by the *Industrial Relations Act,* 1971. A worker who is able to show that he was dismissed, and that the dismissal was not in accordance with equity and the substantial merits of the case, will be able to claim compensation from his employer according to the new rules. This rule is quite independent of those rules governing minimum periods of notice, whether statutory or otherwise. The employee who claims that he has been unfairly dismissed must bring his action before an industrial tribunal. In this action, he is called "the claimant." An appeal will lie from the decisions of the industrial tribunal on points of law only.

23. The action for unfair dismissal. The provisions of the 1971 Act envisage three stages in an action for unfair dismissal:

(a) The claimant must prove that he was *dismissed* within the meaning of the Act.

(b) The employer must show what was the reason for the dismissal and that the reason was one of those specified in the Act.

(c) The claimant must show that, in the circumstances, the employer acted *unreasonably* in treating the reason as sufficient for dismissal. This question is decided in accordance with equity and the substantial merits of the case.

These three stages should be considered separately.

24. Dismissal. The definition of "dismissal" contained in *s.* 23 of the 1971 Act is wider than the concept of dismissal at common law. For the purposes of the unfair dismissal provisions, an employee will be taken to be dismissed by his employer if the contract under which he is employed is terminated by the employer whether it is terminated by notice or without notice, or where under that contract he is employed for a fixed term and that term expires without being renewed. The burden of proving dismissal lies upon the claimant.

25. The reason for dismissal. If the employer wishes to defend himself against a claim for unfair dismissal, *s.* 24 requires him to show:

(a) what was the reason for the dismissal, *and*

(b) that the reason was

(i) related to the capability or qualifications of the employee for performing work of the kind which he was employed to do, *or*

(ii) related to the conduct of the employee, *or*

(iii) that the employee was redundant, *or*

(iv) that the employee could not continue to work in the position which he held without contravention of a statutory duty, *or*

  (v) some other substantial reason of a kind such as to justify
    the dismissal of an employee holding the position which
    the claimant held.

The dismissal will be treated as unfair at this stage of the
action in any of the following circumstances:

  (a) The employer fails to discharge the burden of proving
    that the reason for the dismissal was one of those specified
    above: *s.* 24(1).
  (b) The reason (or, if more than one, the principal reason)
    was that the employee had exercised his rights under
    s. 5(1): *s.* 24(4). This provision applies even in cases
    where the reason for the dismissal was redundancy:
    s. 24(5). (For the employee's rights under *s.* 5(1), *see*
    XX, 17.)
  (c) The claimant was selected for dismissal on grounds of
    redundancy in contravention of customary or agreed
    procedures: *s.* 24(5).

Where none of these three circumstances is shown to exist,
the action proceeds to its third and final stage, namely, the
determination of the question whether the employer acted
reasonably.

  26. Reasonableness. By *s.* 24(6), the determination of the
question whether the dismissal was fair or unfair, having
regard to the reason shown by the employer, will depend on
whether in the circumstances he acted reasonably or unreasonably in treating it as a sufficient reason for dismissing the
employee; and that question must be determined in accordance
with equity and the substantial merits of the case. Presum-
ably, the burden of proving that the employer acted unreasonably will fall on the claimant.

  27. Dismissal during industrial action. The 1971 Act makes
special provision for the case where an employee claims to have
been unfairly dismissed while taking part in a strike or irregular
industrial action short of a strike. If the employer can show that
the reason, or principal reason, for the dismissal was that the
claimant took part in a strike or other industrial action,
the dismissal will not be regarded as unfair unless the claimant is
able to show either (*a*) that one or more employees of the same
employer who also took part in that action were not dismissed

for taking part, or (b) that one or more such employees who were dismissed for taking part in it, were offered re-engagement on the termination of the industrial action and that the claimant was not offered re-engagement. In addition, the claimant must show that the reason, or principal reason, for which he was selected for dismissal, or not offered re-engagement, was his having taken action within the rights conferred upon him by s. 5(1) of the Act. (By s. 5(1), every worker has, as between himself and his employer, (a) the right to be a member of the trade union of his choice, (b) subject to the agency shop and approved closed shop provisions, the right to be a member of no trade union or other organisation of workers or to refuse to be a member of any particular trade union or other organisation of workers, and (c) where he is a member of a trade union, the right at any appropriate time, to take part in the activities of the trade union and the right to seek or accept appointment or election and to hold office as a trade union official.)

28. Remedies. The Act provides for conciliation procedures both during and after the decision of the industrial tribunal.

Where the employee proves that he was unfairly dismissed, and the industrial tribunal considers that it would be practicable, and in accordance with equity, for the employee to be re-engaged by the employer, or to be engaged by a successor of the employer or by an associated employer, then the tribunal *must* make a recommendation to that effect, stating the terms on which it considers that it would be reasonable for the employee to be re-engaged.

Where the tribunal does not make a recommendation for re-engagement, or where the tribunal makes a recommendation for re-engagement, and it is not complied with, then the tribunal *must* make an award of compensation, to be paid by the employer to the employee, in respect of the dismissal. The maximum compensation that can be awarded to the employee is the amount which represents 104 weeks' pay or £4160 whichever is the less.

REDUNDANCY

29. Redundancy Payments Act, 1965. The effect of the Act is, in general, to create property rights in jobs and to make provision for a system of compensation in the event of loss of job through dismissal. Dismissed employees become entitled to lump-sum payments, based on length of service before dismissal. Other factors, such as job prospects of a redundant employee, are not taken into account when calculating the redundancy payment in each case. Nor is an employee's right to redundancy payment affected by the fact that he may find employment with another employer immediately after becoming redundant. His payment will be the same as if he had remained unemployed for a long period after the dismissal.

30. Dismissal and redundancy. For the purposes of the *Redundancy Payments Act*, an employee is taken to have been dismissed by his employer if (a) the contract under which he is employed by the employer is terminated by the employer whether it is so terminated by notice or without notice, or (b) where under that contract he is employed for a fixed term, that term expires without being renewed under the same contract, or (c) the employee terminates that contract without notice in circumstances such that he is entitled so to terminate it by reason of the employer's conduct.

There must be unilateral termination of the contract of employment by the employer. In cases where the employee agrees to take another job which the employer may have found for him in circumstances where he would otherwise have been redundant, that employee has not been dismissed within the meaning of the definition in the Act. And obviously an employee who gives notice to his employer has not been dismissed.

The Act provides that an employee who has been dismissed by his employer will, unless the contrary is proved, be presumed to have been dismissed by reason of redundancy. Thus, the onus is upon the employer to prove, on the balance of probabilities, that the reason for the dismissal of his employee was not redundancy.

Redundancy occurs where an employee has been dismissed and the dismissal is attributable wholly or mainly to:

(a) the fact that his employer has ceased, or intends to cease, to carry on the business for the purposes of which the employee was employed by him, or has ceased, or intends to cease, to carry on that business in the place where the employee was so employed; or

(b) the fact that the requirements of that business for employees to carry out work of a particular kind, or for employees to carry out work of a particular kind in the place where he was so employed, have ceased or diminished or are expected to cease or diminish.

Accordingly, most redundancies occur where an employer's business is closed down or re-organised.

Marriot v. *Oxford & District Co-operative Society Ltd*. (1969): M had worked for some years as an employee of the Oxford & District Co-operative Soc. He was then told that there was insufficient work available for him and that he could be reduced from foreman to supervisor at a reduced wage. M protested and tried unsuccessfully to find work elsewhere. He received a letter from his employer telling him that his wages would be reduced by £1 per week. Again M protested and, several weeks later, he left to take another job. On the question whether he had been dismissed by his employer within the meaning of *s*. 3 of the *Redundancy Payments Act*, HELD: the employer's letter amounted to a termination of the employee's contract of employment unless and until the new terms proposed were accepted by him; since the employee had vigorously protested against the terms of the letter, it was clear that he had not accepted those terms, despite his continuing to work for several weeks after receiving the letter; the contract had been terminated within the meaning of *s*. 3 of the Act. The employee was entitled to redundancy payment.

O'Brien v. *Associated Fire Alarms, Ltd*. (1969): the employer was a company with a branch office at Liverpool. The company had a business which extended into most parts of the United Kingdom, and the Liverpool office controlled an area stretching from mid-Wales to Cumberland. Three of the employees who worked in the area controlled by the Liverpool office and who had their homes in Liverpool and were able to return home each day were requested by the company to work in Cumberland. The employees refused to do this because it would mean their being able to return to their homes only at the weekends. The company thereupon dismissed the employees, who then claimed redundancy payments. The company contended that there was an implied term in their contracts of employment, namely that they should work anywhere in the area controlled from the Liverpool office, and that there had been a breach of this implied term. HELD: the employer had not shown that there was an implied term that the employees could be sent anywhere in the area controlled by the Liverpool office and, accordingly, the employees were presumed to have been dismissed by reason of redundancy.

North Riding Garages, Ltd. v. *Butterwick* (1967): an employee had been employed in a garage for thirty years, during which time he rose to the position of workshop manager in charge of the repairs workshop. He had given good service until the business was taken over by a new employer, who introduced new methods to which the employee found it difficult to adapt. Some months later, the new employer dismissed the employee by giving due notice. The employer then appointed another workshop manager. When the employee applied for a redundancy payment, the employer claimed that he was dismissed on the grounds of incompetence and not by reason of redundancy. On the question whether the employee was dismissed by reason of redundancy, HELD: the employee was not entitled to a redundancy payment because the overall requirements of the employer's business were unchanged. It was not relevant that the duties of the new workshop manager were not identical with the employee's duties before dismissal. *Per* Widgery, J.: "The very fact of dismissal shows that the employee's services are no longer required by his employer and that he may, in a popular sense, be said to have become redundant; but if the dismissal was attributable to age, physical disability or inability to meet his employer's standards, he was not dismissed on account of redundancy within the meaning of the Act. For the purpose of the Act an employee who remains in the same kind of work is expected to adapt himself to new methods and techniques, and cannot complain if his employer insists on higher standards of efficiency than those previously required; but if new methods alter the nature of the work required to be done, it may follow that no requirement remains for employees to do work of the particular kind which has been superseded and that they are truly redundant. Thus, if a motor manufacturer decides to use plastics instead of wood in the bodywork of his cars and dismisses his woodworkers, they may well be entitled to redundancy payments on the footing that their dismissal was attributable to a cessation of the requirements of the business for employees to carry out work of a particular kind, namely, woodworking."

Hindle v. *Percival Boats* (1969): an employee, a highly-skilled craftsman in woodworking, who had been employed most of his life in boat-building, was dismissed because he was "too good and too slow." For several years before his dismissal, the employer's business was in difficulties because of the decline in the work on wooden boats due to the emergence of fibreglass as a boat-building material. For this reason the employer's business suffered some diminution. On the question whether the employee was entitled to a redundancy payment, HELD: there was no entitlement to redundancy payment because the dismissal was not attributable to any diminution of the employer's business but to the fact that he did not come up to the standards required by the employer. *Per* Sachs, L.J.: "The onus placed on the employer by *s.* 9 of the Act of 1965 is simply to show (using the standard test of balance of probabilities applicable where the facts are largely within the knowledge of a party against whom a claim is made) that the dismissal of the employee was not attributable to redundancy; once the tribunal is satisfied that the ground put forward by the employer is genuine and is one to which the dismissal is mainly attributable the onus is discharged; and it ceases to be in point that the ground was unwise or based on a mistaken view of the facts."

An employee is not entitled to a redundancy payment where the employer, being entitled to terminate the contract of employment without notice by reason of the employee's conduct, terminates it either (*a*) without notice, or (*b*) by giving shorter notice than that which would normally be required, or (*c*) by giving full notice, but accompanied by a statement in writing that the employer would, by reason of the employee's conduct, be entitled to terminate the contract without notice.

31. Renewal of employment. The Act provides for cases where there has been a dismissal and, subsequently, the employer discovers that he is able to offer the dismissed employee another job in substitution for the one from which he was dismissed.

Where an employee is dismissed upon redundancy, and the notice of dismissal remains unexpired, if the employer offers re-engagement on the same terms as previously obtaining to take effect on or before the last day of notice, and the employee unreasonably refuses the offer, there will be no entitlement to a redundancy payment.

Where the employer is able to make an offer of suitable *alternative* employment, the provisions are more stringent than where he is able to offer identical employment. The Act provides that an employee will not be entitled to a redundancy payment by reason of dismissal if, before the last day of his dismissal notice, the employer has made him an offer *in writing* to renew his contract of employment, or to re-engage him under a new contract, so that in accordance with the particulars specified in the offer the provisions of the contract as renewed, or of the new contract, as the case may be, as to the capacity and place in which he would be employed, and as to the other terms and conditions of his employment, would differ (wholly or in part) from the corresponding provisions of the contract as in force immediately before his dismissal but (a) the offer constitutes an offer of suitable employment in relation to the employee and (b) the renewal or re-engagement would take effect on or before the last day of the dismissal notice or not later than four weeks after that date, and the employee unreasonably refuses that offer.

Thus, according to these provisions, an employee will lose his right to a redundancy payment if, during the continuance of his dismissal notice, he refuses an offer from his employer of either (a) employment on the same terms as before or (b) employment on suitable alternative terms.

Taylor v. *Kent County Council* (1969): a boys' school was amalgamated with another school, and as a result of this reorganisation a headmaster's employment was terminated, *prima facie*, on the ground of redundancy. The local authority (the employer in this case) offered the headmaster, alternative employment in a mobile pool of teachers serving for short periods in various schools where there was a shortage of staff. The alternative employment offered would require the former headmaster to serve under the authority of the headmaster of each school to which he would be sent. The alternative offer provided for the payment of the same salary as previously paid. The headmaster refused the offer. On the question whether the local authority had made an offer of alternative suitable employment within the Act of 1965, which had unreasonably been refused, HELD: "suitable employment" means employment which is substantially equivalent to the employment which had ceased; the offer of a position in a mobile pool of teachers to a headmaster with the appellant's qualifications, experience and status, and necessitating his moving house, was not suitable; nor could it be made so merely by guaranteeing the same salary. The headmaster was entitled to a redundancy payment.

32. Re-engagement with another employer. Where a redun-

dant employee obtains employment with another employer immediately or soon after becoming redundant, he remains entitled to his redundancy payment. There are, however, two exceptional cases, where re-engagement with another employer deprives the employee of his right to a redundancy payment.

The first case is where an offer of employment is made to a redundant employee by a company associated with the company employing him. If the terms of the offered employment are either identical to the previous employment or if they represent suitable alternative employment, and the requirements of *s.* 2 are met, then there is no dismissal for the purposes of redundancy. For the purposes of this provision, two companies shall be taken to be associated companies if one is a subsidiary of the other, or both are subsidiaries of a third company.

The second case is where an employee's contract has been terminated upon the sale of his employer's business. Where a business is sold as a going concern, it would be unrealistic to say that the employees whose service was transferred from one employer to another had become redundant. The Act, accordingly, provides that if, *by agreement with the employee*, the new owner of the business renews the employee's contract of employment or re-engages him under a new contract of employment, the effect, for the purposes of the Act, is as if the renewal or re-engagement had been a renewal or re-engagement by the previous owner. The provision applies equally where the renewal or re-engagement is on identical terms as the previous employment or on suitably equivalent terms. Again, the offer must be within the provisions of *s.* 2.

In both cases mentioned above, the employee, on subsequently becoming redundant with the new owner of the business, will be able to base his claim for payment on the time he has served with both employers added together.

33. Calculation of benefit. The rules governing the calculation of the redundancy payment to be made in any case are set out in Schedule 1 of the 1965 Act. There are two basic factors involved in the computation: (*a*) a week's pay, and (*b*) the period of continuous employment. The period of continuous employment will not include any week which began before the employee attained the age of eighteen.

The amount of redundancy payment to be paid in any case

must be calculated by reference to the period of continuous employment, by starting at the end of the period and reckoning backwards the number of years of employment falling within the period, and allowing:

(a) one and a half weeks' pay for each year of employment which consists wholly of weeks in which the employee was not below the age of forty-one;

(b) one week's pay for each year of employment (not falling within (a) above) which consists wholly of weeks in which the employee was not below the age of twenty-two;

(c) half a week's pay for each year of employment not falling within either of (a) or (b) above.

Where in reckoning the number of years of employment in this manner twenty years of employment have been reckoned, no account must be taken of any years of employment earlier than those twenty years.

The *Redundancy Payments Act*, 1965, incorporates by reference Schedule 1 of the *Contracts of Employment Act*, 1963, for the purpose of computing the period of employment. By Schedule 1 of the 1963 Act, any week during the whole or part of which the employee's relations with the employer are governed by a contract of employment which normally involves employment for twenty-one hours or more weekly will count in computing a period of employment. But if in any week the employee is, for the whole or part of the week: (*a*) incapable of work in consequence of sickness or injury, or (*b*) absent from work on account of a temporary cessation of work, or (*c*) absent from work in circumstances such that, by arrangement or custom, he is regarded as continuing in the employment of his employer for all or any purposes, that week will, subject to certain exceptions, count as a period of employment.

The upper limit of redundancy payment in any case is governed not only by the rule that the maximum reckonable period of continuous employment is twenty years, but also by the rule that the amount of a week's pay shall not in any case be taken to exceed £40. It is clear, then, that the maximum amount of payment is £1200 at present.

Armstrong Whitworth Rolls, Ltd. v. *Mustard* (1971): an employee began working for the employer in 1953 as a process annealing operator, his normal working hours being 40 hours per week as fixed by the relevant national agreement. The employee, together with two other employees, worked an 8-hour shift for five days a week. They also worked overtime although they were not bound to do so by any express term in their contracts of employment. In 1963, when one of the other employees left, the foreman told the employee and his remaining colleague that they would now have to work 12-hour shifts, five days a week. The employee continued from then on to work a 12-hour shift for five days a week until he was dismissed by reason of redundancy in 1970. On the question whether the employee was entitled to a redundancy payment calculated on the basis of a 60-hour normal working week, or on the basis of a 40-hour normal working week, HELD: the employee was entitled to a redundancy payment calculated on the basis of a normal working week of 60-hours, the natural inference to be drawn from the fact that he was put on a 12-hour shift basis as opposed to an 8-hour shift basis was that the 12-hour shift was something which the respondent was contractually bound to work after his colleague left in 1963. There was no express mutual agreement to vary the terms of the contract of employment, but the conduct of the parties was sufficient to vary the contract by implication.

Fitzgerald v. *Hall Russell & Co., Ltd.* (1969), H.L.: an employee was dismissed on 8 December 1967, by reason of redundancy. He was first employed by the employer on 31 July 1958. There had, however, been an interruption in his employment lasting from 28 November 1962 to 21 January 1963, a period of nearly eight weeks. On the question whether the interruption constituted a break in the employee's period of continuous service, HELD: the interruption for the period of nearly eight weeks did not break the continuity of employment for the purpose of calculating the redundancy payment. It was clear from Schedule 1 of the *Contracts of Employment Act*, 1963, that some weeks may count even though during them the employee was not working and had no contract of employment, and that such weeks do not break the continuity of the period of employment. The whole scheme of these provisions is designed in the interests of employees, and it follows that certain *de facto* breaks in the continuity of employment are to be ignored.

34. Claims for redundancy payments. An employee must make his claim for a redundancy payment by notice in writing given to his employer within six months from the date on which his dismissal notice expired, unless the payment has already been made, or unless the issue of his right to redundancy payment has been referred to an industrial tribunal.

The *Redundancy Payments Act* sets up the Redundancy Fund, to be financed by payments by employers for each person employed. The weekly rate of contribution is, at present, £0·063 for male employees, and £0·029 for female employees. When an employer makes a redundancy payment he becomes entitled to a rebate from the Redundancy Fund. This rebate is calculated as three-quarters of a week's pay for each year of employment of the employee concerned, from the age of forty-one until the year before retirement, a half a week's pay from forty to twenty-two years of age, and a quarter of a week's pay from twenty-one to eighteen years of age.

EMPLOYER'S VICARIOUS LIABILITY

35. The general rule. When an employee commits a tort *in the course of his employment*, the employer is liable to any person who has thereby suffered loss or damage.

36. Course of employment. It is sometimes a matter of difficulty to determine whether an act was done *during the course of employment*. Any of the following factors may be taken into account:

(a) *Manner of working*. Where an employee commits a tort by performing an act of a kind which he is not employed to perform the employer is not liable, but where the employee merely adopts a wrongful method of doing his work, the employer is liable.

> *Century Insurance Co. Ltd.* v. *Northern Ireland Road Transport Board* (1942): an employee struck a match to light a cigarette while he was carrying out his task of transferring petrol from a lorry to an underground tank. The lighted match caused an explosion and a fire. HELD: the employers were liable because the employee was carrying out his authorised duty in an unauthorised manner.

(b) *Prohibition*. Where an employer expressly prohibits his employee from performing certain acts, the prohibition will not protect the employer from liability if its purport is merely to forbid an employee from doing his work in a certain manner. But where an employer's prohibition sets a limit to the sphere of employment, he will not be liable if the employee commits a tort while engaged in the forbidden employment.

(c) *Time and place of the tort.* An employer will not usually be liable for an employee's tort committed outside working hours, or at a place other than where he is authorised to be during working hours. But there is no hard and fast rule on this point, *e.g.* where an employee negligently left a tap running shortly after working hours had ended, the employer was held to be liable to a neighbour whose property was damaged by the flooding: *Ruddiman* v. *Smith* (1889).

In cases where an employee's work involves travelling, any tort committed will usually be within the course of employment. But where the tort is committed while the employee was on an unauthorised detour, difficulties may arise.

The rule was stated in *Joel* v. *Morrison* (1834) by Parke, B., as follows: "If he was going out of his way, against his master's implied commands when driving on his master's business, he will make his master liable; but if he was going on a frolic of his own, without being at all on his master's business, the master will not be liable." Whether or not an employee is on a *frolic of his own* will depend on the circumstances of each case.

(d) *Emergency measures.* An employee has authority to take emergency measures to protect his employer's property when he has reason to believe that it is in danger. Even where the measures taken by the employee are excessive, the employer may be vicariously liable. But where the employee's conduct is outrageous, it will not be within the course of his employment, and the employer will not be liable.

Poland v. *John Parr and Sons* (1927): an employee, seeing a boy tampering with a bag of sugar which was lying on the employer's waggon, struck the boy with his hand. The boy fell under the moving waggon wheel and was seriously injured. HELD: the blow given by the employee was excessive, but not sufficiently excessive to take the act outside the scope of his employment. The employer was, therefore, vicariously liable for the employee's tort.

Warren v. *Henly's Ltd.* (1948): an employee, a garage attendant, accused a customer of trying to leave the garage without paying for his petrol. The language used was violent, and, subsequently, the attendant struck the customer a blow. HELD:

there was no evidence that the assault was so connected with the acts which the employee was authorised to do as to be a mode of doing those acts.

(e) *Criminal conduct.* In certain circumstances criminal conduct on the part of an employee will be regarded as being in the course of his employment. Where this occurs, the employer will be liable for any loss caused to a third party.

Lloyd v. *Grace, Smith & Co.* (1912): S, a solicitor's managing clerk, was authorised to carry out all the conveyancing work of the firm. During the course of his duties, he persuaded L to transfer to him the benefit of a mortgage of which L was the mortgagee, and also the freehold of certain property held by her. S then realised the mortgage and sold the property and kept the proceeds for himself. S's employer, the sole member of the firm, knew nothing of this criminal conduct at the time, nor did he derive any benefit from it. L brought this action against the firm in detinue for the title deeds of the property and for the moneys received by S in respect of the mortgage. HELD: the firm was liable because the fraud was committed in the course of the clerk's employment.

PROGRESS TEST 19

1. Explain the so-called "control" test. Would you expect the courts to apply this test today? Illustrate your answer with decided cases. (1–3)

2. Outline the statutory provisions designed to protect the employee's right to be paid. (5)

3. What written particulars must the employer give to the employee during the first 30 weeks of employment? (6)

4. Examine and illustrate the employer's duty to provide a safe system of work for his employees. (10)

5. Must an employee obey his employer? (13)

6. Explain the employer's right as against his employee in connection with the employer's confidential information. What is the position with respect to an employee's invention? Is there a general duty of fidelity owed by the employee? (14–16)

7. What are the statutory minimum periods of notice? (20)

8. Outline the remedies for breach of contract of employment. (21)

9. What is unfair dismissal? Explain the stages in an action for unfair dismissal. (22–26)

10. "The burden of proving fair dismissal lies on the employer." Examine this statement critically. (23–27)

11. Explain the general effect of the *Redundancy Payments Act*. How are the expressions "dismissal" and "redundancy" defined for the purposes of the Act?   (29, 30)

12. In what circumstances may an employee lose his right to a redundancy payment where he gets an offer of renewal of employment or re-engagement?   (31, 32)

13. How is a redundancy payment calculated?   (33)

14. When is an employer vicariously liable for the tort of his employee?   (35, 36)

CHAPTER XX

INDUSTRIAL RELATIONS

INDUSTRIAL RELATIONS ACT, 1971

1. General effect of the Act. The *Industrial Relations Act*
received the Royal Assent on 5 August 1971, virtually the
whole of the Act coming into effect by 28 February 1972. The
stated purpose of the Act is to promote good industrial relations and, to this end, it introduces some important innova-
tions: in particular, the creation of a new type of civil wrong
to be known as the unfair industrial practice; and the creation
of what is, in effect, a new branch of the High Court, whose
jurisdiction and procedures are very much different from the
other branches of the High Court.

2. The new terminology. It is necessary to grasp at the out-
set the new terminology of the Act:

"Organisation of workers" means an organisation which
either (*a*) consists wholly or mainly of workers of one or more
descriptions and is an organisation whose principal objects
include the regulation of relations between workers of that
description or those descriptions and employers or organisations
of employers, or (*b*) is a federation of workers' organisations.

"Trade union" means an organisation of workers which
is for the time being registered as a trade union under the
Act.

"Organisation of employers" means an organisation which
either (*a*) consists wholly or mainly of employers or individual
proprietors of one or more descriptions and is an organisation
whose principal objects include the regulation of relations
between employers or individual proprietors of that description
or those descriptions and workers or organisations of workers,
or (*b*) is a federation of employers' organisations.

"Employers' association" means an organisation of employers
which is for the time being registered as an employers'
association under the Act.

3. Guiding principles and code. Section 1 of the 1971 Act casts a duty on the Secretary of State for Employment, the Commission on Industrial Relations, the Registrar of Trade Unions and the National Industrial Relations Court, to be guided by four general principles. They are:

First, the principle of collective bargaining freely conducted on behalf of workers and employers and with due regard to the general interests of the community.

Second, the principle of developing and maintaining orderly procedures in industry for the peaceful and expeditious settlement of disputes by negotiation, conciliation or arbitration, with due regard to the general interests of the community.

Third, the principle of free association of workers in independent trade unions, and of employers in employers' associations, so organised as to be representative, responsible and effective bodies for regulating relations between employers and workers.

Fourth, the principle of freedom and security for workers, protected by adequate safeguards against unfair industrial practices, whether on the part of employers or others.

Section 1 expresses the purpose of the entire Act, namely, that of promoting good industrial relations in accordance with these four general principles. In order to assist in the fulfilment of this purpose, a code of practice was issued in February 1972, as required by the Act. The code is intended to give practical guidance to those who are concerned with the promotion of good industrial relations. The code contains two main themes. First, the vital role of collective bargaining carried out in a reasonable and constructive manner between employers and strong representative trade unions. Secondly, the importance of good human relations between employers and employees in every establishment, based on trust and confidence. The code proceeds to deal with the details of the responsibilities of management and trade unions and of the individual employee. Breach of the provisions of the code will not of itself render anyone liable to proceedings under the Act. But, nevertheless, the code has a legal significance. It may be used in evidence in any proceedings before the Industrial Court or the industrial tribunals. And where the code is put into evidence, the court or tribunal must take it into account in reaching its decision.

The scheme of the code is as follows:

(a) *Responsibilities:* management, trade unions, employers' associations and the individual employee.

(b) *Employment policies:* planning and use of manpower, recruitment and selection, training, payment systems, status and security of employees and working conditions.

(c) *Communication and consultation.*

(d) *Collective bargaining:* bargaining units, recognition of trade unions, collective agreements and disclosure of information.

(e) *Employee representation:* functions, appointment and qualifications, status, co-ordination, facilities and training.

(f) *Grievance and disputes procedures:* individual grievance procedures and collective disputes and procedures.

(g) *Disciplinary procedures.*

THE INSTITUTIONS

4. Judicial and advisory bodies. The effectiveness of the provisions of the 1971 Act will depend largely upon the effective functioning of the institutions which the Act creates or modifies. The National Industrial Relations Court, to be known as the Industrial Court, is created as an entirely new institution. The industrial tribunals which were in existence before the passing of the Act have been given an extended jurisdiction, and the Commission on Industrial Relations is converted into a statutory body with new and different functions from those of the Commission as previously constituted. Each of these institutions should be considered separately.

5. The Industrial Court. The Industrial Court is an entirely new court established by the Act. It is equivalent in status to the High Court. Its judges are nominated from among the judges of the High Court, the Court of Appeal and the Court of Session (of Scotland). These judges are assisted by lay members with a special knowledge or experience of industrial relations. Ideally the lay membership should represent both sides of industry. The Industrial Court has a jurisdiction throughout Great Britain. It has offices in London and Edinburgh, and further offices will be opened as and when required. Usually, the court will sit in London or Edinburgh but, where the public interest is served better by the courts sitting in some other place, then this will be done.

When Sir John Donaldson, the President, opened the court, he said that speed, informality and simplicity will be the hall-marks of the court. He was emphasising that the procedure will show no trace of unnecessary formalism and that the court's interest will lie in the substance of each case and not the form.

The court has both an original and appellate jurisdiction. Its original jurisdiction covers most of the matters included in the Act: agency shops (a new shop to replace the closed shop), procedure agreements, sole bargaining agencies, collective agreements, the registration of trade unions and employers' associations, complaints of unfair industrial practices by employers, by trade unions or by individual employees. The Industrial Court as an appellate court will hear appeals on points of law from industrial tribunals. Appeal lies from the Industrial Court to the Court of Appeal on points of law only. The remedies within the jurisdiction of the court are the award of compensation, a declaration of the parties' rights, or an order in the nature of an injunction.

The body previously known as the Industrial Court is now called the Industrial Arbitration Board. This was set up in 1919, comprising employers' and workers' representatives to-gether with independent persons. The Board's present function is to arbitrate claims by employees under the *Terms and Conditions of Employment Act*, 1959.

6. Industrial tribunals. Industrial tribunals were created by the *Industrial Training Act*, 1964, with jurisdiction under the *Contracts of Employment Act*, 1963, the *Redundancy Payments Act*, 1965, the *Equal Pay Act*, 1970, and several other statutes. This piecemeal accumulation of jurisdiction has now been vastly extended by the provisions of the *Industrial Relations Act*. Appeals from industrial tribunals on points of law, pre-viously heard by the High Court, are now to be heard by the Industrial Court. Under the 1971 Act, industrial tribunals will be mainly concerned with complaints by workers that there has been an infringement of rights given to them by the Act, including complaints of unfair dismissal. Perhaps one of the main differences between the industrial tribunals and the

Industrial Court is that in the former, actions will usually be brought by individual workers, and in the latter, actions will generally be brought, in the first instance, by employers, employers' associations and workers' associations and trade unions.

The jurisdiction that has accumulated piecemeal to the industrial tribunals represents a trend—a hiving-off process shifting particular areas of "industrial" jurisdiction away from the High Court. The 1971 Act contains an indication of future developments in this process, namely, a provision which confers upon the Lord Chancellor and the Secretary of State powers to make orders extending the jurisdiction of the tribunals to cover actions for breach of contract of employment.

7. Commission on Industrial Relations. The Commission was established in March 1969 as a Royal Commission. The 1971 Act re-establishes the Commission as a statutory advisory body. Members are appointed by the Secretary of State for Employment, their number varying between six and fifteen. The Commission will be concerned with research, investigation and conciliation of disputes, and will deal with references from the Industrial Court and from the Secretary of State. The Commission will advise and report on agency shops, sole bargaining agents and procedure agreements. The Commission has important functions in connection with the taking of ballots under the Act. The Commission, in order to perform its duties, has power to examine on oath and to require the production of documents. Perhaps the most important role of the Commission is the close connection that it has with the Industrial Court as its advisory body, particularly in connection with agency shop procedure and sole bargaining agent procedure.

REGISTRATION

8. The Registrar. The Act provides for the appointment of a Chief Registrar and assistant Registrars to be responsible for the registration of trade unions and employers' associations. The duties of the Registrar are:

(a) to maintain the *full register* of those organisations which wish to enjoy the rights and privileges granted by the Act;

(b) to ensure that the *rules* of the registered organisations conform to the minimum requirements set out in the Act;

(c) to *investigate complaints* by members of registered organisations that their rights have been denied by the organisation to which they belong.

9. The provisional register. Under the *Trade Union Act, 1871*, which has now been repealed, many trade unions were registered with the Registrar of Friendly Societies. All of these previously registered trade unions were automatically transferred to a register known as the provisional register during October 1971. The Act provided machinery by which, in appropriate cases, there could be automatic transfer from the provisional register to the full register, thus relieving trade unions from any need to make specific application for registration under the new law. The Act, however, permitted trade unions registered under the old law to apply for the cancellation of their automatic provisional registration, and this, in fact, is what the vast majority of trade unions have done.

Those organisations which did not take steps to have their names removed from the provisional register and which the Registrar decided were eligible for full registration, were automatically placed on the full register. It was the Registrar's duty to decide on eligibility during the first six months of provisional registration and his decision was based on the application of the strict test of independence contained in *s.* 67 of the Act.

10. The register. Any organisation of workers may apply to the Registrar for registration as a trade union under the Act. Applications must be accompanied by documents containing the following information: (*a*) a copy of the rules of the organisation and a list of its officers; (*b*) the names and addresses of the branches (if any) of the organisation; and (*c*) if the organisation has been in operation for more than a year before the date of its application, a statement setting out the information that would be required in an annual return, that is to say a report of the activities of the organisation containing audited accounts.

Where an organisation makes an application accompanied by the necessary information, and the Registrar is satisfied that the organisation is eligible for registration as a trade union, the Registrar then becomes duty bound to register the organisation and to issue a certificate of registration. It should be noticed that, at this stage, the Registrar need only satisfy himself on two points. First, whether the organisation has sent the required information with the application. Second, whether the organisation is eligible for registration. The test of eligibility for this purpose is set out in s. 67, which provides that any organisation which: (a) is an independent organisation of workers and (b) has power, without the concurrence of any parent organisation, to alter its own rules and to control the application of its own property and funds, is eligible for registration as a trade union under the Act.

A certificate of registration must specify the name by which the trade union is registered. The name must not be identical with the name by which another trade union or an employers' association has been registered. Nor may the name so nearly resemble the name by which another organisation is registered as, in the opinion of the Registrar, is likely to deceive: s. 73.

When an organisation receives its certificate of registration, it becomes a body corporate by the name specified in the certificate, having perpetual succession and a common seal. Where the organisation was already a body corporate, it becomes a body corporate by the name specified in the certificate of registration, regardless of its previous name if that was different: s. 74.

11. Trade union rules. As soon as is practicable after issuing to an organisation a certificate of registration, the Registrar has a duty to examine the rules of the organisation. He must examine them against the nine guiding principles, and also against the requirements set out in Schedule 4. If the rules of the trade union are in any way inconsistent with the guiding principles or if they do not comply with the requirements of Schedule 4, then the rules are defective. In that case the Registrar must serve notice on the trade union, indicating what alterations in the rules are needed for the purpose of remedying the defect: s. 75(1).

Where the Registrar serves a notice of this kind he must fix a reasonable period for the trade union to alter its rules and to submit them as altered for approval. The Registrar's notice must specify the period fixed by him for this purpose: *s*. 75(2). If a trade union submits its rules to the Registrar before the end of the period specified for alteration, but it appears to the Registrar that the rules have not been altered so as to comply with the requirements of the notice, the Registrar may, if he thinks fit, allow a further reasonable period for the trade union to make the required alterations and to submit the rules as further altered: *s*. 75(3).

Where a trade union fails to alter its defective rules as required, the Registrar may apply to the Industrial Court for an order directing the registration to be cancelled. If the Industrial Court finds that the grounds of the Registrar's application are well founded, the court must make one or other of the following two orders: either (*a*) an order allowing the trade union a further period for altering its rules and submitting them as altered to the Registrar, or (*b*) an order directing the Registrar to cancel the registration of the organisation as a trade union: *s*. 76.

The Act sets out other grounds on which the Registrar may apply to the Industrial Court for an order directing the registration of a trade union to be cancelled. They are:

(a) that the registration was obtained by fraud or mistake;
(b) that, by reason of a change in its rules or other change of circumstances, the organisation has ceased to be eligible for registration;
(c) that the organisation has refused or failed to comply with any requirement imposed on it by or under Part IV of the Act, *i.e.* the Part dealing with registration and conduct of trade unions and employers' associations, and has persisted in its default after the Registrar has given it notice specifying the default and fixing a time for remedying the fault and that time has expired.

If, upon such an application, the Industrial Court finds that the grounds of the application are well founded the court must make one or other of the following orders: either (*a*) an order extending the time for remedying the default, or (*b*) an order directing the Registrar to cancel the registration: *s*. 77.

12. The Registrar's powers of investigation. The Act confers on the Registrar certain powers of investigation. These powers are concerned with registered trade unions and employers' associations only. They have no connection with unregistered organisations. The Registrar may exercise his powers either upon the application of an eligible person, or upon his own initiative.

The following are eligible to make an application to the Registrar to investigate:

(a) Any person who is a member of a registered organisation.
(b) Any person who was a member of a registered organisation and has ceased to be a member otherwise than by voluntary resignation.
(c) Any person who has sought to become a member and has been refused admission or who has been prevented from obtaining admission by action taken by the organisation: *s.* 81.

The application may be made on the grounds that the organisation has been in breach of the guiding principles (*see* **13** below) or of its rules. When the Registrar has made his investigation he must give notice of his conclusions to the applicant and to the organisation concerned. If it appears to him that the grounds of the application are well founded, he must try to promote a settlement without the matter becoming the subject of a complaint to an Industrial Tribunal.

Where the Registrar has reason to suspect that a trade union or an employers' association has been seriously in breach of its rules or has acted in contravention of the guiding principles, he may himself initiate an investigation. If the investigation confirms the Registrar's suspicions, he must give notice of his findings to the organisation concerned and endeavour to secure appropriate action or undertakings as, in his opinion, would put the matter right.

In short, registered organisations must submit to the scrutiny of the Registrar and to retain their registration they must continuously comply with the provisions of the Act. In particular, the Act provides that registered organisations must not arbitrarily refuse membership to those who are appropriately qualified, that members are entitled to take part in the affairs of the organisation, that the rules of natural justice are to be applied in all disciplinary proceedings and that no member is to be penalised on account of his refusal to take part in an unfair industrial practice. Furthermore, the rules of registered organisations must provide for the wide range of specified matters in Schedule 4, including the election and appointment of officers, the alteration of rules and the manner in which the funds of the organisation may be used. The rules must also be consistent with the nine guiding principles set out in *s.* 65.

13. Guiding principles. It is a feature of the 1971 Act that it contains common fundamental guiding principles for the conduct of organisations of workers, regardless of whether they are registered: *s.* 65. Trade union rules must be consistent with these principles, and it is part of the Registrar's duty to ensure that this is so. Furthermore, it is an unfair industrial practice for *any* organisation, registered or unregistered, or any individual, to take *any* action contrary to these principles. The nine principles are as follows:

First, an applicant for membership of an organisation of workers who is a worker of the kind that it organises and represents, and who is appropriately qualified must not be arbitrarily or unreasonably discriminated against by exclusion from membership.

Second, every member of an organisation must have the right, after giving reasonable notice and complying with any reasonable conditions to end his membership at any time.

Third, a member of an organisation must not be arbitrarily or unreasonably discriminated against by exclusion from being a candidate for any office, nominating candidates for any office, voting in any election or ballot, attending and taking part in meetings of the organisation.

Fourth, the voting in any ballot of members of the organisation must be kept secret.

Fifth, every member must have a fair and reasonable opportunity of casting his vote in any ballot without interference or constraint.

Sixth, a member must not be subjected by or on behalf of the organisation to any unfair or unreasonable disciplinary action.

Seventh, a member may not be disciplined except in certain carefully specified circumstances, namely, that he has had a written statement of the charges against him, that he is afforded a full and fair hearing, that he is given a written statement of the findings and has exercised any right of appeal and the appeal has been heard.

Eighth, a person's membership may not be ended unless he has been given reasonable notice and the reason for his expulsion.

Ninth, there must be no restrictions on any member prosecuting or defending proceedings before any court or tribunal, or from giving evidence.

14. Advantages of registration. Registered organisations enjoy immunities and benefits which are denied to those organisations remaining unregistered. To trade unions, the main advantages as against unregistered organisations of workers are as follows:

(a) any person other than a trade union who, in contemplation or furtherance of an industrial dispute, knowingly induces or threatens to induce another person to break a contract (other than a collective agreement) to which that other person is a party will have committed an unfair industrial practice and be liable accordingly. Trade unions are immune from such actions. The difficulties which now face unregistered workers' organisations who wish to take part in industrial action are obvious. It would, clearly, be well-nigh impossible to organise a strike or to carry out serious picketing without inducing breaches of contracts of some kind.

(b) Where an unregistered organisation is found to have committed an unfair industrial practice, there is no limit to the compensation which the Industrial Court may award against that organisation. But for registered trade unions, the Act provides for a maximum amount of compensation. The amount varies with the size of the trade union and ranges from £5000 in the case of the union with less than 5000 members to £100,000 for a union with 100,000 members or more.

(c) The registered trade unions have full corporate status.

(d) The right of a worker to belong to the organisation of workers of his choice and to take part in its activities applies to registered trade unions only.

(e) Only a registered trade union may apply to the Industrial Court for recognition as a sole bargaining agent, for a ballot to establish an agency shop, or for remedial

XX. INDUSTRIAL RELATIONS 267

action where there is no adequate procedure agreement. Unregistered organisations may not make these applications.

(f) Only a trade union may be a party to an agency shop agreement or an approved closed shop agreement.

(g) A trade union is eligible to claim tax relief in respect of its provident expenditure in the same way as under the previous law. It appears that unregistered organisations of workers will lose this right.

COLLECTIVE AGREEMENTS

15. Enforceability. Until the passing of the 1971 Act the vast majority of collective agreements have been regarded as unenforceable except insofar as the terms of such an agreement have been incorporated into individual contracts of employment.

The Act provides that a written collective agreement is enforceable against the parties to it provided it does not contain an express provision to the effect that it is not enforceable. "Enforceability" in this connection does not mean enforceability in the High Court. It means enforceable by the Industrial Court, which has exclusive jurisdiction over collective agreements, a breach of an enforceable collective agreement being an unfair industrial practice.

NOTE
  (i) "*Collective agreement*" is defined by *s.* 166, as any agreement or arrangement which is for the time being in force and
    (a) is an agreement or arrangement made (in whatever way and whatever form) by or on behalf of one or more organisations of workers and either one or more employers, one or more organisations of employers, or a combination of one or more employers and one or more organisations of employers, and
    (b) is either an arrangement or arrangement prescribing (wholly or in part) the terms and conditions of employment of workers of one or more descriptions, or a procedure agreement as defined in the Act, or both.
 (ii) "*Procedure agreement*" means so much of a collective agreement as relates to any of the following matters, that is to say
    (a) machinery for consultation with regard to, or for the

C.I.L—K

> settlement by negotiation or arbitration of, terms and
> conditions of employment;
>
> (b) machinery for consultation with regard to, or for the
> settlement by negotiation or arbitration of, other ques-
> tions arising between an employer or group of employers
> and one or more workers or organisations of workers;
>
> (c) negotiating rights;
>
> (d) facilities for officials of trade unions or other organisa-
> tions of workers;
>
> (e) procedures relating to dismissal;
>
> (f) procedures relating to matters of discipline other than
> dismissal;
>
> (g) procedures relating to grievances of individual workers.

16. Collective bargaining. One of the basic purposes of the
1971 Act is to promote good industrial relations in accordance
with the principle of freely conducted collective bargaining on
behalf of workers and employers with due regard to the general
interests of the community: *s*. 1. In this connection, the
Industrial Court and the Commission on Industrial Relations
have important inter-connected roles to play.

Where a procedure agreement is not effective, or where there
is no procedure agreement in existence, the Secretary of State,
or the employer or the trade union, can make application to
the Industrial Court to have a procedure agreement imposed,
or to have a trade union (or panel of trade unions)—called a
sole bargaining agent—recognised as having exclusive negotiating rights in respect of an identifiable group of employees,
which for this purpose is called a *bargaining unit*. In these
circumstances, it is the duty of the Secretary of State to
persuade the parties to come to some arrangement in preference to bringing the matter before the Industrial Court. He
may not make application to the court before consulting the
parties to this end. But once the matter has been brought
before the court it may be passed between the court and the
Commission on Industrial Relations, in such a way as to give
the parties an opportunity for conciliation at any stage. If
conciliation fails, the Industrial Court may either impose a
procedure agreement, or name a trade union (or panel of trade
unions) as sole bargaining agent, which will then have exclusive
bargaining rights with the employer concerned. If, following
these procedures, the parties have reached an agreement or the
court has made an order, there are a series of unfair industrial

practices defined so as to protect and preserve the effectiveness
of the agreement or the order of the court, as the case may be.
It should be noticed that the court makes an order only as a
last resort, when all efforts at conciliation have come to nought.
It is clearly the policy of the Act to prefer conciliation and
voluntary agreement to an order of the court wherever this is
possible. When the first successful conciliation under the 1971
Act took place in the dispute between the National Union of
Bank Employees and United Dominions Trust, the President
of the Industrial Court said, "We shall measure our success not
so much by the number of decisions we give as by the number
of occasions upon which it becomes unnecessary to give a
decision."

RIGHTS OF WORKERS

17. Three rights. Section 5(1) defines three new rights to be
enjoyed by each worker *as against his employer*.

First, the right to be a member of any trade union that he
may choose.
Second, the right not to be a member of a trade union or other
organisation of workers and to refuse such membership.
Third, the right to take part fully in the activities of a trade
union of which he is a member at appropriate times (limited to
times outside working hours.)

It should be noticed that, by this provision, a worker has no
positive right to belong to an unregistered organisation.

It is an unfair industrial practice to prevent or to deter a
worker from exercising any of these rights, or to dismiss him
or penalise him because he has exercised them. Similarly, it
is an unfair industrial practice for an employer to refuse to
engage a worker because he is a member of a particular trade
union, or because he is not a member of a particular trade
union, or because he is not a member of an unregistered
organisation of workers.

These rights which the worker has in connection with
membership of trade unions and unregistered organisations
must be modified to accord with the opposing principles of the
closed shop, so far as it is permitted by the Act. There are now
two forms of modified post-entry closed shop, namely, the
agency shop and the approved closed shop. Where either of

these forms of closed shop exists, the worker's right not to belong to a trade union must, of necessity, be modified.

18. Agency shop agreements. An agency shop agreement is an agreement made between one or more employers and one or more trade unions (or between an employers' association and one or more trade unions) whereby it is agreed in respect of workers of one or more descriptions specified in the agreement, that their terms and conditions of employment shall include a condition that every such worker must either (*a*) be or become a member of that trade union (or of one of those trade unions, as the case may be) or (*b*) agree to pay appropriate contributions to that trade union (or to one of those trade unions) in lieu of membership or (where permitted to do so) agree to pay equivalent contributions to a charity.

Agency shops may be created by agreement between the parties concerned or by order of the Industrial Court. Only a registered trade union may enter into an enforceable agency shop agreement. The procedures are not available to unregistered organisations of workers.

Where an employer is unwilling to enter into an agency shop agreement with one or more trade unions, the trade union (or trade unions) or the employer may make an application to the Industrial Court specifying (*a*) the description or descriptions of the workers in question, and (*b*) the employer and the trade union or trade unions who would be the parties to the agreement if the agreement were made as desired.

If, on any application of this kind, the Industrial Court is satisfied that it is not precluded by the Act from entertaining the application, and that the trade union (or, as the case may be, each of the trade unions) specified in the application is recognised by the employer as having negotiating rights, or rights corresponding to negotiating rights in respect of workers of the description or descriptions so specified, then the court *must* request the Commission to take the steps required by *s*. 12 of the Act.

By *s*. 12, if the Industrial Court makes a request of this kind, and it appears to the Commission that there is, or there is likely to be, a dispute in connection with recognition of a sole bargaining agent in relation to workers of one or more descriptions specified in the court's application, then the Commission must make a report to that effect to the Industrial Court.

Where there is no likelihood of a dispute as to the recognition of a sole bargaining agent likely to make the proposed agency shop agreement ineffective, the Commission must make arrangements for taking a ballot among the workers affected by the proposed agency shop agreement.

The Commission must report the result of the ballot to the Industrial Court. If the result is that either a majority of the workers eligible to vote in the ballot or not less than two-thirds of those who voted in it have voted in favour of an agency shop agreement, then it becomes the duty of the employer to take all such action as is requisite on his part for the purposes (a) of entering into an agency shop agreement in respect of the description or descriptions of workers comprised in the ballot and (b) after such an agreement has been made, of carrying out the agreement so long as it remains in force.

It is an unfair industrial practice for any person (including any trade union or other organisation of workers or any official of a trade union or unregistered organisation of workers) (a) by calling, organising, procuring or financing a strike, or threatening to do so, or (b) by organising, procuring or financing any irregular industrial action short of a strike, or threatening to do so, knowingly to induce or attempt to induce an employer not to perform a duty imposed on the employer to enter and carry out an agency shop agreement.

If, on the other hand, the result of a ballot is that neither a majority of the workers eligible to vote, nor two-thirds of those who voted in it, have voted in favour of an agency shop agreement, the Industrial Court *must* make an order directing (a) that no agency shop agreement in respect of workers of any description comprised in the ballot shall, during the period of two years beginning with the date on which that result was reported by the Commission to the court, be made between the employer and the trade union (or trade unions) specified in the application, and (b) that any such agency shop agreement purporting to be made between those parties during that period will be void.

19. Approved closed shop agreements. The only closed shop agreements authorised by the provisions of the 1971 Act are those which are approved by the Industrial Court. Application for approval must be made to the court *jointly* by the parties concerned and the application must be accompanied by a copy

of the proposed agreement. The court must refer the application to its advisory body, the Commission on Industrial Relations, whose duty it is to examine the application to discover
whether the proposed closed shop agreement is necessary to
ensure stable collective bargaining arrangements and to prevent collective agreements in that industry from being
frustrated.

The Commission will, in most cases, be able to report that an
agency shop agreement would be effective for the purpose of
the parties to the proposed approved shop agreement. But if
the Commission is of opinion that an agency shop agreement
would not be effective for that purpose, then the Industrial
Court must take further action in the matter.

When the 1971 Act was passed, it was expected that the only
approved closed shop agreements to emerge would be those of
Equity (the actors' union) and the National Union of Seamen.

The definition of "approved closed shop agreement" provided in the Act is "an agreement which:

(a) is made between one or more employers and one or more
    trade unions, or between an organisation of employers
    and one or more trade unions;
(b) is an agreement whereby it is agreed, in respect of
    workers of one or more descriptions specified in the
    agreement, that their terms and conditions of employ-
    ment shall include a condition that every such worker,
    if he is not already a member of that trade union or of
    one of those trade unions, as the case may be, must
    become such a member unless specially exempted; and
(c) is made in accordance with proposals proposed by an
    order of the Industrial Court."

The reference, in that definition, to special exemption, is a
reference to the provision by which any worker who, in accordance with an approved closed shop agreement would, unless
specially exempted, be required to become a member of a trade
union, but objects on grounds of conscience to being a member
of a trade union, may propose to the trade union that, instead
of becoming a member of it, he should agree to pay appropriate
contributions to a charity to be determined by agreement
between him and that trade union. If the worker is unable to
agree with the trade union the dispute will be settled by an
industrial tribunal. It should be noticed that, where an

approved closed shop exists, the only grounds upon which a worker is entitled to refrain from joining the trade union concerned, is where he can show grounds of conscience, and then he *must* make a contribution to charity. Notice that, where an agency shop exists, the worker need not belong to a trade union, but if he does not belong to one, he must pay an appropriate contribution to trade union funds. Where the worker does not want to join or to pay contributions on genuine grounds of conscience, he then becomes entitled to pay an equivalent contribution to charity.

INDUSTRIAL ACTION

20. **Unfair industrial practices.** One of the important effects of the 1971 Act is that the former relationship between industrial action and the law of tort has now lost most of its significance. The question whether industrial action is lawful or unlawful under the new law depends very largely upon whether the industrial action falls within one or other of the statutory unfair industrial practices. The 1971 Act contains a large number of defined unfair industrial practices. The unfair industrial practice is a new form of civil wrong, quite distinct from breach of contract and tort. The jurisdiction over unfair industrial practices belongs exclusively to the Industrial Court. Indeed, if, in any case, the facts are such as to enable proceedings to be brought before the Industrial Court or before an industrial tribunal, an attempt to begin an action in the Queen's Bench Division will probably be stayed. The remedy for an unfair industrial practice is compensation or an order in the nature of an injunction.

Any person who calls, organises, procures or finances industrial action, will be liable before the Industrial Court if his behaviour constitutes one of the defined unfair industrial practices. But a trade union official, acting within the scope of his authority, will not be liable personally. Any other person will bear a personal liability. The liability is to pay compensation or to submit to an order in the nature of an injunction, or both.

Examples of unfair industrial practices of this category are as follows:

(a) It is an unfair industrial practice for any party to a

collective agreement, where the agreement is a legally enforceable contract, to break the agreement: *s*. 36(1).

(b) It is an unfair industrial practice for any person, in contemplation or furtherance of an industrial dispute, knowingly to induce or threaten to induce another person to break a contract to which that other person is a party, unless the person so inducing or threatening to induce the breach of contract is a trade union or an employers' association, or does so within the scope of his authority on behalf of a trade union or an employers' association: *s*. 96(1). (It should be noticed that this protection is not available to unregistered organisations of workers.)

(c) It is an unfair industrial practice for any person, in contemplation or furtherance of an industrial dispute, to take, or to threaten to take, "sympathetic industrial action," in support of an unfair industrial practice taking place in connection with an industrial dispute: *s*. 97.

(d) It is an unfair industrial practice for any person to take or threaten to take industrial action in contemplation or furtherance of an industrial dispute, if his purpose in taking it is knowingly to induce an innocent third party to break a contract other than a contract of employment to which he and the other party to the industrial dispute are both parties: *s*. 98. This provision aims at secondary strikes and boycotts.

(e) It is an unfair industrial practice to organise industrial action or to threaten to do so, in furtherance of a dispute relating to the question of recognition of a sole bargaining agent, after notice of the proposed application has been given to the Secretary of State and so long as the question is pending: *s*. 54(4).

(f) It is an unfair industrial practice knowingly to induce, or to attempt to induce, an employer, by organising industrial action, to refrain from making application for an agency shop agreement: *s*. 16(2)(b).

(g) It is an unfair industrial practice for an employer, by instituting, carrying on, organising, procuring or financing a lock-out, or threatening to do so, knowingly to induce or attempt to induce a trade union to refrain from making application for an agency shop agreement: *s*. 16(1).

(h) It is an unfair industrial practice to organise industrial action, or to threaten to do so, with the purpose of inducing an employer to discriminate contrary to the provisions of the Act in respect of the rights of workers to trade union membership and to take part in trade union activities: s. 33(3)(a).

(i) It is an unfair industrial practice to organise industrial action, or to threaten to do so with the purpose of inducing an employer to dismiss an employee unfairly: s. 33(3)(a).

(j) It is an unfair industrial practice for an organisation of workers to take, or to threaten to take, any action against any member of the organisation or other person, in contravention of the guiding principles of conduct set out in s. 65.

(k) It is an unfair industrial practice for an employer to prevent a worker from exercising any of the rights to trade union membership conferred on him by the Act and to take part in trade union activities: s. 5(2).

These definitions have been constructed so as to catch most of the kinds of industrial action met with in practice. But any strike called by a registered trade union which does not involve the commission of an unfair industrial practice will be lawful. The problem for unregistered organisations is that it will be difficult to engage in strike activity without inducing some person to break a contract. It may emerge that the strike *with due notice* will be the only lawful strike available to an unregistered organisation of workers. The strike notice required must not be less than the notice which an employee should give to terminate his employment. Where this is properly done, there is no unfair industrial practice where a person is induced to break a contract to which he is a party, even though the organisation calling the strike is unregistered.

21. Emergency procedures: "cooling off." Where it appears to the Secretary of State

(a) that, in contemplation or furtherance of an industrial dispute, industrial action, consisting of a strike, any irregular industrial action short of a strike, or a lock-out, has begun or is likely to begin;

(b) that the industrial action has caused, or (as the case may be) would cause, an interruption in the supply of goods or in the provision of services of such a nature, or on such a scale, as to be likely

(i) to be gravely injurious to the national economy, to imperil national security or to create a serious risk of public disorder; or

    (ii) to endanger the lives of a substantial number of persons, or expose a substantial number of persons to serious risk of disease or personal injury; and

  (c) that, having regard to all the circumstances of the industrial dispute, it would be conducive to settlement of it by negotiation, conciliation or arbitration if the industrial action were discontinued or deferred,

the Secretary of State may apply to the Industrial Court for an order for a "cooling off" period.

A "cooling off" order made on an application relating to a strike, or to irregular industrial action short of a strike, must be an order directing that, during the period for which the order remains in force, no person specified in the order may call, organise, procure or finance a strike, or threaten to do so or organise, procure or finance any irregular industrial action short of a strike, or threaten to do so.

22. Emergency procedures: ballot. Where it appears to the Secretary of State

  (a) that in contemplation or furtherance of an industrial dispute a strike or any irregular industrial action short of a strike has begun or is likely to begin;

  (b) that there are reasons for doubting whether the workers who are taking part or are expected to take part in the strike or other industrial action are or would be taking part in it in accordance with their wishes, and whether they have had an adequate opportunity of indicating their wishes in this respect; and

  (c) that either or both of the following conditions are fulfilled:

    (i) that the industrial action in question has caused, or (as the case may be) would cause, an interruption in the supply of goods or in the provision of services of such a nature, or on such a scale, as to be likely to be gravely injurious to the national economy, to imperil national security or to create a serious risk of public disorder, or to endanger the lives of a substantial number of persons, or expose a substantial number of persons to serious risk of disease or personal injury;

    (ii) that the effects of the industrial action in question on a particular industry are, or are likely to be, such as to be

seriously injurious to the livelihood of a substantial
number of workers employed in that industry,

the Secretary of State may apply to the Industrial Court for
an order requiring a ballot to be taken.

If there are sufficient grounds for believing that any one of
these conditions exists, the court must make an order for a
ballot to be taken to discover the views of the workers involved. While the ballot is being taken, no organisation of
workers or employer or organisation of employers or any person
who may be named in the order may take or threaten to take
industrial action. This seems to be the real purpose of the
order, namely, to provide a "cooling off" period coupled with
the ascertainment of the opinion of those workers most closely
involved in the dispute.

PROGRESS TEST 20

1. What are the guiding principles of the *Industrial Relations
Act*? Upon whom do these principles cast a duty?   (3)

2. Explain the legal significance of the Code of Practice.   (3)

3. Outline the jurisdiction of the National Industrial Relations
Court and the industrial tribunals.   (5, 6)

4. What is the role of the Commission on Industrial Relations?
(7)

5. What are the duties of the Registrar?   (8)

6. How may an organisation of workers register as a trade
union?   (10)

7. When does the Registrar examine the rules of a trade union?
What requirements must be met? What happens when the rules
of a trade union are found to be defective?   (11–13)

8. Outline the Registrar's powers of investigation.   (12)

9. List the advantages of registration.   (14)

10. What is a collective agreement and when is it enforceable?
(15)

11. What is a bargaining unit?   (16)

12. What rights has an employee against his employer with
respect to trade union activities?   (17)

13. Explain carefully what you understand by an agency shop
agreement. How does it differ from an approved closed shop
agreement?   (18, 19)

14. What unfair industrial practices have been designed to set
limits to lawful industrial action?   (20)

15. In what emergency circumstances may the Industrial Court
order a "cooling off" period or a ballot?   (21, 22)

CHAPTER XXI

INDUSTRIAL INJURY AND DISABLEMENT

SCOPE OF THE SCHEME

1. The scheme. The *National Insurance (Industrial Injuries) Act*, 1946, set up a scheme to provide benefit for persons in insurable employment who have suffered industrial injuries. The scheme was the result of acceptance by the government of the main recommendations of the Beveridge Report, 1942 (*Report on Social Insurance and Allied Services*), which had advocated the setting up of a national system to insure individuals against a number of contingencies, some of which might result in the interruption, reduction, or termination of earning capacity, while others made additional demands upon the individual or family income. Beveridge recommended the inclusion in the scheme of industrial injury and disablement as insurable risks along with the other main causes of loss of earning capacity—unemployment, sickness and old age. (The benefits relating to unemployment and sickness are discussed in XXII.) This national industrial injuries and disablement scheme replaced a system whereby liability had been placed by statute upon *employers* to compensate their employees for loss of earning capacity arising from an industrial accident or disease. That system was felt to contain a number of disadvantages which the insurance principle would eliminate.

The 1946 Act and subsequent amending legislation were consolidated in the *National Insurance (Industrial Injuries) Act*, 1965, which contains the main provisions of the current scheme. Further amendments are to be found in the *National Insurance Acts*, 1967, 1969 and 1971, and the *Social Security Act*, 1971.

NOTE: It should be noted that there is a third arm to the social security system. In addition to the contributory schemes outlined in XXI and XXII, there is a non-contributory system of benefits known as supplementary benefits. A claimant for supplementary benefit must show that he is not in full-time work, and that his income whether from State benefits or from his own resources is below a certain prescribed limit. It follows that a person who is claiming sickness, unemployment or industrial injuries benefit may also claim supplementary benefit if the total of those benefits does not amount to the sum prescribed as necessary for his requirements. In calculating his requirements, factors such as the number of dependants are taken into account.

2. Insurable employment. The industrial injuries scheme provides cash payments to *insured persons*, that is, those who are engaged in insurable employment. The term *insurable employment* is broadly defined as "employment in Great Britain under any contract of service or apprenticeship whether written or oral and whether expressed or implied" (Schedule 1, Part I). The Act does not, in general, insure self-employed persons who work under a contract for services, but only those who correspond to Class I of the national insurance classification (see XXII). (For a discussion of the difference between a contract of service and a contract for services, *see* XIX. In particular note the decision in *Ready Mixed Concrete (South East) Ltd.* v. *Minister of Pensions and National Insurance* (1968).) However, by *ss.* 74–79 of the main Act, regulations provide for the inclusion and treatment of special classes of individuals as insured for the purposes of the industrial injuries scheme, or for prescribing a person as the insured person's employer for this purpose.

3. Employment treated as insurable. Certain employees for whom Class I contributions into the national insurance scheme are not payable are none the less covered by the industrial injuries benefits. Examples of this category are:

(a) Unpaid apprentices for whom industrial injuries contributions must be paid by their employer. The term "apprentice" includes people articled to solicitors and accountants.

(b) Certain *specified* employments which are usually subsidiary to the main source of livelihood or which require only part-time or occasional services. For example, employment as secretary or clerk of a society, club, committee, philanthropic institution, school, etc., where service is required only occasionally or outside the ordinary hours of work.

4. Excepted employment. The Act, and regulations made under it, exempt certain kinds of employment from the industrial injuries scheme. Examples of these are:

(a) Employment of a wife by her husband or of a husband by his wife.

(b) Employment of a near relation provided the employment is in a private dwelling-house in which both the employer and employee reside and it is not for the purposes of any trade or business which the employer carries on there.

(c) Employment of a casual nature unless the employment is for the purposes of:

  (i) the employer's trade or business, or
  (ii) a game or recreation where the engagement or payment is made through a club.

(d) Employment of a child under school-leaving age. However, the child may be covered for the benefits of the industrial injuries scheme even though no contributions are paid for him.

5. Qualification for benefit. An employee claiming industrial injury benefit or industrial disablement benefit, or on whose death, industrial death benefit is claimed, must fulfil certain conditions. He must be an employed person in insurable employment (*see* 2–4 *above*). This means that he will make weekly contributions into the scheme since it is based on the insurance principle. However, there are no contribution conditions to be fulfilled before benefit can be paid in relation to this part of the scheme, unlike the situation which applies where unemployment or sickness benefit is claimed (*see* XXII, 6). Industrial injury benefit can be paid from the first day of employment in insurable employment. Contribution conditions apply, however, to the payment of short-term earnings-related benefit (*see* 16).

But the insured person must show that he has suffered one of the *two insurable risks* which are covered by the scheme. These will be discussed in more detail in the paragraphs below.

6. Insurable risks. The *National Insurance (Industrial Injuries) Act*, 1965, provides that all persons employed in insurable employment are insured against:

(a) personal injury caused by accident arising out of and in the course of employment; and

(b) a prescribed disease or prescribed personal injury not caused by accident, being a disease or injury due to the nature of that employment and which developed after 4 July 1948.

INDUSTRIAL INJURY

7. Personal injury. A personal injury can consist of either physical or mental injury to the claimant. Mental shock caused by the accident is covered by the scheme. However, the phrase refers to the physical damage and mental attributes of the claimant himself and it is not a personal injury within the meaning of the scheme when damage is caused to personal property, such as clothing. Nor is damage to an artificial addition to the body, such as an artificial limb, false teeth, or a hearing aid, included, even though the damage may result in loss of working capacity.

8. Accident. The injury must have been caused by an accident. There is no definition of the word "accident" in the statute but there have been judicial interpretations of the word which are of some assistance. The courts have defined the word "in the popular and ordinary sense of the word as denoting an unlooked-for mishap or an untoward event which is not expected or designed" (*Fenton* v. *Thorley & Co. Ltd.* (1903)). "The word accident is not a technical legal term with a clearly defined meaning. Speaking generally, but with reference to legal liabilities, an accident means any unintended and unexpected occurrence which produces hurt or loss" (*ibid.*). From these definitions it follows that:

(a) An injury must not arise out of a deliberate act of the claimant which caused injury to himself. Cases of suicide would seem to be outside the definition of an accident, but in certain cases it has been held that self-inflicted injury leading to death entitles beneficiaries of the dead person to claim benefit. The rule seems to be that if, as a result of an accident, or of shock resulting from an accident, a condition of nervous derangement leads to a person committing suicide the applicant can get compensation. On the other hand, the causal connection between the accident and the suicide will be broken if the direct result of the accident is physical injury to the claimant, even though the consequence of the physical injury is that a person's mind becomes unbalanced so that he kills himself. The application of this rule to a particular set of circumstances will be a question of fact in each case.

(b) The *wilful* act of another person may result in an accident as far as the claimant is concerned. It may be an accident although a deliberate act, since it may be an "unlooked for mishap or an untoward event which is not expected or designed" by the claimant.

(c) There must have been a *specific* event for there to have been an accident. Incapacity resulting from exposure to a *process* is not incapacity resulting from an accident. This distinction is also difficult to draw. However, an event will be regarded as an accident even though the effect is to produce a disease: for example, an exertion which results in a hernia; or a trivial scratch which later becomes septic.

9. In the course of employment. To come within this part of the definition, an accident must normally occur during the contractual hours of work, *i.e.* during the period after the daily commencement of work and before its termination. By *s.* 6 of the Act, an accident arising in the course of an insured person's employment is deemed, in the absence of evidence to the contrary, to have arisen out of that employment. In effect, if a person suffers an accident during the time when he is working, there is a general presumption that the accident arose out of the employment. The burden of proof then rests upon the *insurance officer* (*see* **23**) to show that the injury was in fact caused in some manner not connected with the employment. The presumption is, however, rebuttable as is shown by the phrase "in the absence of evidence to the contrary." Should the presumption in *s.* 6 be refuted by evidence to the contrary, "it is then for the applicant to prove that the accident did arise not only in the course of but also out of his employment":

R. v. *National Insurance (Industrial Injuries) Commissioner, ex p. Richardson* [1958].

10. Commencement and termination of work. In general, the course of employment coincides with the contractual hours of work. But there are the following exceptions to this rule:

(a) *Travelling to work.* An accident happening while the insured person is, with the express or implied permission of his employer, travelling as a *passenger* by any vehicle to or from his place of work shall, not withstanding that he is under no obligation to his employer to travel by that vehicle, be deemed to arise out of and in the course of his employment if:

(i) the accident would have been deemed so to have arisen had he been under such an obligation, and

(ii) at the time of the accident the vehicle (1) is being operated by or on behalf of the employer or some other person by whom it is provided in pursuance of arrangements made with his employer, and (2) is not being operated in the ordinary course of a public transport service: *s.* 8.

(b) *Travelling as part of employment.* It seems that in general a claimant will be entitled to benefit for an accident occurring on the highway only if he was under a contractual *duty* and was, with the express or implied permission of his employers, travelling there at the time of the accident. It will therefore be a question of fact whether a person has suffered an industrial accident while on a journey.

(c) *Accidents before and after working hours.* An employed person will be covered by the scheme if he arrives at work at a reasonable time before working hours, in order, for example, to change his clothing or to collect tools. Similarly, should a person remain at the workplace for a reasonable period after the end of the contractual hours of work, an accident occurring during that period may give rise to a successful claim for benefit. What is a reasonable period before and after the commencement and termination of work will be a question of fact in each case.

11. Arising out of employment. To *arise out of* the claimant's
employment, the accident must have occurred while he was
carrying out some task which he was employed to do, or which
was reasonably incidental to it. The test of what is reasonably
incidental to any particular employment must be one of fact in
each instance and the phrase cannot be finally or decisively
defined. Certain aspects of the test are discussed in **12** and **13**.

However, an accident occurring in certain circumstances will
not be regarded as arising out of employment. These include:

(a) *Unauthorised acts.* Where an employee does work which
he is not employed to do, he will not be insured against
an industrial accident which might occur: for example,
if the guard of a train takes it on himself to drive the
train and is injured while driving it, or where a man is
employed to hook goods on to a crane and, instead, takes
it on himself to drive a fork-lift truck.

(b) *Common risks.* A claimant will not generally succeed if
the accident might equally have occurred to any other
member of the community. This general rule, which has
given rise to a number of confusing decisions, is now
subject to the provisions of *s.* 10 of the main Act. This
section provides that accidents are to be treated as
arising out of a person's employment if:

   (i) the accident arises in the course of employment; and

   (ii) the accident either was caused by another person's
conduct, skylarking or negligence, or by the behaviour
or presence of an animal or by the insured person
being struck by lightning; and

   (iii) the insured person did not directly or indirectly contribute to the happening of the accident by his conduct
outside the employment or by any act not incidental
to the employment.

12. Disobeying orders. An accident is deemed to arise out
of and in the course of an insured person's employment, notwithstanding that he is at the time of the accident acting in
contravention of any statutory or other regulations applicable
to his employment, or of any orders given by or on behalf of
his employer, or that he is acting without instructions from his
employer, or that he is acting without instructions from his
employer, if:

(a) the accident would have been deemed so to have arisen

had the act not been done in contravention as aforesaid or without instructions from his employer, as the case may be; and

(b) the act is done for the purposes of and in connection with the employer's trade or business: *s.* 7.

NOTE: The main difference between this situation and the one discussed in **11**(a) seems to be that the section covers an insured person who acts in a wrongful manner but within the terms of his employment. However, a person who takes himself outside the sphere of his employment and suffers an industrial injury as a result is not covered by the scheme.

13. Interruption in working hours. An accident which occurs during an interruption of work may still be in the course of employment if the circumstances are reasonably incidental to work being done. For instance, an employee may take a break to eat a meal, to have a smoke or to have a cup of tea. Whether a claim will succeed seems to depend primarily upon whether it can be found that the employer consents expressly or by implication to the break.

R. v. *Industrial Injuries Commissioner, ex parte A.E.U.* (1966): C was employed in a factory. Employees were entitled to a tea-break of ten minutes in the morning. A buzzer sounded at the end of the tea-break. Smoking was not permitted in the workshops, but was allowed in a small smoking booth which was close to a passage-way. When C reached the booth it was full. He squatted in the passage outside the booth, waiting to go in and smoke. He had overstayed the tea-break by five minutes when he was injured by a fork-lift truck. HELD: the test whether an employee was acting in the course of his employment was whether what he was doing was something incidental to his contract of service, although he might be under no duty to do it. C had taken himself out of the course of his employment in this case.

14. Acting in an emergency. An accident happening to an insured person in or about any premises at which he is for the time being employed for the purposes of his employer's trade or business is deemed to arise out of and in the course of his employment if it happens while he is taking steps, on an actual or supposed emergency at those premises, to rescue, succour or protect persons who are, or are thought to be or possibly to be,

injured or imperilled, or to avert or minimise serious damage
to property (*s.* 9).

INDUSTRIAL DISEASES

15. Prescribed industrial disease. The Secretary of State has
the power to make regulations listing (*a*) certain diseases and
(*b*) certain personal injuries which are not the result of an
accident but are due to the nature of the employment: *s.* 56.
Prescribed diseases and injuries are insured in the same way as
industrial injuries and can attract the same benefits.

A disease or injury may be prescribed in relation to any
insured persons if the Secretary of State is satisfied that:

(a) it ought to be treated, having regard to its causes and
    incidence and any other relevant considerations as a risk
    of their occupations and not as a risk common to all
    persons; and
(b) it is such that, in the absence of special circumstances,
    the attribution of particular cases to the nature of the
    employment can be established or presumed with
    reasonable certainty.

In order to be successful in his claims the insured person
must show that:

(a) he was suffering from a prescribed disease; and
(b) that he has been employed in the occupation for the
    requisite length of time which is listed opposite the
    disease.

Thus, a person suffering from pneumoconiosis would have to
show that he had been employed for the necessary length of
time at mining, quarrying, or working of silica rock.

BENEFIT

16. Industrial injury benefit. This benefit is paid for each day
of incapacity forming part of a period of interruption of
employment for a maximum of 156 days. A period of interruption of employment consists of any two or more days within
a period of six consecutive days. (For this purpose Sundays
are not counted.) Benefit is not paid for the first three days of

incapacity and it is *no longer possible* to claim benefit for these after a further nine days of incapacity. This "twelve day rule" was abolished by the *Social Security Act, 1971.* In effect, a period of interruption of employment cannot begin until the fourth day of incapacity, and benefit will not be paid for an isolated day of incapacity, but only for a period consisting of a minimum of two days occurring within six consecutive days. Any two periods of interruption of employment separated by not more than thirteen weeks are linked to form a single period of interruption of employment.

An insured person who is entitled to earnings-related supplement in case of *unemployment or sickness* will also be entitled to receive it in addition to basic industrial injury benefit from the thirteenth day of interruption of employment for a maximum of six months, up to a maximum of 85 per cent of his normal weekly earnings.

17. Industrial disablement benefit. An industrial disablement occurs:

(a) when permanent effects are left by the injury so that the employee is unable to work at the end of the period of 156 days during which injury benefit was payable; or

(b) where the incapacity, though lasting, is not of such a nature that it causes permanent loss of work. In such a case the claim for industrial disablement benefit can be made after the third day of the period of 156 days.

NOTE: This benefit is not a fixed and unvarying sum. The amount payable will vary according to the extent of the disablement. The assessment is made by means of a medical examination in order to ascertain the degree to which the claimant suffered loss of mental or physical faculty. The loss is assessed in percentages. A loss of both hands is 100 per cent disablement; a loss of a thumb is assessed as 30 per cent loss. The Secretary of State provides a list of disablements with a scale of assessments which guide the medical boards in determining the degree of loss. This assessment is based on a comparison of the employee with the condition of a normal healthy person of the same age and sex.

18. Disablement gratuity and disablement pension. Disablement benefit is paid if the loss of faculty of the insured person is assessed at one per cent or more. Where the loss of faculty is assessed at below 20 per cent a lump sum known as a disablement gratuity is paid, but if the degree of loss is over 20 per cent a disablement pension may be awarded.

19. Additional benefits. In addition to the basic benefits, additional payments can be made as follows:

(a) To supplement industrial injury benefit, an allowance can be claimed for dependent children and dependent adults.

(b) To supplement industrial disablement benefit, an allowance may be made.

  (i) If the loss of faculty is such that the claimant has become incapable of work, an *unemployability supplement* will be paid.

  (ii) If the person in receipt of benefit (1) is incapable of and is likely to remain incapable of following his regular employment and (2) is incapable of following suitable employment of an equivalent standard, a *special hardship allowance* is payable. The supplement together with the benefit granted must not in aggregate amount to more than 100 per cent disablement pension.

  (iii) If the person in receipt of benefit is in need of *constant attendance*, and his disablement is 100 per cent.

  (iv) If the person in receipt of benefit of less than the maximum of 100 per cent *goes into hospital* for treatment, his pension will be increased to the maximum pension rate.

  (v) If the insured person suffers from *exceptionally severe disablement* so that he is in receipt of constant attendance allowance and the need for that allowance is likely to be permanent.

20. Death benefit. Where death is caused by an industrial accident, a claim for payment of the death benefit can be made by certain dependants of the deceased.

(a) A *widow* is entitled to claim if she was living with the deceased or was maintained by him. During the first twenty-six weeks of widowhood the pension is paid at a higher rate plus any earnings-related supplement that would have been payable had she been entitled to national insurance widow's allowance. Thereafter the pension is assessed and paid according to circumstances, such as the number of dependent children. If a widow subsequently remarries, her right to pension ceases, but she will be paid a gratuity which is equal to one year's pension.

(b) A *widower* may claim a pension upon the death of his wife if he can show that he was dependent upon his wife and that he is incapable of earning his living.

(c) *Parents* of the deceased may claim a pension in exceptional circumstances where they were dependent upon him for maintenance.

21. Disqualification from benefit. The Act imposes a duty upon any person claiming or entitled to injury benefit in respect of any injury not to behave in any manner calculated to retard his recovery. Regulations may provide for disqualifying a claimant or beneficiary for *injury benefit* for failure without good cause to comply with this requirement. Regulations may also provide for disqualifying from benefit a claimant or beneficiary for

(a) failure to comply with other requirements of regulations made under the statute, for example, in the case of death benefit, for failure by some other person to give the prescribed notice of the accident;

(b) for wilful obstruction of, or other misconduct in connection with, any examination or treatment to which he is required under regulations to submit himself, or any course which he is required to attend, or any proceedings under the Act for the determination of his right to benefit.

Disqualification from benefit can be for a period up to six weeks in length.

ADMINISTRATION OF THE SCHEME

22. Structure of administration. The Act establishes a structure for running the scheme through the Department of Health and Social Security, which has local offices to deal with individual claims. Claims for benefit are made against the State and not the employer and unlike common law actions for damages, there is no recourse to the law courts except in limited circumstances. The system includes a number of tribunals to which recourse can be made in cases of dispute. The advantage of administrative tribunals are said to be their comparative speed, informality and cheapness.

23. Insurance officers. Initially all claims for benefit are made to a local insurance officer. His main task in the case of any claim or question submitted to him is: (*a*) to decide it in favour of the claimant; or (*b*) to decide it adversely to the claimant; or (*c*) to refer it to a local tribunal. Where a case is referred to a local tribunal, notice in writing must be given to the claimant. However, when a claim involves a "special question" it must be referred (by the insurance officer) to the Secretary of State. "Special questions" relating to industrial injuries include:

(a) whether a person is or was employed in insurable employment;
(b) whether a person so employed or his employer is or was exempt from payment of contributions;
(c) who is or was liable for payment of contributions as the employer of any insured person;
(d) at what rate contributions are or were payable by or in respect of any person or class of persons;
(e) whether the employment is or was one to which special rules as to payment of contributions apply;
(f) whether an increase of disablement benefit in respect of the need of constant attendance is to be granted or renewed, and if so, for what period and of what amount;
(g) how certain limitations on the payment of death benefit are to be applied in the circumstances of any case.

Other questions to be determined by the Secretary of State refer to the person to be treated as maintaining a child, or as to the family in which a child is to be treated as included. Any question of law arising in connection with the determination of a special question may if the Secretary of State thinks fit be referred to the High Court.

24. Local appeal tribunals. A tribunal consists of one or more representatives of employees together with an equal number of representatives of employers. The chairman is independent and is appointed by the Secretary of State. The

representatives are appointed by the Secretary of State from
panels constituted for this purpose. The function of local
appeal tribunals is two-fold:

(a) To determine appeals from claimants against decisions of
an insurance officer.
(b) To decide claims referred by an insurance officer.

25. Medical boards. These consist of two or more medical
practitioners who have to decide on the following questions
referred to them by an insurance officer:

(a) Whether the industrial accident has resulted in a loss of
faculty.
(b) To assess the extent of disablement resulting from a loss
of faculty, and what period is to be taken into account
by the assessment.

Boards have also the task of reviewing previous decisions of
medical boards and medical appeal tribunals:

(a) if satisfied by fresh evidence that the decision was given
as a result of non-disclosure or misrepresentation of the
claimant or any other person;
(b) if satisfied that since making an assessment of disablement, there has been an unforeseen aggravation of the
results of the relevant injury.

26. Medical appeal tribunals. If a claimant is dissatisfied with
the decision of a medical board, he may appeal in the manner,
and within the time limit, which is prescribed, to a medical
appeal tribunal. It may also happen that the Secretary of
State notifies an insurance officer that he is of the opinion that
the decision of the medical board ought to be referred to
a medical appeal tribunal for their consideration, and the
tribunal may confirm, reverse or vary the decision in whole or
in part.

27. National Insurance Commissioners. The function of the
Chief National Insurance Commissioner and other Commissioners is to hear appeals on points of law from local appeal
tribunals and medical appeal tribunals. These officials are
appointed by the Crown from among barristers of at least ten
years' experience. Appeals are heard by the Chief Commissioner

or a deputy but where an appeal involves a point of special difficulty it may be heard by a tribunal which will consist of a number of commissioners sitting together. Appeals to the Commissioner may be made by the claimant, by an association of employed persons of which the claimant was a member at the time of the industrial accident, or by the Secretary of State. However, the consent of the tribunal must first be obtained, and appeals from medical appeal tribunals are allowed only on a point of law. Decisions of the Commissioners cannot be challenged in the High Court except by alleging a breach of natural justice in the hearing of the claim.

28. Jurisdiction. The question whether there has been a "personal injury by accident" is one which is decided by the insurance officer, local appeal tribunal or the Commissioner. The jurisdiction of the medical board or the medical appeal tribunal is confined to a decision as to whether disablement has been suffered by the claimant as a result of the accident.

Minister of Social Security v. *Amalgamated Engineering Union* (1967), H.L.: the claimant felt a pain in his chest when he moved a heavy flagstone in the course of his employment. He claimed industrial benefit on account of suffering a small hiatus hernia. On appeal to the Commissioner, the claim was allowed. Subsequently the workman claimed disablement benefit, which was disallowed by a medical appeal tribunal on the grounds that he had not suffered an industrial injury since it "was not satisfied that the hiatus hernia was either caused or aggravated by the relevant accident." HELD: the decision of the Commissioner that the claimant had suffered personal injury was final and conclusive both for the purpose of the claim to industrial injury and also for the purpose of the subsequent claim to disablement benefit.

NOTE: This decision does not mean that a medical tribunal is debarred from finding that no disablement followed the industrial accident, nor that the disablement which the claimant is alleging did not arise from that accident: (*R.* v. *National Insurance Commissioners, ex parte Hudson & Jones* (1970), C.A.).

29. Declaration of an industrial accident. A claimant may ask for an express declaration that an accident is or is not an *industrial accident*. The declaration can be made even though the claim is disallowed on other grounds, or that no claim for benefit has been made. This section ensures that a person who suffers what appears to be a trivial accident is not barred from making a subsequent claim for benefit should he suffer from ill effects at a later date. An insurance officer, local appeal tribunal or Commissioner may refuse to determine the question whether an accident was an industrial accident if satisfied that it is unlikely that it will be necessary to determine the question for the purposes of any claim for benefit. But a refusal to make a declaration that an accident is or is not an industrial accident is subject to a right of appeal to the local appeal tribunal if the request has been refused by an insurance officer, or to a Commissioner if the request was refused by a local tribunal.

An accident which gives rise to personal injury will be deemed to be an industrial accident if:

(a) it arises out of and in the course of his employment;
(b) that employment is insurable employment; and
(c) payment of benefit is not precluded because the accident happened while he was outside Great Britain.

30. Review of decisions. The decision of an insurance officer, local tribunal or Commissioner may be reviewed by an insurance officer or local tribunal where:

(a) fresh evidence as to a material fact has been received after the original decision was reached;
(b) there has been a material change in circumstances since the original decision was reached;
(c) the decision was based on that of the Secretary of State on a question which has to be decided by him and he has reviewed the previous decision.

LAW REFORM (PERSONAL INJURIES) ACT, 1948

31. Alternative remedies. The *Law Reform (Personal Injuries) Act*, 1948, provides for circumstances where a claimant has alternative remedies, (a) under the National Insurance scheme, (b) under the *Factories Act*, and (c) at common law.

32. Damages at common law. Where an employee sues his employer for breach of his common law duty (*i.e.* in contract

or in tort) the court may award damages. In tort the employee
may claim damages under two heads as follows:

(a) *General damages*, which need not be specially pleaded.
General damages represent the damage or loss which the
law presumes to have been caused by the defendant's
tort, *e.g.* the injured party's pain and suffering.

(b) *Special damages*, which must be specially pleaded, represent the additional loss resulting from the particular
circumstances of the case, *e.g.* the plaintiff's loss of
wages.

33. Adjustment of damages. The *Law Reform (Personal
Injuries) Act* provides that where special damages are awarded
against loss of wages, the court must take into account, in
assessing the sum, any payments made to the plaintiff under
the industrial injuries scheme.

This provision is made because the employer, as well as the
employee, has contributed towards the industrial injuries
scheme. If the employee were allowed to claim the industrial
injuries benefits in full he would be receiving two payments
from the employer to cover the same loss, namely:

(a) the portion of the benefits which has been paid in to the
industrial injuries scheme as a contribution by the
employer, and

(b) special damages awarded by the court, for example, for
loss of wages, should the employee succeed in his action
against the employer for negligence.

34. Sum deducted. The Act provides that where special
damages are awarded the court must deduct from such sum one
half of the plaintiff's benefits for five years under the industrial
injuries scheme. This sum will be deducted before the amount
for contributory negligence should the court find the plaintiff
guilty of such negligence.

EXAMPLE: X suffers injury at work as a result of which he is
incapacitated for some months. He brings an action against
his employer for negligence at common law. The court awards
him general damages of £2000 and special damages of £500
against loss of earnings. They find that X was guilty of contributory negligence to the extent of 50% of the blame. X

will receive £2000 general damages minus 50% for contributory negligence. This assessment will therefore amount to £1000. X will also receive £500 as special damages. The value of his industrial injuries benefits amounts to £100. Half of this sum must first be deducted leaving £450. A deduction will then be made for contributory negligence. 50% of £450 comes to £225. The total damages awarded to X will be £1000 general damages and £225 special damages.

PROGRESS TEST 21

1. Outline the scope of the scheme contained in the *National Insurance (Industrial Injuries) Act,* 1965   (1–5)

2. What contingencies are insured against under the scheme? (6)

3. What is a "personal injury"?   (7)

4. How is an "accident" defined?   (8)

5. Explain the phrase "arising out of and in the course of employment."   (9–14)

6. What is a prescribed industrial disease?   (15)

7. Describe the benefits provided under the scheme.   (16–20)

8. How can a claimant become disqualified for benefit?   (21)

9. Explain the way in which the scheme is administered. (22–27)

10. Which authorities have jurisdiction to determine claims for benefit?   (28)

11. What is the significance of the declaration that an accident is an "industrial accident"?   (29)

12. Under what circumstances can a decision be reviewed? (30)

13. What is the purpose of the *Law Reform (Personal Injuries) Act,* 1948?   (31–34)

CHAPTER XXII

NATIONAL INSURANCE

SCOPE OF THE SCHEME

1. The scheme. The *National Insurance Act*, 1946, also followed the main recommendations of the Beveridge Report, whereby every citizen of working age would contribute into a national insurance scheme according to the security that he needed against certain contingencies. The scheme provides benefit in return for contributions, and, in theory, provides freedom from want for insured persons by providing against interruption and loss of earning power. The *National Insurance Act*, 1965, consolidated the *National Insurance Acts*, 1946–1964, and this statute contains the main provisions with amendments introduced by the *National Insurance Acts*, 1966, 1967, 1969 and 1971, and the *Social Security Act*, 1971.

In order to take into account different needs, the population is divided into six population classes, four main classes of working age, and two others below and above working age. Housewives, that is, married women of working age, are a class to whom special provisions apply since they are entitled to certain benefits by virtue of their husbands' contributions. The three other categories of insured persons are:

(a) *Employed persons*, *i.e.* persons who are gainfully employed under a contract of service.
(b) *Self-employed persons*, *i.e.* persons who are gainfully occupied in employment but who are not employed persons (*e.g.* employers, traders and independent workers of all kinds.)
(c) *Non-employed persons*, *i.e.* persons who are neither employed nor self-employed persons (*e.g.* a person whose income was inherited.)

NOTE
(i) The characteristics of a contract of service are discussed in XIX.

(ii) The question as to the class in which a person is to be placed is determined by the Secretary of State.

2. Persons included in Class I. Provision may be made by regulation for modifying the above classifications where it appears to the Secretary of State desirable to do so by reason of the nature or circumstance of a person's employment or otherwise. Regulations may in particular provide for treating as an employee contributor's employment:

(a) employment under a public or local authority notwithstanding that it is not employment under a contract of service;

(b) employment outside Great Britain in continuation of any employed contributor's employment.

By *ss*. 98–103 of the Act, regulations may be made which modify the Act in its application to special classes of people, such as members of the armed forces.

3. Persons exempt from making contributions. The following persons may be exempt by regulations from making contributions into the scheme, although they may still be entitled to receive benefits:

(a) *Married women* who are occupied in household duties are covered by the insurance contributions made by their husbands. A married woman who is self-employed or who is employed under a contract of service may make contributions into the scheme if she chooses. (Industrial injuries contributions are compulsory for married women.) If she chooses not to pay national insurance contributions, she will remain insured through the contributions of her husband for certain flat-rate benefits. However, a married woman employed under a contract of service must pay graduated contributions on the same terms as other employees (*see* **18**).

(b) *Full-time students and unpaid apprentices.* Full-time students are credited with contributions up to the age of eighteen. They may then choose to pay contributions as non-employed persons. Failure to do so may affect their contribution record. The position of unpaid apprentices is similar.

(c) *Persons whose income falls below a certain limit.*
(d) *Unemployed persons and sick persons* who are credited
    with their contribution during periods of unemployment
    or sickness.

Regulations may also provide for treating as not being an
employed contributor's employment or for disregarding:

(a) Employment which is of a casual or subsidiary nature
    or in which the insured person is engaged only to an
    inconsiderable extent.
(b) Employment in the service, or for the purposes of trade
    or business, or a partner, of the insured person's husband
    or wife.
(c) Employment of a near relation in household duties.

4. Insurable risks. The *National Insurance Act* provides for
the following insurance benefits to be payable:

(a) Unemployment benefit.
(b) Sickness benefit.
(c) Retirement pension.
(d) Maternity benefit.
(e) Widow's benefit.
(f) Guardian's allowance.
(g) Death grant.
(h) Child's special allowance.

Unemployment and sickness benefits are the two kinds of
national insurance benefit which are of primary concern to
employed persons and the provisions concerning them will be
discussed in more detail in the paragraphs below.

CONDITIONS OF UNEMPLOYMENT AND SICKNESS BENEFIT

5. Qualification for benefit. An employee claiming unemployment or sickness benefit must fulfil a number of conditions. As we have seen, he must be an employed person
within the meaning of the Act (*see* **1** *above*). In addition, he
must:

(a) satisfy the conditions as to *contributions* into the scheme;
    and

(b) show that he is *unemployed* or *sick* within the meaning
  of the *National Insurance Acts*.

6. Flat-rate contributions. In order to qualify for the full
rate of unemployment and sickness benefit, the claimant must
have paid not less than twenty-six contributions of the appropriate class since entry into the scheme. (It will not be
sufficient that contributions have been credited.) The *contribution week* begins at midnight on Sunday and contributions
must be paid for any part of the week during which the insured
person was employed. Both the employer and the employed
person make contributions into the scheme, but it is the duty
of the employer to pay both his own and the employee's
contributions. He may then deduct the *employee's* contribution (but not his own) from his wages. Where a person is
employed by two or more persons during a week, the first
employer must make the necessary contributions and stamp
the employed person's card; the first employer may then claim
a share of the contribution from any other employer.

In addition, a claimant must show that he has paid *or been
credited with* at least 50 Class I contributions in the last complete *contribution year*. A contribution year is the period
covered by a contribution card, and it ends five months before
the start of *the benefit year*. The payment of benefit in the
benefit year is dependent upon the insured person's record of
contributions in his contribution year. If the insured person
has paid or been credited with less than 50 but more than
26 contributions in the relevant contribution year, benefit will
be paid, but at a reduced rate.

NOTE: Under the *industrial injuries* scheme there are no conditions as to contributions having been made before benefit can
be paid. An insured person suffering from an industrial injury
at any time after the commencement of employment will be
entitled to full benefit.

7. Graduated contributions. In order to obtain earnings-
related unemployment and sickness benefit, employed persons
who are over the age of eighteen must pay a graduated contribution in any week in which they earn a gross amount which
is over £9, in addition to paying flat-rate contributions. (A
contribution is also paid by the employer.) Except in the case
of those contracted out (*see* Note *below*) the employee pays

C.I.L—L

$4\frac{3}{4}$ per cent of that part of his weekly pay which lies between £9 and £18 and 4.35 per cent of any part which lies between £18 and £42. Where an employee is in contracted-out employment, the employee pays a contribution of $\frac{1}{2}$ per cent of that part of his weekly pay which lies between £9 and £18 and 4.35 per cent of any part which lies between £18 and £42. Unlike flat-rate contributions, graduated contributions are paid at the end of each income tax month to the Collector of Taxes along with P.A.Y.E. income tax. The Inland Revenue then forwards contributions to the Department of Health and Social Security.

NOTE: An employer who provides an adequate pension scheme for his employees can contract employees out of that part of the graduated contributions scheme which relates to earnings between £9 and £18. Such employees pay a lower rate of graduated contributions than those who are not contracted out but they pay a higher flat-rate contribution.

UNEMPLOYMENT

8. Meaning of unemployment. An insured person may claim benefit for any day of unemployment forming part of a *period of interruption of employment*. A period of interruption of employment consists of any two or more days of unemployment within six consecutive days. (For this purpose, Sundays are not counted.) Benefit is not paid for the first three days of unemployment and it is *no longer possible* to claim benefit for these days after a further nine days of unemployment. This "twelve day rule" was abolished by the *Social Security Act*, 1971. In effect, a period of interruption of employment cannot begin until the fourth day of unemployment, and benefit will not be paid for an isolated day of unemployment, but only for a period consisting of a minimum of two days occurring within six consecutive days.

Having established a period of interruption of employment, the claimant must also show that he is, or is deemed by regulation to be "capable of work and available for employment" on any day of unemployment. The *National Insurance (Unemployment and Sickness Benefit) Regulations*, 1967, have made a number of more specific definitions of the term "day of unemployment." For instance, in certain circumstances, a person may still be available for employment although he is doing a part-time job on that day.

9. Disqualification for unemployment benefit. In certain circumstances, a claimant may be disqualified from successfully claiming unemployment benefit:

(a) If a person has lost his employment by reason of a stoppage of work which was due to a *trade dispute at his place of employment*, he will be disqualified *prima facie* from receiving unemployment benefit.
(b) A second set of disqualifications arises out of the claimant's *own conduct* which either causes his dismissal, or which occurs during the period of unemployment.

10. Trade dispute. For the purposes of the Act, the expression "trade dispute" means any dispute between employers and employees or between employees and employees which is connected with the employment or non-employment or the conditions of employment of any persons, whether employees in the employment of the employer with whom the dispute arises or not. The justification for this disqualification is that since the national insurance scheme is run by the State, a financial contribution by it to one of the disputants might appear to favour that party to the dispute.

11. Place of employment. The phrase "place of employment" is also defined in the Act and means the factory, workshop, farm or other premises or place at which he is employed (*s.* 22(6)(a)). A trade dispute resulting in a stoppage at a place of employment other than his own will not disqualify a claimant even though the result is to make him unemployed.

There is a further proviso in this sub-section that where separate branches of work which are commonly carried on as separate businesses in separate premises or at separate places are in any case carried on in separate departments on the same premises or at the same place, *each of those departments* is deemed to be a separate factory or workshop or farm or separate premises or a separate place.

12. Exceptions. The disqualification for benefit will not apply:

(a) where during the stoppage of work a person has become *bona fide* employed elsewhere in the occupation which he usually follows or has become regularly engaged in some other occupation; or

(b) where a person proves:
  (i) that he is not participating in or financing or directly interested in the trade dispute which caused the stoppage of work; *and*
  (ii) that he does not belong to a grade or class of workers of which, immediately before the commencement of the stoppage, there were members employed at his place of employment any of whom are participating or directly interested in the dispute.

NOTE
  (i) A claimant will be considered to be "financing" a trade dispute if his trade union decides to pay dispute money to any of its members at his place of employment.
  (ii) A claimant who wishes to go on working but is prevented by the trade dispute and who is not taking part in the dispute may be precluded from benefit if other workers of the same grade or class are taking part in the dispute.
  (iii) the *dependants* of the disqualified person may claim supplementary benefit which is a benefit awarded on a non-contributory basis for people who are not in full-time work and whose other income, whether from insurance benefits or from their own resources, is not enough to meet their requirements. The *Social Security Act*, 1966, which contains this provision, and which also disqualifies the unemployed person himself from supplementary benefit, makes provision for the payment of benefit in an *urgent case* despite the disqualification.

13. Claimant's conduct. A claimant will be disqualified from receiving unemployment benefit for a period *up to six weeks* in the following circumstances:

(a) If the claimant has lost his employment through his misconduct or has left without just cause.

NOTE
  (i) At common law an employee's misconduct means behaviour which would have given the employer the right to dismiss the employee summarily (*see* XIX, **20**).
  (ii) Whether the claimant left *without just cause* is a question of fact to be decided by the insurance officer (*see* **20**) in the circumstances of each case.

(b) If the claimant has without good cause refused or failed to apply for suitable employment notified to him as vacant, or about to become vacant, by an employment exchange or by or on behalf of an employer.

(c) If the claimant has neglected to avail himself of a reasonable opportunity of suitable employment.

(d) If the claimant has without good cause failed to carry out any reasonable recommendations given to him in writing by an officer of an employment exchange with a view to assisting him to find suitable employment.

(e) If the claimant has without good cause refused or failed to avail himself of a reasonable opportunity of receiving training approved by the Department of Employment for the purpose of becoming fit for entry into or return to regular employment.

14. Suitable employment. The Act provides that employment will *not* be deemed suitable in the following circumstances:

(a) Where a situation has become vacant in consequence of a stoppage of work due to a trade dispute.

(b) Where the employment is *in the claimant's usual occupation in the district where he was last ordinarily employed* but at a lower rate of remuneration or upon conditions less favourable than those which he would have obtained if he were not unemployed or those which he could reasonably have expected to obtain.

(c) Where the employment is in the claimant's *usual occupation in another district* but at a lower rate of remuneration or upon conditions less favourable than those generally observed in that district by agreement between associations of employers and employees, or failing such agreement, than those generally recognised in that district by good employers.

NOTE

(i) The Act does not attempt to define "suitable employment," but simply to state what must be considered unsuitable. What is suitable employment will be a question of fact in each case, depending on such factors as the previous occupation of the claimant.

(ii) The Act provides that after the lapse of a *reasonable time* employment is not to be considered unsuitable merely because it is employment of a kind other than the claimant's usual occupation provided that it is employment at a rate of remuneration not lower, and on conditions not less favourable, than those generally observed by agreement between associations of employers and employees or, failing any such agreement, than those generally recognised by good employers.

SICKNESS

15. Meaning of sickness. An insured person may claim benefit for any day of sickness forming part of a *period of interruption of employment*. A period of interruption of employment is defined in the same way as for unemployment benefit. It should again be noted that the "twelve day rule" has been abolished with respect to sickness benefit.

To be successful in his claim, the insured person must also show that during the period of sickness he is, or is deemed by regulation to be, *incapable of work* by reason of some specific disease or bodily or mental disablement.

16. Disqualification from sickness benefit. A claimant may be disqualified by regulations from receiving sickness benefit for a period of *up to six weeks* in the following circumstances:

(a) Where he has become incapable of work through his own misconduct.
(b) Where he refuses without good cause to attend for or to submit himself to such medical or other examination or treatment as may be required in accordance with the regulations, or to observe any prescribed rules of behaviour.

BENEFITS

17. Flat-rate benefits. If contribution conditions have been fulfilled, unemployment and sickness benefit will be paid from the fourth day of unemployment or incapacity. *Unemployment benefit* is payable up to the 312th day of unemployment. The insured person is thereafter not entitled to benefit for any further day of unemployment unless he has requalified for benefit. A person requalifies for benefit by paying thirteen contributions of the appropriate class.

The rules regarding *sickness benefit* are somewhat different. A person who has paid at least 156 *contributions* into the scheme is entitled to an unlimited period of benefit. (In computing the contributions, only those *paid*, and not credited to the insured person's record, are relevant.) But a person who has paid less than 156 contributions must again requalify for benefit after 312 days, by paying thirteen contributions of the appropriate class.

18. Earnings-related benefit. Unemployment and sickness earnings-related benefit is payable to people who are already in receipt of flat-rate benefit, and who have at least £450 "reckonable earnings" in the relevant income tax year—normally the last complete income tax year. ("Reckonable earnings" refers to those earnings on which income tax is payable under P.A.Y.E.) The benefit is paid from the thirteenth day of unemployment or incapacity for up to 156 days (excluding Sundays). Spells of unemployment and incapacity for work not separated by more than thirteen weeks will be added together to form one period of interruption of employment.

The earnings-related supplement is at the rate of one-third of the amount, up to £20, by which average weekly earnings exceeded £10, and 15 per cent of the amount, up to £12, by which those earnings exceeded £30 (*National Insurance Act,* 1971). The maximum total benefit from flat-rate and earnings-related supplement cannot exceed 85 per cent of the claimant's normal weekly earnings.

NOTE: An employee whose employment is suspended and not terminated, is entitled to flat-rate unemployment benefit from the fourth day of suspension. However, since 1966, he has not been entitled to earnings-related supplement until the eighteenth day of suspension. This is a result of *s.* 3(1)(a) of the *National Insurance Act,* 1966, which provides that benefit for suspension shall be paid only after 7 days of suspension. To this must be added the normal 12 days before qualification for earnings-related benefit begins.

ADMINISTRATION OF THE SCHEME

19. Structure of administration. The structure of this side of the scheme is similar to that for claiming industrial injuries (*see* XXI) except that no medical boards or medical appeal tribunals are necessary. However the "special questions" which must be referred to the Secretary of State are rather different. They are:

   (a) whether contributions conditions for any benefit are satisfied;

   (b) which of two persons is entitled to an increase of benefits where one is awarded;

   (c) as to the class of insured persons in which a person is to be included;

   (d) as to the person to be treated as maintaining a child or as to the family in which a child is to be treated as included.

There is a right of appeal to the High Court on a point of law.

PROGRESS TEST 22

1. Which classes of persons are insured under the *National Insurance Act*, 1965? (1–3)

2. Describe the contribution conditions relating to the scheme. (6, 7)

3. What conditions does a claimant have to fulfil in order to obtain unemployment benefit? (5, 8)

4. How can a claimant be disqualified for unemployment benefit? (9)

5. What is meant by a "trade dispute"? (10, 11)

6. When does the disqualification relating to a trade dispute not apply? (12)

7. What kind of conduct by the claimant will disqualify him for benefit? (13)

8. Does the Act define "suitable employment"? (14)

9. What conditions does a claimant have to fulfil in order to obtain sickness benefit? (5, 15)

10. Describe the benefits provided by the scheme. (17, 18)

CHAPTER XXIII

STATUTORY CONTROL OF WORKING CONDITIONS: FACTORIES

THE FACTORIES ACT, 1961

1. Scope of the Act. The *Factories Act*, 1961, governs working conditions in factories. The Act deals with four main aspects of factory employment:

(a) Health provisions.
(b) Safety provisions.
(c) Welfare provisions.
(d) The employment of women and young persons. (They are protected by more stringent measures, particularly with regard to the length of working hours.)

2. Definition of a factory. The expression *factory* means any premises in which, or within the close or curtilage or precincts of which, persons are employed in manual labour in any process for, or incidental to, any of the following:

(a) The making of any articles or of part of any article, or
(b) The altering, repairing, ornamenting, finishing, cleaning or washing or the breaking up, or the demolition of any article, or
(c) The adapting for sale of any article, or
(d) The slaughtering of cattle, horses and certain other animals, or
(e) The confinement of such animals at certain premises (with certain exceptions) while awaiting slaughter at other premises, in a case where the place of confinement is available in connection with those other premises, is not maintained primarily for agricultural purposes and does not form part of premises used for the holding of a market in respect of such animals,

being premises in which, or within the close or curtilage or precincts of which, the work is carried on in the way of trade or for purposes of gain and to or over which the employer of the persons employed therein has the right of access or control: *s.* 175 (1).

3. Other premises. The Act lists certain kinds of premises which are to be regarded as factories, even though they may not fall within the definition in *s.* 175 (1). These include:

(a) Any yard or dry dock where ships or vessels are constructed, repaired or broken up.

(b) Any premises in which articles are sorted out preliminary to work in a factory.

(c) Any premises where bottles or containers are washed or filled or articles are packed incidentally to the purposes of a factory.

(d) Any premises where yarn or cloth is made up or packed.

(e) Any laundry which is ancillary to a business or public institution.

(f) Any premises in which locomotives or vehicles are constructed or repaired ancillary to a transport, commercial or industrial undertaking.

(g) Any premises where printing or bookbinding is carried out as a trade or incidental to a business.

(h) Any premises in which dresses or properties for film or theatrical productions are made or repaired.

(i) Any premises where films are produced.

(j) Any premises in which articles are made or prepared incidentally to carrying on of operations or works of engineering construction.

4. Employed in manual labour. For premises to be classed as a factory, persons must be employed there in manual labour. Difficulty may arise where occupations of various kinds are found on the same premises. In *Joyce* v. *Boots Cash Chemists (Southern) Ltd.* (1950) it was held that the test to be applied was whether the employment of persons in manual labour was the *substantial purpose* for which the premises were used. In that case the plaintiff was a porter at the defendant's chemist shop. Five other persons were employed there, but the plaintiff was the only one whose work could be described as manual labour. Since the porter's work was *incidental* to the main purpose of the premises, the shop was not a factory. (After the passing of the *Offices, Shops and Railway Premises Act*, 1963, the premises would be covered by different provisions.)

Another difficulty has arisen in defining what kinds of work are to be regarded as manual labour. Most occupations are composed of both elements to varying degrees. It seems that the test which the courts will apply is whether the work is primarily or predominantly manual or primarily and predominantly intellectual in nature. The test is not always easy to apply.

J. F. Stone Lighting and Radio Ltd. v. *Haygarth* (1966), H.L.: S was employed as a radio and television engineer. He worked in a room behind a shop which sold televisions, radios and other electrical goods, and was occupied in repairing faults, replacing faulty parts and adjusting sets, all of which he did by hand. The work also required him to diagnose and to locate faults, a task which was sometimes difficult and sometimes easy. During most of his working time he used his knowledge of television and radio sets and electrical equipment, but his work with his hands occupied the greater part of his time and was an essential part of what he was engaged to do. HELD: the fact that in doing work with his hands a man used technical knowledge did not prevent that work being manual work, so long as it was not primarily or predominantly work of a different kind (*e.g.* intellectual activity) to which work with the hands was merely accessory. On the facts of the case, S was a skilled craftsman applying technical knowledge in doing manual work. The premises were, therefore, a factory.

It is not sufficient that a person is engaged in manual work: he must also be *employed* under a contract of service. In *Pullen* v. *Prison Commissioners* (1957) an ex-prisoner brought an action against the Prison Commissioners alleging that the tuberculosis he had contracted was the result of the dust to which he had been exposed while working in a prison workshop. It was held that the prison workshop was not a factory within the meaning of the Act since there was no relationship of master and servant, or employment for wages in the case of the prisoner.

5. Adapting for sale. It is a question of fact in each case whether an article is being adapted for sale, but something must be done which makes the article different, or more readily saleable. It has been held that adapting for sale includes the

following processes: separating saleable parts of refuse from
the bulk; packaging and arranging sweets into boxes; making
of wreaths; compressing of waste paper into bundles. But the
following have not been regarded as adapting for sale: the
cleaning and cooling of milk; the storage of food by means of
refrigeration.

6. By way of trade or for purposes of gain. The courts have
held that these words include any manufacture, alteration
or adaptation which directly or indirectly results in trading or
gain for the occupier.

> *Stanger* v. *Hendon Borough Council* (1948): a consulting
> engineer tested materials used for building and was paid by the
> builders who supplied him with the materials. He constructed
> concrete blocks, which were then tested for durability by a
> crushing machine. HELD: the premises constituted a factory
> and the process of making and breaking the blocks was carried
> on "for purposes of gain."

Manual work carried on in a technical college does not convert the building into a factory since the work is not by way of
trade, nor for purposes of gain by the occupier. The same
principle has been applied to work carried out in the kitchen
of a hospital: (*Wood* v. *L.C.C.* (1941)).

7. Other purposes. A place which is situated within the
area of the factory which is used solely for some purpose other
than the processes carried out in the factory is not part of the
factory. But this will not apply if the work carried on there
is ancillary to the main purpose of the factory. Thus in
Thorogood v. *Van den Berghs and Jurgens Ltd.* (1951), it was
held that a shed where maintenance of machinery used in the
factory was carried out was a part of the factory and covered
by the *Factories Act*, 1961. But in *King* v. *Magnatex* (1951),
a workshop on the factory premises which had been cleared
of machines in order to hold a Christmas party ceased to be a
factory during that time.

NOTE: *A canteen* within the precincts of a factory used to feed
and entertain persons working there formed part of the factory.
This was a purpose incidental to the main aim of the factory:
Luttman v. *Imperial Chemical Industries Ltd.* (1955). But a
canteen used exclusively for executives and the administrative
staff did not form part of the factory premises even though

occasional meetings between the management and shop stewards were held there. The purpose to which the building was put was not essential "for the welfare of the industrial workers." It was solely used for some purpose other than processes carried on in the factory: *Thomas* v. *British Thomson-Houston Co. Ltd.* (1953).

8. Other premises. Sections 123–127 specify other premises which are not considered factories as defined by *s.* 175, but which are covered by certain measures in the *Factories Act.* These include electrical stations; parts of charitable institutions; docks; wharves and quays, warehouses with mechanical power; the loading, unloading and coaling of ships; building operations and works of engineering construction.

HEALTH (GENERAL PROVISIONS)

9. Cleanliness. The requirements are as follows:

(a) In general *every factory* is to be kept in a clean state and free from effluvia arising from any drain, sanitary convenience or nuisance. Accumulations of dirt and refuse must be removed daily by a suitable method from floors and benches of workrooms and from staircases and passages. The floor of every workroom must be cleaned at least once every week by washing or other effective method.

(b) *All inside walls and partitions* and all ceilings or rooms and passages and staircases must (i) where they have a smooth surface be washed with hot water and soap or cleaned by any other approved method every fourteen months, (ii) where they are painted in a prescribed manner or varnished be repainted or revarnished periodically as may be prescribed (but not more than every seven years.) They must be washed with hot water and soap or cleaned at least once every fourteen months.

(c) In any other case they are to be kept *whitewashed* or colour-washed, which is to be renewed every fourteen months.

These provisions as to methods of cleaning will not apply, except if the inspector so requires, to a factory where mechanical means are not used and less than ten persons are employed: *s.* 1.

NOTE: The Secretary of State may exclude certain factories and parts of factories from these measures where other methods might be appropriate.

10. Overcrowding. In general, a factory must not, while work is carried on, be so overcrowded as to cause risk of injury to the health of the persons employed in it. Every person working in a room must be allowed a space of at least 400 cubic feet. In calculating this space, no space more than 14 feet from the floor shall be taken into account. Special regulations increasing the amount of floor space may be made by the Secretary of State where necessary. A notice must be placed in each workroom specifying the number of persons who may be employed there, unless the district inspector of factories otherwise allows: *s.* 2.

11. Temperature. Effective provision must be made for securing and maintaining a reasonable temperature in each room, but not by means which will cause injury to persons employed there, for example, by the release of fumes. In every workroom where a substantial proportion of work is done sitting and does not involve serious physical effort, a temperature of less than sixty degrees would not be regarded as reasonable after the first hour. At least one thermometer is to be provided in a suitable position in such a room. Regulations may be made to establish a standard of reasonable temperature for any factory: *s.* 3.

12. Ventilation. Effective and suitable provision must be made for securing and maintaining by the circulation of fresh air in each workroom the adequate ventilation of the room, and for rendering harmless, so far as practicable, all such fumes, dust and other impurities generated in the course of any process or work carried on in the factory as may be injurious to health. The Employment Secretary may make regulations to prescribe a standard of adequate ventilation for particular types of factories: *s.* 4.

13. Lighting. Effective provision must be made for securing and maintaining sufficient and suitable lighting, whether natural or artificial, in every part of a factory in which persons are working or passing: *s.* 5. The Secretary of State may, by regulation, prescribe a standard of sufficient and suitable lighting for any class of factory.

Thornton v. *Fisher & Ludlow, Ltd.* (1968), C.A.: the plaintiff, a cleaner, was on her way to work in a factory at 6.45 a.m. on a morning in October. She was walking on a factory roadway when she tripped over a coil of wire, fell and was injured. There were sufficient and suitable lights along a wall by the roadway, but they were not turned on. The plaintiff sued for breach of *s.* 5(i) as well as for negligence at common law. HELD: that the defendants were liable to the cleaner because by not ensuring that the lighting was turned on they failed to make "effective provision" for securing and maintaining sufficient lighting in a part of the factory, and were thus in breach of the Act.

All glazed windows and skylights used for the lighting of workrooms must, so far as is practicable, be kept clean on both the inner and outer surfaces and free from obstruction. This measure does not prevent the whitewashing or shading of windows and skylights in order to lessen heat or glare.

14. Drainage of floors. Where any process is carried on which renders the floor liable to be wet to such an extent that the wet is capable of being removed by drainage, effective means must be provided and maintained for draining: *s.* 6.

15. Sanitary conveniences. Sufficient and suitable sanitary conveniences for the persons employed in the factory must be provided, maintained and kept clean. Effective provision must be made for lighting them. Where persons of both sexes are employed, separate accommodation must be provided for each sex: *s.* 7.

NOTE
  (i) *The Secretary of State may by regulation* prescribe what is sufficient and suitable provision for any class of factory.
 (ii) *Enforcement of this section* and any regulations made under it is the responsibility of each local authority acting through its Medical Officer of Health. The other health provisions of the Act are enforced in the same way in those factories where mechanical power is not used: *s.* 8. An inspector may require a local authority to investigate and remedy any sanitary or other defect in such a factory: *s.* 9. If the Secretary of State is satisfied that a local authority has failed in its duty, he may authorise an inspector to take steps to enforce these provisions: *s.* 10.

16. Medical supervision. In certain circumstances, the Secretary of State may require reasonable arrangements to be made for medical supervision.

If it appears to the Secretary of State that in any class of factory:

- (a) cases of illness have occurred which he believes to be due to the nature of the work done there, or
- (b) there may be a risk to the health of the persons employed in a factory because of a new process, or of new substances used in a process, or because of changes in conditions of work, or
- (c) young persons are employed in work which may cause risk or injury to their health,

he may make special regulations as is necessary: *s.* 11.

SAFETY (GENERAL PROVISIONS)

17. Fencing of machinery. Sections 12–14 of the Act provide that there is a duty to fence the following:

- (a) Prime movers.
- (b) Transmission machinery.
- (c) Every dangerous part of any machinery.

18. Prime mover. *This is machinery such as an engine or motor which provides mechanical energy.* Every flywheel directly connected to any prime mover and every moving part of any prime mover must be securely fenced. Electric generators and flywheels connected to them must be securely fenced unless they are in such a position or of such construction as to be safe to every person employed or working on the premises as it would be if securely fenced: *s.* 12.

19. Transmission machinery. *This is machinery by which the motion of a prime mover is transmitted to or received by any machine.* Every part of the transmission machinery must be securely fenced unless it is in such a position or of such construction as to be safe to every person employed or working on the premises as it would be if securely fenced. Devices or appliances for promptly cutting off power from transmission machinery must be provided in every room or place where work is carried out. The Secretary of State may, where special circumstances exist, direct that this section shall not apply: *s*. 13.

20. Every dangerous part of any machinery. Such parts must be securely fenced unless in such a position or of such construction as to be safe to every person employed or working on the premises as it would be if securely fenced. If such part of a machine cannot by reason of the nature of the operation be secured by means of a fixed guard, it will be sufficient if a device is provided which automatically prevents the operator from coming into contact with that part: *s*. 14.

21. Unfenced machinery. In deciding whether unfenced machinery is safe in accordance with the above tests no account is taken of any person carrying out an examination, lubrication or adjustment of machinery which can only be carried out while the machinery is in motion. This section applies only to male persons over 18 and is subject to conditions specified in the regulations: *s*. 15.

22. Construction and maintenance of fencing. All fencing or safeguards provided under *ss*. 12–14 must be of substantial construction, and constantly maintained and kept in position while parts required to be fenced or safeguarded are *in motion or use*. An exception to this rule is allowed when any such parts are necessarily exposed for examination and for lubrication or adjustment shown by the examination to be immediately necessary, and all such conditions as may be specified in regulations are complied with: *s*. 16. The phrase "in motion" has been discussed in a number of cases. In *Stanbrook* v. *Waterlow & Sons, Ltd.* (1964), it was held that although the movement of a machine was not intended to last for more than a moment of time, yet the machine was in motion for the purpose of *s*. 16 because it was moving at speed, and therefore the defendants were in breach of their statutory duty. However, in *Kelly* v. *John Dale Ltd.* (1964), the machine was not in motion or use within the meaning of the section when a woman supervisor was cleaning a machine and rotating a cylinder gradually by means of an inching button, about every ten minutes. The defendants were, however, in breach of *s*. 20. This was also held in the case in *Denyer* v. *Charles Skipper & East Ltd.* (1970) (*see* 62).

A narrow construction was also placed on the words in *Mitchell* v. *Westin, Ltd.* (1965) in the Court of Appeal, in which an experienced fitter removed a guard off a power driven lathe in order to do some repairs. In order to tighten some screws, he had to turn the lathe round. He could have done so without switching the machine on, but he did it by switching the machine on and almost simultaneously switching it off. While doing this he leaned his left hand on the machine and caught a forefinger in a nip between two cog wheels. It was held that the lathe was not "in motion" within the meaning of *s.* 16 because there was only an intermittent movement, no evidence of high speed, and no substantial movement comparable to the ordinary working of the lathe. According to Pearson, L.J., in deciding whether in a particular case the movement is or is not of such a character that the machinery is "in motion," the factors to be taken into account include the speed of the movement, the duration, the method of starting the machinery and probably to some extent or in some cases also the purpose for which the movement had been instituted.

23. Interpretation by the courts of sections 12–16. The application of these safety measures has been open to judicial consideration in a number of cases:

(a) *"Every dangerous part of every machinery"* (*s.* 14). In *Close* v. *Steel Company of Wales* (1961), the House of Lords gave approval to the test that machinery is dangerous if it is "a reasonably forseeable cause of injury to anybody acting in a way in which a human being may reasonably be expected to act in circumstances which may reasonably be expected to occur."

In *Cross* v. *Midland & Low Moor Iron and Steel Co. Ltd.* (1964) the House of Lords held that this test was to be applied to a machine when it was doing work which it was designed to do; a part of a machine might then become dangerous through the juxtaposition of that part and a piece of material. This decision was applied in the following case:

Johnson v. *F. E. Callow (Engineers), Ltd.* (1970). A horizontal boring bar with a cutting tool in one end was used to bore a workpiece. No guard was provided between the bore and the

workpiece. An automatic coolant system was fitted to the
machine but the plaintiff found it more convenient to use his
own "squeezie" bottle, a practice known to his employers
though not approved by them. The plaintiff slipped while
reaching for the bottle and caught his hand in the nip between
the bore and the rotating workpiece. HELD (*inter alia*): the
boring bar could not be treated in isolation since it became a
dangerous part of the machinery when, in the normal working
of the machine, it was brought into such close juxtaposition with
the workpiece.

(b) *Reasonable foreseeability.* The test of what is reasonably
foreseeable must be applied to the possible behaviour both of
employees and of machines. Machinery which is not intrinsi-
cally dangerous may become so by reference to the behaviour
of an employee. Any behaviour which is reasonably foreseeable
would come within the test, so that it will be a question of fact
in each case whether the employer should have anticipated the
danger. The possibility of careless and inattentive behaviour
by employees must be taken into account as must the behaviour
of a machine when it is being used in the usual course of working.
This point was discussed in *Johnson* v. *F. E. Callow (Engineers),
Ltd.* (*see above*), where it was found that once the defendants
were aware that their employees were using "squeezies" they
could have foreseen that sooner or later someone might slip
or overreach himself or some careless operator might get his
hand too far inside the workpiece with the danger of being
trapped between the boring bar and workpiece.

(c) *Duty to fence.* There is an absolute duty to fence *securely*
and it is no defence to show that it would not be practicable to
fence the machine. If it is not possible to use the machine when
it has been fenced, then it should not be used. The Secretary of
State has power to modify the strictness of this rule by special
regulation under *s.* 76. This has been done, for example, with
regard to the fencing of wood-working machinery.

John Summers v. *Frost* (1954): a fitter injured his thumb
when it came into contact with a power-driven grinding
machine. A fixed guard covered a part only of the grindstone.
HELD: a grindstone was a dangerous part of a machine within
s. 14 and so must be securely fenced even though such fencing
rendered it unusable.

Automatic Woodturning Co. v. *Stringer* (1957): S operated a
power-driven circular saw being used for cutting lengths of

timber. She was provided with a stick to push away the offcuts of timber. While using the push stick her hand came into contact with the saw and she was injured. The saw was fenced in accordance with the *Woodworking Machinery Regulations*. HELD: the saw as a whole complied with the *Woodworking Machinery Regulations* and therefore the provisions of *s*. 14 of the *Factories Act* did not apply.

(d) *Standard of fencing*. By *s*. 16 of the Act all fencing must be of substantial construction and constantly maintained and kept in position while parts are in motion or use, except where the machine is being examined, lubricated or adjusted. The obligation is to fence securely. The test of reasonable foresee-ability, taking into account the possible behaviour of persons employed in deciding what is sufficient fencing, seems to have been modified in the following case:

Millard v. *Serck Tubes, Ltd.* (1969), C.A.: the appellant suffered severe injuries when his hand was dragged into a drilling machine. No accident had ever occurred in this way before. Salmon, L.J., distinguished between the test to be applied here and the test of foreseeability as applied to deciding if a machine is dangerous. Once it is decided that a machine is dangerous, foreseeability of behaviour is no longer relevant. Since this machine was dangerous it ought to have been fenced *properly* and this had not been done. HELD: the occupier of the factory was liable for breach of the statute.

(e) *Extent of duty*. The extent of duty to fence is limited in two ways:

(i) The fencing should be such that it prevents the operator from coming into contact with the machine; it need not prevent parts of the machine from flying out. This prin-ciple has been supported by the House of Lords in *Close* v. *Steel Company of Wales Ltd*. In *Eaves* v. *Morris Motors Ltd*. (1961), it was stated by Holroyd Pearce, L.J., that "there is no protection under *s*. 14 against a class of obvious perils caused by dangerous machinery, namely, perils which arise from a dangerous machine ejecting at the worker pieces of material or even pieces of the machinery itself." It follows that there is no duty to fence against material being ejected whilst being worked on. (The Secretary of State may make regulations requiring that materials or articles which are dangerous while in motion in a machine should be fenced.) Nor need the protection extend to preventing an injury resulting from a tool held by a workman coming into contact with a dangerous part of the machinery: *Sparrow* v. *Fairey Aviation Co., Ltd.* (1961).

Close v. *Steel Company of Wales* (1961): C operated an electric drilling machine, the bit of which shattered and a piece entered his eye. HELD: this was not a dangerous part of machinery, since the harm which had been caused by it was not reasonably foreseeable. Where machinery is dangerous, the duty to fence extends to preventing the body of the operator from coming into contact with the machine. It is not necessary to fence so as to prevent fragments of machinery or material from flying out.

(ii) The machinery which must be fenced is that which is used in the manufacturing processes of a factory. There is no duty to fence machinery which is in a factory for repair or which has been manufactured at the factory.

Parvin v. *Morton Machine Co. Ltd.* (1952): P, an apprentice fitter, was injured while cleaning a dangerous part of a machine which had been manufactured in the factory. This machine, a dough-brake, was unfenced while adjustments were made to it. HELD: the words "any machinery" in *s*. 14 meant machinery used in the factory for production, and there was no duty to fence machinery which had been made there.

Another aspect of this duty was discussed by the House of Lords in *Irwin* v. *White, Tomkins and Courage, Ltd.* (1964). In that case, the deceased was in charge of installation of machinery at the respondent's mill in Northern Ireland. The installation was not complete and the machinery had not been taken into commercial use. The machinery included seven sack hoists to raise sacks to the first floor and corresponding conveyor belts to remove sacks that had been hoisted. The deceased was killed while running one sack hoist which had been completed. It was held that since the sack hoist was an independent entity of machinery which had been *completely installed*, it should have been fenced, notwithstanding that the machine had not been taken into commercial use.

The *mobility* of a piece of machinery does not exclude it from possible inclusion within the terms of the Act. In *British Railway Board* v. *Liptrot* (1967), H.L., the respondent was injured when a revolving body of a mobile crane caught and squeezed him against one of the chassis wheels. It was held (*inter alia*) that the crane was part of the factory equipment and its mobility did not exclude it from the scope of *s*. 14; accordingly *s*. 14 applied to dangerous parts of machinery contained in the mobile crane. No distinction was to be drawn between mobility and immobility but between machinery and vehicles.

24. Construction and sale of new machinery.

Machinery which is to be driven by mechanical power must not be sold, let on hire, or used unless certain parts are effectively guarded so as to prevent danger: *s*. 17.

25. Dangerous substances.

(a) *Vessels containing dangerous liquids* with edge less than three feet above the ground must be securely fenced to that height or securely covered. Where such measures are impracticable, all practicable steps must be taken to prevent any person from falling into the vessel.

(b) Where a vessel containing a dangerous substance is *not securely covered*, no ladder, stair or gangway must be placed above, across or inside it which is not at least eighteen inches wide and securely fenced to a height of at least three feet and securely fixed: *s*. 18.

26. Hoists and lifts.

(a) Every hoist or lift must be of *good mechanical construction*, sound material and adequate strength and must be properly maintained.

(b) Every hoist or lift must be *thoroughly examined* by a competent person at least once every six months.

(c) *A report* must be entered or attached to a general register within twenty-eight days of examination.

(d) *Where a fault is discovered* a copy of the report must be sent to the district inspector within twenty-eight days.

(e) Every hoistway or liftway must be *efficiently enclosed* so as to prevent any person from falling down the way or coming into contact with the lift.

(f) *Gates* to liftways must be fitted with efficient interlocking or other device to ensure that the gate cannot be opened except when the cage or platform is at the landing.

(g) *The maximum working load* must be marked conspicuously on every hoist or lift: *s*. 22.

27. Hoists and lifts used for carrying people. In addition to these precautions, hoists and lifts used to carry people must be equipped with devices to prevent them from over-running: *s*. 23.

28. Teagle openings. Teagle or similar openings used for hoisting or lowering goods must be securely fenced except when in use, and must be provided with secure hand-holds: *s*. 24.

29. Chains, ropes and lifting tackle. With respect to every chain, rope or piece of lifting tackle used for the purpose of raising or lowering people, goods or materials, the following provisions must be complied with:

(a) They must be of good construction, sound material, adequate strength and free from patent defect.

(b) They must not be used for a load exceeding the specified safe working load.

(c) Chains, ropes and lifting tackle must be tested and thoroughly examined by a competent person every six months.

(d) No new equipment of this kind (except fibre ropes) may be taken into use for the first time without being tested and certified: *s*. 26.

Ball v. *Richard Thomas and Baldwins* (1968), C.A.: an overhead crane was used to lift overspill of molten metal known as "scab", off the floor of a steel works. The plaintiff loosened the scab so that the crane could lift it away. As the crane started to lift the scab, on this occasion, the hook straightened or opened dropping the scab, hitting the plaintiff in the face and injuring him. HELD: the operation was one of "raising" materials within the meaning of *s*. 26(1), and, as it had been conceded by the defendant that the hook was not of adequate strength, the employers were in breach of the section.

30. Cranes and other lifting machines.

(a) These must be of *good construction*, sound material, adequate strength and free from patent defect and must be properly maintained.

(b) They must be *thoroughly examined* by a competent person

at least once every fourteen months, and the result
entered on a register.

(c) *Where a fault is discovered* a copy of the report must be
sent to the district inspector within twenty-eight days.

(d) *The safe working load* must be shown and must not be
exceeded except for the purpose of a test.

(e) No lifting machine may be *used for the first time* without
being tested and certified.

(f) *Any person working near* the wheel track of an overhead
crane must be *warned* of its approach or it must be *en-
sured* that the crane does not come within twenty feet of
that place.

(g) *Any person working above floor level* and liable to be
struck by such a crane or its load must be *warned* of its
approach: *s.* 27.

31. Floors, passages and stairs.

(a) All floors, steps, stairs, passages and gangways must be of
sound construction, and must be properly maintained
and must, as far as is reasonably practicable, be kept
free from any obstruction and from any substance
likely to cause people to slip.

(b) Every staircase must be provided with a handrail which,
if the staircase has an open side, must be on that side.
Where there are two open sides or the staircase is
specially liable to cause accidents, a handrail must be
provided on both sides.

(c) All openings in floors must be securely fenced except
where the nature of the work renders this impracticable.

(d) All ladders must be soundly constructed and properly
maintained: *s.* 28.

NOTE

(i) The words "of sound construction and properly maintained"
in *s.* 28(1) establish an *absolute* duty to maintain the structure of floors, steps, stairs, passages and gangways. The
duty does not apply to transient or exceptional conditions
such as sudden flooding due to a heavy storm.

(ii) There is a further duty in this section to keep floors, steps,
stairs, passages and gangways free from any obstruction
and from substances likely to cause persons to slip. This
duty is to do only that which is *reasonably practicable* and it
is not absolute in nature.

Jenkins v. *Allied Ironfounders, Ltd.* (1969), H.L.: the appellant was a labourer at the respondent's factory. Part of his duties were to help two other labourers in decoring castings in the moulding shop. First the castings were removed from the moulding boxes while still hot, and were then put with 40 or 50 castings in a heap. When the castings were cold they were moved again, decored, and piled ready for removal. The castings usually had excrescences of scrap (known as "gates"). Some gates got knocked off when the castings were first emptied but most had to be knocked off when the castings were decored. The appellant was helping to move castings from the first pile to the second when he caught his heel in a gate hidden in the sand which covered the floor. The appellant fell and was injured. HELD: that the respondents were not guilty of breach of statutory duty because it was not reasonably practicable to have a system which would have resulted in the removal of the gate before the accident.

32. Safe means of access and place of work.

So far as it is reasonably practicable there must be safe means of access to every place at which any person has at any time to work. Every such place must, so far as is reasonably practicable, be made and kept safe for any person working there: *s.* 29.

Nimmo v. *Alexander Cowan & Sons, Ltd.* (1967), H.L.: the appellant was unloading railway wagons filled with bales of pulp. He stood on a bale which tipped, and he fell and was injured. The appellant claimed that the bales were insecurely placed in the wagon, but he did not maintain that it was reasonably practicable for the respondents to make the working place safe. HELD: the obligation of proving that it was not reasonably practicable to make the working place any safer was on the occupiers of the factory, and so the case was properly pleaded.

33. Dangerous fumes.

(a) Where work has to be done inside a *chamber or other confined place*, where there are likely to be dangerous fumes (or lack of oxygen) a manhole must be provided in the absence of other adequate means of exit.

(b) Unless a confined space has been *certified* by a responsible person as being safe for entry, no person may enter without wearing suitable breathing apparatus. Where practicable he must also wear a belt with a securely attached rope.

(c) Before being certified as safe, effective steps must be taken to *prevent further entry of fumes*, to remove the source of fumes, and to ensure that the space is adequately ventilated.

(d) Apparatus, belts and ropes must be *examined* at least once a month or as prescribed by a competent person. A sufficient number of persons must be trained in the use of such apparatus: *s.* 30.

34. Explosive and inflammable substances. All practicable precautions must be taken to prevent explosion and restrict its spread: *s.* 31.

35. Steam boilers. The following provisions are contained in *ss.* 32–35, 37, 38, 6th Schedule, para. 5:

(a) Every steam boiler must be of good construction, sound material and adequate strength and free from patent defect.

(b) It must have attached to it: (i) a suitable safety valve so as to prevent the boiler being worked at a pressure greater than maximum permissible pressure, (ii) a suitable stop-valve connecting boiler to steam-pipe, (iii) a correct steam pressure gauge with maximum permissible pressure marked on it, (iv) at least one water gauge of transparent material to show water level in the boiler, (v) where the boiler is one of a number, a plate bearing a distinctive number.

(c) Steam boilers must be thoroughly inspected by a competent person at least once every fourteen months, and after extensive repairs a report must be attached to the general register.

(d) All new boilers must be examined and certified; used boilers must be examined before being taken into use.

36. Air receivers.

(a) They must be of sound construction and properly maintained.

(b) Requirements similar to those for steam boilers apply.

(c) They must be thoroughly cleaned and examined at least once in every period of 26 months, by a competent person and the report attached to the general register. For certain constructions, the examination period may be extended, but not beyond four years: *ss.* 36 and 37.

37. Fire precautions.

(a) The fire provisions of *s.* 40 apply to any factory:

    (i) in which more than 20 persons are employed, or

    (ii) which was built or converted after 30th July 1937, and in which 10 persons are employed in the same building above ground floor, or

    (iii) which was built before that date and in which more than 10 persons are employed above the first floor or more than 20 feet above ground level, or

    (iv) in or under which explosive or inflammable materials are stored or used.

(b) In accordance with *s.* 40, these factories must obtain *fire certificates* from the fire authority stating that the premises have means of escape such as should reasonably be required in case of fire.

(c) *The certificate must specify* precisely and in detail the means of escape provided and give the maximum number of persons to be employed in the factory or in any part of it, and it must give particulars of explosive or highly inflammable material stored or used there.

(d) *All means of escape* must be properly maintained and kept free from obstruction.

(e) *Effective means must be provided and maintained* for giving warning in case of fire, which must be clearly audible throughout the building. These must be tested at least every three months and a report attached to the general register.

(f) In *every* factory there must be provided and maintained appropriate *means for fighting fire*, which must be readily available for use.

(g) While any person is within a factory for the purpose of employment or meals, *the doors of the factory must not be locked* or fastened in such a way that they cannot be easily and immediately opened from the inside.

(h) *Any doors opening on to a staircase or corridor* from any room in which more than 10 persons are employed must open outwards unless they are sliding doors. (This requirement applies to *all* doors affording a means of exit from factories constructed or converted after 30th June 1938.)

(i) *Every hoist and liftway* in a building constructed after June 1938 shall be completely enclosed with fire-resisting materials and all means of access to them must be fitted with doors of fire-resisting materials. The top of unvented hoistways and liftways must be enclosed by material easily broken by fire.

(j) *All fire exits* must be distinctively and conspicuously marked by a notice printed in letters of adequate size.

(k) *In factories employing more than 20 persons* in the same building above the first floor or more than 20 feet above ground level, or if explosive or highly inflammable substances are used or stored in the building, effective steps must be taken to ensure that the workers are familiar with the means of escape and their use.

(l) *The contents of any room* in which persons are employed must be so arranged that there is a free passageway to the means of escape.

(m) The Secretary of State may make *special regulations* as to the measures to be taken to reduce the risk of fire breaking out.

WELFARE (GENERAL PROVISIONS)

38. Supply of drinking water.

(a) *At suitable points* conveniently accessible to all employees there must be an adequate supply of wholesome drinking water from a public main or from some other source approved by the local authority.

(b) *Where the water is not laid on* it must be contained in suitable vessels, and the supply renewed daily. It should be clearly marked as drinking water.

(c) Except where the water is delivered in an upward jet, one or more *suitable cups* must be provided with facilities for rinsing them: *s.* 57.

39. Washing facilities.
Adequate and suitable washing facilities must be provided. These should include the provision

of soap and clean towels (or other means of cleaning or drying) and a supply of clean running hot and cold or warm water. Facilities should be conveniently accessible and be kept in a clean and orderly condition: *s.* 58.

40. Accommodation for clothing. Adequate and suitable accommodation for clothing not worn during working hours must be provided. Arrangements for drying such clothing must also be made when reasonably practicable: *s.* 59.

41. Facilities for sitting. Where any employed persons have in the course of their employment reasonable opportunities for sitting without detriment to their work, there must be provided and maintained for their use suitable facilities for sitting sufficient to enable them to take advantage of these opportunities. Where a substantial proportion of any work can be done sitting, suitable seating must be provided and maintained: *s.* 60.

42. First aid.

(a) *A first-aid box or cupboard* of the prescribed standard must be provided, which must be readily accessible. Where more than 150 persons are employed an additional box must be provided for every additional 150 people.

(b) Each box or cupboard must be *in the charge of a responsible person.* In factories where more than 50 people are employed, this person must be trained in first aid, and must always be available during working hours.

(c) *There must be a notice in every workroom* stating the name of the person in charge of the first-aid box or cupboard.

(d) *If an ambulance room is provided* in which all injuries can be treated, the chief inspector may exempt that factory from certain of these requirements: *s.* 61.

43. Additional regulations. The Secretary of State may make additional regulations to cover certain kinds of employment: *s.* 62.

SPECIAL HEALTH, SAFETY AND WELFARE PROVISIONS

44. Removal of dust and fumes.

(a) *All practicable steps* must be taken to protect employees against inhalation of dust, fumes or other impurities, arising from a process, which are likely to be injurious or offensive or where there is any substantial quantity of dust of any kind.

(b) Where practicable, *exhaust appliances* must be provided and maintained so as to prevent dust and fumes entering the workroom.

(c) *No stationary internal combustion engine* may be used unless:
   (i) provision is made to conduct the exhaust gases into the open air; *and*
   (ii) the engine is partitioned off from any workroom so as to prevent fumes from entering the room: *s.* 63.

NOTE

(i) *Exclusion of s. 63.* The operation of this section may be excluded by special regulations made under the Act.

(ii) *Comparison with s. 4.* The effect of *s.* 63 should be compared to that of *s.* 4(1). Devlin, J., said in *Graham* v. *Co-operative Wholesale Society Ltd.* (1947): "Section 4 is dealing with the circulation of fresh air which gets rid of impurities which come into the air, whereas section 63 is dealing with methods of prevention, of stopping the impurities from ever getting into circulation at all."

(iii) *Nature and quantity of dust.* The two parts of *s.* 63(1) impose duties in relation to two types of circumstances: (1) where the dust given off is likely to be injurious or offensive; (2) where dust of any kind is given off in substantial quantity.

(iv) *Measures must be "practicable."* The duty under *s.* 63 is to take measures which are "practicable." What is practicable depends upon methods of protection which were known to exist at the time of the alleged breach. The onus of proof that injury is a result of a breach of statutory duty lies on the plaintiff.

Richards v. *Highway Ironfounders (West Bromwich) Ltd.* (1955): from 1930 until 1952 the plaintiff was employed in the defendant's factory. The operation of moulding required the use of sand and involved a process known as "knocking out" in which grains of sand had to be knocked out of moulds. Whenever the process took place a substantial quantity of dust was given out. Until about 1950, the dust was not thought to be dangerous but it was then established that after being inhaled over a number of years it was liable to produce silicosis. No steps were taken to protect moulders against inhalation and no exhaust appliances were installed. HELD: since at the time when the plaintiff became seriously affected with silicosis the dust was not known to be injurious, the duty under *s*. 63 did not arise.

45. Meals in dangerous trades.

(a) *Where poisonous substances are used* so as to give rise to dust or fumes, no person may partake of food or drink in that room, nor remain there during meal times.

(b) A person must not remain during meal times in a room in which a process gives rise to *siliceous or asbestos dust*.

(c) Suitable provision must be made for these employees to take their *meals elsewhere* in the factory: *s*. 64.

46. Protection of eyes. The Secretary of State by regulation may specify that certain processes involve special risk of injury to the eyes. Suitable goggles or effective screens must then be provided: *s*. 65.

47. Underground rooms.

(a) *The district inspector may certify* a room unsuitable for work other than for storage purposes or other specified uses.

(b) "*Unsuitable*" means unsuitable as regards height, light or ventilation or on any hygienic ground, or because means of escape in case of fire are not provided: *s*. 69.

48. Lifting excessive weights. A person must not be employed to lift, carry or move any load so heavy as to be likely to cause him injury: *s*. 72.

49. Special regulations for safety and health. The Secretary of State may make special regulations if he is satisfied that any manufacture, machinery, plant or process is of such a nature as to cause risk of bodily injury to employees: *s*. 76.

ACCIDENTS AND INDUSTRIAL DISEASES

50. Notification of accidents. Where an accident in a factory
(a) causes loss of life to an employee, (b) disables an employee
from earning full wages for more than three days at his usual
work, the district inspector must be informed: s. 80.

51. Dangerous occurrences. The Secretary of State has
power to extend the necessity for notification to dangerous
occurrences whether or not death or disablement occur: s. 81.
These dangerous occurrences now include:

(a) *Bursting of a revolving vessel,* wheel or grindstone.
(b) *The collapse or failure* of a crane or hoist.
(c) *Explosion or fire due* to certain causes, resulting in
    damage to the structure of any room, followed by the
    suspension of work for at least five hours.
(d) *Electrical short circuit* or failure of electrical machinery,
    plant or apparatus accompanied by explosion, or fire or
    structural damage resulting in the suspension of work for
    at least five hours.
(e) *Explosion or fire* affecting a workroom and resulting in
    suspension of work for at least five hours.
(f) *Explosion of a receiver or container* used for the storage of
    any gas at a pressure greater than atmospheric pressure.

52. Notification of industrial diseases.

(a) Every medical practitioner attending a patient whom he
    believes to be suffering from lead, phosphorus, arsenical
    or mercurical *poisoning or anthrax* contracted in any
    factory must immediately inform the Chief Inspector of
    Factories.
(b) Where any of the above-mentioned diseases occurs in a
    factory, the *employer* must immediately inform the
    district inspector and the factory doctor: s. 82.
(c) *The statutory list of diseases has been extended* by regu-
    lation to include toxic jaundice, toxic anaemia, ulcera-
    tion and others.

53. Inquest in case of death. Where a coroner holds an
inquest on a person whose death may have been caused by an
accident or disease of which notice has to be given, it must be

adjourned unless an inspector or his representative is present: *s.* 83.

54. Formal investigations.

(a) The Secretary of State may direct a *formal investigation* into any accident or disease contracted in a factory.

(b) *A competent person* may be appointed to hold the *investigation* and the Secretary of State may appoint a person possessing legal or special knowledge to act as assessor.

(c) The investigation is held in an *open court* with the same powers as a *magistrates' court*. It has right of entry into any place or building, the power to summon witnesses, and to require books and documents to be produced.

(d) The court then *reports to the Secretary of State* giving causes and circumstances of the incident and adding any observations which it thinks right to make: *s.* 84.

EMPLOYMENT OF WOMEN AND YOUNG PERSONS

55. Working hours. The *Factories Act*, 1961, contains no restriction as to the length of hours of work of men. But women, and young persons *of either sex under the age of 18*, must not work longer than the hours set down by the statute. The Act imposes the following general conditions of work for women and young persons:

(a) *Total hours of work* excluding intervals allowed for meals and rest must not exceed 9 in any day nor exceed 48 in any week (44 hours for a young person under the age of 16).

(b) *The period of employment shall not exceed* 11 hours in any day and must not begin earlier than 7 o'clock in the morning, nor end later than 6 o'clock at night, for young persons under 16 years, and 8 o'clock in other cases. Work must end at 1 o'clock on Saturday afternoons.

(c) *The maximum continuous spell of work* must not be longer then 4½ hours without a break of at least 30 minutes. However, the spell of work may be extended to 5 hours if at least 10 minutes' break is allowed during this time.

(d) *The period worked and the meal and rest periods* allowed must be the same for all women and young people employed. But a young person under the age of 16 may finish work earlier.

(e) *No woman or young person* must work during meal and rest periods: *s.* 86.

56. Notice of working hours. A notice of hours of work for each day for women and young persons must be posted in the factory, together with the meal and rest intervals: *s.* 88.

NOTE

(i) *Different periods of employment* and different intervals may be fixed for different days of the week.

(ii) *The district inspector must be informed* of any changes in these hours, which cannot be made more frequently than once every three months.

57. Overtime. Pressure of work in a factory may be eased by the overtime employment, within limits, of women and young persons over 16 years of age, subject to the following conditions contained in *ss.* 89–100.

(a) *The total actual hours worked per day* must not exceed 10 (or $10\frac{1}{2}$ where a 5-day week is worked). These hours must be within a maximum period of 12 hours, that is, between 7 a.m. and 9 p.m. or 8 p.m. for young persons.

(b) *The overtime worked* must not exceed an allowance of 100 hours per year for any factory nor 6 hours in any week. This allowance does not vary with the number of women or young persons so employed.

(c) *The period during which overtime is worked* must not exceed 25 weeks in any year.

(d) *The Secretary of State may make regulations* altering in certain circumstances the factory allowance of overtime and substituting a personal allowance. The personal allowance must not exceed 75 hours per year for a woman and 50 hours per year for a young person.

(e) *In factories subject to a seasonal pressure* the Secretary of State may by regulation increase the hours of work of women but not for longer than 8 weeks in any year. The allowance for a factory may be increased to an aggregate not exceeding 150 hours, but no young person must work during more than 100 hours.

(f) The Secretary of State may by regulation allow employment in different parts of a factory or in different processes to be regarded as employment in different factories for the purpose of reckoning hours of overtime: *s*. 89.

58. Shift-work. The Secretary of State may on application of the occupier authorise the employment of women and young persons of under 16 on shifts between 6 a.m. and 10 p.m. and up to 2 p.m. on Saturdays. Generally the shifts must not exceed 8 hours in length. A secret ballot must be held to ascertain the consent of the majority of the employees concerned: *s*. 97.

59. Exceptions. Women in responsible positions of management are not covered by these provisions: *s*. 95. Also, the Secretary of State has power to suspend certain of these provisions in the event of an emergency to avoid serious interference with the ordinary work of the factory: *s*. 96.

60. Exemption orders. Where an application is made to the Secretary of State, he may, when satisfied that it is desirable in the public interest, to maintain or increase efficiency of industry or transport, exempt the employment of women and young persons from the provisions as to working hours: *s*. 117.

Exemption orders may be special or general.

(a) *Special exemption orders* apply only to particular classes of employment.
(b) *General exemption orders* extend to the employment of persons generally, and may be made only on:

    (i) the application of a joint industrial council or similar body, or
    (ii) the application of a wages council, or
    (iii) the joint application of an organisation which appears to represent employers and one representing workmen, or
    (iv) the application of an organisation representative of employers or employees after consultation with the other organisations.

HEALTH AND SAFETY PROVISIONS FOR WOMEN AND YOUNG PERSONS

61. Certificate of fitness. No young person may remain in employment in a factory for longer than 14 days without being medically examined and certified fit by the appointed factory doctor: *s.* 118.

NOTE
(i) The certificate is in force for *12 months* or such shorter period as set out in Departmental regulations: *s.* 118.
(ii) The doctor may issue a *provisional certificate* where he requires further information before granting the certificate. The provisional certificate is operative for up to 21 days only: *s.* 118.
(iii) The factory inspector may require an occupier to *discontinue the employment of young persons* if in his opinion a process is prejudicial to health, until the factory doctor has certified that the young persons concerned are fit for this work: *s.* 119.

62. Cleaning of machinery. A woman or young person must not clean any part of a prime mover or transmission machinery which is in motion; nor any part of any machinery if there is a risk of injury from a moving part of that machine or any adjacent machinery: *s.* 20.

Denyer v. *Charles Skipper & East, Ltd.* (1970), C.A.: While the rollers of a lithographic printing machine were being cleaned, the main current of the machine was turned off. When one length of a roller had been cleaned, it had to be turned by means of an inching button to expose another part for cleaning. When pressing the inching button with his left hand, the plaintiff, a youth of 17, put his right hand too close to the roller so that it was dragged in with the cleaning rag, and he was injured. HELD: the defendants were liable for damages for breach of *s.* 20 since the operation exposed him to risk of injury and the rollers, when being inched, were moving parts of the machinery.

63. Training and supervision. A young person must not work any machine prescribed as dangerous by the Secretary of State unless (*a*) he has received sufficient training in the work, or (b) is under adequate supervision by a person with experience of the machine: *s.* 21.

64. Prohibition of employment. The Act prohibits the employment of women and young persons as follows:

(a) *Female young persons* must not be employed where certain processes involving melting or blowing glass, or the evaporation of brine, are being carried out: *s.* 73.

(b) *Women and young persons* may not be employed in certain processes connected with the manufacture of lead, or the use of lead compounds: *ss.* 74 and 75.

MISCELLANEOUS PROVISIONS

65. Prohibitions of deductions from wages. The employer must not make any deduction from pay for anything he has to do or provide in pursuance of the Act; nor may he allow employees to receive payment from other employees: *s.* 136.

66. Posting of abstract of Act and notices. At the principal entrances of a factory the following must be kept posted:

(a) The prescibed abstract of the *Factories Act*, 1961.
(b) A notice of the address of the district inspector and the superintending inspector for the division.
(c) A notice of the name and address of the appointed factory doctor.
(d) A notice specifying the clock, if any, by which periods of employment and intervals are regulated.
(e) Every notice and document required by the Act to be posted in the factory: *s.* 138.
(f) Copies of all special regulations in force in the factory: *s.* 139.

67. General register. A general register must be kept in every factory in which the following particulars are entered:

(a) The prescribed particulars as to young persons employed in the factory.
(b) The prescribed particulars as to washing, white-washing and painting of the factory.
(c) The prescribed particulars as to every accident and case

of industrial disease occurring in the factory of which notice is to be sent to an inspector.

(d) Particulars of exceptions under certain sections of the Act of which the occupier has availed himself.

(e) All reports and particulars required by the Act to be entered or attached (*e.g.* fire escape certificate).

(f) Particulars of other matters as the Secretary of State may prescribe: *s.* 140.

OBSERVANCE OF THE ACT

68. Duty to observe the provisions of the Act. This duty falls primarily on the occupier of the factory, who may or may not be the owner of the factory: *s.* 155. But in certain circumstances the duty falls on the owner of the factory, or the owner of a machine, or on the employees:

(a) *Liability of owner.* The owner (whether or not he is the occupier) of a tenement factory will be liable for certain contraventions of the Act. A tenement factory is one in which the owner supplies mechanical power to occupiers of different parts of the same premises. Where parts of the same building are let off as separate factories, the owner will again be liable in certain circumstances: *ss.* 120–122.

(b) *Liability of owner of a machine.* The owner or hirer of a machine may be deemed the occupier of the factory for any offence committed to a person employed on the machine who is in the employment of the owner or hirer of the machine: *s.* 163.

(c) *Liability of employee.* A person employed in a factory must not wilfully interfere with or misuse any means, appliance or convenience or other thing provided under the Act for securing health, safety or welfare.

He must use means or appliances provided for his health or safety: *s.* 143.

69. Criminal and civil liability. A person in breach of a duty imposed by the Act is always liable to a prosecution under the criminal law: he may *also* have incurred a civil liability. Broadly, the position is as follows:

(a) *Safety provisions.* A civil right of action is allowed to an employee to claim damages where he has suffered loss due to any breach of a duty imposed by the safety provisions in *ss.* 12–56 of the Act.

(b) *Health and welfare provisions.* There is no clear rule whether the parts of the Act relating to health (*ss.* 1–11) and welfare (*ss.* 57–62) give rise to civil actions or to criminal proceedings only. As regards the health provisions of the Act, there have been a number of decisions in which a civil action was allowed, though the point has not been fully discussed by the courts. There is no general rule as to whether a civil action will be allowed for breach of a welfare provision. Each section must be considered separately. In *McCarthy* v. *Daily Mirror Newspapers Ltd.* (1949) an action was allowed on what is now *s.* 59(1) of the 1961 Act. In Part IV of the Act, which deals with special provisions as to health, safety and welfare, a right of action will depend upon whether the section is concerned to protect health or safety.

70. Exemption from liability. A person prosecuted under the Act may bring forward two defences and have another person charged with the offence. The defences are:

(a) that he has used *all due diligence* to enforce the execution of the Act, and

(b) *that the other person had committed the offence* without his consent, connivance or wilful default: *s.* 161.

ADMINISTRATION OF THE ACT

71. Factory inspectorate. The task of ensuring that the provisions of the Act are observed falls mainly on the factory inspectorate appointed by the Department of Employment. By *s.* 146 an inspector of factories has the following powers:

(a) To enter, inspect and examine at all reasonable times, by day and night, a factory when he has reasonable cause to believe that any person is employed there.

(b) To enter by day any place which he has reasonable cause to believe to be a factory.

(c) To take with him a constable if he has reasonable cause to apprehend any serious obstruction in the execution of his duty.

(d) To require the production of registers, certificates and documents kept in pursuance of the Act and to examine them.

(e) To make any examination and injury as may be necessary to ascertain whether provisions of the Act are being complied with.

(f) To require any person he finds in a factory to give such information as he can as to who is the occupier of the factory.

(g) To examine either alone or in the presence of any other person, every person whom he finds in a factory whom he has reasonable cause to believe has been within the preceding two months employed in a factory and to require such persons to sign a declaration.

(h) To carry out such medical examinations as may be necessary if he is a fully registered medical practitioner.

(i) To exercise such other powers as may be necessary for carrying the Act into effect.

NOTE: An inspector may, where authorised in writing by the Secretary of State, conduct or defend proceedings before a court of summary jurisdiction.

72. Factory doctors. The chief inspector of factories may appoint a sufficient number of medical practitioners as factory doctors. A factory doctor may at all reasonable times inspect the general register of a factory. Every year he must at the prescribed time report to the Secretary of State as to examinations made and other duties carried out under the Act *s.* 151.

73. Medical officers of health. The local authorities have a duty to enforce certain provisions of the statute under Part I and Part VIII. The medical officer of health must report annually to the local authority on the administration of these sections and send a copy to the Department of Employment.

74. Fire authorities. Powers of entry and inspection similar to those conferred by the Act on an inspector (*see* **71** *above*) are exercisable by an officer of a fire authority in certain circumstances. He may, for example, inspect premises for the purposes of granting or withholding a fire certificate.

PROGRESS TEST 23

1. What aspects of working conditions in factories are governed by the *Factories Act*, 1961? (1)

2. How is a factory defined by s. 175 of the Act? What other premises are to be regarded as factories for the purposes of the Act? (2, 3)

3. What difficulties have arisen in connection with the phrase "employed in manual labour"? (4)

4. To what extent are the occupier's purposes relevant to the definition of a factory? (6)

5. Some premises situated within the factory complex may be excluded from the general definition of a factory. On what grounds may this be the case? (7)

6. Outline the main provisions of the *Factories Act* with regard to health. (9–16)

7. List the main provisions of the *Factories Act* with regard to safety. (17–37)

8. What machinery must be fenced in accordance with the *Factories Act*? (17–20)

9. How have the courts interpreted sections 12–16? (23)

10. Discuss the various duties contained in section 28. (31)

11. What factories must obtain a fire certificate in accordance with the provisions of s. 40 of the Act? What other measures apply to these factories? (37)

12. Outline the general provisions of the Act with regard to welfare. (38–43)

13. What is meant by "all practicable steps" in relation to the duty to remove dust and fumes under s. 63. Cite any relevant cases. (44)

14. What industrial accidents and dangerous occurrences must be reported to the district inspector? (50, 51)

15. The Act contains no restriction on the working hours of men. Certain provisions are set out in the Act in relation to women and young persons under eighteen. What are they? (55–58)

16. What persons are made responsible for observing the provisions of the Act? What defences may a person raise if he is prosecuted? (69)

17. What are the powers of the factory inspectorate to enforce the provisions of the Act? (71)

CHAPTER XXIV

STATUTORY CONTROL OF WORKING CONDITIONS: OFFICES, ETC.

THE OFFICES, SHOPS AND RAILWAY PREMISES ACT, 1963

1. Premises to which the Act applies. The Act applies, with certain exceptions, to offices, shops and railway premises where persons are employed to work.

(a) *Offices*. Office premises means a building or part of a building which is solely or principally used as an office or for office purposes. Office purposes include the purposes of administration, clerical work, handling money, and telephone and telegraph operating. Clerical work includes writing, bookkeeping, sorting papers, filing, typing, duplicating, machine calculating, drawing, and the editorial preparation of matter for publication.

(b) *Shops*. The term shop premises is defined to include a building or part of a building which is not a shop but of which the sole or principal use is the carrying on there of retail trade or business. Thus the Act would cover libraries from which books were lent for profit, and restaurants selling food or drink for immediate consumption.

(c) *Railway premises*. The term railway premises means a building occupied by railway undertakers for purposes of the railway undertaking carried on by them and situate in the immediate vicinity of the permanent way: *s.* 1.

NOTE: Staff canteens are included premises.

2. Exceptions. Although the Act applies to most offices, shops and railway buildings, there are certain exceptions. These excepted premises include:

(a) *Premises where self-employed persons work*. The Act applies only to premises where a person is employed under a contract of service or apprenticeship.

(b) *Premises where only certain of the employer's relatives work.*

(c) *Dwellings of outworkers.*

(d) *Premises where employees normally work no longer than a total of 21 hours per week.*

(e) *Premises occupied for a temporary purpose* which is six months in the case of a moveable structure and six weeks in other cases.

HEALTH, SAFETY AND WELFARE PROVISIONS

3. Cleanliness. All premises and all furniture, furnishings and fittings must be kept in a clean state. No dirt or refuse must be allowed to accumulate, and the floors and steps must be cleaned not less than once a week by washing or where suitable by sweeping or other method: *s.* 4.

4. Overcrowding. A room in which people are working must not be overcrowded so as to cause a risk of injury to health. In determining whether a room is overcrowded regard must be had not only to the number of people but also to the space in the room occupied by furniture, furnishings, and other things. The room must be of such a size as to allow 40 square feet of floor space or 400 cubic feet of air space per person: *s.* 5.

5. Temperature. Effective provision must be made to ensure that a reasonable temperature is secured and maintained in every room. No method of heating which might result in the escape of fumes likely to be injurious or offensive may be used. But where a substantial proportion of the work does not involve severe physical effort, a temperature of not less than 16°C (60·8°F) after the first hour is deemed a reasonable temperature. Also, a thermometer must be provided in a conspicuous place on each floor of the premises: *s.* 6.

6. Ventilation. Effective and suitable provision must be made for securing the ventilation of every room by the circulation of adequate supplies of fresh or artificially purified air: *s.* 7.

7. Lighting. Suitable and sufficient lighting, whether natural or artificial, must be provided for every part of the premises. Windows and skylights used for lighting must be, so far as is reasonably practicable, kept clean and free from obstruction. However, windows and skylights may be whitewashed to mitigate glare. All apparatus for producing artificial light must be properly maintained: *s.* 8.

8. Sanitary conveniences. Suitable and sufficient sanitary conveniences must be provided at conveniently accessible places. They must be kept clean and properly maintained and effective provision must be made for lighting and ventilating them: *s.* 9.

9. Washing facilities. Suitable and sufficient washing facilities must be provided including a supply of clean, running hot and cold water or clean running warm water, and soap and clean towels or other suitable means of cleaning and drying. Effective means of lighting must be provided and be kept clean and all apparatus must be kept clean: *s.* 10.

10. Drinking water. An adequate supply of wholesome drinking water must be provided. Where a supply of water is not piped, it must be contained in suitable vessels and must be renewed daily. Where water is supplied other than in a jet, a supply of drinking vessels must be provided of a kind to be discarded after use or other vessels together with facilities for rinsing them in clean water: *s.* 11.

11. Accommodation for clothing. Suitable and sufficient provision must be made for clothing not worn during working hours to be hung up or otherwise accommodated. Such arrangements as are reasonably practicable must be made for drying clothing: *s.* 12.

12. Seating arrangements. Where persons have in the course of their work reasonable opportunities for sitting without detriment to their work, suitable facilities must be provided. The employer must permit employees to use facilities provided whenever this does not interfere with their work: *s.* 13.

NOTE: On shop premises where customers resort, the number

of seats must not be less than one for every three persons employed.

13. Sedentary work. Seats of a suitable design, construction and dimension must be provided for workers whose work is done sitting down. A foot rest must be provided if the employee cannot comfortably support his feet without one: *s.* 14.

14. Eating facilities. Where persons employed in shops eat meals there, suitable and sufficient facilities for eating them must be provided: *s.* 15.

15. Floors, passages and stairs. All floors, stairs, steps, passages and gangways must be soundly constructed and properly maintained and must, so far as is reasonably practicable, be kept free from obstructions and slippery substances. A substantial handrail must be provided for every staircase; if the staircase has an open side, it must be on that side. Where there are two sides or where there is a particular risk of accidents, a handrail or handholds must be provided on both sides: *s.* 16.

16. Fencing of machinery. The provisions of *s.* 17 are similar to those of the *Factories Act*, 1961.

17. Cleaning of machinery. No young person (that is, below 18 years) may clean any machinery if this exposes him to the risk of injury from a moving part of any adjacent machinery: *s.* 18.

18. Training and supervision. No person must work at any machine prescribed as dangerous unless he has been fully instructed as to the dangers arising, and the precautions to be observed and has received sufficient training in the work or is under adequate supervision by a person experienced in the use of the machine: *s.* 19.

19. Prohibition of heavy work. No person should be required to lift, carry or move a load so heavy as to be likely to cause injury to him: *s.* 23.

20. First aid. A first-aid box or cupboard must be provided which is readily accessible to employees. It must contain only first-aid requisites. Where more than 150 persons are employed, an additional box or cupboard must be provided for every 150 persons employed or a fraction of that number. Where more than 150 persons are employed the person in charge of the first-aid box or cupboard must be trained in first-aid treatment in accordance with orders made by the Department of Employment. A notice giving the name of the trained persons must be displayed so as to be easily read by employees.

21. Fire precautions. All premises must be provided with such means of escape in case of fire as may reasonably be required in the circumstances of the case. In determining what means are required, regard must be had not only to the number of employees but also to the number of other persons who may reasonably be expected to be on the premises: *s.* 28.

22. Safety provisions in case of fire. While an employed person is on the premises the doors through which he must pass to get out of the building must not be so locked or fastened that they cannot be immediately opened by him on his way out. Also, the contents of every workroom must be so arranged that the employees have a free passage-way to a means of escape in case of fire: *s.* 33.

23. Provision of fire-fighting equipment. Appropriate means for fighting fire must be provided and maintained. This equipment must be readily available for use: *s.* 38(1).

24. Fire certificates. Unless a fire certificate has been granted or applied for, it is not lawful:

(a) for more than 20 persons to be employed in any premises to which the Act applies, or

(b) for more than 10 persons to be employed other than on the ground floor, or

(c) for any person to be employed to work in premises in or underneath which explosives or highly flammable materials are used or stored, or

(d) for more than a total of 10 persons to be employed elsewhere than on the ground floor in two or more sets of premises in a building to which the *Offices Act* or *Factories Act* applies.

25. Fire alarms. All premises for which a fire certificate is required must provide effective means of giving warning in case of fire. It must be tested every three months or as required by the appropriate authority: *s.* 34.

26. Marking of fire exits. In all premises for which a fire certificate has been granted exits affording or giving access to means of escape must be conspicuously marked by notices printed in letters of adequate size: *s.* 33(3).

27. Fire drills. Effective steps must be taken to ensure that all persons employed in premises for which a fire certificate is required are familiar with the means of escape in case of fire, their use, and the routine to be followed: *s.* 36(1).

28. Right of appeal. There is a right of appeal to a magistrates' court within twenty-one days against a decision by the appropriate authority on any of the following matters:

(a) A refusal to issue a fire certificate.
(b) A refusal to amend a fire certificate.
(c) A requirement to make any alteration to any premises within a specified period.
(d) A prohibition as to putting into effect proposed changes until alterations have been made to premises.
(e) The cancellation of a fire certificate issued with respect to any premises.

29. Notification of accidents. Where an accident in premises to which the Act applies (*a*) causes loss of life to an employee, (*b*) disables an employee from doing his usual work for more than three days, the appropriate authority must be informed. Where death subsequently results from such a disablement, the death must be reported.

Where the occupier of premises is not the actual employer of the person killed or disabled, it is the duty of the employer to inform the occupier of the accident immediately. The occupier should then inform the appropriate authority: *s.* 48.

30. Exemption orders. An application for an order exempting certain premises may be made to the Secretary of State or to an enforcing authority.

31. Exemption by the Secretary of State. The Employment Secretary has power to exempt a *class* of premises from certain provisions of the Act where, because of special circumstances, it would be unreasonable to require compliance. These provisions relate to room space, temperature, sanitary conveniences and washing facilities. Exemption orders may be made without conditions or subject to conditions and with or without a time limit. The Employment Secretary must consult certain organisations before making an order. These must be representatives of workers and employers and other persons concerned: *s.* 45.

32. Exemption by enforcing authority. An enforcing authority has power to exempt *individual* premises from certain provisions of the Act where, by reason of special circumstances it would not be reasonably practicable to require compliance. These provisions relate to room space, temperature, sanitary conveniences and requirements as to running water.

An application must be accompanied by a certificate stating that a notice has been posted on the premises. The notice should contain the following statements:

(a) That an application for exemption is being made.
(b) The requirement from which exemption is being sought.
(c) The period for which the exemption is sought.
(d) The name and address of the authority to whom application is being made.
(e) That written representations may be made to that authority by the persons employed on the premises within fourteen days beginning with the day upon which the notice was first posted: *s.* 26.

MISCELLANEOUS PROVISIONS

33. Levying of charges. The owner or occupier of the premises must not levy any charge upon an employee for anything done or provided in pursuance of the Act: *s.* 47.

34. Information for employees. The Employment Secretary may make regulations under the Act to ensure that employees are informed of the provisions of the Act which affect them: *s.* 50.

OBSERVANCE OF THE ACT

35. Duty to observe the provisions of the Act. This duty falls primarily on the occupier of the premises. But in certain circumstances the duty falls on the employer of any persons employed on the premises, or on the owner of the premises, or on other persons.

36. Liability of occupier. In general, the occupier will be responsible for observing the Act in a building occupied solely by him.

37. Liability of employer. The actual employer of persons working on premises may have responsibilites under the Act if he is different to the occupier of those premises. For example, by *s.* 13(3) it is the duty of the *employer* to permit employees to make use of sitting facilities.

38. Liability of the owner. The owner of a building is liable for observing certain provisions where the building is let to a number of occupiers, or where part only of a building is leased to an occupier. In such cases the owner of the building is liable as follows:

(a) *"Common parts."* By *s.* 42 of the Act the owner is responsible for complying with certain requirements in the "common parts" of the building. The owner must ensure that these parts are kept in a clean state, that suitable lighting is maintained, and that all floors, stairs, steps, passages and gangways are of sound construction and properly maintained.

(b) *Sanitary conveniences and washing facilities.* The owner is responsible for providing sanitary conveniences and washing facilities in accordance with *ss.* 9 and 10 of the Act. He is not responsible for cleaning sanitary conveniences and washing facilities, nor for providing means of cleaning or drying where these are not provided solely for use by the employees of a single occupier.

(c) *Fire precautions.* The responsibility for providing fire precautions in all parts of the building rests on the owner, but an occupier is responsible for taking certain precautions on his premises.

39. Summary of responsibilities. Table 1 shows how responsibility is shared between owners and occupiers in a building let to a number of occupiers or where part only of a building is leased to an occupier.

TABLE 1

	Occupier	Owner
	Responsibility allocated to	
(1) Common parts (cleaning, lighting, safety).		X
(2) Provision of sanitary conveniences and washing facilities (including maintenance, lighting and ventilation, as required).		X
(3) Cleaning of sanitary conveniences and washing facilities provided for joint use by two or more occupiers.		X
(4) Cleaning of sanitary conveniences and washing facilities provided for sole use of one occupier.	X	
(5) Provision of soap and towels or other means of cleaning and drying.	X	
(6) All provisions relating to fire precautions, except those in (7).		X
(7) Taking precautions within individual premises so as to provide free access to means of escape, making employees familiar with the escape routine, and provision of fire-fighting equipment.	X	

40. Liability of owners in plural ownership. A building may be divided into different parts owned by different persons. Each owner is responsible for the part owned by him except that there is a joint responsibility for maintaining fire precautions under the Act.

41. Liability of other persons. Any person who wilfully and without reasonable cause does anything to endanger health or

safety of employees is liable under the Act. This section also
covers wilful misuse of equipment provided under the statute
and its removal without reasonable excuse: *s.* 27.

42. Defences. Where a person is prosecuted under the Act
it is a defence for him to show that he used all due diligence
to comply with the provision.

ADMINISTRATION OF THE ACT

43. The administration of the Act is in the hands of enforcing
authorities. These include local authorities, the factory inspectorate and fire authorities.

44. Local authorities. It is the duty of every local authority
to enforce the provisions of the Act in respect of premises
within their areas (except provisions with regard to fire precautions). But the responsibility for inspecting premises
directly under the control of local authorities, or closely connected with their work, is given to the factory inspectorate.

45. Factory inspectorate. Some of the duties of ensuring that
the provisions of the Act are observed fall on the factory inspectorate appointed by the Employment Secretary. By *s.* 53,
an inspector of factories has the following powers:

(a) To enter and inspect any premises to which the Act
applies, or any common parts of a building to which the
Act applies.

(b) To enter and inspect premises which he has reasonable
cause to believe are covered by the provisions of the Act.

(c) To enter and inspect premises underneath premises to
which the Act applies if he has reasonable cause to believe that explosive or flammable materials are kept there.

(d) To ask any questions as he thinks fit of any person whom
he finds on such premises to discover whether the provisions of the Act are being complied with.

(e) To require production of certificates and notices kept in
pursuance of the Act.

(f) To take with him a constable if he has reasonable cause
to apprehend any serious obstruction in the exercise of
the powers conferred on him under the Act.

TABLE 2

Class of Premises	General Provisions other than Fire (Sections 4–27 and 46–50)	Means of Escape (Sections 28, 29, 30, 32, 35)	Other Fire Provisions (Sections 33, 34, 36–38)
Premises owned or occupied by the Crown	H.M. Factory Inspector[1]	H.M. Factory Inspector[1]	H.M. Factory Inspector[1]
Premises occupied by county councils, local, fire[2] and police authorities; probation committees	H.M. Factory Inspector	H.M. Factory Inspector	H.M. Factory Inspector
Premises provided and maintained by county councils and local authorities for purposes connected with the administration of justice	H.M. Factory Inspector	H.M. Factory Inspector	H.M. Factory Inspector
Premises in a school maintained by L.E.A.	H.M. Factory Inspector	H.M. Factory Inspector	H.M. Factory Inspector
U.K. Atomic Energy Authority premises	H.M. Factory Inspector	H.M. Factory Inspector	H.M. Factory Inspector
Offices and shops in factories and other places covered by The *Factories Act, 1961*	H.M. Factory Inspector	H.M. Factory Inspector	H.M. Factory Inspector
Railway premises and railway offices (except offices in railway hotels and those not situated in the immediate vicinity of the permanent way). Fuel storage premises on land owned by railway undertakers	H.M. Factory Inspector	Fire Authority	H.M. Factory Inspector
Offices and shops in places of public entertainment in London	H.M. Factory Inspector	Fire Authority	H.M. Factory Inspector
Offices, shops and fuel storage premises at mines and quarries	Greater London Council H.M. Inspector of Mines and Quarries	Fire Authority[3] Fire Authority	Fire Authority[3] H.M. Inspector of Mines and Quarries
Other offices and shops	Local Authority[4]	Fire Authority	Fire Authority

[1] References to H.M. Factory Inspector mean the Factory Inspector in whose District the premises are situated.
[2] Where the Crown is the occupier, inspection will take place by administrative arrangement.
[3] The fire authority in this case will in fact be the Greater London Council.
[4] In the Inner and Middle Temples, these provisions will be enforced by the respective overseers by virtue of s. 89 of the Act.

(g) To exercise such other powers as may be necessary for carrying the Act into effect.

46. Fire authorities. Local fire authorities have the duty to enforce provisions with regard to fire precautions in certain premises.

47. Summary of responsibilities. Table 2 shows how responsibility for enforcing provisions of the Act in different classes of premises is divided between the various authorities.

48. Powers of magistrates' courts. Where a complaint is made by an enforcing authority, a magistrates' court has power to make orders with regard to the following matters:

(a) That any part of the premises is in such condition or is so constructed that it cannot be used without risk of bodily injury or injury to health, or

(b) That any machinery, plant equipment or appliance used in the premises is in such a condition, is so constructed or is so placed that it cannot be used without such a risk, or

(c) That an operation carried on in the premises, or a process used therein, is so carried on or used in such a manner as to cause such risk.

The court order may prohibit such use absolutely unless it is satisfied that repair or alteration will remove the risk: *s.* 22(1).

49. Imminent risk. Where the court is satisfied that there is imminent risk of bodily injury or injury to health from the use of premises or appliances or a process, an interim order may be made prohibiting their use either absolutely or subject to conditions until a court hearing is held. The occupier must be given three clear days' notice of intention to apply for an interim order: *s.* 22(2).

PROGRESS TEST 24

1. To which premises does the *Offices, Shops and Railway Premises Act*, 1963, apply? Mention any exceptions. **(1, 2)**
2. What is the scope and purpose of the Act? **(1, 2)**
3. What provision does the Act make for the following:

(a) cleanliness, (b) overcrowding, (c) temperature and ventilation, (d) lighting, and (e) sanitary and washing facilities. (3–9)

4. What are the rules as to the fencing, cleaning and use of machinery? (16–18; XXII, 18)

5. To what extent does the Act provide for the possibility of fire? (21–28)

6. In what circumstances must accidents be notified? Who must give the notification to the appropriate authority? (29)

7. May premises be exempted from the provisions of the Act? (30, 32)

8. Explain the liability of (a) the occupier, (b) the employer, and (c) the owner, of premises covered by the Act. What are the provisions as to *common parts* and *plural ownership*? (35–39)

9. The administration of the Act is in the hands of *enforcing authorities*. Which are these authorities, and what are their responsibilities? (43–46)

10. What are the powers of magistrates' courts where a complaint is made by an enforcing authority? (48, 49)

EXAMINATION TECHNIQUE

1. Two types of question. A student preparing for a law examination must train himself to answer two kinds of question:

(a) *Textbook questions, i.e.* those requiring exposition or discussion of a particular topic.

(b) *Problems, i.e.* those requiring the application of legal principles to a given situation.

2. Textbook questions. These are designed to test the student's knowledge and understanding of the subject. Such questions require the statement, criticism, or discussion of principles. Here are some points for guidance:

(a) *Read the question carefully.* In any examination, there are always students who fail to do this. *Underline* any parts of the question which seem to you to be significant. Notice particularly what you are told to do.

(b) *Make an outline plan of your answer.* In order to do this, you must try to see exactly what the examiner *wants*. If the question is widely drawn you will need a widely drawn plan. If the question is narrowly drawn, you will need a narrowly drawn plan. Make sure that the aim and scope of your plan exactly satisfy the question. It is at this stage that you must settle what goes into your answer. Your outline plan will probably consist of four or five key sentences arranged in logical sequence. (Each of these key sentences will probably develop into a paragraph of your final answer.) Jot down the names of cases and statutes you wish to cite.

(c) *Write an answer based on the plan.* Stick to the plan and try to set out the answer in an attractive way. Let the plan "show through" the answer so that your work has an obvious shape to it. If you think that sub-headings will help to underline the form of your answer, then delineate them clearly (*e.g.* by numbering and under-lining them).

(d) *Express yourself with clarity and precision.* Your style of writing is personal, but in law examinations it is usually best to aim at simplicity. Never use a long sentence when a shorter one will do. Never use a long sentence when the ideas contained in it can be more simply expressed in two or three short sentences. Keep close to the line of argument in your outline plan. Above all, do not "waffle": the examiner will always recognise this for what it is, and it will gain you no marks.

3. Problems. These questions are designed to discover whether the student can (i) recognise the legal principles which are applicable to the given situation, and (ii) apply these principles. Here are some points for guidance:

(a) *Read the problem carefully.* Be sure that you have con-sidered all the facts stated. Do not bother how these facts could be proved: just accept them as facts. Notice what the instructions are. If, for instance, you are asked to "advise X" you should carry out these instructions exactly.

(b) *Decide what principles should be applied.*

(c) *Make an outline plan of your answer.* This should con-sist of the principles briefly stated, the sequence being such as to allow you to bring out the relationship between these principles, *e.g.* where you need to apply a rule which is an exception to the general rule, state the general rule and follow it with the exception; also, where two conflicting rules seem to apply, state both rules. Jot down the names of cases and statutes to be cited. Complete your plan by making a *brief note* of the result when relevant principles are applied to the case in question.

(d) *Write an answer based on the plan.* Aim at a *concise* state-ment of the rules applicable, and give an authority for each rule stated if you can: the name of a case is usually sufficient. Do not launch out a long rigmarole about the facts of cited cases. The examiner is looking mainly for an ability to solve legal problems, not trying to test your memory as to facts of cases.

When your summary of the law applicable is complete,

come immediately to the solution of the problem. A good problem frequently has no definite answer; therefore you should deal in possibilities rather than certainties. Your advice should take the form "If so-and-so then so-and-so, but if so-and-so then so-and-so." The examiner does not expect you to reach a hundred per cent correct solution; he wants you to display a lawyerly ability to suggest possible answers to a hypothetical case.

INDEX

A

Acceptance, 6
  communication of, 8
  manner of, 9
  subject to contract, 7
  tender, of, 7
Account stated, 98
Agency:
  creation of, 100
  estoppel, by, 100, 101
  necessity, of, 101
  ratification, 102
  termination of, 106
  third parties, 102
Agency shop, 270
Agent:
  appointment of, 100
  capacity of, 100
  classes of, 101, 107
  mercantile, 108
  obligations of, 104
  principal and, 100, 104
  warranty of authority, 105
Agreement, 2
Arbitration:
  agreement for, 171
  reference to, 169
Articles of association, 189
Assignment, 70
  automatic, 72
  equitable, 71
  obligations, of, 73
  statutory, 70
Auction sales, 159
Auctioneers, 108
Auditors, 204

B

Bills of Exchange:
  acceptance of, 125
  cheques, 136
  consideration for, 132
  definition of, 123
  demand, 124
  discharge of, 135
  dishonour of, 130
  forgeries, 134
  holders, 132
  indorsement of, 128
  inland and foreign, 124
  negotiation of, 128
  noting of, 132
  parties to, 134
  payment of, 125, 129
  protesting of, 132
Breach of contract, 3, 76
  discharge by, 82
  remedies for, 83
Brokers, 108

C

Capacity:
  contractual, 28
  corporations, of, 32, 188, 206
  infants, of, 28
  insane persons, of, 31
Cheques, 136
Chose in action, 70
Closed shop, 271
Collective agreements, 267
Commission on Industrial
  Relations, 260
Common mistake, 34, 36
Companies:
  accounts of, 201
  articles, 189
  auditors, 204
  borrowing, 207
  capacity, 188, 206
  directors, 197

Companies—*contd.*
  dividends, 194
  formation of, 182, 184
  kinds of, 183
  meetings, 198
  memorandum, 187
  promoters, 184, 186
  reconstruction, 220
  shares, 190, 191
  trading certificate, 185
  winding up, 212
Condition, 24
Conditional sale, 142, 163
Consideration, 15
  bill, for, 17, 132
  waiver, in support of, 18
Contract:
  breach of, 3, 76, 82
  capacity, 28
  conditions, 24
  construction of, 20
  discharge of, 76
  effect of, 3
  formation of, 1
  illegal, 52
  infant's, 28
  privity of, 69
  service, of, 222
  specialty, 1, 92
  terms of, 19
  unenforceable, 31
  validity of, 25
  void, 28, 56
  voidable, 29
Control test, 223
Cooling-off period, 275
Counter offer, 6
Credit-sale, 142, 165

D
Damages:
  liquidated, 87
  measure of, 85
  specific sum as, 89
  unliquidated, 85
Debentures, 208

Del credere agent, 108
Directors, 197
Discharge, 76
  agreement, by, 78
  breach, by, 82
  frustration, by, 79
  performance, by, 76
Dismissal, 238, 244
  unfair, 240
Dividends, 194
Duress, 48

E
Employee's duties, 234
Employer's duties, 228
Employment:
  contract of, 222
  excepted, 280
  insurable, 279
Estoppel:
  agency by, 100, 101
  equitable, 19
Exemption clauses, 20

F
Factories Act, 1961:
  accidents, 330
  administration of, 337
  factory, 307
  health, 311, 328
  industrial diseases, 330
  manual labour, 308
  safety, 314, 328
  special provisions, 328
  welfare, 326, 328
  women and young persons, 331, 334
Firm-name, 111
Fraud, 45
Frustration, 79

G
Guarantee, 64

H
Hire-purchase, 66, 163
  at common law, 163

implied terms, 166
statutory, 164
Holder in due course, 74

I

Illegality, 52
Implied terms, 23, 166
Impossibility, 79
Indemnity, 64
Industrial Court, 258
Industrial injuries, 278, 281
    accident, 281, 292
    benefit, 280, 286, 287
    Commissioners, 291
    diseases, 286
    insurable employment, 279
    insurable risks, 281
    insurance officers, 290
    medical boards, 291
    scheme, 278, 289
Industrial Relations Act, 1971:
    agency shop, 270
    approved closed shop, 271
    code, 257
    emergency measures, 275
    register, 261, 266
    Registrar, 260
    terminology, 256
    unfair dismissal, 240
    unfair industrial practices 273
    workers' rights, 269
Industrial tribunals, 259
Infants, 28
Inunction, 93
Intention, 12, 24
Invitation to treat, 4

L

Limitation of actions, 92

M

Master and servant, 222
Meetings, 198
Memorandum of association, 32, 187
Misrepresentation, 43

fraudulent, 45
innocent, 45
remedies for, 45, 46
Mistake, 34
    equity, in, 35, 42
    operative, 35

N

National Insurance:
    administration, 305
    benefits, 304
    contributions, 299
    disqualifications, 301, 304
    persons exempt, 297
    scheme, 293
    unemployment, 300
Negotiability, 73, 123
Negotiable instruments, 73, 123

O

Offer, 3
    communication of, 5
    lapse of, 11
    rejection of, 12
    revocation of, 10
Offices, Shops, etc., Act, 1963:
    administration, 349
    health and safety, 341
    observance of, 347
    premises, 340
Ownership, 149

P

Part performance, 65
Partners, 110, 112
    agents, as, 114
    liability of, 114, 116
Partnership, 110
    dissolution of, 118
    limited, 121
    third parties and, 114
Penalty, 87
Price, 91, 155
Principal:
    agent and, 100, 104
    obligations of, 105

Principal—*contd.*
  third parties and, 102
  undisclosed, 103
Privity of contract, 69
Promissory notes, 139
Public policy, 61

Q
Quantum meruit, 90
Quasi-contract, 96

R
Ratification, 102
Reconstruction, 220
Redundancy, 243
Representation, 43
Repudiation, 30, 83, 84
Resale price, 63, 179
Resolutions, 200
Restraint of trade, 58
Restrictive practices, 58, 62, 175
  price maintenance, 63, 179
Restrictive Trade Practices Acts:
  registration, 175
  Restrictive Practices Court, 176

S
Sale of goods, 142
  auctions, 159
  buyer's duties, 149
  buyer's remedies, 156
  international, 160
  ownership, 149
  seller's duties, 144
  seller's remedies, 154
  unpaid seller, 153

Shares, 190
Simple contracts, 1
Specialties, 1, 92

T
Tender, legal, 77
Tenders, 8
Terms of contract, 19, 43
  express, 20, 43
  implied, 23
Title, 149
Trade unions:
  collective bargaining, 268
  industrial action, 273
  registration, 260, 266
  rules, 262
  workers' rights, 269

U
Undue influence, 49
Unenforceable contracts, 31, 63
Unilateral mistake, 37

V
Vicarious performance, 73
Vitiating factors, 25
Void contracts, 28, 56
  at common law, 56, 61
  by statute, 57
Voidable contracts, 29

W
Waiver, 18
Warranties, 24
Warranty of authority, 105
Winding up, 212
Workers' rights, 269